SOLID GROUND

25 YEARS OF EVANGELICAL THEOLOGY

SOLID GROUND

25 YEARS OF EVANGELICAL THEOLOGY

Edited by

CARL R. TRUEMAN

TONY J. GRAY

CRAIG L. BLOMBERG

APOLLOS

APOLLOS (an imprint of Inter-Varsity Press),
38 De Montfort Street, Leicester LE1 7GP, England

This collection © Inter-Varsity Press 2000

First published in book form 2000

British Library Cataloguing in Publication Data
A catalogue record for this book is available from the British Library.

ISBN 0–85111–465–2

Set in Minion Condensed
Typeset in Great Britain
Printed and bound in Great Britain by Creative Print and Design (Wales),
Ebbw Vale

Contents

Preface

This volume celebrates the twenty-fifth anniversary of the journal *Themelios*. Written specifically for undergraduate students of theology and religious studies, *Themelios* has always been consciously evangelical, aiming to serve students, ministers and thoughtful lay people with up-to-date articles on a range of academic and missiological issues. *Themelios* has been produced by the Universities and Colleges Christian Fellowship, the Religious and Theological Studies Fellowship (part of the UCCF, which aims to serve and equip theology and RS students), and the International Fellowship of Evangelical Students, which all share a common doctrinal basis. The essays collected here are only a snapshot of the numerous excellent articles that have appeared in the journal during the past quarter-century, but hopefully they represent the breadth of evangelical theology in its best sense – covering diverse issues, representing a variety of positions, and coming from a variety of backgrounds.

In selecting these essays, we have not intended to indicate criticism of essays not included. Space has indeed been at a premium. It must also be kept in mind that each essay was written at a specific time on a specific occasion, and hence the original dates are given in order to help the reader to contextualize each contribution. Nevertheless, it is hoped that this collection will serve a number of purposes: first, to provide today's students of theology and RS with a solid ground to which they can refer as they begin their studies; second, to celebrate the achievements and strengths of the past generation of evangelical scholars; and third, to challenge and encourage a new generation of evangelical scholars whose desire is to serve the church with their minds through a faithful, articulate and principled scholarship.

Thanks are expressed to all the contributors who gave their permission for their articles to be reprinted here, to Elizabeth Fraser for her tireless work in the RTSF office, and to the various staff at IVP for their hard labours in seeing this project through to completion.

Carl R. Trueman
Tony Gray
Craig L. Blomberg

Abbreviations

AV	Authorized (King James) Version of the Bible (1611)
BASOR	*Bulletin of the American Schools of Oriental Research*
BDB	F. Brown, S. R. Driver and C. A. Briggs, *Hebrew and English Lexicon of the Old Testament*, 1906
BETS	*Bulletin of the Evangelical Theological Society*
Bib	*Biblica*
BibOr	*Bibliotheca Orientalis*
BJRL	*Bulletin of the John Rylands Library*
BR	*Biblical Research*
CBQ	*Catholic Biblical Quarterly*
Con	*Concilium*
CSR	*Christian Scholar's Review*
CTJ	*Calvin Theological Journal*
CTR	*Criswell Theological Review*
EQ	*Evangelical Quarterly*
ET	English translation
EvTh	*Evangelische Theologie*
ExpT	*Expository Times*
GTJ	*Grace Theological Journal*
HAR	*Harvard Annual Review*
HJ	*Heythrop Journal*
HTR	*Harvard Theological Review*
HUCA	*Hebrew Union College Annual*
IEJ	*Israel Exploration Journal*
Int	*Interpretation*
IRM	*International Review of Missions*
JAOS	*Journal of the American Oriental Society*
JBL	*Journal of Biblical Literature*
JCR	*Journal of Contemporary Religion*
JCS	*Journal of Cuneiform Studies*
JETS	*Journal of the Evangelical Theological Society*
JFSR	*Journal of Feminist Studies in Religion*
JGES	*Journal of the Grace Evangelical Society*
JJS	*Journal of Jewish Studies*
JNES	*Journal of Near Eastern Studies*

JRE	*Journal of Religious Ethics*
JSNT	*Journal of the Study of the New Testament*
JSSR	*Journal for the Scientific Study of Religion*
JTC	*Journal for Theology and Church*
JTS	*Journal of Theological Studies*
MFAR	*Mission Focus Annual Review*
NIVI	New International Version of the Bible, inclusive language edition (1995–6)
NovT	*Novum Testamentum*
NRB	*Nouvell Revue Théologique*
NS	New series
NTS	*New Testament Studies*
PSB	*Princeton Seminary Bulletin*
RB	*Revue Biblique*
RGG	*Religion in Geschichte und Gegenwart*
RHR	*Revue de l'Histoire des Religions*
RJCM	*Rutherford Journal of Church and Ministry*
RSR	*Recherches de Science Religieuse*
RSV	Revised Standard Version of the Bible (NT 1946, second edition 1971; OT 1952)
RT	*Religion Today*
RTR	*Reformed Theological Review*
RV	Revised Version of the Bible (1881–5)
SBET	*Scottish Bulletin of Evangelical Theology*
SJT	*Scottish Journal of Theology*
Sup	*Supplement*
TB	*Tyndale Bulletin*
ThV	*Theologia Viatorum*
TJ	*Trinity Journal*
TSAJ	*Texte und Studien zum Antiken Judentum*
USQR	*Union Seminary Quarterly Review*
VoxEv	*Vox Evangelica*
VoxR	*Vox Reformata*
VT	*Vetus Testamentum*
WTJ	*Westminster Theological Journal*
WUNT	*Wissenschaftliche Untersuchungen zum Neuen Testament*
ZAW	*Zeitschrift für die alttestamentliche Wissenschaft*
ZK	*Zeitschrift für die Kirchengeschichte*
ZNW	*Zeitschrift für die neutestamentliche Wissenschaft*
ZTK	*Zeitschrift für Theologie und Kirche*

Introduction

Athens, Jerusalem and the evangelical contribution

Tony Gray

I must admit to feeling slightly inadequate to write an essay looking at the past twenty-five years of evangelical scholarship as reflected in the journal *Themelios*. First of all, I am barely older than those twenty-five years myself, and so may be unqualified to comment on what was happening while I was still at school. In addition, I first developed an interest in evangelical theology during my undergraduate degree at Exeter University, and so have really been only something of a spectator of the academic scene in the past ten years – and then usually at some distance. Evangelicalism, and evangelical theology, have of course a history that is much richer and more developed than my few years. However, I hope that my involvement in the task of evangelical theology, and in the publishing of the journal *Themelios*, gives me some credentials with which to speak.

When I left the sixth form, having *just* scraped through a higher education certificate in Religious Studies and intending to study theology, a concerned and pastorally minded teacher gave me an old copy of *Themelios*. I knew no Greek, and nothing of the issues in academic theology, and so the edition lay at the bottom of my cupboard for the following year as a I worked for an evangelistic mission with no mind of what was to come. Yet when I arrived at university, *Themelios* was one element of a lifeboat that got me through the first term of university.

Leaving home took its toll, as it does for many teenagers, and coping away from the home environment brought its challenges and upsets. Together with this went the sudden realization that my chosen theology degree was not going to be three years of dedicated Bible study which would equip me to be a better

Christian! Within weeks I was desperate to return home and stack shelves in the local supermarket, and given half a chance I would have done so. That prospect was thankfully closed off to me by family, friends and the discovery of a support network that would help me with theological issues. Although this appears all too much like a corny advert for *Themelios*, the journal was also part of this package, and that first copy soon emerged from the bottom of the cupboard to help me re-establish the foundations of my faith.

Of course, ministers and well-meaning Christians had warned me of the dangers of doing academic theology. Many times, before I studied patristic theology, people misquoted the famous lines of Tertullian at me: 'What has Athens to do with Jerusalem?' What has the church to do with the academy? Their advice was loving and concerned, if not simplistic. Stay in the church, devote yourself to the service of the church, and avoid the pitfalls of academic theology by not doing a theology degree. That path will lead only to doubt, suspicion and temptation. This was not only scaremongering; it had actually happened to many other young and naïve undergraduates. It would be best to avoid that route altogether.

Ten years later I am deeply convinced that far from being a half-truth, that advice and those conclusions are made up of untruths. Of course people do have doubts and sometimes fall away from the faith because of their theological education. That is not to be questioned, and it is a serious concern. What I think is dangerous is the conviction that the church should have nothing to do with the academy, Jerusalem nothing to do with Athens. The Christian 'battle for the mind' is not only crucial if Christians are going to have a voice in the marketplace; it is central to what it means to be a Christian, to being an adopted child of the Father. If Christ is Lord of all creation, then He is also Lord of our minds, wherever they may be active. God is surely not to be restricted to Sunday mornings and evangelistic meetings; his kingdom is also to be proclaimed in the debating chamber, in the world of commerce and in the theological textbooks.

Others have already articulated this in much more detail, and in much more effective ways, than I can. In the twentieth century popular figures such as C. S. Lewis, Francis Schaeffer and John Stott were fierce advocates of this battle for the mind, and heavyweight academics such as C. F. H. Henry demonstrated how their allegiance to Christ cannot be excluded from the academic battlefield. Christians are not to escape from the world of the mind, hoping that it will have no effect on them. There are battles to be fought and won, as the pages of *Themelios* have witnessed. Contemporary historian Mark Noll has ably charted the debates within evangelicalism concerning the battle for the mind.[1] His most recent work, *The Scandal of the Evangelical Mind*,[2] continues his assessment and evaluation of the present situation. In various fields of the academy, in addition to theology, Noll finds the evangelical contribution still wanting and facing challenges, despite the progress made. Nevertheless, he is optimistic about the evangelical contribution waiting to be made, and the progress that engagement with the academy can achieve. David Wells, in a trilogy of recent works on the state of evangelicalism,[3] is more pessimistic, yet is still engaged in a similar 'battle for the mind'.

My own commitment to the evangelical engagement with the academy was, initially at least, much more pragmatic. Either get involved by wrestling with the problems, hoping to make some headway, or give up and give in to the liberal conclusions presented. The third option was to ignore the dichotomy between Jerusalem and Athens, embracing the world of Jerusalem on a Sunday morning, and agreeing to the conclusions of the academy in my essays during the rest of the week. So I and a few other evangelical students met, prayed over and discussed our questions, ordered *Themelios* and evangelical books, and began to discover the legacy of evangelical scholarship which was there for us to mine and use. We soon realized that we were not on our own, that we were not the first to consider and wrestle with these questions, and that there may even be some sensible answers that would help us maintain our faith while remaining academically credible.

Part of that process involved learning to challenge some of what was accepted as 'academically' credible. The presuppositions of academic theology were often anathema to those of evangelical theology, and so questions of methodology and presuppositions became extremely important. It is perhaps this lesson which was the most valuable to learn. In the essay at the end of this volume, the current editor of *Themelios*, Carl Trueman, examines some of the dangers facing evangelical scholarship, and how much it might actually buy into these presuppositions. There is of course that danger, and we must always be reminded of it. Nevertheless, in my early experience we soon realized that what we were doing was very much against the grain of what we were being taught. In order to make headway, we had to think deeply about the issues involved, challenge the presuppositions of what we were being taught or were reading, and come up with our own answers.

Ironically, I came to realize later that our teachers also understood this. Although not evangelical in their theology, I am grateful to all of them for introducing the joys of theology to me. To give them their due, they were also astute enough to realize that students who met and discussed theology often made better students. A number of those involved in that discussion group, who met together to pray and wrestle with issues, worked hard enough to become first-class students.

Biblical studies

Although this is only anecdotal evidence, the impact of this engagement on the wider scene of theology can be seen in particular with reference to biblical studies. The growth of the market for commentaries, and the number of well-researched works being produced for this market by evangelicals, demonstrates the fruit of this battling. It was natural that in the early years of evangelical theology the concentration of effort would be on biblical studies, answering the questions and criticisms of the text, form and redaction critics. J, D, E, P and Q became letters that the evangelical student recognized as dangerous and important to engage with. Some evangelical scholars went on to accept or modify these various theses, others to reject them and to offer alternatives. A few generations on, the result is a wealth of evangelical biblical scholars worldwide, fed and resourced by such institutions as Tyndale House and its library in Cambridge, a major supporter in the work and publishing of *Themelios*.

A small sample of the fruit of this labour is seen in the first chapter of this collection. As in all sections, a wealth of material across a wealth of subjects made selection extremely difficult. Yet here both the authors and the articles give a snapshot of what has been achieved in evangelical scholarship. Howard Marshall, recently retired from official teaching responsibilities, has made an enormous contribution to the advancement of evangelical biblical studies across the world. During his many years as Professor of New Testament Exegesis at Aberdeen, he attracted doctoral students from different continents to this Scottish outpost to complete their research under his guidance. They returned to teach and to make an evangelical contribution in a wide variety of contexts and countries. Here, his article 'Orthodoxy and heresy in earlier Christianity' deals with an issue which is vital both to the New Testament and also to the theological student. In terms of its context, Marshall deals with the controversial thesis of Bauer, establishing that the earliest Christians were in fact concerned to discern what was 'right' teaching. One of the questions I wrestled with early on, and continue to wrestle with, concerns the boundaries of belief. When does an academic position step outside that which is considered to be 'sound'? Perhaps, more biblically, what is Christian belief and what is not Christian belief? With careful biblical exegesis Professor Marshall returns us to the criteria which the Bible itself proposes, rather than to currently accepted norms regarding who is 'in' and who is 'out'.

When I started as a student, one of the first evangelical books I purchased was Marshall's *The Origins of New Testament Christology*.[4] As I studied the Synoptic and Johannine material, one of the crucial questions in my first year concerned the identity of Jesus. At the same time, a course on Christianity and other religions brought me face to face with issues of religious pluralism, which questioned the uniqueness of Jesus and doubted the traditional interpretation of Jesus as presented throughout the history of the church. If I was to have an answer to this second area, my foundations in the first needed to be secure. Marshall's work, together with that by Dick France (as former editor of *Themelios*), John Wenham and C. F. D. Moule became my staple diet.[5] (John Wenham, one of the founding members of the Tyndale Fellowship, took a continuing interest in *Themelios*. One of his sons, David, became its editor and an established New Testament scholar in his own right, while another, Gordon, became a leading Old Testament scholar.) And so I began to wrestle with the critical issues involved. More recently, the work of Larry Hurtado has made an enormous and impressive contribution to these questions, focusing in the essay reprinted here on 'The origins of the worship of Christ'. Hurtado's work, *One God, One Lord*,[6] is a powerful examination of how Christology developed in the experience of the first Christians. This is among a handful of questions that can correctly be classed as *crucial* for the theological student.

Richard Bauckham's essay, from the pen of a scholar who has made enormous contributions to the fields of both systematic theology and biblical studies (a rare quality among evangelicals), calls attention to the rise and influence of apocalyptic ideas within Scripture, and asks both historical and theological questions of the relationship between apocalyptic and the two Testaments. Together with the more recent article by Craig Blomberg on 'Eschatology and the church', these two essays illustrate that evangelical scholarship is at its best when critically engaging with the issues of the day. Eschatology, including apocalyptic, has been a major subject for discussion in all branches of theology in the past fifty years. Blomberg provides a useful and precise overview of current issues, whilst Bauckham illustrates the benefit of detailed and original research. Although New Testament scholarship seems to have accepted the fact that eschatology is essential to the theology of the Gospels and of the Pauline material, scholars still hotly debate what this actually means and what implications it had for Jesus' ministry. Blomberg draws attention to just one evangelical scholar who is at the cutting edge of this discussion, N. T. Wright. His claim that the temple was the focus of Jesus' eschatological expectations, and the apparent downplaying of a future return of Christ, needs careful interaction by other evangelicals.

In the sphere of Old Testament studies, *Themelios* has been well served both by excellent articles and also by an editor (Chris Wright, now Principal of All Nations Christian College, a missionary training college in the UK). Included here are two articles reflecting different areas of concern. The first deals with a textual issue (one which is also presented by the New Testament), in Joyce Baldwin's article, 'Is there pseudonymity in the Old Testament?' What would it mean for our view of Scripture if a work claiming to be written by one author were not actually written by that person? Baldwin sets out a more traditional response, whereas other *Themelios* contributors (such as John Goldingay and Richard Bauckham) have been happier to accept pseudonymity. Secondly, Desmond Alexander's article on 'The Old Testament view of life after death' confronts a theological issue from the Old Testament that has been challenged by liberal theology in many ways. Does a unified view of life after death exist in the Old Testament, and if so, is there continuity between this view and the view of the New? Alexander challenges the liberal assumption that the views of life after death in the Old Testament are not unified, and are in such conflict that the Old Testament could not be used to develop such a theology. This is important not only for this issue in particular, but also for wider issues of unity and diversity in both Testaments, and in the Bible as a whole. This specific article also became of particular interest for me as I proceeded to doctoral work, examining the doctrine of hell and how it is understood in systematic theology. Many theologians from systematics, cut off from the world of biblical theology, had assumed the conclusions of the liberal Old Testament scholars and had thus decided that the Old Testament offered no unified picture. In his article at the end of this volume, Trueman points out the danger of specialization which separates the worlds of biblical and systematic theologies. The work of those such as Frances Watson, who calls for a bringing together of the two, is to be welcomed.[7]

Hermeneutics

The issue of the relationship between biblical studies and systematic theology raises important hermeneutical questions. The discipline of hermeneutics has grown rapidly over the years that *Themelios* has been in production, and has become increasingly central to theology. However, basic hermeneutical questions have always been present. I mentioned earlier the handful of crucial questions that face any theological student, and the major one that I faced embarking on a career in theology was that of scriptural authority. In what way is the Bible an authority? Where does its authority come from? What about apparent contradictions and clashes with science? Can we argue that the Bible is an authority? All these questions and more threaten the evangelical student, and can be in danger of toppling the student from his or her solid rock, the foundation of the Scriptures. The name of *Themelios* was chosen for this very reason. 'Foundation', 'cornerstone', 'firm basis' – Scripture is clear that our foundation is Christ, the cornerstone of the new people of God that is being built. And our access to this foundation? Revelation, the revelation of Jesus in and through the Scriptures.[8] When I started theology I expected three years of Bible study. What I seemed to be getting when I arrived was three years of criticizing the Bible, of trying to destroy my foundation stone. Consequently, the articles that I valued most, and read and reread most frequently, were those in *Themelios* and other journals and books which tackled this central question.

The work of J. I. Packer is without doubt seminal in evangelical theology. In 1958, his *'Fundamentalism' and the Word of God*[9] responded to attacks on the Bible by liberal scholars who viewed evangelical convictions about scriptural authority as fundamentalistic. (This issue raises its head again later on in this collection with the reprinting of David Wright's critical review of the work of James Barr.) In his biography of Packer, Alister McGrath observes that this work by Packer 'moulded the thinking of evangelical students in the late 1950s and early 1960s … Packer allowed this new generation of evangelicals to realize that they were in possession of a coherent and credible understanding of the inspiration and authority of Scripture.'[10] Here, one of Packer's essays on this subject is reprinted from a special volume on hermeneutics. If the evangelical is to engage in the hermeneutical task, what implication does this have for scriptural authority?

As Watson highlights, and as all hermeneutics illustrates, the relationship between text and doctrine is vital, especially for the evangelical church. If the text is to be preached to change lives, then evangelicals must be teaching the right doctrines from the right texts. Central to this is the issue of the relationship between the Testaments and, as a supreme example of this, of how Jesus himself used the Scriptures to preach. Therefore Greg Beale's essay, 'Did Jesus and his followers preach the right doctrine from the wrong texts?', addresses a vital issue for all hermeneutics. Bringing the discussion more up to date, the essay by John Goldingay on biblical narrative addresses contemporary concerns over the role of narrative in biblical tradition. How do stories work, and more importantly, how do we, the readers, make sense?

The inclusion of a section on hermeneutics reflects the growth and increasing influence of this field on theology. It is fair to say that some of the major players in the discussion have been either evangelicals or scholars strongly influenced by the evangelical tradition.[11]

Systematic and historical theology

In many evangelical scholarly circles, systematic theology has been somewhat neglected. The reasons for this, as Trueman hints in his article, may have been to do with historical priorities, where resources and time were given to areas considered most significant. As I contemplated the almost suicidal path of doing theological research, systematic theology appealed for two reasons. First (and most honestly), my lack of expertise in the biblical languages, and secondly, the lack of evangelical presence in systematic theology, spurred me on to try to make a contribution. However, as I have progressed in the discipline, I have become more aware of the wealth of contributions that have been, and are being, made.

Historically, the creeds have played an enormous role in traditional theology, not only within evangelicalism. Gerald Bray considers the case for and against Chalcedon, and the important role the creeds play in the history of the church. Bray wrote this article in the light of *The Myth of God Incarnate* debate. In the face of challenges by pluralist theologians, and the non-incarnational theologies of the likes of John Hick, reconsideration of the creeds is vital. Does a Chalcedonian Christology make sense, both philosophically and biblically? Orthodox Christianity bases itself on the incarnation, and excludes all those with errant Christologies as heretics. As an evangelical theology student, the question of who was an evangelical was important. The question of who was a Christian was even more so.

Concerning definitions, the work of James Barr on *Fundamentalism* was often brought into discussion to challenge evangelical theology students. Barr's work on semantics and biblical literature is well known, and vital to any student of the biblical texts. However, his work on defining fundamentalism and evangelicalism aroused perhaps even more debate, and the evangelical reaction to it was vociferous and usually indignant. David Wright's review of the book offers a measured and sensible approach, responding to an issue that is vital for a proper historical understanding of evangelicalism and evangelical theology. Since then, works by scholars such as David Bebbington have attempted to clarify the differences between fundamentalists and evangelicals,[12] and more recent studies claim that the attacks on Barr may indeed need to be re-evaluated.[13] At the very least, Barr's work meant that evangelical theology was being taken seriously as one voice among many. The growth of evangelical theology since then has been enormous, obviously with both positive steps forward and other more negative developments.

If Barr is considered to be a critic of evangelicalism, perhaps even better known are Don Cupitt and David Jenkins. Jenkins, in the UK at least, has had his fair share of media limelight, questioning traditional doctrines such as the virgin birth while installed as Bishop of Durham in the Church of England. Don Cupitt, who continues to write extensively and who heads the Sea of Faith Society, developed a non-realist theology which doubts whether we can decide if God does in fact exist. Such questions may ultimately be pointless. What is of ultimate concern is that communities are formed which change the individual. In 'A taproot of radicalism', philosopher of religion Paul Helm offers a fascinating analysis of this sort of radical theology, suggesting possible responses to these positions. Although not many are signed-up followers of Cupitt, this type of thinking is more common than is often assumed, and so Helm's analysis of the legacy of Kant still proves useful.[14]

Application

If Jerusalem has nothing to do with Athens – if there is no engagement between the church and the academy, or even better the church and the world – what point is there in Jerusalem's doing anything? As a theological student I wanted to know how my evangelical theology affected all the current student issues of the day. As an evangelical theologian, what did I have to say to the Thatcherite social policies of the day, and how different should that make me? As the university Christian Union considered debating with the growing Islamic society, were there any resources from my theological understanding that made it easier to think my way through this decision? As several of my close friends, Christian and non-Christian, confided in me their belief that they were homosexuals, how I was to respond without condemnation or compromise? And as many fellow students looked for spiritual fulfilment elsewhere, how could the Christian church best express itself to a generation lacking guidance for the church yet desperate for the things of God?

This last section deals with a number of these issues of application. Of course these essays do not provide all the answers, nor do they cover all the bases. Nevertheless, they point to the growing effort among evangelicals to try to make theology relevant. That last statement sticks in my throat (or in my keyboard) a little. I am always wary of theology that has to try to *make* itself relevant. Is it really true theology if it is trying to do that, or have we then misunderstood what theology is really about? Controversially, I think that this last section reflects poverty in evangelical scholarship, and perhaps also poverty in the back-catalogue of *Themelios*. Not that these essays are not excellent. They are. Yet evangelicalism has only relatively recently rediscovered its social conscience, and its awareness that what we do must be relevant to the world, or we will be shouting at ourselves. My one fear for this volume is that it will just become another collection of evangelical words read by evangelicals who will go on to talk to evangelicals about it. If that is so, then this book will betray the intentions of this last set of authors.

The need to proclaim a gospel that is heard in and beyond the public square is highlighted by the essay by David Lyon on secularization. Being involved in academic theology, and working for a Christian missionary organization, I can have two reactions to this reality: either horror that things really are as secularized as they are (thus rushing headlong into activism and proclamation), or concern that such environments cause me to forget what the rest of the world really is like – that I know a lot of Christians because most of my time and energy is spent with Christians, and that beyond these comfort boundaries are deeply entrenched worlds without God. Lyon analyses the fate of faith in modern society and helps us to understand the implications of secularization.

Similarly, the next two essays present the reality of worlds without God's revelation, yet worlds that are desperately seeking the truth. Ida Glaser, with a wealth of experience in mission, writes on 'The concept of relationship as a key to the comparative understanding of Christianity and Islam'. Here is a deep commitment to mutual understanding, twinned with mission. This surely must be one of the goals which evangelical scholarship and a journal like *Themelios* should aim for – that we should understand as much as possible the particular issues we are trying to deal with. The Christian battle for the mind should not merely be an attempt to get some proof-text answers and some battle-winning one-liners, but a desire to work as deeply as possible at the issues involved, dependent always, of course, on the final truths revealed in Scripture rather than on the sinful mistakes of our fallen human minds. On this level, the work of John Drane on the New Age is widely known and respected. Here he presents a survey and analysis of 'Methods and perspectives in understanding the New Age'. Evangelical response to the New Age has often been simplistic and offensive, ignoring both the deep diversity within the movement and, often, the antipathy to what is usually the traditional 'rational' method of theology in discussing religious ideas.

These two essays are important because they bring an evangelical voice to bear on religious studies. It is surely in this field of enormous growth that evangelicals need do the hardest and most serious work. When asked by students in the UK today, "Who can come and talk on issues in RS as a committed evangelical?", I can often count them on the fingers of one hand. Of course, there are some brilliant minds working in RS. Yet we need many more, many prepared to do the hard technical work of understanding religions, anthropology, sociology, psychology and all the associated disciplines, so that they can contribute a sensible voice to this field as evangelicals have done in others. If it is true that more and more people are becoming interested in religion at the beginning of the third millennium, then the evangelical voice must be ready to be heard.

The final essay reprinted is orientated towards ethical issues, where J. Glen Taylor looks at the Bible and homosexuality. For many evangelical Christians, this issue has become one of the major points of difficulty. This is not necessarily because they themselves have a homosexual orientation and so struggle with the relationship between that and their faith, although the reality of these struggles must not be ignored. More commonly, it is because evangelicals, especially evangelical students, come face to face with friends and family who are themselves homosexual. Tolerance may be the watchword of modern society which evangelicals often criticize, but it is an extremely powerful and palatable watchword that many find attractive. Taylor's essay is a helpful starting-point, and, although there is much more to be said, hopefully it will act as a resource that will then send students in many other directions. The issue promises to remain large on the horizon for the church, and so no-one should claim innocence and ignore it. [15]

Conclusion

Is Jerusalem interacting with and answering Athens? Or is Athens overrunning Jerusalem? This collection of essays demonstrates that the former has happened and is certainly taking place. However, it cannot be denied that at times the latter has been the reality, and perhaps the truth is somewhere in the middle. Yet in some respects this is to be welcomed, for at least discussion and debate are taking place. There are larger questions, then, at stake, and these are taken up by the last two essays in this volume. Carl Trueman looks at them from a UK perspective, while Craig Blomberg offers an American reflection. How is evangelical scholarship to build on this heritage, and proceed into the third millennium? Perhaps going further, what are the implications for theological education, especially for the education of those involved in ministry in the churches? In the UK today I hear a number of voices, some calling for more involvement in the academy, some calling for reforming of the academy, and still others calling for total withdrawal and establishment of Christian seminary environments similar to those in the US.

Of course, there are even deeper questions – the relationship between faith and reason, the role and suitability of apologetics, and the possibility of Christian morality finding a voice in the marketplace. I hope that some of the essays in this collection have pointed towards initial thoughts on such weighty issues. My personal plea is a simple one – that churches take the academy more seriously, and the academy take the church more seriously. Common to all the contributors to this volume whom I have had the pleasure of knowing personally is the commitment to academic rigour that serves the church. Many of them have acted as an inspiration and role model for me, even when I have disagreed with their conclusions. I hope that they will do so to others of my generation, and to generations to come.

Notes

1. His first volume, *Between Faith and Criticism* (Leicester: Apollos, 1991), charts the history of evangelical theology most specifically in the United States, and the battles with fundamentalism and liberalism, providing some fascinating insights into what has gone before. As a young scholar I discovered this volume to be a great inspiration and insight into what evangelical theologians had fought for during the twentieth century. Noll also deals briefly in this volume with the enormous contribution made by British evangelicals, many of whom were inspirational in the work of the Tyndale Fellowship, the academic body linked with the UCCF and IFES, both of whom co-publish *Themelios*. He writes on page 106 concerning *Themelios*, 'That journal, its predecessor the British *TSF Bulletin*, and the annual *Tyndale Bulletin* have been for many years the finest regular sources of serious evangelical writing on the modern study of the Bible in the English-speaking world.'
2. Leicester: IVP, 1994.
3. *No Place for Truth* (Leicester: IVP, 1993); *God in the Wasteland* (Leicester: IVP, 1994); *Losing our Virtue* (Leicester: IVP, 1998).
4. 1976; second edition Leicester: Apollos, 1990.
5. R. T. France, *Jesus in the Old Testament* (London: IVP, 1971), John Wenham, *Christ and the Bible* (Guildford: Eagle, latest edition 1993); C. F. D. Moule, *The Origin of Christology* (Cambridge: Cambridge University Press, 1977).
6. Edinburgh: T and T. Clark, 1988.
7. Frances Watson, *Text, Church and World* (Edinburgh: T. and T. Clark, 1994); *Text and Truth* (Edinburgh: T. and T. Clark, 1997).
8. In the first editorial, the then Chairman of the Theological Students' Fellowship (now RTSF), Trevor Morrow, wrote the following, with reference to Paul's use of the term in Ephesians 2:20: 'The foundation is of paramount importance. If our foundation is not Paul then neither is our temple. The Church of Christ which is being built is grounded in the authoritative witness of the apostles and prophets to Jesus Christ (the chief cornerstone). It is only upon such a foundation that our theological bricks and mortar can be of value in the erection of a holy edifice to the glory of God' (vol. 1.1, p. 1).
9. London: IVF, 1958.
10. Alister McGrath, *To Know and Serve God* (London: Hodder and Stoughton, 1997), p. 86.
11. For example, see A. C. Thiselton, *The Two Horizons* (Carlisle: Paternoster, 1980) and *New Horizons in Hermeneutics* (London: HarperCollins, 1992), and Kevin Vanhoozer, *Is There a Meaning in this Text?* (Leicester: Apollos, 1998).
12. David Bebbington, *Evangelicalism and Modern Britain* (London: Unwin Hyman, 1989).
13. Harriet Harris, *Fundamentalism and Evangelicals* (Oxford: Clarendon, 1998).
14. For evangelical responses to two other pressing issues in systematics, see Miroslav Volf's reflection on liberation theology in vol. 8.3, and GrahamTomlin on postmodernity in vol. 23.1, which also addresses the central issue of the cross in evangelical theology.
15. One of the most important contributions on ethics by an evangelical is Oliver O'Donovan, *Resurrection and Moral Order* (1986; revised edition Leicester: Apollos, 1994). Stephen Williams, former editor of *Themelios*, offers an extremely helpful assessment of this in vol. 13.3.

Part 1
Biblical studies

1

Orthodoxy and heresy in earlier Christianity

I. Howard Marshall   Vol. 2.1 (1976)

There is a story, possibly apocryphal, which tells how the Roman Catholics once advertised a public meeting in Sydney, Australia; on their posters they presented their claim to be the upholders of pure Christianity by means of the slogan 'The Faith of our Fathers'. Not to be outdone, the Protestants arranged a rival meeting with the redoubtable T. C. Hammond as their speaker, and they advertised as their title, 'The Faith of our Grandfathers'. The title of this essay is somewhat similar to the Protestant parody. It is a secondary elaboration of a more famous phrase, and will be readily recognized as a parody of the title of a well-known book by Walter Bauer, *Orthodoxy and Heresy in Earliest Christianity*. As with a number of other significant German books, the importance of this one was not recognized in this country until long after its original publication. English-reading students have had to wait until the last twelve years to see translations of the works of William Wrede, Wilhelm Bousset and Rudolf Bultmann, and with them of W. Bauer, first published in 1934 and not available in English until 1972 (in America, 1971).[1] Unlike the others, however, which hit the headlines on the Continent at the time of publication, Bauer's work came at a time when the German church was preoccupied with other more pressing issues, and it had to wait till after the war for due recognition.

Bauer's basic thesis was a polemical one and is best summed up in his own words: he argued that, according to the generally accepted interpretation of the situation, 'Jesus revealed the true teaching to his apostles who in their turn went out into all the world after the ascension to hand on the unadulterated gospel to the peoples. It was only after their death that obstacles arose for the preaching from the Christian side. For now some people who were misled by the devil gave up the apostolic preaching which had been the means of their conversion and put in its place their own human ideas. Thus in the post-apostolic period there arose heresies of various kinds which could certainly be very annoying to the church but never in any form really dangerous.

'This conception [he went on] must be tested for its accuracy by means of history. Did the order: unbelief, orthodox belief, false belief, which is said to have been the case everywhere, really correspond with the facts or not, or was it the case to a limited extent that must be worked out and expressed?'[2]

In order to settle this question Bauer thought it best to start outside the disputed area of the New Testament writings. And so he proceeded to do a package tour of the world of early second-century Christianity in order to discover whether the rise of what came to be called heresy was always preceded by orthodox teaching from which it had deviated. A close study of the rise of the church in Edessa and Alexandria suggested to him that in the beginning so-called unorthodox groups were predominant; what was later regarded as orthodoxy was represented at best by small groups, so that from the very beginning so-called heretical and orthodox forms of the faith existed side by side. The churches were more 'orthodox' in Asia Minor, but various arguments suggest that there were strong pockets of unorthodox Christianity in this area. If the position was different in Corinth, where the church certainly began with strong heretical tendencies, this was due to the influence of Rome imposing its views on the church. It could be said that 'the form which Christianity gained in Rome was led to victory by Rome and thus established as orthodoxy'.[3] Bauer then went on to show how Rome established its own doctrinal position as the orthodox one. It was largely because the heretics were independent of one another and unable to unite with one another in opposition to Rome that they eventually succumbed to her influence. The great mass of middle-of-the-road Christians who might well have been won over by either wing of the church in fact threw in their lot with Rome.

Bauer thus concluded that what later came to be regarded as orthodoxy was only one of several competing systems of Christian belief, with no closer links to any original, so-called 'apostolic Christianity' than its rivals, and that it owed its victory in the competition more to what we might call political influences than to its inherent merits.

The corollary to be drawn from Bauer's discussion is that things were no different in the first century. Thus R. Bultmann, who fully accepted Bauer's arguments, stated: 'The diversity of theological interests and ideas is at first great. A norm or an authoritative court of appeal for doctrine is still lacking, and the proponents of directions of thought which were later rejected as heretical consider themselves completely Christian, such as Christian Gnosticism. In the beginning, faith is the term which distinguishes the Christian Congregation from Jews and the heathen, not *orthodoxy* (right doctrine). The latter along with its correlate, *heresy*, arises out of the differences which develop within the Christian congregations.'[4] It is interesting, however, that Bultmann proceeds to say, 'In the nature of the case this takes place very early.'

The argument was taken further by G. Strecker in an investigation of Jewish Christianity in an appendix to the 1964 edition of Bauer's book; he argued that Jewish Christianity was diverse in character and that what must be considered as historically primary in the first century was seen to be heretical when compared with what later was regarded as orthodoxy.[5]

A somewhat similar point of view appears to be represented by Stephen S. Smalley in his examination of 'Diversity and Development in John'. He submits that in the Gospel of John, as distinct from the Epistles, we have a considerable diversity of views expressed, some of which could be seized upon as supporting their cause by later, orthodox writers, others of which could be seized upon by the heretics. He therefore states that 'John's diversity can hardly be regarded as consciously orthodox *or* heretical; it is neither one nor the other. If such considerations had influenced John's writing, it is very unlikely that he would have left so much on the "orthodox" side unsaid, and so much on the "heretical" side open to misconstruction, to be used eventually in evidence against him.'[6]

The scope of the present essay, confined as it is to the first century, enables me to side-step a discussion of the correctness or otherwise of Bauer's thesis as it applies to post-apostolic Christianity – although it must be observed that if it is inapplicable to the second century, it can hardly be applied to the first century. On the whole, it seems to have been subjected to considerable modification in detail, but few have been willing to contradict its main lines. If it has done nothing else it has emphasized the prevalence of diversity in the second-century church and the difficulty that existed in attempting to draw clear boundaries between what was orthodox and what was heretical.[7] My starting-point is rather the fact that Bauer had the effrontery to label the second century as *'earliest* Christianity', and I want to look at the period which is in fact earlier than this, the period of the New Testament itself.

Unity, variety and diversity

In the essay which I have already quoted, S. S. Smalley suggests that the key to our problem in John's Gospel may lie in the categories of diversity and development. These two terms give us a set of co-ordinates against which the ideas of the early church might be plotted in such a way that the variety of ideas at any one given time may be seen, and also the differences in ideas between one period of time and another. A recent book of essays by H. Koester and J. M. Robinson has used the term 'trajectories' to give expression to this kind of approach, although it is obvious that the name, like the word 'canon', is simply a new invention to describe a concept of which scholars have long been conscious.[8]

Granted that there is diversity and development in the theologies expressed in the New Testament, the question is whether this is the same thing as saying that no distinction between orthodoxy and heresy was being made, or that this concept did not exist prior to the development of a vocabulary to describe it. And at once it is obvious that the two things are not the same. It is possible, in other words, for there to be a variety in presentation of the Christian faith without the varied presentations being incompatible with one another. It is probable that in the church at Corinth different cliques attached themselves to the names of Paul, Apollos and Cephas. No doubt these three men presented the gospel in different ways, and it may well be that their followers developed their own individual ideas, but Paul was quite clear that there was no fundamental incompatibility between himself and his colleagues in the presentation of the gospel. 'We are fellow workers for God'; 'All things are yours, whether Paul, or Apollos, or Cephas ... all are yours' (1 Cor. 3:9, 21f.). In the same way, while it was judged politic for there to be two Christian missions, one to the circumcised and one to the uncircumcised, they were in fellowship with one another, and there is no suggestion of any fundamental disagreement between them (Gal. 2:7–9). Bauer's attempt to interpret Paul's statement otherwise is somewhat mischievous.

The fact of such a basic unity was emphasized by A. M. Hunter in a book which is of importance out of proportion to its size. In *The Unity of the New Testament*[9] he argued that the major writers of the New Testament show a basic unity in their testimony to one Lord, one church and one salvation. Writing in 1943, Hunter was working against a background of stress on the diversity within the New Testament. This was presented in another product of Scottish theology by E. F. Scott in *The Varieties of New Testament Religion*.[10] He was equally rightly concerned to emphasize the lack of uniformity in the New Testament: the writers 'are all inspired by the one faith, but every teacher interprets it differently, as he has known it in his own soul'.[11] Both of these points of view need to be heard, but perhaps it is the voice of Hunter which has had less attention than it deserves in our own day. Where Scott is distinctly woolly in his survey and makes generalizations do duty in place of hard facts,

Hunter is careful to give evidence for his statements and to argue a case which is the more impressive by reason of its restraint and caution.

But Hunter was concerned with the writers of the New Testament. He made no attempt to claim that Paul and his opponents in Galatia had a basic unity in their theology. The question that now arises concerns the degree of variety in the life and thought of the early church which is reflected in the New Testament: at what point, if any, does variety become a deviation from the truth?

The later books of the New Testament

We shall now make an attempt to look at the evidence relevant to this second question. It may be helpful to begin, like Bauer, with what are usually thought to be the latest writings in the New Testament, and then turn to the generally accepted letters of Paul, and finally to the Gospels.

In the *Pastoral Epistles*[12] we have a writer who is confronted by teaching which he regards as false in the churches for which he has a responsibility. At the outset of 1 Timothy there is an instruction not to allow people to teach 'different doctrine'; it is associated with speculation about myths and genealogies and it leads to vain discussion instead of growth in faith. Such teaching appears to have rested on what the author regarded as a misunderstanding of the law, and to have led to an intellectual type of religion which ignored the claims of conscience. Over against it the author places 'healthy doctrine', which he characterizes as being in accordance with the gospel (1 Tim. 1:3–11). This basic theme is repeated throughout the Pastorals, most clearly in 1 Timothy and Titus. It is probable that the writer was confronted by a type of Gnosticizing teaching with strong Jewish elements, which laid stress on knowledge and which led both to asceticism and to moral licence. What is important is that he is clearly aware of its existence and of its distinction from what he regards as the truth. The lines are firmly drawn. The teaching is 'other' and does not conduce to spiritual 'health'. It produces moral behaviour which is incompatible with godliness. Over against it the writer places healthy teaching, and he clearly reckons with the existence of traditions in the church, such as the 'faithful sayings', which enshrine the truth of the gospel. He regards the church as being the pillar and bulwark of the truth.

It is impossible to avoid the conclusion that in these Epistles the writer is conscious of being the defender of truth and that he is prepared to take disciplinary measures against those who persist in erroneous beliefs. The very word *hairetikos* is used in this connection. It is perhaps not unfair to say that the Pastorals were composed in a situation of false teaching threatening the truth, and that their basic purpose is to deal with this situation by outlining the true nature of Christian living, and by equipping the church with leaders who will be able to promote the cause of orthodoxy.

This understanding of the Pastorals was, of course, shared by Bauer, but it did not basically affect his thesis because he was prepared to put them at a rather late date and to see them as directed against Marcionite teaching. If this late dating is wrong, an obvious weakness in Bauer's case is opened up. The trend in recent scholarship is in fact to date the Epistles in the first decade of the second century, and this is a significant shift in placing them historically.[13] Even this date is probably too late, and there is good reason to place them considerably earlier. But the commonly accepted date is sufficient to allow us to make our point, that *a distinction between orthodoxy and heresy had come into existence by the end of the first century or just after.*

The *Revelation* can probably be dated in the last decade of the first century. Its author's main concern was to strengthen the church to face persecution, but in order to achieve this aim he realized that the church must be purified of false belief and immorality; otherwise it would fall under the judgments of God on the world at large. His attack is directed mainly against attempts to combine idolatry and idolatrous practices with Christian faith. The apostolic decree requiring abstinence from food sacrificed to idols and from immorality (Acts 15:29) was evidently being flouted. There were people around who called themselves apostles, and there was a prophetess who gave the weight of her authority to idolatrous practices and immorality (Rev. 2:2, 20). The implication is that the upholders of this position felt it necessary to claim support for their views by appeal to ecclesiastical office and to Spirit-inspired revelations. It looks as though they formed a definite group in the church. Their teaching may well have had a Gnosticizing tinge, as is suggested by the allusion to the deep things of Satan (Rev. 2:24). The other members of the church are said to have tested the false prophets and found them wanting; they are criticized for not throwing out Jezebel as well. But what is perhaps of greatest interest is that the group attacked by John are referred to as Nicolaitans, followers of Nicolaus (Rev. 2:6, 15). They are thus known by the name of their leader, real or imaginary, in the same way as later groups of heretics were identified. This is to my knowledge the first example of such a procedure, and it is highly significant as showing that already within New Testament times *it was possible to identify and label a group regarded as heretical.* In other words, the lines were already being clearly drawn. Unfortunately, much is left obscure; we should like to know how the heretics saw themselves, how they established their claim to authority, and how they regarded their opponents.

We are not surprised to find the word *hairesis* being used in its developed sense in what is often regarded as the latest writing in the New Testament, *2 Peter* (2:1). The writer is concerned about the rise of false teachers in the church. Their behaviour was licentious; it appears to have involved a rejection of the morality enshrined in the law, and to have questioned some aspects of Christian teaching, including the hope of the parousia. Above all they despised and reviled the accepted authority in the church. They evidently appealed to the writings of Paul in support of their teaching, and imposed what the author regarded as a false interpretation upon them. They also claimed prophetic inspiration. The picture is similar to that in Revelation, but the heresy appears to have gone further, and to have taken the step of claiming Pauline support. We should naturally like to know how they interpreted Paul. It seems probable that some of his teaching may have been understood as sanctioning antinomianism, although it is hard to find passages in his existing Epistles which give much support to such views.

The situation reflected in *Jude* appears to have been similar to that in 2 Peter. Here again opponents of the writer are to be found in the church, and have not yet been ejected. They are castigated for their immorality and contentiousness which have caused divisions in the church. We learn nothing about the actual content of their teaching. The author's reply is to call his readers back to the tradition which they have received, to the faith once for all delivered to the saints; he has no doubt that this stands in opposition to the teaching which he is criticizing. This may reflect a slightly earlier stage than in 2 Peter, since the heretical appeal to tradition may well have followed the orthodox appeal by claiming that the orthodox were misinterpreting it.

A clear consciousness of differing opinions in the church is found in *1 – 3 John*. In 2 John the writer speaks of deceivers who deny the coming of Jesus Christ in the flesh. There are people who do not abide in the doctrine of Christ. It is probable that some off-beat Christological teaching is in mind, possibly a docetic denial that Jesus really was the Christ, or that the Christ really became incarnate in Jesus. In 1 John the group has come out into the open and begun a separate existence. Three important facts characterize the Elder's reply. One is that he attacks this point of view on the intellectual level by asserting that the doctrine of God is jeopardized by this teaching. One cannot truly believe in the Father without also believing in the Son. In other words, a heresy which may have seemed innocuous or marginal is shown to affect understanding of basic doctrine. This point is stressed throughout 1 John. Second, the writer's stress on the need for love, shown in practical ways, is a flank attack on his opponents' position, but he does not indulge in empty abuse against them; rather he invites his readers to apply the test of 'By their fruits you shall know them'. The third point is that the writer holds that fellowship should not be extended to those who maintain this point of view; we may compare the similar command in Titus 3:1f. Those who adopt such teaching are equated with antichrist *(*i.e. the opponent of Christ, rather than somebody taking the place of Christ). A distinction between different groups with different doctrines is consciously taking place.

It is not clear whether a situation of heresy is reflected in 3 John. It is well known that E. Käsemann has proposed that Diotrephes was really the champion of orthodoxy, attempting to stifle the influence of the unorthodox Elder, but there is good reason to reject this interpretation.[14] On the other hand, there is no proof that Diotrephes was unorthodox; at the most he appears to have been ambitious and curt with his possible rivals.

We can quickly pass over *James* and *1 Peter* in our survey. The writer of the former letter, it is true, has been thought to be critical of Paul, but his real bone of contention is with Christians lacking in the works of love who probably claimed Paul in support of their own position. From both James and 2 Peter it can be seen that appeal was made to Paul in support of opinions that were denied by other New Testament writers; but both 2 Peter and James regard Paul as being on their side, and James does not give the impression of regarding the people whom he is criticizing as heretics.

We may summarize our conclusions so far by noting that in the late first-century church there was a consciousness of the distinction between orthodoxy and heresy. Appeal was made on both sides to the teaching of the apostles and to the voice of prophecy. There was a consciousness of an inherited body of belief, 'the faith', and excommunication was beginning to be used as a weapon. There is no reason to suppose that these ideas developed without previous preparation: we are justified in examining the other New Testament documents to see whether they reflect a development towards this position.

Paul

We turn, therefore, back to Paul. Almost everywhere in his writings we can detect the presence of opponents who questioned his teaching or put up some other teaching instead of it. To be sure, it is unlikely that this is the case in *1 Thessalonians*, where such problems as arose were probably due simply to the inadequate grounding in his teaching which his converts had had before he was forced to leave them. The situation is one of questions and uncertainties rather than opposition to his teaching. The situation in *2 Thessalonians* is at first sight very similar, but it is interesting that in attacking the view that the day of the Lord has already arrived Paul should refer to the possibility of a spirit or word or letter purporting to be from himself, and that he urges the readers to hold fast to the traditions which he has taught them orally or by letter. Further, he lays stress on the importance of what he says in this letter to the extent that anyone who does not accept its teaching is to be solemnly warned and disciplined. Such strict discipline is not unparalleled in Paul (1 Cor. 5). The significant facts are rather that Paul considers the error which he is opposing to be so serious and that he suspects that his own authority has been used to defend it. It is not surprising that this Epistle has been thought to be post-Pauline, and to reflect an attempt by the orthodox to claim Paul's authority for their own position instead of that of their rivals. There appears to be an organized opposition against the Pauline position. But the situation is comprehensible if the life of the church is in danger of being crippled by an apocalyptic enthusiasm which has upset normal daily life. Nor would it be surprising if a prophet claimed to speak in the name of the Lord, and even claimed the authority of Paul (cf. Acts 19:13). The Pauline situation remains the more probable, and, if correct, it shows that at an early date teaching opposed to that of Paul was being promulgated with a false appeal to his authority, and that the answer to this teaching was for Paul himself to claim that he had been wrongly interpreted. It was presumably because of this direct misrepresentation of his own views that Paul spoke out so strongly against those who rejected his authority in Thessalonica.

Nobody denies that Paul himself faced opposition when he composed *Galatians*, but the situation is more than a little complex. We need to distinguish between the opposition in Galatia itself, and that which Paul experienced in Jerusalem and Antioch. Then we must assess correctly the nature of the opposition experienced by Paul. There are two main views of this, namely that it was either Judaizing or Gnostic, but the case that it was Judaizing is the stronger of the two. If so, this means that the same type of opposition was prevalent in Galatia and on the home front. The opposition in Galatia was Jewish or Jewish-Christian in inspiration, and it received the full force of Paul's opposition because it compromised the doctrine of faith in Christ which he regarded as all-important. Acceptance of the contrary point of view called the mission to the Gentiles in question. Paul's defence, as is well known, rested on an appeal to history, to experience and to Scripture. He was able to claim that his message had been accepted by the leaders of the church in Jerusalem; the weakness in this argument was the strange case at Antioch where Peter and Barnabas sided against him, and Paul never says that they changed their minds, although the friendly allusions to them in 1 Corinthians would imply that they did in fact do so. But, while it is possible that Paul passed over their initial reaction with a discreet silence, it is more likely that he was simply carried away by the force of his own argument. His second appeal was to experience, both his own and that of his converts; he could point to his own revelation of Jesus at his conversion, which for him had immediate authority, and he could also point to the way in which his converts received the gift of the Spirit apart from the law. His third appeal was to Scripture, showing from the Old Testament that God's principle of working with men, even in the era of the law, was by faith. Since his converts had not yet apparently succumbed to what he regarded as error, he was able to address them in terms of appeal rather than condemnation; but he spoke in no uncertain terms about those who were leading them astray. He called down God's curse on anybody who was doing this. There could be no other gospel than Paul's gospel. There is no appeal to apostolic authority here other than his own; Paul argues from his own experience of Christ.

By the time of *1 Corinthians*, however, Paul is more conscious of the significance of tradition, to which he makes appeal more than once. His bases for argument include the commands of the Lord, as well as his own consciousness of inspiration by the Spirit. He can appeal to the practice of other apostles. This suggests that the opposition to Paul stood outside the mainstream of the church, even if there was appeal to Apollos and Cephas. Basically, Paul appears to have been confronted by two groups in the church, one Jewish-Christian and the other incipient Gnostic. The former were 'weak' in faith, but not heretical; Paul thinks they are wrong, but does not condemn their error, and indeed seeks a sympathetic approach to them from the rest of the church. On the point at issue, he tended to side with the strong Christians. But the impression we gain is of a church with tendencies that could lead to error, judged by Pauline standards, rather than with full-blown heresy. There was immoral and licentious behaviour to be corrected. There was an overemphasis on spiritual gifts unaccompanied by love. There may have been a false understanding of the resurrection. But the whole tone of the letter is that of a wise pastor, rather than that of someone determined to stamp out organized opposition at any cost. The extent of the opposition to Paul in Corinth at this point can easily be exaggerated.

The fact of opposition is clearer in *2 Corinthians 10 – 13*, but in this middle period of Paul's work the problems of interpretation are complex. Here we do hear of preaching of *another Jesus*, a *different spirit* and a *different gospel* which did not lead to reformation of life (2 Cor. 11:4). There was opposition to Paul by persons who claimed apostolic status, who regarded themselves as engaged on a mission similar to his own and under superior auspices. They were in danger of assuming control of the church at Corinth. Paul was strenuously opposed to them, as they were to him. He speaks of them in the strongest terms as servants of Satan, and it may well be that they regarded him in similar terms. There is no doubt, then, that lines were being drawn between opposing sides. But what was the basis of the disagreement with them? I am not convinced by the theory that they were Gnostics, nor that they thought of themselves as divine men preaching a Jesus who was similarly a divine man. The truth is that the nature of the doctrinal disagreement scarcely comes to the surface in this section of the Epistle. They were Jews, possibly claiming special credentials from Jerusalem, people whom Paul regarded as proud of their position and making extravagant claims and demands for themselves in virtue of it, people who claimed spiritual visions and revelations. But it is extraordinarily hard to discern exactly what they believed and taught. Paul simply places his own claims over against theirs and attacks their claims rather than their message. Nor is it clear why they were so opposed to Paul. Did they regard his teaching as false, or were they simply jealous of his success, or what? And suppose some third party came along: how could he tell which group was 'orthodox'? These questions can hardly be answered for lack of information.

In *Romans* we have evidence of people who create dissensions and stand in opposition to the doctrine which Paul taught; they are not in Paul's eyes true servants of Jesus, but they serve their own carnal natures. Schmithals regards them as Gnostics, but it is doubtful whether the evidence takes us that far. But it may be that the same sort of rival mission as we found in 2 Corinthians is reflected here, and that Paul feared persons travelling around in his footsteps and contradicting his teaching. Once again we note that their teaching is not detailed or refuted by Paul; he simply warns against them and their deceitful methods of establishing their views. This is significant as regards the later Epistles which, it is sometimes said, reflect a lack of argument with heresy in contrast to Paul's own earlier attempts to deal more rationally with it.

In *Philippians* again there is danger to the church from persons who uphold circumcision. Here the most plausible identification of the opponents of Paul is as Judaizers. But the situation is complicated by the mention of people who claimed some kind of perfection and those whom Paul regarded as enemies of the cross who pandered to their own fleshly desires. This wording is similar to that in Romans and suggests that the same group were on their rounds. They could be antinomians. The danger comes from outside the church, and perhaps this is why Paul does not deal with its errors in detail; it may be a potential rather than a real situation.

The same is possibly true of *Colossians*. Here it has been traditional to find evidence of a developed Gnostic heresy, but recently M. D. Hooker has strongly challenged this assumption, and shown that it is doubtful whether there was a coherent, organized heresy.[15] Paul's teaching, it is said, 'seems to us to be quite as appropriate to a situation in which young Christians are under pressure to conform to the beliefs and practices of their pagan and Jewish neighbours, as to a situation in which their faith is endangered by the deliberate attacks of false teachers'.[16] Whatever be the situation, Paul's reply is to call the church back to the way in which it received Christ as Lord, and to the gospel which it preached throughout all the world. The doctrines of the person of Christ and of union with him leading to ethical behaviour are his reply to false versions of the gospel.

The Gospels

We turn, finally, to the Gospels before attempting to draw some conclusions. Traces of polemic have been found in all of them. This is least obvious in the case of *Luke* along with its companion, Acts. Certainly there is one clear warning against the rise of heresy in the church in the post-Pauline period, which may well reflect earlier struggles, but on the whole little is said about the nature of such troubles. The attempt by C. H. Talbert to find Gnostics under Luke's bed seems to me singularly unsuccessful.[17] What we do have is the early struggle of the church to deal with Judaizing tendencies, and this struggle is regarded as being successfully resolved in favour of the Pauline position. There is a point of view which is resisted and shown to be wrong, and the proof is found in the manifest willingness of God to accept the Gentiles and bestow the Spirit upon them apart from acceptance of circumcision. The argument is not dissimilar to that in Galatians.

In *Matthew* E. Schweizer has found opposition to a group of enthusiasts who sat loose to the ethical teaching of Jesus.[18] It is this Gospel more than any other which bears witness to the fact of a mixed church with true and false believers in it. But the nature of a Gospel prevents direct address to such people, and all that can be done is to present the relevant teaching of Jesus, in some cases carefully underlined to bring out the significant points for the situation.

It is chiefly in *Mark* that recent students have found polemic against heresy. Especially in the work of T. J. Weeden[19] and N. Perrin[20] we have the suggestion that the disciples are identified with a false view of the person of Jesus over against which Jesus himself presents the truth. They were tempted to think of him as Messiah and Son of God in terms of a divine man working miracles, whereas Mark insisted that this view must be qualified by the preaching of Jesus as the Son of man who must suffer and die before being glorified. The main essentials of this position are accepted by R. P. Martin, who, however, does not identify the disciples as the carriers of the false view.[21]

With respect to *John* something similar has been claimed, John being seen as the corrector of a too-simple view of Jesus as a docetic figure, a worker of signs; but there is too much uncertainty here for us to offer any assured conclusions.[22]

Historical conclusions

We have now surveyed the evidence relative to the positions of the writers of the New Testament. What have we found?

1. We have found that *teaching regarded by them as false was extremely common*. In nearly every book of the New Testament this has been evident. The significance of this must not be overestimated. Van Unnik has rightly observed that we must not seek heresy everywhere as the determinative factor in the composition of the New Testament.[23] Alongside the need to combat it there was what is probably more important, the proclamation of the gospel. 'The development of the earliest church was not set in motion by the almost unbridgeable tensions between Christians, but by the positive task of being witnesses of Jesus Christ in a world whose demands continually summoned them to provide answers.' Nevertheless, it is clear that from New Testament times the New Testament writers were conscious of rivalry and teaching opposed to their own.

2. There is a *development* in the presence of false teaching. The New Testament writings reflect an early stage in which the church was formulating its attitude on the question of circumcision and the Mosaic law. But from Galatians onwards Paul regards that issue as settled, and is intolerant of any who impose Jewish legalism on Gentiles. He does not object to Jews keeping up their own practices, although on the whole he thinks them unnecessary and a source of possible danger. But from the period of his letters onwards various types of problems arise. (a) There is *sheer rivalry* in the proclamation of the gospel. This Paul was prepared to put up with, but he drew the line when his own mission and apostolate were called in question. (b) There was *unethical behaviour*, which Paul condemned, especially if it arose from false teaching. (c) There was the possibility of Christians being *misled* as a result of pagan ideas, through lack of Christian instruction, through false deductions from the gospel. (d) There was the possibility of *teaching which differed from Paul's understanding* of the gospel. This included Judaizing, which jeopardized faith in Christ, and antinomianism, which went contrary to Paul's understanding of the nature of the new life in Christ. There may have been erroneous views of the work of the Spirit, especially in relation to spiritual gifts, and false views of

the death and resurrection of Jesus. *Another Jesus, another gospel, another Spirit* – these three phrases sum up the dangers faced by Paul. This was how he saw heresy. Similar dangers are found in the other New Testament writings.

3. *Paul's method* of treatment varied. Sometimes he was simply warning his churches against possible influences, and we do not learn much about the character of the problems faced. At other times, the error seems to have got a firmer hold on the church. Then there may be a full-scale argument to show its falsity, as in Galatians, or a restatement of doctrine, as in Colossians. There is appeal to the nature of Christian experience, to the gospel as he preached it, and as he had received it, and to his own calling. Those who persist in false teaching may be removed from fellowship in the church. The church needs to appoint teachers who will stand firmly in the succession of sound doctrine and themselves be apt to teach others.

Now if this survey is sound, it shows that certain people in the first century, namely the writers of the New Testament, were conscious of the existence of opinions different from their own in the church, that they wrote and used other means to state or show that they were incompatible with the gospel which they believed themselves to have inherited, and that certain groups of people were regarded by them as deviationists and were excluded from the church or took themselves off to form their own groups. And this in my opinion is evidence that Bauer's thesis does not work when it is applied to the first century. Smalley's version of it with regard to John cannot be applied to the rest of the New Testament, and I am doubtful whether it is true even of John. For Bauer said in effect that there was considerable variety of belief in the early church, and that what later came to be regarded as orthodoxy was not conscious of being such at first, nor were there clear boundaries between different sorts of Christian belief, nor was what later came to be regarded as orthodox necessarily first on the ground. But the only valid point in this is that *there was variety of belief in the first century*. The New Testament writers one and all regard themselves as upholders of the truth of the gospel, and they often see quite clearly where the lines of what is compatible with the gospel and what is not compatible are to be drawn. And while it is possible that in some places the beginnings of Christianity came from people later regarded as heretical, it is not the case that orthodoxy was a later development.

Areas for further exploration

What factors might be placed over against this conclusion?

1. Basically, there is the question whether the New Testament writers were in fact in such agreement that any one of them would have recognized any

other as 'sound in the faith'. Did James think that Paul was sound? If Paul had read Revelation, would he have agreed with it? Did John write his Gospel because he thought the others needed correction or even supersession, and did any of the other Gospel writers think the same way? These questions cannot be given a facile answer in the brief space left at my disposal, but I make bold to say that they would have recognized one another as brothers and colleagues in the defence of the gospel.

2. What were the groups criticized by the New Testament writers as heretical really like? Until a sort of first-century Nag Hammadi library comes to light, this question cannot be fully answered. But it may be worth noting that when the Nag Hammadi library was first discovered, H. Chadwick expressed his opinion that it would not cause any major alteration in our assessment of the nature of Gnosticism as we had learned it from the church fathers who wrote against it. The same may well be true of the New Testament. Thus I find no reason to doubt that Paul was justified in his accusations of immorality against those who rejected his gospel. Did such people regard themselves as the defenders of truth? We have seen that some did, but this reinforces the view that the idea of orthodoxy was prevalent in the first century.

3. How did such groups regard persons like Paul or John? Were they regarded as heretical, and if so, by whom? And in such cases how do we decide which was right? Was Diotrephes the defender of 'orthodoxy' against the Elder? The church's answer was to canonize Paul and John, and not their opponents. But how did the situation seem during their period of ministry? One answer is that Paul evidently had some respect for the Jerusalem church, and he wanted to have its assurance that he was not, as he puts it, running in vain. But he was accepted by it, and could build on that fact. It was to the apostles that appeal was made. And if a Peter or Barnabas could deviate from Paul on occasion, it was only temporary and an inevitable risk during the growing period. There must undoubtedly have been a growing period during which the situation was flexible and ideas were not hard and fast, but some basic essentials were probably settled quite early, certainly earlier than Bauer suggests.

4. Perhaps the biggest problem concerns the relations between the various groups which lie behind the New Testament writers. There is the problem of the relation between Hebrews and Hellenists in the Jerusalem church, and the whole question of Jewish-orientated and Gentile-orientated types of Christians. This has been stressed by U. Wilckens in an essay discussing the place of Jesus-traditions in the church; he suggests that there were two communities, one passing on these traditions, and the other comparatively unaffected by them; the one orientated to the earthly Jesus, the other to the

exalted Christ. These were later brought together, but at first there were in effect two quite different types of Christianity.[24]

Somewhat similar is the attempt of H. Koester to show that there were four different types of Gospel material in the early church, effecting different Christologies. These were (1) the collection of *sayings of Jesus*, assembled by those who thought that the essence of Christianity was to perpetuate the teaching of Jesus as a teacher of wisdom. (2) The *aretalogy*, presenting Jesus as a divine man who performed supernatural actions. (3) The *revelation*, in which the risen Jesus gives esoteric instruction to his disciples. (4) The *kerygma* of the death and resurrection of Jesus historicized into a narrative form. Our canonical Gospels represent to some extent corrections of these earlier outlooks – a feature we have already noticed in the case of Mark.[25]

The question would then be how far these different points of view represented varieties of Christian belief, and how far they required the rejection of other points of view as heretical. But a more basic question would be how far this is a correct analysis of the position in the early church, and I would suggest that Koester's view is in fact a misleading description of the situation. This point cannot be developed in detail here. But if Koester's view contains elements of truth, it poses questions for us.

These four problems indicate that I have not provided all the answers to the historical questions posed by orthodoxy and heresy in New Testament times. None of them, however, is sufficient in my opinion to call in question my basic thesis, namely that the first-century church was conscious of the difference between orthodoxy and heresy, and that from an early date there was a body of belief which could be regarded as apostolic and orthodox.

The theological consequences

I have left myself no space to discuss the theological and contemporary significance of the material we have been discussing. It must suffice simply to pose some questions that arise.

1. We have travelled thus far without raising the basic question of what we are talking about. *What in fact is heresy?* It is dangerous to work with undefined terms. W. Bauer at one point speaks of a heretic as 'a fellow Christian concerning whom one is convinced that his divergent stance with regard to the faith bars him from the path of salvation'.[26] That is perhaps an extreme definition. At the opposite extreme there have been those who regard any deviation from their particular brand of Christianity as heresy. I can think of one distinguished writer on baptism who certainly came near to thinking that anybody who had doubts about the validity of infant baptism ought not to

be a candidate for the ministry in his particular denomination. Somewhere in between these extremes there may be the idea of heresy as teaching which is regarded as contrary to the basic confession of the church in some central point or points, such that the confession is endangered by it.

2. A second question concerns *the rise of heresy*. H. Koester suggests that it arises from two possible dangers: either the time-bound historical shaping of the Christian revelation was absolutized and the quality of revelation was credited to a temporary form, or as a result of the consciousness that the revelation had a supra-historical quality, the link with its historical origin was surrendered, and foreign ideas were able to claim admission.[27] One might see Judaizing as an example of the first of these dangers and Gnosticizing as an example of the second. The question then arises as to whether heresies in general can be subsumed most fruitfully under these two headings.

3. The early church took up *a stance against heresy*, and in some cases acted against heretics. Does this provide a pattern for the church today to follow? In a brief article written at the time of the Pike controversy, J. Macquarrie suggested that the category of heresy was no longer applicable in the church today. Christianity can exist in a variety of forms, and the lines between orthodoxy and heresy cannot be drawn sharply. Excommunication for heresy is no longer a viable possibility, especially when today's heresy may become tomorrow's orthodoxy.[28]

This approach certainly suggests the need for caution, but it may well be that it does not take the New Testament seriously enough. For the essence of heresy is that it presents itself as a form of the real thing, as distinct from, say, an atheistic position which is confessedly anti-Christian, and therefore it presents the greater danger to the faith since, from the point of view of orthodoxy, error is masquerading as truth. A church which takes its confession seriously must surely be prepared to speak out against what it believes to be error, and if necessary to discipline those who profess to uphold its confession while effectively denying or contradicting it. A confessional church has a right and necessity to do so. Whether the same thing is possible in a non-confessional church may be more difficult to argue; perhaps indeed it is an argument against a non-confessional church that it is unable to apply the categories of orthodoxy and heresy.[29]

Notes

1. W. Bauer, *Rechtgläubigkeit und Ketzerei im ältesten Christentum* (Tübingen, 1934; reprinted 1964); ET *Orthodoxy and Heresy in Earliest Christianity* (London, 1972).

2. From W. Bauer's own summary statement of his thesis in his *Aufsätze und kleine Schriften* (ed. G. Strecker, Tübingen, 1967), pp. 229–233 (my translation).

42 Solid Ground

3. Ibid.
4. R. Bultmann, *Theology of the New Testament* 2 (London, 1955), p. 135.
5. G. Strecker, 'On the problem of Jewish Christianity', in W. Bauer, *Orthodoxy and Heresy*, pp. 241–285.
6. S. S. Smalley, 'Diversity and development in John', *NTS* 17 (1970–71), pp. 276–292, quotation from p. 279.
7. 'For a survey of reactions to Bauer's thesis, see the appendix to his book by G. Strecker and R. A. Kraft (op. cit., pp. 286–316). More recent discussions include: H.-D. Altendorf, 'Zum Stichwort: Rechtgläubigkeit und Ketzerei im ältesten Christentum', *ZK* 80 (1969), pp. 61–74; M. Elze, 'Häresie und Einheit der Kirche im 2. Jahrhundert', *ZTK* 71 (1974), pp. 389–409; A. I. C. Heron, 'The Interpretation of I Clement in Walter Bauer's "Rechtgläubigkeit und Ketzerei in ältesten Christentum"', *Ekklesiastikos Pharos* 4 (1973) (NE), pp. 517–545.
8. H. Koester and J. M. Robinson, *Trajectories through Early Christianity* (Philadelphia, 1971).
9. A. M. Hunter, *The Unity of the New Testament* (London, 1943).
10. E. F. Scott, *The Varieties of New Testament Religion* (New York, 1946).
11. Op. cit., p. 305.
12. Since most scholars hold that the Pastoral Epistles are post-Pauline and are some of the latest writings in the New Testament, our discussion assumes that view for the sake of the argument. In other words, our discussion is intended to show that even on the assumption of a late date for the Epistles they testify to the existence of a clear distinction between orthodoxy and heresy at the end of the first century. Our point, therefore, does not depend on acceptance of a conservative view of the authorship and date of the Epistles, although conservative scholars who believe that there are good grounds for substituting 'Paul' for 'the writer' in the text will be able to claim that there was a concern for right doctrine at an earlier date than most critical scholars would allow.
13. The date assigned by W. G. Kümmel, *Introduction to the New Testament* (London, 1966), p. 272, is typical of recent study. For arguments in favour of Pauline authorship see D. Guthrie, *The Pastoral Epistles* (London, 1957); J. N. D. Kelly, *The Pastoral Epistles* (London, 1963).
14. E. Käsemann, 'Ketzer und Zeuge', *ZTK* 48 (1951), pp. 292–311.
15. M. D. Hooker, 'Were there false teachers in Colossae?', in B. Lindars and S. S. Smalley (eds.), *Christ and Spirit In the New Testament* (Cambridge, 1973), pp. 315–331.
16. Op. cit., p. 329.
17. C. H. Talbert, *Luke and the Gnostics* (Nashville, 1966).
18. E. Schweizer, 'Observance of the law and charismatic activity in Matthew', *NTS* 16 (1969–70), pp. 213–230.
19. T. J. Weeden, *Mark – Traditions in Conflict* (Philadelphia, 1971).
20. N. Perrin, *A Modern Pilgrimage in New Testament Christology* (Philadelphia, 1974), pp. 84–93.
21. R. P. Martin, *Mark: Evangelist and Theologian* (Exeter, 1972).
22. On this view John was correcting the viewpoint of a more naïve 'signs source' which he has incorporated in his Gospel.
23. W. C. van Unnik, 'Die Apostelgeschichte und die Häresien', *ZNW* 58 (1967), pp. 240–246.
24. U. Wilckens, 'Jesusüberlieferung und Christuskerygma – zwei Wege urchristlicher Uberlieferungsgeschichte', *ThV* 10 (1965–6), pp. 310–339.
25. H. Koester, 'One Jesus and four primitive Gospels', *HTR* 61 (1968), pp. 203–247; reprinted in H. Koester and J. M. Robinson, op. cit.
26. W. Bauer, op. cit., pp. 234f.
27. H. Koester, 'The theological aspects of primitive Christian heresy', in J. M. Robinson (ed.), *The Future of our Religious Past* (London, 1971), pp. 65–83.
28. J. Macquarrie, *Thinking about God* (London, 1975), pp. 44–45.
29. For a survey of heresy in the New Testament see H. Koester, 'Häretiker im Urchristentum', in *RGG*, III. 3, cols. 17–21.

2

The rise of apocalyptic

Richard J. Bauckham   Vol. 3.2 (1978)

Apocalyptic is currently a growth area in biblical studies. Fresh study, more reliable texts, new editions, even hitherto unpublished documents are enriching our understanding of the intertestamental apocalyptic literature. In addition, there has been fresh debate over the origins of apocalyptic and its relation to Old Testament prophecy, while in the wake of E. Käsemann's notorious claim that 'apocalyptic is the mother of all Christian theology'[1] the importance of apocalyptic as the intellectual matrix of primitive Christianity is increasingly recognized. More and more, apocalyptic must be seen as a crucial historical bridge between the Testaments.

All this raises serious theological questions. Is apocalyptic a legitimate development of Old Testament religion? The historical investigation of apocalyptic origins cannot avoid a theological assessment, which has its implications also for New Testament theology to the extent that apocalyptic was a formative factor in early Christian theological development. In this way the question of the theological continuity between the two Testaments themselves is involved in the problem of the status of apocalyptic. Moreover, as James Barr points out,[2] the status of apocalyptic raises the question of the status of the canon in which it is only marginally represented. Can an *intertestamental* development be seen as providing theological continuity between the Testaments?

In this article we shall be concerned primarily with the rise of apocalyptic up to the flowering of Hasidic apocalyptic in the mid-second century BC. We shall be asking (in Part I) the *historical* question of the origins of apocalyptic, in the light of some recent studies, and (in Part II) the *theological* question of the theological legitimacy of apocalyptic as a development of Old Testament religion.

I. Origins

Apocalyptic in the prophets

The most important recent investigation of the origins of apocalyptic in Old Testament prophecy is that of Paul D. Hanson.[3] Hanson argues that apocalyptic eschatology developed in the early post-exilic period (late sixth and early fifth centuries) as a development rooted in the prophetic tradition. The extent of the development of apocalyptic in this period, as he estimates it, is indicated by his revision of the usual terminology: he uses the term 'proto-apocalyptic' for Second Isaiah, since he points in the apocalyptic direction; Third Isaiah and other prophetic material from the early Persian period (Zech. 9 – 13; Is. 24 – 27) he calls 'early apocalyptic'; Zechariah 14, which he dates in the mid-fifth century and thinks marks the point at which apocalyptic eschatology is fully developed, is 'middle apocalyptic'; Daniel, from the mid-second century, is already 'late apocalyptic'.[4] (To avoid confusion, in this article I shall use the term 'apocalyptic prophecy' to designate apocalyptic material within the Old Testament prophetic books, i.e. Hanson's 'early' and 'middle' apocalyptic.) Hanson admits a chronological gulf between Zechariah 14 and 'late' apocalyptic, but the special characteristic of his thesis is that he considers apocalyptic eschatology to have already developed in all essentials *before* this gulf. This enables him to stress the continuity between prophecy and apocalyptic to an unusual degree, and to deny the importance of the non-Israelite influences (Iranian and Hellenistic) which have so often been regarded as contributing significantly to the development of apocalyptic. Such influences, he argues, enter the picture only at a late stage when apocalyptic's essential character was already developed.

Of course such a thesis can only be maintained if an appropriate definition of apocalyptic is used. Hanson's definition focuses on apocalyptic *eschatology* and relates it to prophetic eschatology, distinguishing the two in terms of the kind of balance which each maintains between myth and history. The characteristic of classical prophecy is the dialectic it maintains between the cosmic vision of Yahweh's plans and the prophet's responsibility to translate that vision into concrete historical terms. Prophetic eschatology is 'a religious perspective which focuses on the prophetic announcement to the nation of the divine plans for Israel and the world which the prophet has witnessed unfolding in the divine council and which he translates into terms of plain history, real politics and human instrumentality'.[5] What apocalyptic lacks is that last clause. The balance between vision and history is lost. Despairing of the realization of the vision in the historical sphere, the apocalyptists were increasingly content to leave it in the realm of myth. Apocalyptic eschatology is 'a religious perspective which focuses on the disclosure ... to the elect of the cosmic vision of Yahweh's sovereignty – especially as it relates to his acting to deliver his faithful – which disclosure the visionaries have largely ceased to translate into terms of plain history, real politics, and human instrumentality'.[6]

This apocalyptic eschatology developed among the disciples of Second Isaiah (to whose tradition belong not only Is. 56 – 66 but also Zech. 9 – 14) in the post-exilic Palestinian community. Second Isaiah's prophecies of glorious restoration remained unfulfilled, and in the bleak conditions of the early Persian period the visionary group which maintained his eschatological hope increasingly presented it in purely mythical terms, in images of sheer divine intervention and cosmic transformation. To the possibility of fulfilment through human agency and favourable historical conditions they became indifferent.

As the sociological context for the development of apocalyptic eschatology Hanson postulates an intra-community struggle between this visionary group on the one hand, and on the other hand the hierocratic group, a Zadokite priestly group which adopted a pragmatic approach to restoration. By contrast with the visionary programme of Second Isaiah and his followers, this latter group were at first inspired by the more pragmatic restoration programme of Ezekiel, and through the preaching of Haggai and Zechariah they succeeded in harnessing eschatological enthusiasm to their policies. After the rebuilding of the temple they won control in the community and thereafter discouraged all eschatological expectation as a threat to the stability of their achievement. The visionary group, on the other hand, consistently opposed the rebuilding of the temple in the name of their transcendent eschatology and waged the most bitter polemic against the hierocratic party. Their own political powerlessness encouraged their visionary indifference to the sphere of political responsibility.

Hanson's reconstruction of this community struggle is speculative at best and probably the weakest part of his thesis. In particular it leads him to a polarization of the prophetic tradition of Second Isaiah, Third Isaiah and Zechariah 9 – 14 on the one hand, and on the other hand the tradition of Ezekiel and Zechariah 1 – 8. The former he regards as the tradition in which apocalyptic emerged, while the latter only used apocalyptic motifs to legitimate a pragmatic political programme. Such a polarization does far less than justice to the significance of Ezekiel and Zechariah 1 – 8 in the development of apocalyptic,[7] as Hanson himself has begun to recognize in a subsequent modification of his treatment of Zechariah.[8] To treat Zechariah 9 – 14 as belonging to the tradition of Third Isaiah *rather than* to the tradition of Ezekiel and Zechariah 1 – 8 is to ignore the evidence that these chapters are quite heavily dependent on Ezekiel and relatively little dependent on Isaiah 40 – 66.[9] This in itself suggests that the emergence of apocalyptic must be reconstructed according to a less rigid classification of prophetic traditions.

This is not the place to attempt an alternative reconstruction in detail, but what seems needed is greater recognition of the common features of the various post-exilic prophecies. Despite the varying emphases there is a common conviction that the eschatological promises of restoration in Second Isaiah and Ezekiel remained largely outstanding despite the restored city and temple. In all of these prophecies there is therefore a degree of dependence on and reinterpretation of the earlier prophecies, and all are more or less apocalyptic (according to Hanson's definition) in the extent to which they depict the coming salvation in terms of Yahweh's direct intervention and radical transformation of historical conditions. The distinctive aspect of Haggai and Zechariah (1 – 8) is that they focused these apocalyptic hopes on the rebuilding of the temple and the leadership of Joshua and Zerubbabel, But these historical realities soon proved incapable of measuring up to the hopes aroused, and so those who subsequently kept alive the eschatological expectation were not opponents of Haggai and Zechariah but successors who sought to remain faithful to their prophecy.

There is, however, a great deal of value in Hanson's analyses of Isaiah 56 – 66 and Zechariah 9 – 14. He shows convincingly how various features of apocalyptic eschatology emerge in these passages. Thus, judgment and salvation are no longer prophesied for the nation as a whole but respectively for the faithless and the faithful within Israel.[10] The doctrine of a *universal* judgment is adumbrated in Isaiah 63:6; 66:l6,[11] and eschatology takes on cosmic dimensions. Beyond the judgment lies a new age radically different from the present age and inaugurated by a new act of creation: this idea has its background in Second Isaiah and is already developed in such passages as Isaiah 65:17-25; Zechariah 14:6-9.[12] These elements compose the trans-cendent eschatology of divine intervention and cosmic transformation which forms the central core of apocalyptic belief.

Hanson also shows how this development entails the revivification of ancient mythical material, especially the Divine Warrior myth, to depict the coming eschatological triumph of Yahweh.[13] Here Hanson follows the pioneering work of his teacher F. M. Cross, whose studies of Canaanite myth in relation to the Old Testament revealed the extent to which 'old mythological themes rise to a new crescendo' in apocalyptic.[14] Other studies have shown the extent to which Canaanite myth continues to be used even in Daniel and Enoch,[15] while the apocalyptic assimilation of myth extended also to Babylonian, Iranian and Hellenistic material. This 'remythologization' of Israelite religion was not, however, a reversion to an historical worldview, but serves to represent an eschatological future which is now understood to transcend the categories of ordinary history.

Hanson has succeeded in demonstrating that the transcendent eschatology which characterizes apocalyptic emerged in post-exilic prophecy as an internal development in the Israelite prophetic tradition in response to the historical conditions of the post-exilic community. This is an important conclusion. On the other hand, there remains a significant gulf, which is not only chronological, between this apocalyptic prophecy of the fifth century and the Hasidic apocalyptic of the second century. Apocalyptic prophecy is not pseudonymous, though it is often anonymous. It does not include extensive surveys of history in the form of *vaticinia ex eventu*. Its angelology is relatively undeveloped. The temporal dualism of two ages is emerging, but the spatial dualism of heaven and earth, which also characterizes intertestamental apocalyptic, is not yet apparent. Moreover, the transcendent eschatology of apocalyptic prophecy does not yet include the transcendence of death, so central to later apocalyptic belief.[16]

In other words, although Hanson has demonstrated the continuity between prophecy and the apocalyptic prophecy of the early Persian period, there still remains a problem of continuity between this apocalyptic prophecy and the later apocalyptic of Daniel and the intertestamental literature.

To the origins of this later apocalyptic we now turn. We shall see that it is really the heir of post-exilic prophecy and owes its transcendent eschatology to that source. But we shall also see that this is not the whole story, for the alternative derivation of apocalyptic from wisdom has some validity, and there is moreover a significant discontinuity between the self-understanding of apocalyptic prophecy and that of the later apocalyptists.

Daniel and mantic wisdom

The most radical rejection of the derivation of apocalyptic from prophecy is that of Gerhard von Rad, who argued that apocalyptic is not the child of prophecy but the offspring of wisdom.[17] This proposal has been widely criticized,[18] as being at least one-sided. In this section and the next, we shall argue that, while von Rad's thesis was too generalized and cannot be treated as an *alternative* to the derivation from prophecy, it does have some validity in relation to the background of the books of Daniel and Enoch. In both cases, however, the wisdom background needs more careful definition than von Rad gave it.

An important attempt to refine von Rad's argument is H. P. Müller's proposal to derive apocalyptic not from proverbial but from *mantic* wisdom.[19] For alongside the wise men whose type of wisdom is represented by the book of Proverbs, the ancient Near East had also mantic wise men, whose function was to divine the secrets of the future by various methods including the interpretation of dreams, omens, mysterious oracles, and the stars.[20] There is little trace of a class of mantic wise men in Israel, but two Old Testament figures who rose to prominence in foreign courts did so by virtue of their successful competition with the court diviners in the practice of the mantic arts: Joseph at the court of Pharaoh and Daniel at the court of Nebuchadnezzar. It is the case of Daniel which suggests that one of the roots of apocalyptic lies in mantic wisdom.

Daniel was not a prophet in the sense of classical Israelite prophecy.[21] His activity in chapters 2, 4, and 5 consists in the interpretation of Nebuchadnezzar's dreams and of the mysterious message on Belshazzar's palace wall. In each case he is called in after the failure of the other diviners at court. Clearly he belongs among them (2:18), and as a result of his success becomes their chief (2:48; 4:9; 5:11). His *function* is exactly theirs: the disclosure of secrets of the future. Of course the source of his supernatural knowledge is the God of Israel, and his success is designed to bring glory to the God of Israel as the God who is sovereign over the political future. Daniel is the representative of the God of Israel among the magicians and astrologers of the Babylonian court, but he represents him *in the practice of mantic wisdom* (cf. 5: 12).

It is, moreover, this aspect of the Daniel of chapters 1 – 6 which most plausibly accounts for the ascription to him of the apocalypse of chapters 7 – 12. We must therefore take seriously the claim that apocalyptic has roots in mantic wisdom.

There are strong formal resemblances between the symbolic dream with its interpretation in mantic wisdom and the apocalyptic dream or vision with its interpretation. The latter also has roots in prophecy (especially Ezekiel and Zech. 1 – 6), but the connection with mantic wisdom is hard to deny in the case of Daniel, where Nebuchadnezzar's dream and its interpretation in chapter 2 corresponds so well to Daniel's dream-visions and their interpretation in chapters 7 and 8. Besides their dream-interpretation, the mantic wise men were doubtless responsible for the literary prophecies of the ancient east, such as the Mesopotamian 'apocalypses' which have been compared with Jewish apocalyptic in certain respects.[22] These provide precedent, which cannot be found in Israelite prophecy, for the long reviews of history in the form of predictions from a standpoint in the past, such as we find in Daniel 11 and other Jewish apocalypses.[23] The astrological aspect of mantic wisdom is naturally less well represented in Jewish parallel material, but it is noteworthy that interest in astrological prediction recurs at Qumran.

The argument about the date of Daniel may have been conducted too simply in terms of a choice between the sixth and second centuries. We may now be able to recognize the book's dual affinities, with Babylonian mantic wisdom on the one hand and with Hasidic apocalyptic on the other, which indicate the probability of a developing Daniel tradition,[24] which has its roots as far back as the exile in Jewish debate with and participation in mantic wisdom, developed in the Eastern diaspora, and finally produced Daniel apocalypses on Palestinian soil in the time of Antiochus Epiphanes.[25] This is all the more probable in view of the similar chronological development which the Enoch tradition underwent (see below).

The key to the emergence of apocalyptic in such a tradition is undoubtedly a growing concern with eschatology. Apocalyptic, like mantic wisdom, is the revelation of the secrets of the *future*, but in its concern with the *eschatological* future apocalyptic moves beyond the scope at least of *Babylonian* mantic wisdom.[26] Thus, while Daniel's interpretations of the dream of chapter 4 and the oracle of chapter 5 belong to the typical activities of the Babylonian diviners, his *eschatological* interpretation of the dream of chapter 2 is already in the sphere of apocalyptic. Hence it is chapter 2 which provides the point of departure for the apocalypse of chapters 7 – 12, which interprets the future according to the pattern of the four pagan empires succeeded by the eschatological kingdom. But even this contrast between mantic wisdom and apocalyptic may be too sharply drawn. If Nebuchadnezzar's prognosticators would not have given his dream an eschatological sense, the Zoroastrian magi who succeeded them at the court of Darius might well have done.[27] Precisely the four-empires scheme of chapter 2, with its metals symbolism and its eschatological outcome, has close parallels in the Iranian material which has been plausibly suggested as its source.[28] We touch here on an old debate about apocalyptic origins: the question of the influence of Iranian eschatology.[29] Whatever the extent of the *influence*, it is clear that there are *parallels*, of which the Jews of the diaspora cannot have been unaware. Not even eschatology decisively differentiates Jewish apocalyptic from the products of mantic wisdom, insofar as eschatology developed also to some extent in non-Jewish mantic circles.

It becomes increasingly clear that apocalyptic, from its roots in mantic wisdom, is a phenomenon with an unusually close relationship to its non-Jewish environment. At every stage there are parallels with the oracles and prophecies of the pagan world. This is equally true as we move from the Persian to the Hellenistic age. Hellenistic Egypt has an 'apocalyptic' literature of its own: pseudonymous oracles set in the past, predicting political events, eschatological woes, and a final golden age.[30] There is an extensive Hellenistic literature of heavenly revelations and celestial journeys sometimes remarkably similar in form to those of the apocalyptic seers.[31] It is not surprising that H. D. Betz concludes that 'we must learn to understand apocalypticism as a peculiar manifestation within the entire course of Hellenistic-oriental syncretism'.[32]

Nevertheless this close relationship of Jewish apocalyptic to its non-Jewish environment is misunderstood if it is treated merely as syncretistic. Undoubtedly there is considerable borrowing of motifs, symbols, literary forms – not only by Jew from Gentile but also *vice versa*.[33] Undoubtedly Judaism after the exile, especially in the diaspora but increasingly also in Palestine, was not immune from the moods and concerns of the international religious scene. The relationship, however, was not one of passive absorption of alien influence, but of creative encounter and debate in which the essence of Israelite faith was reasserted in new forms.   .

This element of debate is already in evidence in the encounter with Babylonian mantic wisdom. Daniel, as we have seen, practises it among but also in competition with the Babylonian diviners, to show that it is the God of Israel who is sovereign over the future and gives real revelation of the secrets of destiny (2:27f., 46). Such a tradition of debate found one of its most natural expressions in the Jewish *Sibylline Oracles*, in which an internationally known pagan form of prophetic oracle was adopted as a vehicle for a Jewish eschatological message. The message, drawn from Old Testament prophecy, of God's judgment on idolatry and his purpose of establishing his kingdom, was attributed to the ancient prophetesses, the Sibyls, largely, it seems, with an apologetic aim, to gain it a hearing in the non-Jewish world. Of course the bulk of Jewish apocalyptic was written for an exclusively Jewish audience, but behind it lay a close but critical interaction with its non-Jewish environment such as the *Sibyllines* bring to more deliberate expression. This kind of relationship is hazardous. The appropriation of pagan forms and motifs can become insufficiently critical and the voice of authentic Jewish faith can become muffled or stifled. We cannot suppose that the Jewish apocalyptists never succumbed to this danger, but on the whole the risk they took was justified by the achievement of an expression of prophetic faith which spoke to their own age.

From its potentially ambiguous relationship with paganism, apocalyptic emerged in the crisis of hellenization under Antiochus, *not* as the expression of hellenizing syncretism, but as the literature of the Hasidic movement, which stood for uncompromising resistance to pagan influence. How did apocalyptic succeed in retaining its Jewish authenticity and avoiding the perils of syncretism? This is the point at which the derivation of apocalyptic from mantic wisdom fails us, and needs to be supplemented with the derivation from Old Testament prophecy. The two are after all not entirely dissimilar. While Jewish practitioners of mantic wisdom were entering into competition with the Babylonian fortune-tellers, Second Isaiah, the father of apocalyptic prophecy, was also engaged, at a greater distance, in debate with his pagan counterparts, exposing the impotence of the Babylonian gods and their prognosticators (Is. 44:25; 47:13) by contrast with Yahweh's sovereignty over the future revealed to his servants the prophets (Is. 44:26; 46:9-11). The apocalyptic heirs of Jewish mantic wisdom were not prophets, but their concern with God's revelation of the future made them students of Old Testament prophecy, and the more they concerned themselves with the *eschatological* future, the more they sought their inspiration in the prophets. With the cessation of prophecy in Israel, the apocalyptists became the interpreters of Old Testament prophecy for their own age. So while the *form* of their work was stamped by its continuity with pagan oracular literature, its *content* was frequently inspired by Old Testament prophecy. Again we can see this in Daniel. His eschatological dream-interpretation in chapter 2 is, if not inspired by, at least congruous with the eschatological hope of the prophets. Taken as the fundamental idea of the apocalypse of chapters 7 - 12, it is then filled out by means of the interpretation of Old Testament prophecy. Thus the Hasidic apocalyptists stood in a tradition with its origins in mantic wisdom, but filled it with their own dominant concern to achieve a fresh understanding of prophecy for their own time. In that sense they were also the heirs of post-exilic apocalyptic prophecy.

Enoch and the cosmological wisdom

We have traced the emergence of apocalyptic between the exile and the Maccabees, between prophecy and mantic wisdom, in the tradition which produced our book of Daniel. We must now look at the emergence of apocalyptic in another tradition which spans the same period, the Enoch tradition.

The discovery of the Aramaic fragments of *Enoch* at Qumran, now available in J. T. Milik's edition,[34] is most important for the study of apocalyptic origins. With the exception of the *Similitudes* (*1 Enoch* 37 - 71), fragments of all sections of *1 Enoch* have been found: the *Book of Watchers* (1 - 36), the *Astronomical Book* (72 - 82), the *Book of Dreams* (83 - 90), and the *Epistle of*

Enoch (91 – 107). There are also fragments of a hitherto unknown *Book of Giants.*

These discoveries clarify the issue of the relative dates of the parts of the Enoch corpus.[35] The generally accepted date of the *Book of Dreams* (165 or 164 BC) may stand, but the pre-Maccabean date of the *Astronomical Book* and the *Book of Watchers*, hitherto disputed, is now certainly established on palaeographic evidence. The *Astronomical Book* (now known to have been much longer than the abridged version in *Ethiopic Enoch* 72 – 82) cannot be later than the beginning of the second century, and Milik would date it in the early Persian period.[36] The *Book of Watchers* cannot be later than c. 150 BC, and Milik thinks it was written in Palestine in the mid-third century.[37] He is almost certainly correct in regarding chapters 6 – 19 as an earlier written source incorporated in the *Book of Watchers*; these chapters he regards as contemporary with or older than the *Astronomical Book*.[38] While Milik's very early dating of the *Astronomical Book* and chapters 6 – 19 is uncertain, the important point for our purpose is their relative date as the earliest part of the Enoch corpus. This means that apocalyptic was not originally the dominant concern in the Enoch tradition, for the apocalyptic elements in these sections are not prominent.[39] The expansion of chapters 6 – 19 with chapters 1 – 5, 21 – 36 to form the *Book of Watchers* had the effect of adding much more eschatological content to this part of the tradition. Then in the Maccabean period a full-blown Enoch apocalypse appeared for the first time in the *Book of Dreams*. So we have a development parallel to that in the Daniel tradition.

Also like the Daniel tradition, the Enoch tradition has its roots in the Jewish encounter with Babylonian culture, but in this case over a wider area than mantic wisdom.[40] The circles which gave rise to the tradition had an encyclopedic interest in all kinds of wisdom, especially of a cosmological kind: astronomy and the calendar, meteorology, geography, and the mythical geography of paradise. In all these areas of knowledge they were indebted to Babylonian scholarship,[41] while the picture of Enoch himself as the initiator of civilization, who received heavenly revelations of the secrets of the universe and transmitted them in writing to later generations, is modelled on the antediluvian sages of Mesopotamian myth.[42]

But, once again as in the Jewish involvement in mantic wisdom, this Jewish encyclopedic wisdom is not only indebted to but also in competition with its pagan counterpart. Civilization is represented as an ambiguous phenomenon, with its sinful origins in the rebellion of the fallen angels (*1 Enoch* 7:1; cf. 69:6–14) as well as an authentic basis in the divine revelations to Enoch.[43] The true astronomy which Enoch learns from the archangel Uriel is not known to the pagan astrologers who take the stars to be gods (80:7) and distort the calendar (82:4f.). The true wisdom which Enoch teaches is inseparably connected with the worship of the true God. So the scientific curiosity of the Enoch circles retains a genuinely Jewish religious core.

Von Rad's derivation of apocalyptic from wisdom relied heavily on the evidence of *1 Enoch*, but he was mistaken to generalize from this evidence. Only in the Enoch tradition was encyclopedic wisdom (as distinct from the mantic wisdom of the Daniel tradition) the context for the development of apocalyptic. Von Rad explained this development simply from the wise men's thirst for knowledge, which led them to embrace eschatology and the divine ordering of history within the sphere of their wisdom. There may be some truth in this, but the increasing dominance of eschatology in the Enoch tradition demands a more specific explanation. Perhaps the most promising is that the Enoch tradition shows from the start a preoccupation with *theodicy*, with the origin and judgment of sin. The myth of the Watchers, the fallen angels who corrupted the antediluvian world, is a myth of the origin of evil. Though the Watchers were imprisoned and the antediluvian world annihilated in the flood, the spirits of their offspring the giants became the evil spirits who continue to corrupt the world until the last judgment (15:8 – 16:1). Already in the earliest section of the *Book of Watchers* (6 – 19), eschatology emerges in this context: the judgment of the antediluvian world prefigures the final judgment[44] when the wickedness of men will receive its ultimate punishment (10:14 = 4QEn^{c}1:5:1f.) and supernatural evil be entirely eliminated (16:1; 19:1). With the expansion of the *Book of Watchers*, the emphasis on the final judgment increases. Enoch, who in chapters 6 – 19 was primarily the prophet of God's judgment on the Watchers at the time of the flood, now becomes, naturally enough, the prophet of the last judgment (1 – 5). Also, for the first time in Jewish literature, a doctrine of rewards and punishments for all men after death is expounded (22 = 4QEn^{c}1:22):[45] this too expresses a concern with the problem of evil, the problem of the suffering of the righteous at the hands of the wicked (22:5–7, 12).

So the Enoch tradition included a strong interest in the problem of evil, which was first expressed in the antediluvian legends of chapters 6 – 13, but also gave rise to increasing preoccupation with eschatology. This was its point of contact with apocalyptic prophecy, which therefore began to provide the content of Enoch's prophecies of the end.[46] Apocalyptic prophecy was also much concerned with theodicy, specifically with the problem of Israel's continued subjection to the Gentile powers, but this specific problem does not (at least explicitly) appear in the Enoch tradition until the *Book of Dreams*, in which the tradition at last related itself to the prophetic concern with Israelite salvation history. The special mark of the Enoch tradition, linked as it was to prehistoric universal history, was its treatment of theodicy as a cosmic problem. This proved a reinforcement of a general tendency in apocalyptic to set the problem of God's dealings with Israel within a context of universal history and cosmic eschatology.

The pre-Maccabean Enoch tradition left a double legacy. On the one hand, much as in the Daniel tradition, the tradition became a vehicle for the interpretation of Old Testament prophecy. In the Hasidic *Book of Dreams* and the (probably later) *Epistle of Enoch*, we have classic expressions of the apocalyptic view of history and eschatology, inspired by Old Testament prophetic faith. On the other hand, however, Enoch's journeys in angelic company through the heavens and the realms of the dead, discovering the secrets of the universe, are the first examples of another aspect of later apocalyptic literature. We need to distinguish two types of apocalypse. There are those which reveal the secrets of *history*: the divine plan of history and the coming triumph of God at the end of history. These could be called 'eschatological apocalypses'. But there are also apocalypses which reveal the mysteries of the *cosmos*: the contents of heaven and earth, or the seven heavens, or heaven and hell. These could be called 'cosmological apocalypses'.[47] The Hasidic apocalypses – Daniel, the Enochic *Book of Dreams*, the *Testament of Moses*[48] – are eschatological apocalypses. But the cosmological interest did not die out, and was by no means divorced from eschatological apocalyptic, since the secrets of heaven were believed to include the pre-existing realities of the eschatological age. Cosmology really came into its own in the late Hellenistic apocalypses of the Christian era, such as *2 Enoch* and *3 Baruch*, in which the eschatological hope has disappeared and apocalyptic is well on the way to the pure cosmology of Gnosticism. As the revelation of cosmic secrets the apocalypse became the typical literary form of Gnosticism.

So we see once more how apocalyptic, from its origins in the Jewish encounter with the Gentile cultures of the diaspora, retained a somewhat ambiguous position between Jewish and Gentile religion. Its continuity with Old Testament prophetic faith cannot be taken for granted. Each apocalyptist had to achieve this continuity by creative reinterpretation of prophecy in apocalyptic forms. His success depended on the vitality of his eschatological hope inspired by the prophets, and when this hope faded apocalyptic easily degenerated into cosmological speculation of a fundamentally pagan character.

Apocalyptic as interpretation of prophecy

The continuity between prophecy and apocalyptic occurred when the apocalyptists assumed the role of interpreters of prophecy. They did not always do this nor always to the same extent, for as we have seen there are other aspects of apocalyptic literature, but this was the dominant aspect of the major tradition of eschatological apocalypses. In this tradition the transcendent eschatology of post-exilic prophecy was taken up and further developed in a conscious process of reinterpreting the prophets for the apocalyptists' own age.

The apocalyptists understood themselves not as prophets but as inspired interpreters of prophecy.[49] The process of reinterpreting prophecy was already a prominent feature of post-exilic prophecy, but the post-exilic prophets were still prophets in their own right. The apocalyptists, however, lived in an age when the prophetic spirit was quenched (1 Macc. 4: 46). Their inspiration was not a source of new prophetic revelation, but of interpretation of the already given revelation. There is therefore a decisive difference of self-understanding between prophets and apocalyptists, which implies also a difference of authority. The authority of the apocalyptists' message is only derivative from that of the prophets.

So when Jewish writers with a background in the mantic wisdom of the Daniel tradition or the cosmological wisdom of the Enoch tradition inherited the legacy of post-exilic prophecy, they did so as non-prophetic interpreters of the prophetic tradition which had come to an end. There may of course have been other groups without a wisdom or diaspora background who stood in greater *sociological* continuity with the prophetic tradition, maintaining the eschatological hope of the disciples of Second Isaiah and influencing the Enoch and Daniel traditions. The strong influence of Isaiah 40 – 66 on the apocalyptic of the *Book of Watchers*[50] and Daniel[51] is suggestive in this respect. To such a group we might attribute the eventual compilation of the book of Isaiah. But even in such a tradition a *theological* discontinuity occurred (perhaps gradually) when consciousness of independent prophetic vocation disappeared.

The puzzling apocalyptic device of pseudonymity is at least partly connected with this apocalyptic role of interpreting prophecy. The *Testament of Moses*, which may well be a Hasidic work contemporary with Daniel,[52] is the least problematic example: as an interpretation of Deuteronomy 31 – 34 it puts its interpretation of Moses' prophecies into Moses' mouth. Similarly Daniel 7 – 12 has been attributed to Daniel because its fundamental idea is the scheme of the four empires followed by the eschatological kingdom, which derives from Daniel's prediction in chapter 2. Of course the apocalyptist does not interpret only the prophecies of his pseudonym, but the pseudonym indicates his primary inspiration.[53] Pseudonymity is therefore a device expressing the apocalyptist's consciousness that the age of prophecy has passed: not in the sense that he fraudulently wishes to pass off his work as belonging to the age of prophecy, but in the sense that he thereby acknowledges his work to be mere interpretation of the revelation given in the prophetic age. Similarly the *vaticinia ex eventu* are not a fraudulent device to give spurious legitimation to the apocalyptist's work; they are his interpretation of the prophecies of the past, rewritten in the light of their fulfilment in order to show how they have been fulfilled and what still remains to be fulfilled. In pseudonymity and *vaticinia ex eventu* the apocalyptists adopted a form which was common in pagan oracular literature and made it a vehicle of their self-understanding as interpreters of Israelite prophecy.

II. Theological issues

The problem of theological evaluation

Discussion of the origins of apocalyptic cannot really be isolated from a theological evaluation of apocalyptic. Implicitly or explicitly, much recent discussion has involved the judgment that apocalyptic is a more or less degenerate form of Israelite faith. Von Rad, for example, was clearly led to deny the connection between prophecy and apocalyptic because he believed the apocalyptic understanding of history compared so badly with the prophetic, and even Hanson, despite his strong argument for the continuity of prophecy and apocalyptic, still treats pre-exilic prophecy as the high point of Old Testament theology, from which apocalyptic is a regrettable decline, however much it may be an understandable development in post-exilic circumstances.

Moreover, the general theological outlook of the scholar can determine which new theological developments in the rise of apocalyptic he selects as the really significant ones. An older generation of scholars regarded the development of Jewish belief in life after death as a major landmark in the history of revelation, and so, however unsympathetic they may have been to other aspects of apocalyptic, this feature alone guaranteed the positive importance of apocalyptic. Recent scholarship in this area has paid remarkably little attention to this central apocalyptic belief, so that von Rad barely mentions it, and Hanson can argue that apocalyptic eschatology was in all essentials already developed before the introduction of a doctrine of immortality or resurrection.

Almost all modern attempts either to denigrate or to rehabilitate apocalyptic focus on its attitude to history. So discussion of Wolfhart Pannenberg's evaluation of apocalyptic in his systematic theology has centred on whether he is correct in supposing that apocalyptic gave real significance to universal history as the sphere of God's self-revelation.[54]

To a large extent recent discussion has rightly concentrated on the apocalyptic view of history in relation to eschatology, since this takes us to the heart of the problem. The real issue is whether theology may seek the ultimate meaning of human life and the ultimate achievement of God's purpose *beyond* the history of this world. For many modern scholars, pre-exilic prophecy is the Old Testament theological norm partly because it did not do this, while apocalyptic is a serious decline from the norm, even a relapse into paganism, because it did. Thus for Hanson the transcendent eschatology of apocalyptic prophecy is 'myth' not merely in the literary sense (which is undeniable) but in a sense akin to Bultmann's. In their literal expectation that Yahweh was going to establish his kingdom by direct personal intervention rather than human agency, and in a way which involved radical transformation of this world beyond the possibilities of ordinary history, the disciples of Second Isaiah were *mistaken*. Such language of divine intervention and cosmic transformation could only be valid as a mythical way of illuminating the possibilities of ordinary history. So when the apocalyptists did not translate it into pragmatic political policies but took it to mean that ordinary history would really be transcended with the arrival of salvation, they were engaged in an illusory flight from the real world of history into the timeless realm of myth.

For the Christian the validity of transcendent eschatology is in the last resort a problem of New Testament theology. While the apocalyptic hope was certainly modified by the historical event of Jesus Christ, the New Testament interprets this event as presupposing and even endorsing a transcendent eschatology of divine intervention, cosmic transformation and the transcendence of death. The final achievement of God's purposes and the ultimate fulfilment of humanity in Christ really do lie beyond the possibilities of this world of sin and suffering and death, in a new creation such as apocalyptic prophecy first began to hope for on the strength of the promises of God. Of course the new creation is the transformation of *this world* – *this* distinguishes Christian eschatology from the cosmological dualism of Gnosticism – but it transcends the possibilities of ordinary history. So it seems that a serious commitment to the New Testament revelation requires us to see apocalyptic eschatology as essentially a theological advance in which God's promises through the prophets were stirring his people to hope for a greater salvation than their forefathers had guessed. This must be the broad context for our evaluation of apocalyptic.

It still remains, however, a serious question whether the apocalyptists in fact abandoned the prophetic faith in God's action *within* history, and the prophetic demand for man's free and responsible action in history. Have they in fact *substituted* transcendent eschatology for history, so that history itself is emptied of meaning, as a sphere in which God cannot act salvifically and man can only wait for the End? To answer this we must look more closely at the apocalyptic attitude to history in the context of the post-exilic experience of history to which it was a response.

The negative view of history

The apocalyptic attitude to history is commonly characterized by a series of derogatory terms: radically dualistic, pessimistic, deterministic. The apocalyptists are said to work with an absolute contrast between this age and the age to come. This age is irremediably evil, under the domination of the powers of evil, and therefore all hope is placed on God's coming intervention at the end, when he will annihilate the present evil age and inaugurate the eternal future age. In the history of this age God does not act salvifically; he has given up his people to suffering and evil, and reserved the blessings of life in his kingdom wholly for the age to come. So the apocalyptists were indifferent to the real business of living in this world, and indulged their fantasy in mere escapist speculation about a transcendent world to come. It is true that they engage in elaborate schematizations of history and emphasize God's predetermination of history, but this is purely to show that God is bringing history to an end, while their extreme determinism again has the effect of leaving man with no motive for responsible involvement in the course of history.

This is the wholly negative view of history commonly attributed to the apocalyptists. Like so much that is said about apocalyptic, it suffers from hasty generalization. It would not be difficult to make it appear plausible by quoting a secondhand collection of proof-texts, and especially by preferring later to earlier apocalyptic, and emphasizing texts which are closer to Iranian dualism at the expense of those most influenced by Old Testament prophecy. We have seen that the apocalyptic enterprise, with its potentially ambiguous relationship to its non-Jewish environment, was hazardous, and the above sketch has at least the merit of illustrating the hazard. But it does no justice to the apocalyptists to draw the extreme conclusions from a selection of the evidence.

The apocalyptic view of history must be understood from its starting-point in the post-exilic experience of history, in which the returned exiles remained under the domination of the Gentile powers and God's promises, through Second Isaiah and Ezekiel, of glorious restoration, remained unfulfilled. Those who now denigrate apocalyptic rarely face the mounting problem of theodicy which the apocalyptists faced in the extended period of contradiction between the promises of God and the continued subjection and suffering of his people. The apocalyptists refused the spurious solution of a realized eschatology accommodated to Gentile rule and the cult of the second temple: they insisted on believing that the prophecies meant what they said, and undertook the role of Third Isaiah's watchmen, who are to 'put the LORD in remembrance, take no rest, and give him no rest until he establishes Jerusalem' (Is. 62:6f., RSV).

So the apocalyptists did not begin with a dogma about the nature of history: that God cannot act in the history of this world. They began with an empirical observation of God's relative absence from history *since the fall of Jerusalem.* It did not appear to them that he had been active on behalf of his people during this period. Consequently the common apocalyptic view, which goes back to Third Isaiah,[55] was that the exile had never really ended.[56] Daniel 9 therefore multiplies Jeremiah's seventy years of exile into seventy weeks of years to cover the whole period since 586. It was of the history of this period that the apocalyptists took a negative view. Daniel's four world empires are not a scheme embracing all history, but specifically history since Nebuchadnezzar and the exile. The Enochic *Book of Dreams* contains an allegorical account of the whole history of the world since creation (*1 Enoch* 85 – 90), but again the negative view characterizes only the period since the end of the monarchy. in this period (89:59 – 90:17) God is represented as no longer ruling Israel directly but as delegating his rule to seventy 'shepherds', angelic beings who rule Israel successively during the period from the fall of Jerusalem to the end. The number seventy indicates that the author is reinterpreting the seventy years of exile of Jeremiah's prophecy. God in the vision commands the shepherds to punish the apostates of Israel by means of the pagan nations which oppress Israel during the whole of the post-exilic period, but in fact they exceed their commission and allow the righteous also to be oppressed and killed. God is represented as repeatedly and deliberately refusing to intervene in this situation. Evidently this is a theologically somewhat crude attempt to explain what the author felt to be God's absence from the history of his people since the exile. Later the idea of angelic delegates developed into the idea of Israel's being under the dominion of Satan during this period. It was the 'age of wrath' (CD 1:5) in which Satan was 'unleashed against Israel' (CD 4:12).

This view of post-exilic history came to a head in the crisis of Jewish faith under Antiochus Epiphanes. This was the climax of the age of wrath, 'a time of trouble, such as never has been' (Dan. 12:1; cf. *Testament of Moses* 8:1). The Hasidic movement, which produced the apocalypses of this period, was therefore a movement of repentance and suffering intercession,[57] seeking the promised divine intervention to deliver the faithful. This was not a retreat from history but precisely an expectation that God would vindicate his people and his justice on the stage of history, though in such a way as to transcend ordinary historical possibility.

The apocalyptists faced not only the absence of God's saving activity from history since the exile, but also the silence of God in the period since the cessation of prophecy. 'There is no longer any prophet, and there is none among us who knows how long' (Ps. 74:9). Behind apocalyptic lurks a fear that God had simply abandoned his people, and against that fear apocalyptic is a tremendous reassertion of the prophetic faith. In apocalyptic God's silence was broken by the renewal of his past promises in their relevance to the present. God had not abandoned his people; his promised salvation was coming. Sometimes, perhaps, the apocalyptists broke God's silence with speculations of their own, forced too much contemporary relevance out of the prophecies, answered too precisely the unanswerable 'how long?'[58] But their work ensured the survival of hope.

It is true that the act of divine deliverance for which the apocalyptists looked far transcended the great events of the salvation-history of the past. So the image of a new exodus is less common in apocalyptic than the image of a new creation. In the Enoch literature the dominant type of the end is the deluge, in which a whole universe was destroyed.[59] This universalization of eschatology resulted in part from the historical involvement of post-exilic Israel in the destiny of the world empires, and in part from the pressure of a universal theodicy which looked for the triumph of God over every form of evil: we saw how this developed in the Enochic *Book of Watchers*. The apocalyptists dared to believe that even death would be conquered. So they expected an act of God within the temporal future which would so far transcend his acts in past history that they could only call it new creation.

This is the expectation which gives rise to the temporal dualism of apocalyptic: its distinction between this age and the age to come which follows the new creation. The terminology of the two ages does not emerge in apocalyptic until a late stage, becoming popular only in the first century AD, as the New Testament evidences.[60] This is significant because it shows that apocalyptic did not begin from a dualistic dogma, but from an experience of history. For this reason the contrast between the two ages is never absolute. There is no denial that God has been active in the past history of Israel, and this can even be emphasized, as in the Enochic *Book of Dreams*. His coming eschatological intervention transcends, but is not wholly different in kind from his past acts.[61] Even in late apocalyptic where the dualism is sharpened, this world remains God's world. It is not totally given over to the powers of evil. So the temporal dualism of apocalyptic is not cosmological dualism.

Apocalyptic eschatology does not therefore arise from an abandonment of the prophetic faith that God acts in history. It would be better to say that the apocalyptists held on to this faith in the face of the doubt which the universal experience of history provokes. Because they believed he had acted in the past they hoped for his action in the future. But they saw the world in terms which demanded the hope of total transformation as the only appropriate expression of faith in a God who rules history.

In a sense, then, the prophetic faith could only survive the post-exilic experience by giving birth to eschatological faith. We may be grateful for that. Nevertheless, there was surely a danger. The apocalyptists might be so intent on eschatology that they could forget that God does act in history before the end. They might despair of history altogether, and the experience of God's absence from their own history might become the dogma of his absence from all history.

So the Hasidic apocalyptists have often been contrasted with their contemporaries the Maccabees. The former are said to have deduced from their eschatology a quietist attitude of waiting for divine intervention, so that they held aloof from the Maccabean revolt and were unable to see the hand of God in the Maccabean victories. We can see how this might have happened, but it is not really clear that it did. It is true that the book of Daniel refers to the Maccabees only as 'a little help' for the martyred Hasidim (11:34), but this need not be as disparaging a reference as is often thought. More probably it indicates that Daniel was written when the Maccabean resistance had only just begun. The Enochic *Book of Dreams*, written a year or so later, regards the Maccabean victories as the beginning of God's eschatological victory and Judas Maccabaeus as a practically messianic agent of God's eschatological intervention (*1 Enoch* 90:8–18). The truth would seem to be that the apocalyptic hope mobilized support for the Maccabees. Of course the Maccabean revolt did not turn out actually to be the messianic war, though it was a notable deliverance, but it does not follow that the apocalyptists must have concluded that their expectations of it were entirely misplaced. The fact that the Hasidic apocalypses were preserved without modification, and Daniel was even canonized, suggests otherwise. An historical event like the Maccabean deliverance could be regarded as a provisional realization of God's promises, an act of God within history which anticipated and kept alive the hope of the greater deliverance still to come. Transcendent eschatology need not empty history of divine action; it can on the contrary facilitate the recognition and interpretation of God's action in history.

Again I do not wish to say that this was always the case. In this as in other respects the apocalyptists were walking a theological tightrope, and there was no guarantee that they would keep their balance, other than their study of Old

Testament prophecy. It seems that in the end they did not. The overwhelming disappointment of Jewish apocalyptic hopes in the period AD 70–140 proved too great for the healthy survival of the apocalyptic hope. The great apocalypses of that period – the *Apocalypse of Abraham, 2 Baruch,* and *4 Ezra* – are the last great eschatological apocalypses of Judaism, In *4 Ezra* in particular we can see the strain under which the apocalyptic theodicy was labouring. There is a deepening pessimism, an almost totally negative evaluation of the whole history of this age from Adam to the end, a stark dualism of the two ages. This apocalyptist does not surrender his eschatological faith, but we can see how short a step it now was to cosmological dualism and outright Gnosticism.

Apocalyptic eschatology at its best spoke to a contemporary need. It was not identical with the faith of the pre-exilic prophets, but nor was the experience of history in which it belonged. Perhaps it is true that transcendent eschatology was gained at the cost of a certain loss of awareness of the significance of present history. This loss was recovered in the New Testament revelation, but it is worth noticing that it was recovered in a way which so far from repudiating the apocalyptic development, took it for granted. The significance of present history was guaranteed for the New Testament writers by their belief that in the death and resurrection of Jesus God had *already* acted in an *eschatological* way, the new age had invaded the old, the new creation was under way, and the interim period of the overlap of the ages was filled with the eschatological mission of the church. So it is true that the apocalyptic tendency to a negative evaluation of history is not to be found in New Testament thought, but this is not because the New Testament church reverted to a pre-apocalyptic kind of salvation history.[62] It is because the apocalyptic expectation had entered a phase of decisive fulfilment.

Apocalyptic determinism

We have still to answer the charge of determinism against the apocalyptic view of history. Von Rad made this a major reason for denying apocalyptic an origin in prophecy.[63] He correctly stresses the apocalyptic doctrine that God has determined the whole course of the world's history from the beginning: 'All things which should be in this world, he foresaw and lo! it is brought forth' (*Testament of Moses* 12:5). This is the presupposition of the comprehensive reviews of future history and of the conviction that the end can come only at the time which God has appointed (Dan. 11:27, 29, 35f.). It is the secrets of the divine plan, written on the heavenly tablets of destiny, which the apocalyptist is privileged to know: 'what is inscribed in the book of truth' (Dan. 10:21); the heavenly tablets ... the book of all the deeds of mankind, and of all the children of flesh that shall be upon the earth to the remotest generations' (*1 Enoch* 81:2). Von Rad correctly points out that this differs from the prophetic conception, in which Yahweh makes continually fresh decisions, and issues threats and promises which are conditional on men's sin or repentance (Jer. 18:7–10). Granted that the apocalyptists share the prophetic concern for Yahweh's sovereignty over history, is their deterministic way of expressing it a denial of human freedom and responsibility and so a retreat from human involvement in history?

Determinism certainly belongs more obviously in the context of apocalyptic's continuity with the pagan oracles than it does in the context of its debt to Old Testament prophecy. Pagan divination was generally wedded to a notion of unalterable fate. There are no threats or promises calling for an ethical response, simply the revelation that what will be will be. The forms of oracle which apocalyptic shares with its pagan neighbours, including the *vaticinia ex eventu*, tend to reflect this outlook. Their popularity in the centuries when apocalyptic flourished may partly reflect the fact that the nations of the Near East had lost the power to shape their political future. A genre which made the seer and his audience mere spectators of the course of history corresponded to the mood of the time.

Again we can see the hazardous nature of apocalyptic's relationship to its environment. In its attempt to express in this context the sovereignty of the personal and ethical God of Israel there was the risk of confusing him with fate. The avoidance of this risk depended on the apocalyptists' ability to place alongside a passage like Daniel 11, with its deterministic emphasis, a passage like Daniel's prayer in Daniel 9, with its conviction that God judges his people for their rebellion and responds in mercy to their repentance and to the prayers of intercessors like Daniel. It is no solution to this paradox to excise Daniel's prayer as later interpolation,[64] for the conviction that God would respond to repentance and intercession was at the heart of the Hasidic movement and appears in all their apocalypses. All their pseudonymous seers were noted intercessors: Daniel (Dan. 9; *Testament of Moses* 4:1–4), Enoch (*1 Enoch* 83f.), Moses (*Testament of Moses* 11:14, 17; 12:6).[65] Belief in the divine determination of all events clearly exists in tension with the conviction that the covenant God responds to his people's free and responsible action. The former does not result in fatalism because it is only one side of the apocalyptic faith.

Positively, the apocalyptic belief in divine determination of history functioned to support eschatological faith in the face of the negative experience of history. In an age when it was tempting to believe that God had simply abandoned the historical process and with it his promises to his people, the need was for a strong assertion of his sovereignty. This functions, first, to relativize the power of the pagan empires in stressing that it is God 'who removes kings and sets up kings' (Dan. 2:21). So his purpose of giving the kingdom to his own people is assured of success at its appointed time. Secondly, the apocalyptic belief emphasizes that in the last resort the promise of eschatological salvation is unconditional, as it was also for the prophets. For their sins, Moses predicts, Israel 'will be punished by the nations with many torments. Yet it is not possible that he should wholly destroy and forsake them. For God has gone forth, who foresaw all things from the beginning, and his covenant is established by the oath' (*Testament of Moses* 12:11–13). Similarly Second Isaiah had met the despair of the exiles with the message of Yahweh's sovereignty over the nations and his irrevocable purpose of salvation for his people.

So the determinism of apocalyptic must be judged not as an abstract philosophy, but by its function within its context, which is precisely to counter fatalistic despair, to lay open to men the eschatological future, and call men to appropriate action. In terms of that function the gulf between the prophetic and apocalyptic concepts of history is by no means so unbridgeable as von Rad assumes.[66]

Apocalyptic and the canon

We have defended the apocalyptists as interpreters of prophecy for their own generation. A literature as varied as the apocalyptic literature must be evaluated with discrimination rather than generalization, and we have recognized the theological hazards which the apocalyptists did not always avoid. But they lived in an age whose dominant mood encouraged just such a flight from historical reality as eventually issued in Gnosticism. So if their hold on the full reality of Old Testament salvation history seems sometimes precarious we should not be surprised It is more surprising that they kept hold of it as well as they did. They faced the problem of believing in the God of the prophets against the evidence of history. Their transcendent eschatology was both a solution, in that the problem of history demands a solution which transcends history, and an aggravation of the problem, as apocalyptic hopes remained unfulfilled. But with New Testament hindsight, we can see that this was their theological role between the Testaments: to keep Jewish faith wide open to the future in hope.

The apocalyptists occupy an essentially intertestamental position. They interpret the prophets to an age when prophecy has ceased but fulfilment is still awaited. They understand their inspiration and their authority to be of a secondary, derivative kind. Their transcendent eschatology, which is apocalyptic's theological centre, is already developed in post-exilic prophecy,[67] and the apocalyptists' role is to intensify it and enable their own generation to live by it. It was by means of apocalyptic that the Old Testament retained its eschatological orientation through the intertestamental age, in this sense apocalyptic is the bridge between the Testaments, and it corresponds to the character of apocalyptic that it is represented, but not extensively represented, in the Old Testament canon.

Notes

1. 'The beginnings of Christian theology', *JTC* 6 (1969), p. 40 (= E. Käsemann, *New Testament Questions of Today*, London: SCM, 1969, p. 102).
2. 'Jewish apocalyptic in recent scholarly study', *BJRL* 58 (1975–6), pp. 28–29.
3. *The Dawn of Apocalyptic* (Philadelphia: Fortress Press, 1975). See also Hanson's articles: 'Jewish apocalyptic against its Near Eastern environment', *RB* 78 (1971), pp. 31–58; 'Old Testament apocalyptic re-examined', *Int* 25 (1971), pp. 454–479; 'Zechariah 9 and the recapitulation of an ancient ritual pattern', *JBL* 92 (1973), pp. 37–59; 'Apocalypticism', *Interpreter's Dictionary of the Bible: Supplementary Volume* (Nashville, Tennessee: Abingdon, 1976), pp. 28–34.
4. In this article I accept, as Hanson does, the usual critical conclusions as to the unity and date of the books of Isaiah, Zechariah and Daniel. Readers who maintain the traditional conservative views on these issues will naturally have to differ very radically from both Hanson's and my own reconstructions of the rise of apocalyptic. For the consistency of these critical conclusions with an evangelical doctrine of Scripture, see J. E. Goldingay, 'Inspiration, infallibility, and criticism', *The Churchman* 90 (1976), pp. 6–23; idem, 'The book of Daniel: three issues', *Themelios* 2.2 (1977), pp. 45–49. The honesty of the pseudepigraphal device in Daniel is defended below.
5. Hanson, *The Dawn of Apocalyptic*, p. 11.
6. Ibid.
7. For the contrary view that apocalyptic arises in the tradition of Ezekiel and Zechariah, cf. H. Gese, *ZTK* 70 (1973), pp. 20–49; R. North, 'Prophecy to apocalyptic via Zechariah', *VTSup* 22 (Congress Volume, Uppsala 1971), pp. 47–71.
8. *Interpreter's Dictionary of the Bible: Supplementary Volume*, pp. 32, 982–983.
9. M. Delcor, *RB* 59 (1952), pp. 385–411: contacts with Ezekiel listed, p. 386, relation to Third Isaiah discussed, pp. 387–390. R. A. Mason, *ZAW* 88 (1976), pp. 227–238, claims that continuity of themes shows that Zech. 9 – 14 stands in the tradition of Zech. 1 – 8.
10. E.g. *Dawn*, pp. 143f., 150–151.
11. Ibid., pp. 185, 207.
12. Ibid., pp. 155–161, 376–379, 397.
13. On the Divine Warrior myth: ibid., pp. 300–323, 328–333.
14. F. M. Cross, *Canaanite Myth and Hebrew Epic* (Cambridge, MA: Harvard University Press, 1973), p. 90, cf. pp. 144, 170, 343–346.
15. *Daniel*: J. A. Emerton, *JTS* (NS) 9 (1958), pp. 225–242; Cross, op. cit., p. 17; M. Delcor, *VT* 18 (1968), pp. 290–312; idem, *Le livre de Daniel* (Paris: Gabalda, 1971), pp. 32, 210–211. *Enoch*: M. Delcor, *RHR* 190 (1976), pp. 3–53; R. J. Clifford, *The Cosmic Mountain In Canaan and the Old Testament* (Cambridge, MA: Harvard University Press, 1972), pp. 182–189; J. T. Milik, *The Books of Enoch* (Oxford: Clarendon Press, 1976), pp. 29, 39.
16. Probably a doctrine of resurrection appears in Is. 26:19, which Hanson considers 'early apocalyptic' (op. cit., pp. 313f.), but he does not discuss it.
17. G. von Rad, *Old Testament Theology* 2 (ET Edinburgh and London: Oliver and Boyd, 1965), pp. 301–308, is the original version of his argument; this was completely revised for the fourth German edition: *Theologie des Alten Testaments* 2 (Munich: Kaiser, 1965), pp. 316ff. (not in ET); and developed again in *Wisdom in Israel* (ET London: SCM, 1972), pp. 263–282.
18. For criticism see P. Vielhauer in *New Testament Apocrypha* 2, ed. W. Schneemelcher and R. McL.

Wilson (London: Lutterworth, 1965), pp. 597–598; W. Zimmerli, *Man and his Hope in the Old Testament* (London: SCM, 1971), p. 140; K. Koch, *The Rediscovery of Apocalyptic* (London: SCM, 1972), pp. 42–47; W. Schmithals, *The Apocalyptic Movement* (Nashville, TN: Abingdon, 1975), pp. 128–131; J. Barr, art. cit., p. 25.

19. 'Mantische Weisheit und Apokalyptik', *VTSup* 22 (Congress Volume, Uppsala 1971), pp. 268–293. Müller's argument takes up von Rad's in the sense that, although von Rad failed to distinguish mantic from proverbial wisdom, his thesis did in the end concentrate on the mantic aspect of wisdom: *Wisdom in Israel*, pp. 280–281. Cf. also J. J. Collins, *JBL* 94 (1975), pp. 218–234.

20. Old Testament references to mantic wise men: Gen. 41:8; Est. 1:13; Is. 44:25; 47:10–13; Jer. 50:35–36; Dan. 2:2, 48; 4:4–5; 5:7, 11. On mantic wisdom in Mesopotamia, see A. L. Oppenheim, *Ancient Mesopotamia* (Chicago: University of Chicago Press, 1964), pp. 206–227; on interpretation of dreams in particular, see idem, *The Interpretation of Dreams in the ancient Near East: With a Translation of an Assyrian Dream-book* (Philadelphia: American Philosophical Society, 1956).

21. In later times he could be loosely called a prophet (Mark 13:14), as could David (Acts 2:30), in the sense that they gave inspired predictions.

22. A.K. Grayson and W. G. Lambert, *JCS* 18 (1964), pp. 7–30; W. W. Hallo, *IEJ* 16 (1966), pp. 231–242; R. D. Biggs, *Iraq* 29 (1967), pp. 117–132; W. W. Hallo and R. Borger, *BibOr* 28 (1971), pp. 3–24; H. Hunger and S. A. Kaufman, *JAOS* 95 (1975), pp. 371–375. Note that Hunger and Kaufman (p. 374) suggest that their text dates from the reign of Amel-Marduk, son of Nebuchadnezzar II.

23. The device of *vaticinia ex eventu* is used in the texts published by Grayson and Lambert, Hunger and Kaufman, and in Hallo and Borger's Sulgi text. Most of these texts are probably anonymous, but Hallo and Borger's (like the Jewish apocalypses) are pseudonymous.

24. The products of the Daniel tradition are not limited to our book of Daniel: to the 'court-tales' of Dan. 1 – 6 must be added 4Q *Prayer of Nabonidus* and the LXX *Additions to Daniel*; and to the 'apocalypse' of Dan. 7 – 12 must be added the (still unpublished) fragments of a Daniel apocalypse from Qumran: 4QpsDan^{a-c}.

25. That Dan. 1 – 6 originated in circles of Jewish mantic wise men in the east diaspora, and Dan. 7 – 12 in the same circles after their return to Palestine, is argued by Collins, art. cit. (n. 19).

26. Mesopotamian 'apocalyptic' (n. 22 above) has no properly eschatological features, at most a cyclical view of history: cf. Hallo, art. cit., p. 241.

27. For the mantic activity of the magi at the courts of Media and Persia, cf. S. K. Eddy, *The King is Dead* (Lincoln, NB: University of Nebraska Press, 1961), pp. 65–71.

28. D. Flusser, *Israel Oriental Studies* 2 (1972), pp. 148–175. The Iranian sources are late, but are based on a lost passage of the *Avesta* and the parallels are too close to be fortuitous. Note how the passage from the *Zand-i Vohuman Yasn* (p. 166) incorporates precisely the connection between mantic wisdom and apocalyptic in terms of symbolic dream/vision: Ahuramazda gives Zarathustra a vision of a tree with branches of four metals, which he explains as four periods. M. Hengel, *Judaism and Hellenism* 1 (London: SCM, 1974), pp. 182–183, prefers to trace Dan. 2 to Hellenistic Greek sources.

29. Cf. Hengel, op. cit., p. 193; J. J. Collins, *VT* 25 (1975), pp. 604–608.

30. C. C. McCown, *HTR* 18 (1925), pp. 357–411; Hengel, op. cit., pp. 184–185.

31. Ibid., pp. 210–218.

32. 'On the problem of the religio-historical understanding of apocalypticism', *JTC* 6 (1969), p. 138.

33. Hengel, op. cit., p. 185: 'It is not improbable that Egyptian "apocalypticism"... and its Jewish counterpart had a mutual influence on each other.'

34. *The Books of Enoch* (Oxford: Clarendon, 1976).

35. On the relative dates, cf. also P. Grelot, *RB* 82 (1975), pp. 481–500.

36. Milik, op. cit., pp. 7–9.

37. Ibid., pp. 22–25, 28.

38. Ibid., pp. 25, 31.

39. Eschatological material appears only in 10:12 – 11:2 (which may have been expanded when chs. 6 – 19 were incorporated in the *Book of Watchers*); 16:1; 72:1; 80.

40. The debate with mantic wisdom is reflected in *1 Enoch* 7:1; 8:3.

41. Milik, op. cit., pp. 14–18, 29–31, 33, 37–38, 277; P. Grelot, *RB* 65 (1958), pp. 33–69.

42. P. Grelot, 'La Légende d'Hénoch dans les apocryphes et dans la Bible: origine et signification', *RSR* 46 (1958), pp. 5–26, 181–210; R. Borger, *JNES* 33 (1974), pp. 183–196. Grelot, 'Légende', p. 195,

concludes that the Babylonian exile was the *Sitz im Leben* of the origin of the Enoch legend, whence a continuous tradition reached the Hasidim of the Maccabean age. It is not always easy to distinguish Canaanite and Babylonian sources: cf. Grelot, 'Légende', pp. 24–26; *RB* 65 (1958), p. 68; and n. 15 above.

43. So the Enoch writings do not *identify* Enoch with an antediluvian sage of pagan myth. They present Enoch *in opposition to* the pagan heroes and sages, who are identified rather with the fallen angels and their offspring the giants: cf Milik, op. cit., pp. 29, 313.

44. In 10:20, 22 it is clear that the deluge and the final judgment are assimilated; cf. also the description of the deluge as 'the first end' in 93:4 (*Epistle of Enoch*).

45. On this passage see Milik, op. cit., p. 219. In view of the mention of Cain's descendants (22:7), 'the souls of all the children of men' (22:3) must mean all men, not just all Israelites, as R. H. Charles thought: *The Book of Enoch* (Oxford: Clarendon, 1912), p. 46. So a doctrine of general rewards and punishments after death was already developed in pre-Maccabean apocalyptic tradition. This is a decisive refutation of the thesis of G. W. E. Nickelsburg Jr, *Resurrection, Immortality, and Eternal Life in Intertestamental Judaism* (Harvard Theological Studies 26: Cambridge, MA: Harvard University Press, 1972), who argues that a doctrine of rewards and punishments after death developed at the time of the Antiochan crisis with reference only to the martyrs and persecutors of the time. His discussion of *1 Enoch* 22 assumes a post-Maccabean date (p. 134 n. 15, p. 143), which the 4QEn fragments now render impossible. *1 Enoch* 22 (cf. also 10:14; 27:2–3) is therefore of crucial importance for the origins of Jewish beliefs about the afterlife, as is the fact that the Enoch tradition, unlike other apocalyptic traditions, never expresses belief in bodily resurrection, but rather the doctrine of spiritual immortality which is also found in Jubilees and probably at Qumran. This is a striking instance of the continuing distinct identity of the various apocalyptic traditions.

46. The apocalyptic passages of the pre-Maccabean parts of *1 Enoch* are especially indebted to Third Isaiah: 5:6 (cf. Is. 65:15); 5:9 (cf. Is. 65: 19 – 20, 22); 10:17 (cf. Is. 65:20); 10:21 (cf. Is. 66:23; Zech. 14:16); 25:6 (cf. Is. 65:19f.); 27:3 (cf. Is. 66:24); 72:1 (cf. Is. 65:17; 66:22); 81:9 (cf. Is. 57: 1).

47. This distinction, in different terminology, is made by I. Willi-Plein, *VT* 27 (1977), p. 79.

48. For the date of the *Testament of Moses*, see n. 52 below.

49. This is argued most recently by Willi-Plein, art. cit. Cf. also D. S. Russell, *The Method and Message of Jewish Apocalyptic* (London: SCM, 1964), ch. 7.

50. See n. 46 above.

51. For Daniel's (and general Hasidic) dependence on Third Isaiah, cf. Nickelsburg, op. cit., pp. 19–22.

52. There are two possible dates for the *Testament of Moses* (also called *Assumption of Moses*): c. 165 BC (with ch. 6 as a later interpolation) or early first century AD. The former is supported by J. Licht, *JJS* 12 (1961), pp. 95–103; Nickelsburg, op. cit., pp. 43–45, and in *Studies on the Testament of Moses*, ed. G. W. E. Nickelsburg (Cambridge, MA: SBL, 1973), pp. 33–37; J. A. Goldstein in ibid., pp. 44–47.

53. In later apocalypses, such as those attributed to Ezra and Baruch, there is no longer any question of interpreting the pseudonym's prophecies. The authors of *4 Ezra* and *2 Baruch* doubtless chose their pseudonyms because they identified with the historical situation of Ezra and Baruch after the fall of Jerusalem.

54. E.g. H. D. Betz, *JTC* 6 (1969), pp. 192–207; W. R. Murdock, *Int* 21 (1967), pp. 167–187.

55. C. Westermann, *Isaiah 40 – 66* (London: SCM, 1969), pp. 348–349.

56. M. A. Knibb, *HJ* 17 (1976), pp. 253–272.

57. Hengel, op. cit., pp. 179–180.; cf. Dan. 9; 11:33; 12:3; *1 Enoch* 83f.; *Testament of Moses* 9; 12: 6.

58. In fact the apocalyptists were less addicted to setting dates for the end than is often thought: L. Hartman, *NTS* 22 (1975–6), pp. 1–14.

59. *1 Enoch* 83 makes the flood a cosmic catastrophe; cf. n. 44 above.

60. In *1 Enoch* the terminology of the two ages appears only in the *Similitudes*, now almost universally admitted to be no earlier than the first century AD. The classic statement of the doctrine of the two ages, from the end of the first century AD, is *4 Ezra* 7:50: 'The Most High has made not one age but two.' For possible rabbinic examples from the first century BC, see M. Delcor, *Le Testament d'Abraham* (Leiden: Brill, 1973), pp. 41–42.

61. A typological view of history is still quite clear in *2 Baruch*, a late first-century AD work which reflects growing dualism. *2 Baruch* 63 tells of the deliverance of Jerusalem from Sennacherib in

terms which prefigure the end.

62. *Contra* W. G. Rollins, *NTS* 17 (1970–71) pp. 454–476.
63. *Wisdom in Israel*, pp. 268–277.
64. As von Rad does: *Old Testament Theology* 2, p. 309 n. 19.
65. On the significance of this theme in *Testament of Moses*, A. B. Kolenkow in *Studies on the Testament of Moses*, pp. 72–74.
66. *Wisdom in Israel*, p. 270.
67. Probably even resurrection: Is. 26:19. But the development of this doctrine remains a very significant development in the intertestamental period.

3

The origins of the worship of Christ

L. W. Hurtado   Vol. 19.2 (1994)

Introduction

The great German scholar Johannes Weiss called the worship of Christ 'the most significant step of all in the history of the origins of Christianity'.[1] The American scholar David Aune has written, 'Perhaps the single most important historical development within the early church was the rise of the cultic worship of the exalted Jesus within the primitive Palestinian church.'[2] In this essay I wish to discuss the origins of this fascinating feature of early Christianity. I begin with a quotation from 1 Corinthians 8:5–6 (RSV), from a letter of the apostle Paul written c. AD 52–55, scarcely twenty years after the death of Jesus.

> Although there may be so-called gods in heaven or on earth – as indeed there are many 'gods' and many 'lords' – yet for us there is one God, the Father, from whom are all things and for whom we exist, and one Lord, Jesus Christ, through whom are all things and through whom we exist.

In these words we find succinctly expressed the distinctive 'binitarian pattern' of early Christian devotion, in which Christ is reverenced along with God within a firm monotheistic commitment to the one God of the Bible. I would like to comment on a few important matters about early devotion to Christ reflected in this passage. After these comments, I shall then offer some observations on the historical factors that contributed to this binitarian pattern of devotion.[3]

Early devotion to Christ

Scriptural background

First, the wording Paul uses here appears to be a deliberate adaptation of the ancient Jewish expression of faith in the one God of the Bible, the *Shema* (constructed from Deut. 6:4–9; 11:13–21; Num. 15:37–41), whose initial words can be rendered, 'Hear, O Israel: The Lord our God is one Lord.'[4] Over against the readiness characteristic of all other forms of ancient religion to worship the many deities of the ancient world, the Jewish stance may be called an 'exclusivist monotheism': the one God of the Bible is to be worshipped exclusively.[5] This is the firm faith within which Saul of Tarsus was formed, and it is the commitment within which he continued to live as a Christian apostle. Here Paul rejects the other deities of the Greco-Roman world as 'so-called gods', and insists that there is only one true God.

But for Paul and for other Jewish Christians of the first few decades of the Christian movement, their monotheistic commitment to the one God of the Bible accommodated a second figure as worthy of devotion, namely the resurrected and exalted Jesus. That is, within the firm monotheism of these early Christians there was a definitive duality, of God the Father and Christ. There was a binitarian 'shape' to their monotheistic faith and devotion. In this passage, without hesitation, Paul immediately follows his exclusivistic expression of monotheistic faith ('one God, the Father, from whom are all things') with an equally firm reference to the 'one Lord, Jesus Christ, through whom are all things'. It appears that Paul actually adapts the wording of the *Shema* to make room for both the one 'God' and Jesus as the one 'Lord'. This means that this passage exhibits a most exalted reverence for Christ, reverence expressed in terms normally applied only to God.

This is shown in the application to Christ of the titles and language used to refer to God in the Old Testament. In this passage, Christ is the one 'Lord' (*kyrios*), using the title by which God is designated in Deuteronomy 6. In many other passages as well, Paul and other early Christian writers apply to Christ the language and functions associated with God in the Old Testament.[6] That is, the early Christians seem to use the most exalted language and conceptions available to them in their religious tradition by which to refer to Christ.

Over the 400 years following Paul, the early church struggled to develop doctrines adequate to express and to justify this binitarian monotheism. The Nicene Creed of AD 325 and the Chalcedonian Creed of AD 451 are the classic formulations.[7] But well before these developments – indeed, driving these developments – was the binitarian pattern of early Christian devotion and worship reflected in 1 Corinthians 8:5–6. In other words, it is not an exaggeration to say that the 400 years of doctrinal controversy which followed Paul were essentially an attempt to form doctrine adequate to the pattern of religious life which had taken shape within the first twenty years of the Christian movement.

Early and undisputed

Secondly, we should also note that here as everywhere in Paul's undisputed letters (written between approximately AD 50 and 60), this inclusion of Christ in Christian devotional life is taken for granted as the established pattern. Controversies between Paul and other Christians are reflected in his letters, but there is no hint of a controversy over this matter. He has disagreements with other Jewish Christians over the divine plan of salvation for Gentiles, and does not hesitate to indicate that his own views are controversial. Consequently, the lack of any evidence of disagreement over the status of Christ is a most eloquent silence that suggests that the evidence of Christian devotion in the Pauline letters can be taken as representative of at least many circles of Christians beyond Paul's own churches.[8]

Indeed, there are strong confirmations that the devotional pattern involving both God and Christ goes back to the earliest 'layers' of the Christian movement. One of the most striking pieces of evidence for this is the little Aramaic phrase in 1 Corinthians 16:22, *marana tha*, 'Our Lord, come!' This phrase is probably an invocation of the risen Christ by the gathered Aramaic-speaking Christian community, an invocation uttered as part of the worship gathering, a corporate prayer to the risen Christ. The fact that Paul uses the phrase in his letter to Greek-speaking converts and without translating it suggests that the phrase was already a piece of sacred Christian tradition, a liturgical formula carried over into Greek-speaking churches and preserved because it derived from the earliest circles of Jewish Christians.

In addition, there are other passages in Paul's letters commonly identified by scholars as pieces of Christian faith and practice from years earlier than the letters in which they appear. These include confessional forms such as 'Jesus is Lord' (1 Cor. 12:3; Rom. 10:9), and perhaps hymns such as the much-discussed passage in Philippians 2:6–11.[9] It is also commonly thought that Paul's letter openings and closings, which feature both God and Christ as sources of grace and objects of devotion, take up the language of early Christian liturgy that had become well established by the time of his letters.

In my book *One God, One Lord: Early Christian Devotion and Ancient Jewish Monotheism* (1988), I have described six major phenomena of the devotional life of the early Christians which show that this binitarian pattern was firmly embedded within the first decades of the Christian movement.[10] These six phenomena are (1) early Christian hymns concerning Christ and probably sung to Christ, (2) prayer to Christ, (3) liturgical use of the 'name' of Christ, such as 'calling upon the name' of Christ (probably corporate invocation/praise of Christ in the worship setting) and baptizing 'in/into the name' of Jesus, (4) the understanding of the Christian common meal as 'the Lord's supper', which identifies this marker of Christian fellowship as belonging to Christ, (5) 'confessing' Jesus, another ritual probably set within the Christian community gathered for worship, and (6) prophecy in the name of Jesus and inspired by the 'Spirit of Christ'. Taken together, these things amount to clear evidence of a conscious and significant inclusion of Christ into the devotional life of early Christianity. They show a pattern of devotion in which Christ, with God, receives the sort of prominence and cultic actions that in monotheistic religion are normally reserved for God alone.

I wish to underscore the fact that 1 Corinthians 8:5-6 reflects the actual incorporation of Christ as an object of devotion in the worship life of early Christianity. In the context of this passage, the contrast is between reverence for idols on the one hand and, on the other hand, proper reverence for the one true God and the one Lord Jesus. Scholars have tended to focus on the doctrinal concepts of the early Christians. Perhaps it is to be expected that scholars, who spend their days developing ideas, would approach early Christianity primarily asking about its ideas and doctrines. Also, of course, the historical investigation of the New Testament emerged during the Reformation as Protestants contended with Rome and with one another over right doctrine. Consequently, scholars went looking first and foremost for doctrines and regarded the New Testament mainly as a record of early doctrinal developments.[11]

The New Testament certainly reflects early Christian doctrinal developments, but it is also very much a record of the larger religious life of early Christianity. We must recognize that behind the New Testament lies, not primarily doctrinal discussions, but the mission, community formation and worship of the churches.[12] In the context of ancient Jewish scruples about worship, I suggest that the incorporation of Christ with God into the devotional life of the churches amounted to a momentous development. This development in the worship pattern of early Christianity is in fact a much more significant development than any of the Christological doctrines, such as pre-existence and incarnation, with which scholars have usually been so very preoccupied. As I have argued in *One God, One Lord*, the ancient Jewish religious tradition made scruples about the legitimate object of worship the key dividing line between right piety and blasphemy.[13] The acceptance of Christ with God as worthy of cultic veneration within the early years of Christianity and among Jews sensitive to the scruples of their ancestral religion can only be regarded as a most striking phenomenon. It deserves far more attention than it has been given in critical scholarship.[14]

Not pagan divinization

Thirdly, this treatment of Christ as worthy of divine honours cannot correctly be understood as a divinization of Christ after the pattern of pagan heroes and demi-gods. The people among whom Christ was first given cultic devotion were Jews loyal to their ancestral traditions, not pagans or syncretistic Jews who had assimilated to paganism. Although the doctrinal reflection on Christ continued and developed over several centuries, the essential steps in treating the exalted Christ as divine were taken while Christianity was still almost entirely made up of Jews and dominated by Jewish theological categories.

This is shown, for example, in the larger context of 1 Corinthians 8 – 10, where Paul instructs his converts to avoid the worship of idols, reflecting the attitudes and the language characteristic of ancient Jewish monotheistic disdain for pagan religions. The early Christian readiness to worship Jesus cannot be seen as a late development: it begins within the first two decades of the church. It cannot be explained as the result of Gentile influences: it begins during the period when the church is essentially a new movement within the Jewish tradition. The worship of Jesus does not reflect a readiness to accommodate additional deities: the Christians among whom Jesus was first reverenced continue to show the disdain for pagan gods that characterized Jewish monotheism of the Greco-Roman era.

I wish to emphasize also that this inclusion of Christ as object of cultic/liturgical devotion was not intended or understood in any way as diminishing or threatening the sovereignty of the one God. Paul's language here suggests that for him the reverence of Christ is an extension of reverence for the one God. This is confirmed in other passages, for example Philippians 2:9–11, which emphasizes that it is God who has 'highly exalted' Jesus and given Jesus 'the name which is above every name'. The same passage predicts a universal acclamation of Jesus as 'Lord' (*kyrios*), likening Jesus' acclamation to the acclamation of God's universal sovereignty by using the wording from Isaiah 45:23 (another example of the use of Old Testament language and passages concerning God to refer to Christ).[15] My point here, however, is that this universal acclamation of Christ is also 'to the glory of God the Father' (2:11). There is absolutely no intention to reverence Christ at the expense of

God the Father. Reverence for Christ is seen as reverence for God the Father.[16]

Likewise, in 1 Corinthians 15:20–28 Christ is portrayed as the risen Son to whom everything is to be made subject, including death. But note that it is *God* who puts all things 'in subjection under him' (15:27), making Christ's rule an extension of God's sovereignty. And the outcome of Christ's victory over all things is that Christ will deliver the kingdom to God (15:24), manifesting his subjection to the Father, so that God may be magnified above all (15:27).

This too shows plainly that the religious viewpoint of the early Christians was directly contrary to that of the pagan religious environment with its readiness to recognize many deities. The veneration of Christ as divine in earliest Christianity remained firmly within the tradition of Jewish monotheistic concern for the universal sovereignty and uniqueness of the one God of Israel. The incorporation of Christ with God produced an apparently unusual form of monotheism, but was never intended to violate the monotheistic commitment of the biblical tradition.[17]

Historical factors that shaped devotion to Jesus

If I have correctly sketched the binitarian devotional pattern of early Christianity reflected in 1 Corinthians 8:5–6, and if it reflects a development as important as I have asserted, then what could have caused this development? Unfortunately for modern historical enquiry, the early Christians did not spend a lot of time analysing the historical factors that led them to worship Christ, and they have left us no records of discussion about this matter. Therefore, we have to use what early Christian evidence we have and try to make inferences. In what follows, I offer my own reflections, which have been stimulated and informed very much by the work of many other scholars, to whom I am greatly indebted. I suggest that there were four major historical factors involved in shaping the binitarian pattern of early Christian devotion, which involved the worship of Christ alongside God the Father.[18]

The ministry of Jesus

First, we have to grant the importance of the ministry of Jesus. There are sharp differences among scholars about the precise features of Jesus' ministry and message, and it would take much more time than is available here to develop a very specific picture of Jesus' ministry.[19] I suggest, however, that we must grant that Jesus had a very high impact on his followers during his earthly ministry. He summoned his closest followers to fellowship with him in his mission, and his own validity was the central question for both his followers and his opponents. His execution on charges against Roman order (probably as 'king of the Jews'), and his probable rejection by the priestly authorities as a false teacher or blasphemer (perhaps against the temple), further combined to make the question of Jesus' person the central one for his followers, even after his death. The choice was either to agree with his opponents and regard him as a failure, and perhaps even as a dangerous man (a false prophet and/or rebel), or to find in him the decisive figure around whom to gather before God.

In other words, Jesus' own earthly ministry and its immediate outcome produced a profound crisis in the lives of his followers. The apparently bold, even audacious, way he presented himself as decisive spokesman and representative of the divine kingdom made it difficult to take him as one teacher among others. The priestly and governmental rejection of him in the strongest possible measure available (crucifixion!) made the choice rather stark: either they were right and Jesus should be rejected, or they were wrong and Jesus was in fact God's decisive representative, with a validity far higher than those who condemned him. This crisis in the religious lives of Jesus' followers must be taken as one of the historical factors that contributed to his being at the centre of their religious life so soon after his earthly ministry.[20]

Jewish tradition: God's principal agent

Secondly, ancient Jewish religious tradition provided the earliest Christians with precedents and a basic category for accommodating Jesus in a heavenly position next to God. I have discussed this at some length in *One God, One Lord*, and can only summarize that material here very briefly.[21]

In a variety of ancient Jewish texts we have references to this or that figure who is pictured as what we might call the divine vizier, God's chief agent. In some cases this figure is one of the heroes of the Old Testament, such as Moses. Another such figure less well known today is Enoch, around whom developed a very great deal of interest and speculation in at least some ancient Jewish circles. Such Old Testament heroes are pictured as sitting on God's throne and exercising God's sovereignty on God's behalf as his appointed representatives.

In some texts we have a divine attribute such as Wisdom or the divine Word (*Logos*) personified and described as God's chosen representative, even as God's companion in the creation of the world (see e.g. Prov. 8:22ff.; Wisdom of Solomon 9 - 10). There continues to be a debate among scholars as to whether the personification of these divine attributes was essentially a form of colourful religious language or represented a belief that Wisdom or the divine Word really existed as distinct beings.[22] I tend to think that the language is highly rhetorical, but that is not the issue before us in this essay. My point here is that these references to divine attributes picture them in the role of God's principal agent, almost as God's partner in the exercise of his sovereignty over the rest of creation.

There are also important cases where a principal angel is portrayed in this position.[23] Indeed, I think that the idea of God having such a principal agent or vizier probably originated in connection with speculations about God's angels, and was then appropriated in speculations about revered Old Testament heroes and divine attributes. In any case, principal angels are certainly portrayed as God's chief agent, his vizier, second only to God in comparison with all other beings. In Daniel 12:1 we have a reference to 'Michael, the great prince' who will arise to lead the redemption of the elect in the last days. Even more striking, however, are references to principal angels such as Yahoel in the apocryphal writing called the *Apocalypse of Abraham*.[24] Here (10:3–4) Yahoel is appointed by God as the angel in whom the divine name dwells, as is indicated by his name, which is a compound of *Yahweh* and *El*, two names of the God of the Bible. The details vary from text to text, but this sort of principal angel who acts as God's chief agent is described as exercising divine powers and attributes. When such a being is described visually, there seems to be a deliberate use of language from the Old Testament 'theophanic' accounts, such as Daniel 7, where God is pictured and manifests his glory. In some cases, the appearance of such a principal angel to a human causes the human being to confuse the angel with God until corrected, so much is the principal angel like God.[25]

As texts such as *Enoch* show (esp. chs. 3 – 1), various motifs could be combined, from royal traditions about the Davidic king and messianic expectations, speculations about Old Testament heroes such as Enoch, and principal-angel speculations. My main point here is that, though the names and particular features vary across the many Jewish texts, we seem to have a recurring idea in them all that God can be thought of as having a specially chosen agent who is far above all other beings except God. That is, there seems to have been a widespread notion that pictured God as like a great emperor exercising sovereignty over all creation, with a massive and glorious retinue of heavenly beings to serve him. Also, as appropriate for a great emperor, God has a particular figure who holds the position of vizier, chief prince, principal agent of the divine sovereignty. The fact that a variety of identities were given to this figure, e.g. Old Testament heroes, personified attributes, principal angels, shows that the basic idea of such a principal agent was widespread. It also shows that the principal-agent position or category was a popular way of exalting this or that figure next to God within the fundamentally monotheistic orientation of ancient Jewish religion.

These traditions about God's principal agent allowed considerable scope for the exaltation of the figure put in this position. The principal agent or heavenly vizier is essentially the highest position imaginable without threatening the position of God or moving into a notion of multiple gods. I suggest that, when the earliest Christians became convinced through encounters with the resurrected Jesus that he was in fact really sent from God and had been chosen by God, the principal-agent traditions provided them with a category for placing Jesus next to God in the divine plan. We have to allow for a powerful (and perhaps complex) interaction back and forth between their experiences of the risen/exalted Jesus and the Jewish monotheistic traditions I have referred to as principal-agent traditions. The resurrection experiences convinced the earliest Christians that Jesus was totally vindicated by God against all those who had condemned him (see e.g. Acts 2:36). Also, as the one man singled out for eschatological glorification, Jesus was specially chosen by God to be the leader of the eschatological resurrection (e.g. 1 Thess. 1:10; 1 Cor. 15:20). But, I suggest, these experiences were interpreted with the aid of categories provided to the earliest Christians in their Jewish monotheistic religious tradition, though these categories were also adapted in the process. Among the traditions that were much used in the period of the origins of Christianity, there was the idea that God has a principal agent, exalted far above all others, second only to God in rank.

This category of principal-agent seems to lie behind nearly all the Christological terms and expressions used in the New Testament. Space permits me only a few illustrations. The text we considered at the beginning, 1 Corinthians 8:5–6, is a good example. All things come from God and are for God, but come *through* Christ. Christ is here the principal agent of creation and redemption. Likewise, in 1 Corinthians 15:20–28, Christ is the divinely designated leader through whom comes resurrection (15:22), and the one appointed by God to manifest the divine rule over all opposing forces (15:24–26). Christ rules by divine appointment, as God's chosen agent, and demonstrates his position as agent to God ultimately by subjecting himself to God (15:28). Even the most exalted Christological expressions in the New Testament, such as John 1, Hebrews 1, Colossians 1, or in the book of Revelation, all seem to be appropriations of the principal-agent category we have identified.[26]

In the Christian adaptation of Jewish divine-agent traditions and categories, however, there were momentous and apparently unparalleled developments. For one thing, it was an astonishing move to identify a recently executed contemporary as holding this position. I know of no analogy of an authentically Jewish group identifying its leader or founder as the heavenly vizier of God. The Qumran sect referred to its 'Righteous Teacher' (commonly thought to be a designation of the founder or some major figure in the history of the group) with great respect, but this does not compare with what the early Christians made of the risen Jesus. The other examples of divine vizier in the Jewish tradition are either angels, divine attributes or heroic figures of the distant (and more glorious) past, such as Moses.

The principal-agent traditions provide us with some of the religious background and may help us to understand what the earliest Christians were trying to say about Jesus. But these traditions do not explain *why* they said these things about Jesus. It would have been quite possible for them to have portrayed Jesus as the vindicated prophet of the last days, or even as the vindicated Messiah who is to return as God's chosen king over the elect. But something seems to have driven the earliest Christians to put the risen Jesus in the highest category afforded to them by their ancestral tradition, seeing him as God's heavenly vizier, second only to God both on earth and in heaven.

Moreover, nothing in the principal-agent traditions prepares us for the worship of God's principal agent.[27] There is no evidence of cultus devoted to any of the other principal-agent figures in Jewish tradition. There are no sacrifices to Moses, Michael, or Enoch in the Jerusalem temple of the first century. There are no prayers or hymns to such figures that seem to have been actually used in Jewish worship gatherings, no indication that in Jewish gatherings such figures were the objects of religious devotion. The Qumran sect speculated about the worship offered by angels in heaven but did not worship angels. They had a special common meal, but did not identify it with any principal agent of God. Nor were the initiation rites of any known Jewish group identified with the name of such a figure.

In the apocalyptic texts which show such interest in God's heavenly retinue, the prayers and worship are always directed to God alone. In fact, in several texts where a principal angel appears to a human being who initially confuses the angel with God, the angel corrects the human's confusion and refuses the attempts of the human being to offer him worship.[28] That is, in the very writings which show the strongest interest in God's principal agent and describe such a figure in glorious terms, there is a clear recognition that it is not appropriate to offer worship to this figure.

In short, though the principal-agent traditions are important as the basic conceptual categories appropriated by early Christians in accommodating Jesus as God's uniquely chosen agent, these traditions do not suffice to explain all that happened. The early Christian development went beyond any analogy in the Jewish principal-agent traditions, in identifying a recent contemporary as God's heavenly vizier, and in taking the momentous step of offering worship to this figure. We have to look for other factors that might have contributed to these unparalleled developments.

Experience of the glorified Jesus

A third historical factor, particularly important for the rise of the worship of Jesus, was the powerful effect of religious experiences in the earliest Christian circles. I have in mind the Easter experiences, subsequent visions of the glorified Christ and prophetic revelations and oracles in the name of Christ.[29] As is the case with all the material in the Gospels, the stories of the disciples' encounters with the risen Jesus have all been shaped by the process of being retold and adapted by the individual evangelists. This makes it difficult to reconstruct the actual experiences of the disciples in any detail, though I think it most likely that real experiences do lie beyond these traditions.[30]

Paul claims his own powerful experiences of the risen Jesus in 1 Corinthians 9:1 and 2 Corinthians 12:1. He describes his change from persecutor to advocate of the Christian faith as caused by a 'revelation' of God's Son (Gal. 1:15–16).[31] Acts 7:55–56 attributes to the dying Stephen a vision of the glorified Christ 'at the right hand of God', and in Revelation 5 we have another, more detailed description of a Christian visionary's ascent into heaven, where he sees the glorified Christ receiving heavenly reverence with God. In short, the religious life of the earliest Christian communities was marked by many such powerful experiences of 'revelation'.

In 1 Corinthians 14:26, Paul includes several such charismatic experiences as regular features of the Christian worship gathering. It seems likely that the worship gathering may well have been a characteristic setting for times when the glory of Christ was made known experientially.[32]

I suggest that the only way we can account for devoutly monotheistic Jews taking the unparalleled step of offering worship to God's principal agent is to posit that they must have felt required by God to do this. They must have come to believe that it was not only permitted to offer devotion to Jesus, it was required of them. It may well be that they came to this conviction as a result of visions of Christ receiving reverence in heaven (as, e.g., in Rev. 5), and then patterned their own worship after the heavenly ideal. They may well have had divine confirmation given to them in revelatory oracles from God, endorsing Jesus as the divine agent and requiring the elect to obey God by reverencing Jesus. Certainly the history of religions seems to furnish analogous cases of major modifications to religious traditions arising from the powerful religious experiences of individuals and groups.[33]

The effect of opposition

Fourthly, I propose that we have to allow for the effect of opposition. We may assume that earliest Christian reverence of Jesus was received quite negatively by at least some Jewish religious authorities, who probably regarded Christians as endangering the integrity of Jewish religion.[34] Paul's 'persecution' of Jewish Christians (from his pre-Christian standpoint, a form of religious discipline against Jewish Christians whom he saw as seriously problematic in their religious practice) is early evidence that Christian Jews encountered opposition right away. If opposition was, in part at least, directed against the Christian reverence given to Jesus (as I think quite likely), it is reasonable to suppose that one Christian response may well have been to withstand such opposition by emphasizing still more the importance of offering Jesus reverence. We may see a prime example of such a hardening of (Jewish) Christian convictions about the exalted significance of Jesus in the Gospel of John, which devotes a lot of space to the theme of opposition from other Jews directed against Jesus and those who revere him (e.g. John 9).

Conclusion

In this discussion I have been able only to sketch the nature of early Christian devotion to Christ and the possible historical factors that prompted it. Scholars will continue to attempt to understand better how the earliest Christians interpreted Jesus' significance and the factors that influenced them to reshape monotheistic tradition to accommodate devotion to Christ. A vigorous dialogue (and sometimes heated disagreement!) characterizes the current discussion of the matter, and my own suggestions will not all be persuasive to everyone else engaged in the subject. In any case, I hope that I have helped readers to see how important this topic is in the development of early Christianity, and that some among research students will join in the investigation of the phenomena involved in the early Christian redefinition of monotheistic devotion to accommodate the worship of Christ.

Notes

1. Johannes Weiss, *Earliest Christianity* 1(New York: Harper and Row, 1959), p. 37.
2. David Aune, *The Cultic Setting of Realized Eschatology in Early Christianity*, in *NovTSup* 28 (Leiden: Brill, 1972), p. 5.
3. For a more extensive discussion of these matters, see my book *One God, One Lord: Early Christian Devotion and Ancient Jewish Monotheism* (Philadelphia: Fortress; London: SCM, 1988). Of course, the classical Christian doctrine is a trinitarian understanding of God. But the earliest

developments in what became the doctrine of the Trinity had to do with incorporating Christ along with God the 'Father', both in doctrine and in the devotional life of early Christianity. The Spirit has never become an object of devotion in the way that God the Father and Christ were and are for Christians.

4. See e.g. R. A. Horsley, 'The background of the confessional formula in 1 Kor. 8:6', in *ZNW* 69 (1978), pp. 130-134. On the evidence for early Jewish use of the *Shema*, see e.g. E. P. Sanders, *Judaism: Practice and Belief 63 BCE - 66 CE* (London: SCM; Philadelphia: Trinity Press International, 1992), pp. 241-251.

5. See L. W. Hurtado, 'What do we mean by "first-century Jewish monotheism"?', in *Society of Biblical Literature 1993 Seminar Papers* (Atlanta: Scholars Press, 1993) for discussion of the nature of Greco-Roman Jewish monotheism and for interaction with recent suggestions that the term is not appropriate. See also Yehoshua Amir, 'Die Begegnung des biblischen und des philosophischen Monotheismus als Grundthema des jüdischen Hellenismus', in *EvTh* 38 (1978), pp. 2-19; and R. M. Grant, *Gods and the One God* (Philadelphia: Westminster, 1986).

6. See e.g. L. J. Kreitzer, *Jesus and God in Paul's Eschatology*, in JSNTSup 19 (Sheffield: JSOT Press, 1987); Carey C. Newman, *Paul's Glory-Christology: Tradition and Rhetoric*, in NovTSup 69 (Leiden: Brill, 1992).

7. English translations of these and other creeds are in H. Bettenson, *Documents of the Christian Church* (London: Oxford University Press, 2nd edn 1963). Good surveys of the doctrinal developments are in J. N. D. Kelly, *Early Christian Doctrines* (New York: Harper and Row, 2nd edn 1960); and W. H. C. Frend, *The Rise of Christianity* (Philadelphia: Fortress, 1984).

8. Here and in what follows, I draw upon the fuller discussion in my book *One God, One Lord: Early Christian Devotion and Ancient Jewish Monotheism* (London: SCM, 1988), esp. pp. 93-124, to which I refer the reader for citation of recent scholarly literature.

9. R. Deichgraber, *Gotteshymnus und Christushymnus in der frühen Christenheit* (Göttingen: Vandenhoeck und Ruprecht, 1967); M. Hengel, *Between Jesus and Paul* (London: SCM; Philadelphia: Fortress, 1984), pp. 78-96; R. P. Martin, 'Some Reflections on New Testament Hymns', in *Christ the Lord: Studies in Christology Presented to Donald Guthrie*, ed. H. H. Rowdon (Leicester: IVP, 1982), pp. 37-49.

10. *One God, One Lord*, pp. 100-114.

11. It is still the case that the study of early Christian worship is left mainly to historians of liturgy, who in turn often focus on formal features of worship and attempt to trace origins of later liturgical practices, while neglecting the all-important question of the *content* and *objects* of early Christian worship as historically significant in the context of ancient Jewish monotheistic scruples. For a helpful introduction to historical investigation of liturgical developments, see Paul Bradshaw, *The Search for the Origins of Christian Worship* (London: SPCK, 1992).

12. Whatever one may think of particular positions advocated by the old *religionsgeschichtliche Schule* and scholars of similar orientation (e.g. Bousset, Weiss, Wrede, Deissmann), it seems to me that they can be applauded for this emphasis on the religious life of early Christianity.

13. See also my essay, 'What do we mean by "first-century Jewish monotheism"?', in the first work referred to in n. 5 above.

14. Other scholars who have pointed to the historical significance of early Christian worship of Christ include R. Bauckham, 'The worship of Jesus in apocalyptic Christianity', *NTS* 27 (1980-81), pp. 322-341; R. T. France, 'The worship of Jesus: a neglected factor in Christological debate?', in *Christ the Lord: Studies in Christology Presented to Donald Guthrie* (see n. 9 above), pp. 17-36. For responses to my emphasis on this matter, see e.g. Paul A. Rainbow, 'Jewish monotheism as the matrix for New Testament Christology', *NovT* 33 (1991), pp. 78-91; J. D. G. Dunn, *The Partings of the Ways between Christianity and Judaism and their Significance for the Character of Christianity* (London: SCM; Philadelphia: Trinity Press International, 1991), ch. 10, esp. pp. 203-206. See my comments on Rainbow later in this essay. I do not find persuasive Dunn's attempt to play down the evidence of early Christian reverence of Christ in the worship setting. Also, his claim that Paul's letters convey no evidence that Jewish authorities found Christian reverence for Christ objectionable fails to take account of three things: (1) 1 Cor. 12:3 may in fact be such evidence, perhaps alluding to Jewish pressure to curse Christ (see W. Horbury, 'The benediction of the *minim* and early Jewish–Christian controversy', *JTS* 33 (1982), pp. 19-61; (2) Paul's letters are intra-Christian communications and the issues they contain are almost entirely intramural questions, so a paucity of information about Jewish attitudes toward Christian worship is not

surprising, and is by no means indicative of the absence of hostility toward Christian worship practices; (3) the Gospel accounts of Jesus' trial and condemnation for blasphemy may well have been shaped by early Jewish–Christian experiences of being charged with blasphemy by synagogue councils, and may thus be indirect evidence of Jewish opposition to Christian reverence of Christ.

15. David B. Capes, *Old Testament Yahweh Texts in Paul's Christology* (WUNT 2.47; Tübingen: Mohr [Siebeck], 1992), is a recent study of this phenomenon, but his discussion is flawed at some points by simplistic categories. See my review forthcoming in *JBL*. On Paul's use of *kyrios* as a Christological title, see my article 'Lord', in *Dictionary of Paul and his Letters*, eds. G. F. Hawthorne and R. P. Martin (Downers Grove and Leicester: IVP, 1993).

16. Indeed, the classical dogma of the Trinity was essentially intended to teach the divinity of Christ while professing a monotheistic stance in which there is only one God, and in which reverence for Christ (and the Spirit) is seen as glorifying, not diminishing, the one God. But concepts of divine 'substance' shared by Father, Son and Spirit were appropriated and used later than the New Testament. Within the New Testament, the way of referring to Christ's divinity is more in terms of his status, glory, attributes and titles, which all amount to an honorific rhetoric of divinity.

17. Of course, the classical Christian understanding of the Trinity grants the same divine 'nature' to Christ and the Spirit as to God the Father. But the functional subordination of Christ and the Spirit to God the Father expressed in these New Testament passages is retained in classical trinitarian dogma as well.

18. Students should recognize that an attempt to analyse the historical process involved in the emergence of devotion to Christ is not necessarily in conflict with a view of the process as divinely directed and as conveying authoritative revelation. A committed Christian could be just as capable as anyone else of engaging in vigorous historical enquiry, and might have special motivation for wanting to understand in historical terms the process by which the truths he or she holds dear came to expression.

19. Personally, I find Dunn's discussion of Jesus' ministry and its connections with post-Easter Christian developments largely persuasive in *The Partings of the Ways*, chs. 3, 6 and 9. Among recent studies of Jesus' ministry, we may single out E. P. Sanders, *Jesus and Judaism* (London: SCM; Philadelphia: Fortress, 1985), as particularly influential, though some of his positions have received telling criticism.

20. For a classic discussion of the importance of Jesus' crucifixion for subsequent Christian estimation of him, see N. A. Dahl, *The Crucified Messiah and Other Essays* (Minneapolis: Augsburg, 1974), pp. 10–36.

21. See chs. 1–4 for references to primary texts and scholarly literature.

22. See Saul M. Olyan, *A Thousand Thousands Served Him: Exegesis and the Naming of Angels in Ancient Judaism* (TSAJ 36; Tübingen: Mohr [Siebeck], 1993), esp. pp. 89–91.

23. On Jewish angel speculation, see ibid. and Michael Mach, *Entwicklungsstadien des jüdischen Engelglaubens in vorrabinischer Zeit* (TSAJ 34; Tübingen: Mohr [Siebeck], 1992).

24. For introductions and English translations of this and many other relevant non-canonical Jewish texts, see J. H. Charlesworth (ed.), *The Old Testament Pseudepigrapha*, 2 vols. (Garden City: Doubleday, 1983, 1985).

25. On this phenomenon, see esp. R. Bauckham, 'The Worship of Jesus' (see n. 14 above).

26. My argument has been taken by E. E. Ellis (in a review of *One God, One Lord*) as promoting an 'Arian' Christology, a suggestion I regard as bizarre on account of its anachronism, its use of dogmatic categories to evaluate historical enquiry, and the failure involved to recognize that I emphasize the innovative *adaptation* of divine agent traditions in the New Testament as summarized in the following paragraphs, an adaptation that involved the worship of the divine agent in the actions and terms normally reserved for God alone. This cultic development was in fact later the major factor that militated against Arian Christology being accepted, as Arius could not justify the worship of Christ and still call himself a monotheist.

27. This is a major point, for which I have argued in *One God, One Lord* in discussing the references to divine-agent figures in the Jewish sources. See also my discussion in 'What do we mean by "first-century Jewish monotheism"?' (n. 5 above).

28. The evidence is discussed in R. Bauckham, 'The worship of Jesus in apocalyptic Christianity' (n. 14 above). The key references are *Apoc. Zeph.* 6:15; *Ascen. Is.* 7:21–22; *Rev.* 19:10; 22:8–9.

29. J. D. G. Dunn, *Jesus and the Spirit* (London: SCM; Philadelphia: Westminster, 1975), is a good

discussion of religious experience in early Christianity. On early Christian prophecy, see D. E. Aune, *Prophecy in Early Christianity and the Ancient Mediterranean World* (Grand Rapids: Eerdmans, 1983), though Aune focuses more on the form than on the contents of prophetic speech.

30. The *narratives* have been so shaped. This does not necessarily mean that the *events* behind the narratives were created in the process.

31. See my essay 'Convert, apostate or prophet to the nations? The "conversion" of Paul in recent scholarship', in *Studies in Religion / Sciences religieuses* 22 (1993), pp. 273-284, for a review of recent issues and literature on Paul's conversion.

32. See *One God, One Lord,* esp. pp. 161–168, for references to scholarly studies of earliest Christian worship.

33. Paul Rainbow's view ('Jewish monotheism as the matrix for New Testament Christology', pp. 86–87) that religious experiences can only reflect previously formed religious beliefs seems to me simplistic. To be sure, his view is correct for human experiences normally. But there are also perceptions that appear to be novel, introducing innovation, invention, revelation in religion, experiences that seem to require (and help generate) revised new understandings of things. On innovation, see e.g. H. G. Barnett, *Innovation: The Basis of Cultural Change* (New York: McGraw-Hill, 1953).

34. See my comments about early Jewish opposition to Christ devotion in n. 14 above.

© L. W. Hurtado 1994

4

Eschatology and the church[1]

Some New Testament perspectives

Craig L. Blomberg   Vol. 23.3 (1998)

For many in the church today, eschatology seems to be one of the least relevant of the historic Christian doctrines. On the one hand, those who question the possibility of the supernatural in a scientific age find the cataclysmic irruption of God's power into human history at the end of the ages unpalatable. On the other hand, notable fundamentalists have repeatedly put forward clear-cut apocalyptic scenarios correlating current events with the signs of the end in ways which have been repeatedly disproved by subsequent history and which have in the process tarnished all conservative Christian expectation as misguided.[2] At the same time, a substantial amount of significant scholarship, particularly in evangelical circles, goes largely unnoticed by the church of Jesus Christ at large. This scholarship not only addresses key theological and exegetical cruxes but has direct relevance for Christian living on the threshold of the twenty-first century.

The topic is immense, so before I proceed I need to make several disclaimers and mark out the parameters of this brief study.

1. I am neither a systematic theologian nor an Old Testament specialist, so, as my title indicates, my comments will be primarily limited to those who have grappled with key themes and texts in the New Testament. In this connection I have sometimes ventured an opinion on a range of questions which I know require more careful and sustained consideration.

2. Although there is a time and a place to use the term 'eschatology' broadly to refer to the goal and direction of human history under God's sovereignty at each stage of the biblical revelation,[3] I will restrict my comments to issues dealing with the end of life or the end of human history as we know it.

3. My remarks are highly selective and do not reflect an exhaustive survey of the contemporary literature, although I have tried to read widely.

4. I will concentrate primarily on key trends in the last two decades of scholarly conversation and focus almost entirely on English-language material.

5. Despite my attempts to keep abreast with trends in the UK, my immediate context of teaching in a North American theological seminary will undoubtedly colour my perceptions and analyses of these trends. Hopefully this will not be entirely inappropriate. My own experience of living in several cultures has regularly reminded me of the value of seeing things from the 'outsider's' perspective. Indeed, there are some trends in North American evangelicalism that I believe merit wider exposure, even as I confess my indebtedness to British evangelicalism for many of the formative stimuli in my own theological pilgrimage.

Key themes in personal eschatology

The annihilationist debate

A flurry of discussion continues in response to John Stott's famous admission of a decade ago that he wondered whether the data of the New Testament might direct one to the annihilationist perspective. This has normally implied that the unbeliever simply ceases all conscious existence upon death, although Stott seems to allow for people to suffer temporarily in a conscious state of 'hell'.[4] Four arguments have proved influential among those who have defended this perspective:

1. the repeated scriptural language about the 'destruction' of the impenitent;

2. the metaphor of fire as implying destruction;

3. the apparent injustice of infinite punishment for finite sin; and

4. the apparent irreconcilability of the promise of eternal bliss for God's people with their consciousness of others being eternally tormented.

Despite the inherent attractiveness of annihilationism to anyone with a heart of Christian compassion, this position must be finally judged as inadequate.[5] The Greek words for 'punishment' and 'destruction' (*olethros, kolasis, apollymi* and its nominatival forms) can refer to 'ruin', carrying the sense of the cessation of life as we know it in this world, with the possibility of influence by good, to be replaced by a state of eternal punishment. Several texts seem to demand a bodily resurrection of the unrighteous to a conscious existence of eternal separation from God, occurring in contexts in which they directly parallel descriptions of eternal life (cf. esp. Dan. 12:2; Matt. 25:41, 46;

and John 5:24–30).[6] Several texts warn against hell by declaring that it would be better for those in danger of going there never to have been born, a statement that makes little sense if the wicked at some point merely cease to exist (cf. esp. Matt. 18:8–9; 26:24; and note a similar comparative logic dealing with degrees of eternal punishment in Matt. 10:15).[7] Second, the fires of hell are said to be unquenchable (Matt. 3:12; Mark 9:43), suggesting that whatever fuels them remains for eternity. Third, the problem of infinite punishment for finite sin is not resolved by annihilationism; those who would cease to exist would still do so for an infinite period of time. Indeed, this disparity is a problem for all perspectives on the fate of the impenitent short of full-fledged universalism, and its solution probably requires something along the lines of C. S. Lewis's famous descriptions of those who are unsaved eternally resisting any desire for salvation[8] (cf. Rev. 9:20–21; 16:9–10). Fourth, the existence of any finally impenitent, whether conscious or destroyed, remains a datum of Scripture which apparently clashes with *God's* perfect happiness and victory. So, again, it is not clear that anything short of complete universalism solves this problem. And if we had a greater appreciation of divine holiness, one of the communicable attributes which we can look forward to sharing in some measure in the life to come, we probably would not sense this same tension over the destruction of the wicked that we do now.[9]

The implications for the church are potentially enormous, particularly with respect to its outreach. Wildly different definitions of evangelism in fact compete with one another for acceptance.[10] There is little doubt that a proper, biblical, evangelistic zeal for reconciling men and women to God is easily quenched if one seriously believes that the worst that can happen to the non-Christian is that he or she simply ceases to exist.[11] I would love to find out in the next life that I am wrong and that proponents of annihilationism are right on this issue, but I wonder if the risk is worth taking, if indeed it turns out that this view is wrong and the more traditional Christian view is right, and if in the process my enthusiasm for sharing Christ with the lost has so waned that sinners are consigned to an endless agony that might otherwise not have been their plight.

The nature of hell

None of the above remarks, however, necessarily commits one to a particular position on a second recently much-debated issue. A discussion of four Christian views on hell itemizes the literal, the metaphorical, the purgatorial, and the conditional views.[12] The last of these, conditional immortality, is only slightly different from the annihilationist view already discussed.[13] The third, or purgatorial view, is largely limited to Roman Catholic circles and, by the admission of its own supporters, not clearly defensible from the Protestant canon. But increasingly, interpreters are recognizing that the language of eternal destruction in the New Testament consistently employs a variety of metaphors, most notably fire and outer darkness which, if absolutized, contradict one another.[14] 2 Thessalonians 1:9 may be one of the most literal descriptions of the fate of the wicked, as it explains, 'They will be punished with everlasting destruction and shut out from the presence of the Lord and from the majesty of his power' (NIVI).[15] Much of the offence in the concept of conscious eternal punishment may be mitigated if one refuses to include literal bodily torments in one's description, seeing rather a state of profound agony and awareness of being separated from God and all things good.[16] Yet this metaphorical view does not so remove the sting of death as to quash evangelistic zeal.

A second point, less widely noted, addresses further objections. Is it not unjust that the generally kind, decent, non-Christian neighbour in our pluralist world should suffer the same fate as the Idi Amins or Pol Pots of our day? I think the answer is 'yes', but then one must immediately add that nothing in Scripture consigns us to believing that the fate of all of hell's inhabitants should be the same. Particularly significant in this light is Luke 12:47–48, verses unique to Luke's version of the parable of the faithful and unfaithful servants: 'The servant who knows the master's will and does not get ready or does not do what the master wants will be beaten with many blows. But the one who does not know and does things deserving punishment will be beaten with few blows.' Given that damnation in Scripture is consistently linked with judgment according to one's works, it makes eminent sense to speak of a widespread gradation of degrees of punishment in hell.[17]

The fate of the unevangelized

Speaking of those who do not know their master's will leads us directly into a third much-debated area of personal eschatology. What about those who have never had a clear presentation of the Christian gospel? Numerous recent anthologies of essays addressing this question from a variety of perspectives have appeared in evangelical literature.[18] Indeed, two triennial conferences ago, the Tyndale Fellowship addressed this question as part of its major theme of responding to the pluralism of our modern world.[19] John Sanders has provided the most extensive taxonomy of historic Christian options, complete with the biblical data to which each appeals, the strengths and weaknesses of each case, and the list of key Christian writers over the centuries who have advocated each view. Sanders' categories include: (1) restrictivism (all those who have not heard are damned); (2) universal evangelization before death (subdivided into the options that (a) God will send the message to those who are genuinely seeking him; (b) there will be a universal opportunity for salvation just before death; and (c) God's middle knowledge – his pre-understanding of what all possible beings would do in all possible created worlds – leaves no-one without excuse); (3) eschatological evangelization (i.e. the possibility of repentance in a post-mortem state); and (4) universally accessible salvation apart from evangelization (God, through his prevenient grace or general revelation, making it possible for all those who truly seek him to be saved).[20] Perhaps the most important lesson to be derived from Sanders' study is that there is not one and only one traditional, historic Christian position on this question, despite the claims of some to the contrary. And while, on the one hand, in an age of rampant pluralism it is clearly crucial to reassert the distinctive claims of the gospel, it is not as clear that we are required to adopt the restrictivist position. Sir Norman Anderson, arguably evangelicalism's leading spokesman of the past generation in the area of comparative religions, spoke cogently when he wrote just over two decades ago,

> May this not provide us with a guideline to the solution of the burning problem of those in other religions who have never heard – or never heard with understanding – of the Saviour? It is not, of course, that they can earn salvation through their religious devotion or moral achievements, great though these sometimes are – for the NT is emphatic that no man can ever earn salvation. But what if the Spirit of God convicts them, as he alone can, of something of their sin and need; and what if he enables them, in the darkness or twilight, somehow to cast themselves on the mercy of God and cry out, as it were, for his forgiveness and salvation? Will they not then be accepted and forgiven in the one and only Saviour?[21]

Our understanding of how deeply embedded the concept of 'works-righteousness' is in the vast majority of human religions does not generate great optimism that large numbers of people would come into the kingdom by this method. But the wisdom of Anderson's position at the same time allows us to carry on with our evangelism more intelligently and perhaps more effectively. For indeed one of the biggest stumbling-blocks to coming to faith in Christ for many today is the apparently unsatisfactory nature of the arguments of the restrictivist position basing universal accountability on general revelation. Anderson's cautious 'wider hope' does not require one to imagine the grotesque scenario of somebody having been saved apart from the knowledge of Christ and then refusing the gospel upon hearing it, only to find himself or herself lost. Presumably anyone already seeking a knowledge of the one, true, living God would be empowered by him to respond positively to the Christian message. Nor is this version of the position Sanders calls 'universally accessible salvation apart from evangelization' without scriptural support. Several recent writers have insisted that this is precisely what Romans 2:12–16 implies, even if it is never explicitly stated.[22] The alternative options all fail at key points: those who 'show that the requirements of the law are written on their hearts, their consciences also bearing witness, and their thoughts now accusing, now even defending them' (Rom. 2:15) could be a merely hypothetical category, but this explanation does not work nearly as well with the parallel statements in 7–11 and 25–29 (about those who do good, are circumcised by the Spirit and receive eternal life). As J. D. G. Dunn has stressed, the culmination of this section of Romans in 3:20 does not state that no-one is justified apart from having heard of Christ, but rather that no-one is justified by the works of the law.[23] But the view of C. E. B. Cranfield, that in all three of these excerpts in Romans 2 only Christians are in view,[24] runs foul of the larger narrative flow of the epistle, in which the role of the Christian gospel does not seem to be unpacked until 3:21. So, at the very least, we have a precedent in Romans 2 for the faithful *Jew* under the old covenant responding by grace with faith in God's promises. But the reference to the *Gentiles* in verse 14 then most naturally raises the question whether all those who have not heard might not be theologically 'BC', even if they are chronologically living in the Christian dispensation.

Eternal life for Christians

It is a little ironic that so much study has concentrated on the fate of unbelievers without a corresponding focus on the glory to which Christians can look forward.[25] Two areas of study to which only slight attention has been devoted deserve further exploration. First is the issue of rewards for believers. I have argued elsewhere that, contrary to one popular strand of thought, believers should not expect eternal degrees of reward in heaven. The imagery of the parable of the vineyard labourers (Matt. 20:1–16) points us away from such an expectation, as does the logic of heaven itself (how can there be degrees of perfection?). The so-called 'crown' passages (1 Cor. 9:25; 1 Thess. 2:19; 2 Tim. 4:8; James 1:12; 1 Pet. 5:4), as well as numerous other New Testament texts, speak merely of eternal life in general as the reward for Christian commitment. I do not dispute for one minute that the New

Testament teaches that each believer will have an entirely unique experience before God on judgment day (esp. Matt. 25:14–30; 1 Cor. 3:11–15; 2 Cor. 5:1–10). I merely dispute whether any passages commit us to seeing such unique experiences as perpetuated throughout all eternity.[26]

The issue is a significant one, for a fair amount of motivation for living the Christian life is often based on these alleged degrees of reward, rather than, as Luther saw most clearly among the Protestant Reformers, on the motive of profound gratitude for God in Christ having already done what we could never do or merit.[27] Ironically, those who most emphasize rewards often also have a very broad definition of who (under the heading of the carnal Christian) can still just barely squeeze into heaven. By missing the point of the New Testament texts, they may be in fact including people that Scripture excludes, a point that becomes more obvious once we realize that several warning passages are about Christian entrance into the kingdom, rather than degrees of reward within it (e.g. 1 Cor. 9:24–27; Phil. 3:10–14).[28] Indeed, if one couples the theme of equality in heaven with that of degrees of punishment in hell, the results fit in well with a consistent biblical asymmetry: that salvation is always entirely by grace, whereas judgment is just as consistently according to one's works. Grace leaves no room for gradation; works allow for endless degrees of differentiation. I am afraid that some popular Christian thought has entirely inverted this biblical model, promising degrees of reward in heaven, but seeing those who suffer in hell as experiencing identical agony.

The intermediate state

Second, more attention needs to be devoted to the classic Christian understanding of the intermediate state. An important work which goes against the grain of much recent thought in this respect is John Cooper's *Body, Soul, and Life Everlasting*.[29] We are told these days by various philosophers, psychologists and biologists that the human person must be viewed as an indivisibly monistic whole. This claim has spawned major reinterpretations of what happens to a believer upon death, prior to the general resurrection accompanying the parousia. Either believers look forward to 'soul-sleep', whereby their next conscious moment of existence is at their resurrection, or they receive a resurrection body immediately upon death.[30] But the former option commands almost no exegetical support, except for the use of the common Greek euphemism 'sleep' for death. And the latter view, arguably present in 2 Corinthians 5:1–10, seems to require an understanding of Pauline 'development' in which the apostle actually contradicts, or changes his mind from, his earlier views (see esp. 1 Thess. 4:13–18; 1 Cor. 15:51–55). The traditional exegesis of 2 Corinthians 5 remains the best.[31] Paul does not desire to be absent from the body and home with the Lord as his ideal, but it is preferable to remaining in this life apart from the direct presence of God, if indeed it turns out that he will not live until Christ returns.[32] It is not clear that philosophy or science has proved that no intangible or immaterial dimension of the human person exists apart from his or her body.[33] Exegesis, at any rate, dare not take apparent findings of modern, non-biblical worldviews as its starting-point.

The issue is not an insignificant one. The classic conception of the intermediate state allows Christians to console loved ones who have lost believers to death with the assurance that they are immediately in the presence of Jesus. It enables us to continue to defend one essential part of the *imago Dei*: humans are unique among the forms of life God created in having the capacity to be in a spiritual relationship with him.[34] And it makes sense of the rash of near-death experiences being reported these days of individuals sensing a disembodied life beyond the grave, without forcing us to view all of these experiences either as some biologically caused illusion or as necessarily accurate descriptions of the eternal state.[35] The intermediate state does not necessarily correspond to the nature of resurrection life, for either a believer or an unbeliever.

At the same time, we must insist that even the glory of disembodied presence with God in Christ is not the ideal. Bodily resurrection vindicates God's initial purpose for creating men and women, just as the new heavens and the new earth re-establish God's original intention for the rest of his creation. Again, our popular Christian mindset, not to mention the culture of recent films enamoured of life after death, does not consistently appreciate how earthy and bodily the Christian hope is for the age to come. God originally created this world as 'good' and humans as 'very good' (Gen. 1:4, 10, 12, 18, 21, 25, 31). We have corrupted ourselves and creation, but he will have the last word, redeeming and demonstrating as utterly good all of the material world. Much popular Christianity, as well as alternative worldviews, not least in the so-called New Age movement, are neo-Gnostic in comparison.[36]

Exegesis of key New Testament texts

The Olivet discourse

Professor G. R. Beasley-Murray has put us in his debt with an update and restatement of his classic analysis of Jesus' eschatological discourse (Mark 13 and pars.).[37] After sketching out in comprehensive detail exegetical alternatives, he again cogently defends a 'historic' or 'classic premillennialist' interpretation.[38] The sermon begins (vv. 5–13) with things that must happen 'but the end is still to come' (v. 7). Verses 14–23 introduce us to 'the abomination that causes desolation' (v. 14), depicting the destruction of the temple by Rome in AD 70. Not until verses 24–27 is the parousia directly in view, but no sign is ever given that enables us to calculate its timing. Not even Jesus, in the human limits of his incarnation, had access to this information (v. 32). The enigmatic verse 30, with its reference to 'this generation' (*hē genea hautē*) not passing away 'until all these things have happened,' must be interpreted in light of verse 29. The Greek word for 'these things' (*tauta*) in verse 30 is identical to its antecedent in verse 29. But verse 29 speaks of 'these things' happening so that 'you know' that 'it' (i.e. Christ or his return) 'is near, right at the door'. It makes no sense therefore for 'these things' to include Christ's actual return because then the parousia would no longer be simply near, close at hand; it would have arrived. *Tauta* must therefore refer to the preliminary events of verses 5–23, all of which were fulfilled, at least provisionally, within the first century, enabling the church to have the lively hope of an imminent return of Christ in numerous eras of its history ever since.[39] Indeed, the application with which Mark's version of the discourse closes (and which extends for an entire additional chapter in Matthew) stresses the practical application of Jesus' words (vv. 33–37). Far from encouraging contemporary events-watching, Jesus discourages attempts to discern when the end is at hand, mandating faithful, obedient service all the while instead. T. J. Geddert's fine study persuasively demonstrates that this interpretation of the Olivet discourse matches Mark's purpose and structure more generally: to deter a theology of signs and promote humble discipleship that follows Jesus on the road to the cross.[40] Several other recent evangelical commentators and essay-writers have taken a roughly similar tack to Mark 13 and parallels, at times dubbing it a preterist-futurist approach.[41] But I do not sense that it has become well known in our churches, and certainly not as well known as the purely preterist or purely futurist options that consign all of Jesus' teaching (and like passages elsewhere in the New Testament) either to the first century or to an entirely future time.

As we approach the intriguing year 2000, I'm afraid we shall again encounter a rash of date-setters, much as we have seen, particularly in North America and in Korea, over the past decade.[42] The argument lies ready at hand. It was an ancient Jewish belief, adopted by some early Christian writers, on the basis of Psalm 90:4 ('a thousand years ... are like a day'), that the millennium would come as God's sabbath rest for human history during its seventh thousand-year period.[43] When a date of roughly 4,000 BC is accepted for the creation of the earth, it is a short step to concluding that we are on the verge of that seventh millennium. But the sole New Testament citation of this Psalm (2 Pet. 3:8–9) applies it quite differently – as a rationale for the delay of the parousia, rather than as a basis for predicting its arrival. And the uniquely Matthean sequence of parables created by Matthew's longer ending to the Olivet discourse depicts quite poignantly all of the options for the timing of Christ's return. In the parable of the thief in the night (Matt. 24:42–44), Christ returns entirely unexpectedly. In the parable of the faithful and unfaithful servants (vv. 45–51), he comes unexpectedly early. And in the story of the ten bridesmaids (25:1–13), he is unexpectedly delayed. Surely this calls Christians to prepare for all three logical possibilities[44] and rules out any attempt to imply, however cautiously, that we can ever predict a particular generation (or any period of time) in which Christ is most likely to come back.

Romans 11:25–26

An enormous amount of scholarly literature continues to address Paul's treatment of Israel in Romans 9 – 11. Particularly controversial is the climax of his discussion in 11:25–26. Is there justification here for a future hope for ethnic Israel? One's views at this point will most likely colour one's interpretation of a variety of other scattered references in the New Testament that impinge on the debate. We are particularly in debt to P. Walker for his recent book-length treatment of Jerusalem in the New Testament.[45] On this subject, Walker follows N. T. Wright's lead with respect to New Testament eschatology more generally, believing that the church has entirely superseded Israel as the chosen people of God.[46] This situation should not cause Christians to gloat; it led both Jesus and Paul to express great sorrow for their countrymen who were not responding to the gospel (Matt. 23:37–29 par.; Rom. 9:1–5). But there is no New Testament justification for seeing a final stage of eschatological blessing for literal Jews after 'the times of the Gentiles are fulfilled' (Luke 21:24). Walker and Wright give us, I believe, profound insights into vast sections of the New Testament that are directly applicable to a debate that until recently went on almost entirely outside of evangelical circles. I speak of the so-called 'two covenants' approach to salvation: Jesus is Messiah for the Gentiles but Jews may be saved by remaining faithful to the Mosaic covenant. Inasmuch as one begins to find evangelical Christians articulating this position,[47] Walker and Wright provide massive evidence that the relevant texts will simply not bear this interpretation.

To the extent that many North American Christians uncritically support the current State of Israel, seeing it even as some fulfilment of prophecy, these correctives prove crucial. No text of the New Testament suggests any future for a socio-political entity such as the modern nation of Israel. Even less substantiable are views that require Jewish presence in Jerusalem to rebuild a literal temple just prior to Christ's return, given that the foundational role of the temple was to be the one divinely ordained place for offering sacrifices. The Epistle to the Hebrews surely dispenses with the notion that literal animal sacrifices could ever again play a part in God's plans for his people. Writers like C. Chapman and G. Burge have pursued this theme in a related direction, noting that the vast majority of all Christians currently living in Israel are Palestinian.[48] And if there is no biblical mandate for a current socio-political entity in the historic lands bequeathed to the Jews, then a certain sympathy for the plight of the Palestinians must certainly be at the forefront of any Christian's social agenda.

But I fear that at times, particularly in the evangelicalism of the British Commonwealth, these points are taken for granted, and possibly balancing emphases in the New Testament of a future, at least for *ethnic* Jews, is too hastily dismissed. Hints appear in Matthew 23:39 (par. Luke 13:35);[49] Luke 21:24; Acts 3:19–21; and elsewhere, but ultimately discussion must focus attention on the more detailed conclusions of Romans.

At first glance, the approach adopted by Walker and Wright makes eminent sense. Romans 11:26 begins with a 'so' or 'thus', not a clearly temporal connective such as 'then'. In the earlier stages of salvation history Jews were God's chosen people; then came the Christian age in which Gentiles predominated (v. 25). *Thus* together 'all Israel' (that is, God's people of all ages or dispensations) 'will be saved' (v. 25a). On the other hand, the immediate, surrounding context of verses 23 and 28 promises literal Jews that they can be grafted in again to God's people if they do not persist in unbelief. And the larger narrative flow of chapters 9 – 11, speaking of a succession of ages in salvation history, makes it most natural to take the 'thus' of verse 26 as referring to a third and final stage in conjunction with the parousia (vv. 26b–27). While it is true that Romans 9:6–13 and other passages distinguish between literal, ethnic Israel and a remnant who are the true spiritual Israel, and while Paul may even refer to the entire Christian church as 'the Israel of God' (Gal. 6:16), it is not clear that the immediate context of Romans 11:25–26 allows any distinction in meaning between the literal Jews of 'Israel' in verse 25 and the people implied by 'all Israel' in verse 26. It is better, therefore, to follow the majority of commentators in seeing Paul as promising a large-scale outpouring of belief in Jesus as Messiah among literal, ethnic Jews, not necessarily concentrated in any piece of geography, in conjunction with events immediately leading up to Christ's return.[50]

If this is so, then the church needs to rethink carefully its relationship with Jewish people. On the one hand, in a post-Holocaust age any form of dialogue that is not highly sensitive to the horrors and prejudice of anti-Semitism throughout Christian history does not deserve the title 'Christian' and is, in any event, likely to prove counter-productive. On the other hand, engaging contemporary Jews as partners only in a religious dialogue that sidesteps the unique, salvific claims of Jesus in the New Testament risks ultimate irrelevancy. D. Bloesch puts it more pointedly: 'The church is betraying its evangelistic mandate if it withholds the gospel of salvation from the very people who gave us the Messiah and Saviour of the world. Such an attitude could be construed as the worst kind of anti-Semitism ...'[51] It is even arguable, on the basis of the salvation-historical priority of the Christian mission to the Jews in Romans 1:16, and the pattern of early Christian preaching in the book of Acts more generally, a pattern which even the end of the book of Acts does not seem finally to abolish,[52] that evangelizing Jewish people might still retain a certain priority in our age.[53]

The book of Revelation and apocalyptic

A huge bibliography of recent works again attaches itself to this third significant portion of Scripture. There is now widespread agreement that the book of Revelation must be seen in light of three biblical genres: apocalyptic, prophecy, and epistolary literature. But the greatest of these is apocalyptic. A widely quoted and highly influential definition of apocalyptic comes from John Collins in his *Semeia* symposium:

> 'Apocalypse' is a genre of revelatory literature with a narrative framework in which a revelation is mediated by an other-worldly being to a human recipient, disclosing a transcendent reality which is both temporal insofar as it envisages eschatological salvation, and spatial insofar as it involves another, supernatural world.[54]

A comprehensive anthology of English translations of the so-called pseudepigrapha has appeared in two volumes, one of them entirely devoted to apocalyptic and related literature, under the editorship of Princeton scholar James Charlesworth.[55] A more selective and readable collection, for one wishing to familiarize himself or herself with snippets of Jewish, Christian and Greco-Roman apocalyptic most relevant for interpreting the Bible, is now found in the volume edited by Reddish.[56] Large, even multi-volume, commentaries on Revelation have either appeared or are imminent, and, as with the interpretation of Jesus' Olivet discourse, tend to defend the classic preterist (or amillennial) and futurist (or dispensational) option.[57] But again, a historic or classical premillennialist (and post-tribulational) view, to be sharply distinguished from the better-known and more widespread dispensational (and pre-tribulational) premillennialism, still remains best. The trio of commentaries by Mounce, Ladd, and Beasley-Murray, all from the 1970s and, with varying nuances, all reflecting the classical premillennialist view, probably remains the best and most manageable package to hand a would-be interpreter of the final book of the New Testament canon.[58] The entire Revelation is written from a clear end-of-the-first-century perspective. John's visions, symbolism, and imagery would have all been more quickly understood by a first-century Christian audience in western Asia Minor than they often are today. As Fee and Stuart in their hermeneutical handbook put it so aptly, 'The primary meaning of the Revelation is what John intended it to mean, which in turn must also have been something his readers could have understood it to mean.'[59] Yet at the same time, from at least chapter 7 onwards, it seems crucial to insist that the events to which John's visions point have not yet been consummated.

None of this commits us to discount the greatest strength of the non-futurist positions, namely, an appreciation that Revelation is not attempting to depict events immediately preceding the parousia in any consistently literal fashion. Nor dare our readings lead us to dilute a healthy Christian social ethic, based on the assumption that things immediately preceding the end will merely go from bad to worse anyway. We must recognize that the primary purpose of apocalyptic is increasingly agreed to be to provide comfort for those who are experiencing persecution, oppression, or some other form of social marginalization, or who at least form part of a community who perceive themselves to be subject to such marginalization.[60] Again, with writers out of the recent African and Latin American strands of liberation theology, we must remember that Revelation, like much apocalyptic literature more generally, functions as a literature of protest, though without any clear indications that such protest may ever turn violent.[61] By depicting the perfect justice of the world to come, the injustices of present socio-political realities are unmasked. Governments may be divinely ordained (Rom. 13) but they may also be demonic, requiring civil disobedience (Rev. 13).[62]

In the final analysis, the case for historic premillennialism rests on the narrative flow of Revelation 19 – 20. It seems impossible to insert a literary seam in between Revelation 19:20–21 and 20:1 as amillennial and post-millennial perspectives are forced to do. Chapter 19 ends with the eternal punishment of two-thirds of the unholy trinity of chapters 12 to 13: the first beast and the false prophet. But what is the fate of the dragon, i.e. Satan, the third individual and chief person of this demonic trio? This question is not answered until 20:1–3. But, given that there is no logical or chronological break before verse 4, the millennium that is described in the rest of chapter 20 must of necessity follow the return of Christ, with which chapter 19 concludes.[63]

Nor is this merely a literary observation. Theologically, just as it is crucial to insist that human bodies will be redeemed via their resurrection, so also God's initial plans for this world, not merely in a wholly re-created heavens and earth, will be vindicated in a millennium that falls just short of the utter perfection of the new cosmos described in Revelation 21 – 22. Far from being a disincentive to an appropriate Christian social or environmental ethic, a healthy chiliasm, akin to the dominant strand of the pre-Augustinian church in the first centuries of its history,[64] and shorn of nineteenth-century dispensationalist novelties (most notably a pre-tribulational rapture),[65] flows directly from the conviction that God himself in Christ will complete with this current earth precisely what Christians through his power are unable to complete prior to the parousia. Nevertheless, there is wisdom in the old line about the individual who, at the end of tedious debates among the various branches of millennialism, declared himself simply to be a pan-millennialist: 'I believe that it will just all pan out in the end.' Few exegetical conundra in Revelation need prove divisive, particularly in light of apocalyptic's avowed purpose of offering comfort to the oppressed (cf. also 1 Cor. 15:58). If we can agree that Christ is indeed coming back and that this is the central eschatological theme of Revelation, we can disagree amicably on almost everything else.[66]

Demythologizing the parousia?

The final significant development in recent evangelical eschatology which I wish to address nevertheless challenges even this broad conclusion. It has long been noted that certain passages in the New Testament, often taken to refer to the parousia, may make better sense on a different interpretation. For example, in evangelical circles R. T. France has championed a view of Mark 13:24–27 and parallels that sees Jesus' coming on the clouds not as a reference to his return at the end of human history as we know it, but to God's coming through Jesus in judgment on the nation of Israel at the time of the destruction of the temple in AD 70.[67] Whether or not this is the best interpretation of this passage, it is an approach that fits the text's immediate context about the destruction of the temple. But now N. T. Wright has pressed the case substantially further. In a massive and magnificent recent publication, *Jesus and the Victory of God*,[68]

Wright disputes the traditional interpretations of all of the so-called parousia passages in the Gospels, taking them apparently in their entirety to refer to Jesus' invisible coming in judgment on Jerusalem in the first century.

Before placing a significant question mark in front of this perspective, I want to commend Wright's work for offering perhaps the most important contribution to the so-called third quest of the historical Jesus of any in our time.[69] Wright begins with an impressive demolition of the increasingly popular view, particularly in the United States, that sees the core of the Gospels that can be attributed to the historical Jesus as portraying a radically non-eschatological and non-apocalyptic, itinerant Cynic sage.[70] Wright's own thesis that Jesus must be placed into a thoroughly intelligible Jewish milieu that was above all grappling with the problem of the Jews' failure to experience God's promises of freedom, peace and prosperity in their land is almost certainly on target. He correctly emphasizes the corporate dimension of this plight, reading afresh many texts in the Gospels as the unique answer of Jesus and his followers to the question of what is to be done about the Romans. In short, for Wright the biggest problem for the Jews was not human oppression but satanic enslavement. The greatest distinctives of Jesus' ministry and message were his claims that the kingdom had arrived, the Messiah was present, the resurrection had begun, and the problem of Jewish exile had been solved, all despite no appearance of any outward socio-political changes in Israel. It would be a pity if evangelicals, who I suspect will widely question what Wright does with the parousia passages, would miss in the process the immense contribution he has made to historical Jesus research more generally. Nevertheless, in the context of this brief discussion of eschatology, serious questions do need to be raised about Wright's reinterpretation of Christ's return, even as we agree that we must restore a historically plausible, Jewish, apocalyptic dimension to our reading of the Gospels.

In short, Wright's claim is that Jewish apocalyptic literature never looked forward to the end of history in terms of a changed space-time order of the universe as we know it. Instead, passages that refer to cosmic upheaval regularly stand as ciphers for socio-political transformation. Within a spectrum of seven possible definitions of eschatology, ranging from one extreme in which it refers to the end of the world, that is, the end of the space-time universe, to the opposite end in which it functions merely as a 'critique of the present socio-political scene, perhaps with proposals for adjustments', Wright believes that the best definition of eschatology is 'the climax of Israel's history, involving events for which end-of-the-world language is the only set of metaphors adequate to express the significance of what will happen, but resulting in a new and quite different phase *within* space-time history'.[71] But between the first of these definitions and Wright's preferred definition, he allows only for the alternative, 'eschatology as the climax of Israel's history, involving the end of the space-time universe'. Granted that Israel's future hope was always grounded in restoration from exile, if not in a restored earth more broadly, it seems that Wright has left out the option that most adequately encompasses a substantial percentage of Jewish apocalyptic (including New Testament perspectives), namely, eschatology as the climax of Israel's history, using metaphorical language for *both* socio-political transformation *and* cosmic renewal of a kind made possible only by God's supernatural intervention into history, yet still without bringing about the end of the space-time universe.[72]

Certainly this is the way the vast majority of scholars of eschatology and apocalyptic across all major theological traditions have read the relevant Jewish literature. Given the proper concern to situate Jesus squarely within this milieu, it is not clear why we must use certain metaphorical texts about socio-political upheavals (e.g. Is. 13:9–11; 39:3–4; Ezek. 32:5–8) monolithically to label all metaphorical language in apocalyptic as no different.[73] Given the Christian conviction that what happened to Jesus at his resurrection happened within this space-time universe and yet involved God acting supernaturally to transform the nature of Jesus' existence into something that transcended what socio-political liberation could accomplish, and given the consistent Christian linkage between what happened at Jesus' resurrection and what will happen at the general resurrection of believers at the end of time (see esp. 1 Cor. 15:12–28), surely the most consistent view is to adopt this 'both/and' approach of *both* social transformation *and* cosmic intervention for the eschatology of the New Testament in general. Specific texts and exegetical details further support this suggestion. In Mark 14:62 Jesus' reply to the high priest that 'you will see the Son of Man sitting at the right hand of the Mighty One and coming on the clouds of heaven' does not easily fit Jesus' *invisible* coming to God to receive authority, as some have argued.[74] Granted that Daniel 7:13–14 has the Son of Man coming on the clouds as he goes to God's heavenly throne, rather than to earth, the sequence of Jesus' wording reverses these actions here. He is *first* sitting at the right hand of the Mighty One and *then* coming on the clouds of heaven. In this context, only the earth can be the destination for the Son of Man's travel.[75] This interpretation meshes with Luke's words in Acts 1:11, quoting the angels' declaration, 'This same Jesus, who has been taken from you into heaven, will come back in the same way you have seen him go into heaven.' But the claim that the disciples literally saw Jesus disappear from their midst suggests that his return must be a similar public, visible, and glorious event, ruling out the interpretation of the parousia as Christ's invisible coming to earth in judgment on the temple in AD 70. Space precludes an exegesis of the various parousia passages in Paul or of the imagery of cosmic destruction and renewal in 2 Peter 3:10–13, but it is hard to see how Wright's consistent interpretation of the parousia motif in the Gospels could be convincingly extended to the rest of the New Testament.[76]

For the credibility of Christian witness, Wright's reinterpretation of the classic Christian hope for Christ's visible return at the end of human history differs little from Bultmann's better-known existentialist, demythologizing programme,[77] save that it is at least conceivable in a first-century Jewish milieu. As we focus on relevance for the church, it is important to stress that theologically Wright's reinterpretation may not grant any more hope for the future than Bultmann's. It is true that the seemingly mythological language of the New Testament can prove an embarrassment today, and that great edifices can be erected on the hypothesis that New Testament theology changed in substantial ways after early Christians perceived an apparent delay in Jesus' return. But as R. Bauckham helpfully pointed out almost two decades ago, and as C. Holman has stressed in a recent book-length treatment, the so-called delay of the parousia was not a distinctively Christian problem.[78] Jews from the eighth century BC on had been wrestling with the fact that their prophets declared that the day of the Lord was at hand without any apparent fulfilment. Jewish and Christian use of Psalm 90:4 consistently stressed simply that God's time was not the same as human time. If God seems to delay, it is so that more will have an opportunity to repent. The church at the end of the twentieth century may be embarrassed by the seemingly mythological language of the New Testament with respect to Christ's return and by the apparent delay of two millennia that a waiting for a literal fulfilment of the parousia passages appears to create. But we would do well to take a similar tack and recognize God's compassionate strategy in allowing for more time for us to fulfil the Great Commission and get his message out.

Conclusions

At the beginning of our paper we suggested that too often Christians have either neglected the theme of eschatology as irrelevant or fuelled the fires of those who would stereotype and caricature us as grotesquely misinterpreting apocalyptic in terms of current events-watching. A third approach, particularly in mainline Protestant and Roman Catholic circles, has attempted to rehabilitate the relevance of apocalyptic and eschatology for the church in our day by pointing to the real horrors of worldwide wars experienced throughout this century and to the even more horrible threat of a nuclear holocaust.[79] But in its own way, this attempt to make eschatology relevant also demythologizes it. Unless we recognize a supernatural dimension to New Testament eschatology that goes beyond the good and evil that human structures can generate we will not do full justice to the text. Nor, paradoxically, will we prove to be as relevant, once we realize how limited the long-term changes are that human institutions can create.

The most important thing that needs to be said about the eschatology of the New Testament is that it shares with the message of the kingdom, and with New Testament theology more generally, the same 'already-but-not-yet' framework. In the words of A. Cunningham,

> We ... the church – are called to proclaim that the world is oriented not to catastrophe and disaster, but to final transformation, assured in the victory of a peace that is not the world's to give. That is the reason for our search to live a life worthy of the gospel: a life of hope, love, service, and transformation of suffering and evil through faith and worship.[80]

It is precisely because we understand God's plans to transform our universe supernaturally that we can function as little outposts of heaven to model his designs for the universe. We pray, 'your will be done on earth as it is in heaven' (Matt. 6:10). A healthy understanding of the inaugurated eschatology of the New Testament will save us from the twin errors of a despair or defeatism that attempts to do nothing for this world but save souls from it and the currently more prominent mistake of replacing a hope for a supernaturally re-created universe with utopian socio-political programme for this world. Only God knows how much good we as Christians can bring about socially, politically, ethically, and ideologically in our world. We have seen in our time relatively peaceful revolutions in Europe and the former Soviet Union due in part at least to Christian intercession and non-violent action. It is not a little perverse when certain North American dispensationalists continue to see European unity as a sign of the fulfilment of prophecies in the book of Revelation of satanic activity.[81] But euphoria over the collapse of the Iron Curtain quickly gave way to grief over mass genocide in Rwanda, a country boasting 80% of its population as professingly Christian! So quickly on the heels of events seemingly influenced by the divine came the demonic again, and the tribalism that generated that African holocaust in less extreme ways tends to fragment our world on every continent at the end of this second Christian millennium, notwithstanding all attempts to create structures reflecting socio-political or even ecclesiastical unity.

Reflecting on several of the key themes of Revelation may provide an apt summary and conclusion to a survey of New Testament eschatology more generally. It is ultimately only eschatology which completes an adequate Christian theodicy.[82] Christ began the decisive work of defeating sin and evil on the cross. But that process will not be completed until his return. Meanwhile we may be assured of and confidently proclaim at least four key propositions: (1) God is still sovereign, even when circumstances, personally, nationally, or even globally, suggest otherwise. (2) History has a goal and terminus, in which justice will prevail. When we ask why God does not intervene to bring about perfect justice now and destroy his enemies, a major part of our answer must be that such intervention would require destroying ourselves as well and hence history as know it, inasmuch as we are all intricately involved in the perpetration of evil. (3) We need not avenge those who wrong us, however prophetically we may speak out in critique of injustice in our day, precisely because we have the confidence that ultimately God will right all wrongs. (4) In the words of the shortest summary of New Testament eschatology that I have ever heard, 'Jesus wins.'[83] That hope is enough – or should be – to sustain us until the day when we see it accomplished in our midst.

The scholar in whose name this lecture was originally given retitled his best-selling book *The Goodness of God*, in a revised edition, *The Enigma of Evil*.[84] Questions of theodicy were a major concern for John Wenham in this work that has helped a large number of theological students and other Christians around the globe for many years. Among other points, Dr Wenham stressed that suffering is limited and that retribution, however beneficent, is real. Although he also supported one of the doctrines that this lecture has called into question, namely, annihilationism,[85] I believe that he would have well applauded our concluding insistence that Christian eschatology continue to make room at its centre for a belief in a visible, public return of Christ to initiate an age of justice that will make all of our current injustices pale in comparison.

If there is a theme that unites the disparate topics treated in this rapid survey, it may be that we ought not lightly to dismiss classic Christian options with respect to the future and the last days, even while recognizing at times the diversity of answers that historic Christianity has given to those questions. Ultimately, we can but echo the apostle Paul, who marvelled, 'Behold, therefore, the goodness and severity of God' (Rom. 11:22, AV). We dare not jettison either attribute in our study or in our ministry. Or, to quote Dr Wenham at some length,

It is contrary both to Scripture and to experience to believe that all will yield to gentle persuasion. It is not true even of those who are soundly converted. When we pray 'Thy kingdom come,' we pray for the overthrow of evil. We know that the answer to that prayer will be partly by grace and partly by judgment. It is not for us to choose which it shall be. We shall rejoice with the angels over the sinner that repents. And when God himself makes plain that they will not yield to his love and that the day for anguished intercession is over, we shall rejoice with all the servants of God at the destruction of those who sought to destroy God's fair earth.[86]

Meanwhile we long for God to establish his kingdom in all its fullness and we work by the Spirit to create a colony of that kingdom in the communities of the redeemed we call his church. *Maranatha*; our Lord, come!

Notes

1. An initial draft of this paper was delivered as the John Wenham Lecture to the Tyndale Associates as part of the July 1997 Tyndale Fellowship conference on 'Eschatology' in Swanwick.
2. For a mainline Protestant survey of responses to several of these, see S. L. Cook, 'Reflections on apocalypticism at the approach of the year 2000', *USQR* 49 (1995), pp. 3–16.
3. As in the excellent study by W. J. Dumbrell, *The Search for Order: Biblical Eschatology in Focus* (Grand Rapids: Baker, 1994).
4. D. L. Edwards with J. Stott, *Essentials: A Liberal-Evangelical Dialogue* (London: Hodder and Stoughton; Downers Grove: IVP, 1988), pp. 313–320. Cf. C. H. Pinnock, 'The destruction of the finally impenitent', *CTR* 4 (1990), pp. 243–259. The debate, of course, has emerged in many periods of church history, and has had other modern defenders, but none has recently generated so much response as Stott (particularly in the UK) and Pinnock (particularly in the US). Stott has also stressed in response to his critics how tentatively he holds his view.
5. R. A. Peterson, 'A traditionalist response to John Stott's arguments for annihilationism', *JETS* 37 (1994), pp. 553–568; R. L. Reymond, 'Dr John Stott on Hell', *Presbyterion* 16 (1990), pp. 41–59; J. I. Packer, 'The problem of eternal punishment', *Crux* 26.3 (1990), pp. 18–25; H. O. J. Brown, 'Will the lost suffer forever?' *CTR* 4 (1990), pp. 261–278.
6. E. E. Ellis, 'Forum on conditional immortality' (Swanwick: Tyndale Conference, 1997), argues that the parallelism consists of a one-time event with eternal consequences. But the fate of the unbeliever is to depart 'into the eternal fire prepared for the devil and his angels' (Matt. 25:41), a fire that is said to torment 'day and night for ever and ever' (Rev. 20:10). Cf. also Rev. 14:10–11.
7. This would seem to be true even if hell were conceived as potentially temporal, as in D. Cheetham, 'Hell as potentially temporal', *ExpT* 108 (1997), pp. 260–263.
8. C. S. Lewis, *The Great Divorce* (London: Geoffrey Bles, 1946).
9. For a more detailed, recent presentation and analysis of the issues at stake in this debate, see T. Gray, 'Destroyed forever: an examination of the debates concerning annihilation and conditional immortality', *Themelios* 21.2 (1996), pp. 14–18.
10. Most notably, with respect to the question of to what extent spiritual salvation to prepare one for a life beyond this world should even still be included in the concept. Particularly significant for theological students' reflection are the diverse contributions to R. Evans et al., eds., *The Globalization of Theological Education* (Maryknoll: Orbis, 1993).
11. This is not to say it will inevitably be quashed; happily, some act inconsistently with their premises and continue in faithful obedience in this arena.

12. *Four Views on Hell*, ed. W. Crockett (Grand Rapids: Zondervan, 1992).

13. Technically, 'conditional immortality' deals only with the issue of whether humans have an innately immortal soul. Even if they do not, God might choose to raise *both* believers and unbelievers to an everlasting conscious existence. But usually proponents of conditional immortality go on to affirm the annihilation of the unbeliever.

14. See e.g. G. E. Ladd, *A Theology of the New Testament*, rev. D. A. Hagner (Grand Rapids: Eerdmans, 1993; Cambridge: Lutterworth, 1994), p. 196.

15. All quotations in this paper follow the New International Version, Inclusive Language Edition (London: Hodder and Stoughton, 1996).

16. Cf. esp. I. H. Marshall, *1 and 2 Thessalonians* (London: Marshall, Morgan and Scott; Grand Rapids: Eerdmans, 1983), pp. 178–180.

17. N. Geldenhuys, *Commentary on the Gospel of Luke* (Grand Rapids: Eerdmans; London: Marshall, Morgan and Scott, 1951), p. 365; cf. D. Gooding, *According to Luke* (Leicester: IVP, 1987), p. 246; J. A. Fitzmyer, *The Gospel According to Luke* 2 (Garden City: Doubleday, 1985), p. 992, at the level of the historical Jesus but not of Lukan redaction. Curiously, most commentators assume that Jesus is still speaking of his disciples in vv. 47–48. But vv. 45–46 depict a faithless servant who contrasts with the faithful steward of vv. 42–44 and who is assigned 'a place with the unbelievers' (v. 46). 'The servant' of v. 47, then, is taken most naturally as elaborating on the faithless servant of the immediately preceding verses. Verses 47–48 thus consider two kinds of faithless servants who take their place among unbelievers.

18. See esp. *What About Those Who Have Never Heard? Three Views on the Destiny of the Unevangelized*, ed. J. Sanders (Downers Grove: IVP, 1995); *Through No Fault of Their Own? The Fate of Those Who Have Never Heard*, eds. W. V. Crockett and J. G. Sigountos (Grand Rapids: Baker, 1991).

19. Many of these papers were published in *One God, One Lord in a World of Religious Pluralism*, eds. A .D. Clarke and B. W. Winter (Cambridge: Tyndale House, 1991).

20. J. Sanders, *No Other Name: An Investigation Into the Destiny of the Unevangelized* (Grand Rapids: Eerdmans, 1992; London: SPCK, 1994).

21. N. Anderson, *The World's Religions* (London: IVP, 1975; Grand Rapids: Eerdmans, 1976), p. 234.

22. See esp. G. N. Davies, *Faith and Obedience in Romans* (Sheffield: JSOT, 1990), pp. 53–71; K. Snodgrass, 'Justification by grace – to the doers: an analysis of the place of Romans 2 in the theology of Paul', *NTS* 32 (1986), pp. 72–93; J. D. G. Dunn, *Romans 1 – 8* (Dallas: Word, 1988), p. 107.

23. Ibid., pp. 158–160.

24. C. E. B. Cranfield, *A Critical and Exegetical Commentary on the Epistle to the Romans* 1 (Edinburgh: T. and T. Clark, 1975), pp. 151–153, 155–163.

25. Though see P. Toon, *Heaven and Hell* (Nashville: Nelson, 1986).

26. See further C. L. Blomberg, 'Degrees of reward in the kingdom of heaven?' *JETS* 35 (1992), pp. 159–172. In fact, E. Disley ('Degrees of glory: Protestant doctrine and the concept of rewards hereafter', *JTS* 42 (1991), pp. 77–105) notes that the development of the doctrine of differentiating degrees of reward was in part the legacy of non-Lutheran reformers trying to salvage something of the Roman Catholic notion of purgatory. The most recent attempt to argue for eternal rewards distinct from salvation (R. N. Wilkin, 'The biblical distinction between eternal salvation and eternal rewards: A key to proper exegesis', *JGES* 9, 1996, pp. 15–24) is aware of my article, misleads in its summary of my views and fails entirely to address its main arguments.

27. Cf. e.g. Luther's *Works* (Philadelphia: Muhlenberg, 1959), 51.282–283.

28. This misunderstanding of Scripture has been epitomized in recent years perhaps best by Z. C. Hodges in his numerous writings.

29. Grand Rapids: Eerdmans, 1989.

30. The former is the more common recourse; the latter has become well known via M. J. Harris, *Raised Immortal* (London: Marshall, Morgan and Scott, 1983; Grand Rapids: Eerdmans, 1985), pp. 98–101; following F. F. Bruce, *1 and 2 Corinthians* (London: Marshall, Morgan and Scott, 1971; Grand Rapids: Eerdmans, 1980), p. 204.

31. Cf. also I. K. Smith, 'Does 2 Corinthians 5:1–8 refer to an intermediate state?' *RTR* 55 (1996), pp. 14–23.

32. On the logic here, see esp. W. L. Craig, 'Paul's dilemma in 2 Corinthians 5.1–10: A "Catch 22"?', *NTS* 34 (1988), pp. 145–147. On the exegetical evidence for an intermediate state more generally,

see J. Osei-Bonsu, 'The Intermediate State in the New Testament', *SJT* 44 (1991), pp. 169–194. Osei-Bonsu also deals well with the Corinthian text in idem, 'Does 2 Cor. 5.1–10 teach the reception of the resurrection body at the moment of death?' *JSNT* 28 (1986), pp. 81–101.

33. On the contrary, see the important research on the 'mind–brain' distinction by J. C. Eccles, *The Human Mystery* (Berlin and New York: Springer, 1979); idem, *The Human Psyche* (New York: Springer, 1980; London: Routledge, 1992).

34. On which, see R. W. Wilson and C. L. Blomberg, 'The image of God in humanity: A biblical-psychological perspective', *Themelios* 18.3 (1993), pp. 8–15.

35. See esp. D. Groothuis, *Deceived by the Light* (Eugene, OR: Harvest House, 1995).

36. Cf. idem, *Unmasking the New Age* (Downers Grove and Leicester: IVP, 1991).

37. G. R. Beasley-Murray, *Jesus and the Last Days* (Peabody: Hendrickson, 1993). Cf. idem, *Jesus and the Future* (London: Macmillan, 1954).

38. To be differentiated from amillennialism and postmillennialism, on the one hand, and the better-known dispensational form of premillennialism, on the other hand.

39. Alternative approaches prove less convincing. 'This generation' cannot easily be made to mean the last generation before the parousia in view of its consistent usage elsewhere in the Gospels (cf. Mark 8:12, 38; 9:19; Matt. 11:16; 12:41–42, 45; 17:17, 23:36, etc.). Nor is the NIV marginal reading 'race' a lexically common meaning of the term.

40. T. J. Geddert, *Watchwords: Mark 13 in Markan Eschatology* (Sheffield: JSOT, 1989).

41. Cf. e.g. D. A. Carson, 'Matthew', in *Expositor's Bible Commentary*, ed. F. E. Gaebelein, 8 (Grand Rapids: Zondervan, 1984), pp. 488–508; R. H. Gundry, *Mark: A Commentary on His Apology for the Cross* (Grand Rapids: Eerdmans, 1993), pp. 733–800; D. E. Garland, *Mark* (Grand Rapids: Zondervan, 1996), pp. 487–512. The term itself is found in D. L. Turner, 'The structure and sequence of Matthew 24:1–21: Interaction with evangelical treatments', *GTJ* 10 (1989), pp. 327, who adopts this approach as well. For an advocate of a similar position outside of explicitly evangelical circles see B. K. Blount, 'Preaching the kingdom: Mark's apocalyptic call for prophetic engagement', *PSBSup* 3 (1994), pp. 33–56.

42. For a survey and helpful reply to a number of these at a popular level, see B. J. Oropeza, *99 Reasons Why No One Knows When Christ Will Return* (Downers Grove: IVP, 1994).

43. The oldest Christian version of this belief preserved is found in the *Epistle of Barnabas* 15.

44. So also D. A. Hagner, *Matthew 14 – 28* (Dallas: Word, 1995), p. 718.

45. P. W. L. Walker, *Jesus and the Holy City: New Testament Perspectives on Jerusalem* (Grand Rapids and Cambridge: Eerdmans, 1997).

46. Cf. N. T. Wright, *The Climax of the Covenant* (Edinburgh: T. and T. Clark, 1991), pp. 231–257.

47. I am not aware of any *bona fide* scholarly defences of this view by avowed evangelicals, but I have increasingly heard it promoted orally in both the US and the UK at the grass-roots level. A variation of this view, in which *all* Jews of all time are saved at the parousia of Christ/general resurrection, by faith in Jesus in response to *his* preaching the gospel, appears in R. H. Bell, *Provoked to Jealousy* (Tübingen: Mohr, 1994), pp. 134–145. For representative recent literature of all the major exegetical options surrounding vv. 25–27, see D. J. Moo, *The Epistle to the Romans* (Grand Rapids and Cambridge: Eerdmans, 1996), pp. 713–729.

48. C. Chapman, *Whose Promised Land?* (Tring: Lion, 1983); G. M. Burge, *Who Are God's People in the Middle East?* (Grand Rapids: Zondervan, 1993).

49. On which, see esp. D. C. Allison Jr, 'Mt 23:39 = Lk 13:35b as a conditional prophecy', *JSNT* 18 (1983), pp. 75–84.

50. E.g. Cranfield, *Romans* 2, pp. 574–579; Dunn, *Romans 9 – 16* (1988), pp. 690–693; Moo, *Romans*, pp. 719–726. B. W. Longenecker ('Different answers to different issues: Israel, the Gentiles and salvation history in Romans 9 – 11', *JSNT* 36, 1989, pp. 95–123) is particularly helpful in showing how Paul's logic here develops out of thoroughly Jewish (and esp. Old Testament) eschatology.

51. D .G. Bloesch, ' "All Israel will be saved": supersessionism and the biblical witness', *Int* 43 (1989), pp. 140–141. Some have argued that God will save Israel through faith in Christ by extraordinary means apart from the preaching of the gospel, but cf. S. Hafemann, 'The salvation of Israel in Romans 11:25–32: A response to Krister Stendahl', *Ex Auditu* 4 (1988), pp. 54: 'The future salvation of ethnic Israel must correspond to the nature of the remnant's salvation in the present, since the future nature of ethnic Israel is inextricably tied to the present nature of the remnant (11:16).'

52. See esp. R. C. Tannehill, 'Israel in Luke–Acts: A tragic story', *JBL* 104 (1985), pp. 69–85.

53. F. D. Bruner, *The Christbook: Matthew 1 – 12* (Waco: Word, 1987), p. 372, 'Israel always has precedence.'

54. J. J. Collins, 'Introduction: morphology of a genre', *Semeia* 14 (1979), p. 9.

55. J. H. Charlesworth (ed.), *The Old Testament Pseudepigrapha*, 2 vols. (Garden City, NY; London: Darton, Longman and Todd, 1983, 1985).

56. M. G. Reddish (ed.), *Apocalyptic Literature: A Reader* (Nashville: Abingdon, 1990; subsequently reprinted by Hendrickson).

57. Contrast D. E. Aune, *Revelation*, 3 vols. (Dallas: Word, 1997–), with R. L. Thomas, *Revelation*, 2 vols. (Chicago: Moody, 1992, 1995). G. K. Beale's forthcoming New International Greek Testament Commentary offering on Revelation will be bound as one volume but is long enough to have been easily divided in two.

58. R. H. Mounce, *The Book of Revelation* (Grand Rapids: Eerdmans, 1977; currently being revised); G. E. Ladd, *A Commentary on the Revelation of John* (Grand Rapids: Eerdmans, 1972); G. R. Beasley-Murray, *The Book of Revelation*, 2nd edn (London: Marshall, Morgan and Scott, 1978).

59. G. D. Fee and D. Stuart, *How to Read the Bible for All Its Worth* (Grand Rapids: Zondervan, 1982), p. 209.

60. Cf. esp. A. Y. Collins, *Crisis and Catharsis: The Power of the Apocalypse* (Philadelphia: Westminster, 1984); with E. S. Fiorenza, *The Book of Revelation: Justice and Judgment* (Philadelphia: Fortress, 1985). Collins has now advanced her discussion considerably in *Cosmology and Eschatology in Jewish and Christian Apocalypticism* (Leiden: Brill, 1996).

61. For an extreme liberation theology reading that turns Revelation into a mandate for merely socio-political change, see P. Richard, *Apocalypse: A People's Commentary on the Book of Revelation* (Maryknoll, NY: Orbis, 1995). For a balanced blend of evangelical historic premillennialism with a cautious liberation theology, see R. Foulkes, *El Apocalipsis de San Juan: Una Lectura desde América Latina* (Grand Rapids: Eerdmans; Buenos Aires: Nueva Creación, 1989).

62. From South Africa at the height of apartheid, cf. A. A. Boesak, *Comfort and Protest: Reflections on the Apocalypse of John of Patmos* (Philadelphia: Westminster; Edinburgh: T. and T. Clark, 1987); cf. also C. Rowland, 'The Apocalypse: hope, resistance and the revelation of reality', *Ex Auditu* 6 (1990), pp. 129–144.

63. Cf. Beasley-Murray, *Revelation*, pp. 283–292.

64. A. W. Wainwright, *Mysterious Apocalypse: Interpreting the Book of Revelation* (Nashville: Abingdon, 1993), pp. 21–31. Wainwright's book is also an excellent, readable history of the interpretation of Revelation more broadly.

65. Of particular value for lay people now is B. Gundry's updated popular-level defence of post-tribulationism: *First the Antichrist* (Grand Rapids: Baker, 1997).

66. Recent study of Revelation has generated several helpful studies of its theology, demonstrating the rich breadth of topics, even besides eschatology, that are addressed. See esp. G. Goldsworthy, *The Gospel in Revelation* (Exeter: Paternoster, 1984); D. Guthrie, *The Relevance of John's Apocalypse* (Exeter: Paternoster; Grand Rapids: Eerdmans, 1987); R. Bauckham, *The Theology of the Book of Revelation* (Cambridge: Cambridge University Press, 1993); idem, *The Climax of Prophecy: Studies on the Book of Revelation* (Edinburgh: T. and T. Clark, 1993); S. S. Smalley, *Thunder and Love: John's Revelation and John's Community* (Milton Keynes: Nelson; Grand Rapids: Baker, 1994).

67. R. T. France, *The Gospel according to Matthew* (Leicester: IVP; Grand Rapids: Eerdmans, 1985), pp. 333–336, 343–348.

68. London: SPCK; Minneapolis: Fortress, 1996 esp. pp. 360–367; building on idem, *The New Testament and the People of God* (London: SPCK; Minneapolis: Fortress, 1992), pp. 280–338.

69. A full-orbed, multi-author critique of Wright's work from a mostly evangelical perspective is *Jesus and the Restoration of Israel* (Downers Grove: IVP, 1999) under the editorship of C. Newman.

70. Esp. B. L. Mack, *A Myth of Innocence: Mark and Christian Origins* (Philadelphia: Fortress, 1988); M. J. Borg, *Jesus: A New Vision* (San Francisco: HarperSanFrancisco, 1987); J. D. Crossan, *The Historical Jesus* (San Francisco: HarperSanFrancisco; Edinburgh: T. and T. Clark, 1991).

71. Wright, *Jesus and the Victory of God*, p. 208. Wright is building especially on various brief treatments by his former doctoral supervisor, G. B. Caird.

72. Cf. esp. D. C. Allison Jr, 'A plea for thoroughgoing eschatology', *JBL* 113 (1994), pp. 651–668; with idem, *The End of the Ages Has Come* (Philadelphia: Fortress; Edinburgh: T. and T. Clark, 1985), pp. 84–90.

73. See the data assembled in Wright, *Jesus and the Victory of God*, pp. 354–360.

74. E.g. France, *Matthew*, p. 381.

75. B. Witherington III, *Jesus, Paul and the End of the World* (Downers Grove: IVP; Exeter: Paternoster, 1992), p. 172 – in another enormously useful recent evangelical treatment of New Testament eschatology.

76. In private conversation, P. Walker informs me that Wright, in a recent seminar, did not wish to extend this interpretation but left unanswered the subsequent question of where this new motif originated. To distinguish Jesus' pre-resurrection parousia hope from later New Testament teaching is particularly difficult given the verbal allusions to Jesus' teaching on the topic in Paul and elsewhere. See esp. D. Wenham, *Paul: Follower of Jesus or Founder of Christianity?* (Grand Rapids and Cambridge: Eerdmans, 1995), pp. 305–328.

77. R. Bultmann, *Theology of the New Testament* 1 (London: SCM; New York: Scribner's, 1952), pp. 4–11. Cf., too, the quite recent study by J. D. G. Dunn, 'He will come again', *Int* 51 (1997), pp. 42–56, in which affirmation of Christ's return means simply that the end of human history is particularly Christ-centred and empowered.

78. R. Bauckham, 'The delay of the parousia', *TB 31* (1980), pp. 3–36; C. L. Holman, *Till Jesus Comes: Origins of Christian Apocalyptic Expectation* (Peabody: Hendrickson, 1996).

79. Of many possible examples, see D. S. Russell, *Divine Disclosure: An Introduction to Jewish Apocalyptic* (Minneapolis: Fortress; London: SCM, 1992), p. xx, whose work overall remains an excellent introduction to the topic.

80. A. Cunningham, 'From strangers to citizens: Eschatology in the patristic era', *Ex Auditu* 6 (1990), p. 83.

81. Particularly balanced, in part as a response to this mentality, is F. Catherwood, *Pro-Europe?* (Leicester: IVP, 1991).

82. On Revelation as theodicy, see esp. G. R. Osborne, 'Theodicy in the Apocalypse', *TJ* 14 (1993), pp. 63–77.

83. Attributed to A. Y. Collins at a conference at North Park Seminary in the early 1990s and reported to me by my former colleague and one of the conference participants, Dr T. P. Weber.

84. J. Wenham, *The Enigma of Evil* (Leicester: IVP; Grand Rapids: Baker, 1985; original edn, *The Goodness of God*, Leicester and Downers Grove: IVP, 1974).

85. J. Wenham, *Goodness*, pp. 27–41.

86. J. Wenham, *Enigma*, p. 165.

5

Is there pseudonymity in the Old Testament?

Joyce G. Baldwin   Vol. 4.1 (1978)

A pseudonymous work, by definition written under a false or assumed name, is meant to conceal the identity of the writer. No more may be involved than the choice of a fictitious name, so that when it comes to light that Helen Morgan is our old friend Rhena Taylor under a pseudonym[1] we dismiss the matter with a smile or a shrug, scarcely even wondering what lay behind her secrecy. If she had chosen the name Hector Morgan or had called herself H. Morgan we should have concluded that she was another George Eliot or George Sand, avoiding any prejudice on the grounds of her sex. If, however, she had taken the name Dewi Morgan or G. Campell Morgan she would have risked a court action for infringing the copyright laws.

So much for our modern presuppositions, but what bearing have they on the world of the Bible? Since the rise of historical criticism in the nineteenth century it has been asserted that there are pseudonymous works in the canonical Scriptures, that pseudonymity was common in the ancient world, and that we may reassure ourselves that nothing fraudulent was either intended or involved.

So far as the New Testament is concerned, the subject has received considerable recent attention.[2] Kurt Aland, as the title of his paper implies, sees the need to examine the subject in the broad perspective of Christian literature generally in the first two centuries. Guthrie's historical approach faces the subject from the period of the Reformation. He calls in question the assumption that orthodox Christians would have used an apostolic name to authenticate their writing, and if they did that the practice would be sanctioned by the whole church. Such use of an authoritative name and not merely a fictitious one is known as 'pseudepigraphy', and raises the question of forgery, taken up by Metzger. Collins notes that the very book which provided the term 'apocalyptic', the Apocalypse of John, did not share the pseudonymity which many allege to have been characteristic of that genre. Nevertheless, he would not disqualify its inclusion as apocalyptic on that ground.

In the Old Testament field L. H. Brockington[3] mapped the problem in a short article twenty-five years ago; since then, as this paper will show, more relevant material has come to light and interest in the subject has grown accordingly. There is a sense in which the subject of this paper is basic also to pseudonymity in the New Testament for, if the Old Testament Scriptures can be proved to have included pseudonymous writings, an important precedent would have been set for the New. We shall begin by assembling information from the world of the Old Testament on the subject of pseudonymity and then look more closely at three books which are alleged to be or to contain within them pseudonymous writings.

Pseudonymity in the world of the Old Testament

Hard evidence as opposed to theory is hard to come by, but relevant fragments from the library of the Assyrian King Ashurbanipal (66 – c. 627 BC), who made a collection of texts from many archives and religious centres, have been published by Professor W. U. Lambert.[4] He tells us that these provide an insight into the question of authorship as it confronted Babylonian scholars in the early first millennium BC.

A librarian in the ancient world who came to the task of compiling a catalogue had to contend with the fact that the vast majority of texts circulated anonymously. In this royal library the scribes undertook to draw up a list of authors' names, 'a task comparable with modern discussion on the origin of Homer or the Fourth Gospel. The big difference is that modern writers on problems of authorship expose every detail of their materials and reasoning, while the Babylonian author gives results only.'[5] This catalogue is the earliest document of any civilization dealing with authorship, but Professor Lambert does not find this unexpected for ancient Mesopotamia, which had sign lists c. 3,000 BC, pronouncing dictionaries by 1800 BC and a mass of lexical texts, commentaries, analyses of the Sumerian verb, and other philological materials by 800 BC. This reminder that scholarship, like wisdom, goes back to ancient times is an important one.

The method in this catalogue is first to give the name of the author: 'These are by …' and then to quote the first line of his writings. The authors whose names are preserved fall into four classes: gods, legendary and other humans of great antiquity, men without indication of family origin and men described as 'son' of an ancestral figure. The human author was often looked on only as the intermediary while incantations, rituals and omens were attributed to a god or a number of gods. 'The incantation is not mine, it is the incantation of Ea and …' Such a note at the end of an incantation would hardly rank as an example of pseudonymity. Indeed, Professor Lambert explains that authorship is not the point here, but rather attention is drawn to the powers which would be operative when the incantations were recited. 'The difficulty of explaining the multiple authorship does not therefore arise.'[6]

Now these librarians must often have been hard pressed to find an author, and the attribution of works to gods and ancient worthies may be their last resort; but what is of special interest for our subject is the evidence that scribes profess descent from ancestors, some of whom are known from other sources as authors or editors of literary texts. But they do not profess to *be* those ancestors. From the evidence of these texts, therefore, the conclusion is that, so far as can be judged, anonymity rather than pseudonymity was characteristic of early first-millennium Babylonian authors, a number of whom specifically avoided opportunities for pseudepigraphy.

This fact is important in the light of frequent assertions that in ancient literature the adoption of a pseudonym was one of the most familiar of literary expedients. The question has to be asked, what period is in mind and what evidence can be given? The word 'ancient' is used to cover millennia and needs to be defined. The earliest indisputable evidence for pseudonymity comes from the third century BC, and James S. Candlish may well have been right in his judgment that before that time book learning was not so much cultivated as to give facility and motive to literary fictions.[7] That century saw the foundation of the Museum of Alexandria by Ptolemy Philadelphus (283–247 BC), to be followed in the next by that of Pergamum, founded by Eumenes II (197–159).

These centres of learning created a great demand for works by famous authors so that it became a lucrative occupation to write what appeared to be ancient works and pass them off as genuine. Bruce Metzger refers to the evidence of Galen (second century AD) that 'literary forgeries were first multiplied in numbers when the kings of Egypt and of Pergamum sought to outdo each other in their efforts to increase the holdings in their respective libraries. Monetary rewards were offered to those who would provide a copy of some ancient author, and, in consequence, many imitations of ancient works were composed and palmed off as genuine.'[8] The condemnation implied by Galen, who himself suffered from fraudulent imitators, is obvious.

But deliberate forgeries of this kind are not significant for our purpose. No-one claims that the Old Testament contains this kind of material. Another kind of forgery referred to by Metzger should, however, be mentioned. Two of the earliest forgeries in Greek history, 'perpetrated in the interests of securing greater credence for certain doctrines and claims', date from the sixth century BC and concern interpolations into the *Iliad* and into the *Oracles of Musaeus*. Both were detected and one of the offenders was identified and banished from Athens.[9] The evidence is important because it proves that to interpolate additions into an ancient text, at least with an ulterior motive, was not only not tolerated in Greece in the sixth century BC but was regarded as a serious crime.

It is significant that within the period covered by the Old Testament no example has so far come to light of a pseudepigraphon which was approved or cherished as an authoritative book, and, on the evidence just quoted, there was opposition to the interpolation of new material into a text.[10]

Alleged pseudonymity in the Old Testament

The earliest example of pseudonymity in the Old Testament is usually held to be the book of Deuteronomy, for, under the heading 'These are the words that Moses spoke ...' (1:1, RSV), it consists in the main of speeches in the first person. A similar Mosaic origin is claimed, however, by the introductory formula 'The LORD said to Moses' for much of the books of Exodus, Leviticus and Numbers, and since the Pentateuch would require a study all its own we shall not attempt to include these books in this article.[11]

Ecclesiastes

The book we know as Ecclesiastes has a special claim to consideration because its writer evidently wanted to remain anonymous. In the Hebrew he calls himself Qoheleth, which means something like 'the preacher-philosopher', and yet he adds 'the son of David, king in Jerusalem' (1:1). No king of that name is known in David's line. Taken literally, 'son of David' suggests Solomon, though his name appears nowhere in the book and he seems to be ruled out by 'all who were before me in Jerusalem' (2:9). The most likely explanation of this enigma is to see in his impersonation a literary device, a dramatization of his anti-secularism. The author 'pictures for us a super-Solomon (as he implies by the word "surpassing", in 1:16) to demonstrate that the most gifted man conceivable, who could outstrip every king who ever occupied the throne of David, would still return empty-handed from the quest for self-fulfilment'.[12]

Martin Hengel, who speaks of the unique semi-pseudonymity of the work, points out that the pseudonymity applies only to 1:12 – 2:12b; 'later the individuality of the author breaks through the pseudonymous form'.[13] But it seems better to avoid the term altogether. Qoheleth is no more pretending to be Solomon than Shakespeare is pretending to be Hamlet, but he is inviting his readers to see life through the eyes of that superbly endowed king. He does not belong to the era of Solomon and he has no intention of pretending he does, but as a learned professor in the school of the wise he inherits the wisdom by which kings reign and rulers decree what is just (Prov. 8:15). Presuming that there was no longer a king in Jerusalem, and the likely date of writing in the late fourth or early third century BC[14] makes this virtually certain, he claims the authority to which kings of old appealed and to which they were indebted for such wise and just administration as they achieved. There was a sense in which the Wise reigned when kings and thrones were a nostalgic memory in Israel, and Qoheleth thus claimed to be 'king'.[15]

Prophecy: Zechariah

Composite authorship of the prophetic books is another alleged source of pseudonymous, or at least anonymous, writings in the Old Testament. The theory that the whole prophetic movement became suspect after the exile has been deduced from Zechariah 13:2–6. 'A generation which knew Babylonian divination and accepted the law of Moses thought that the Prophets' methods of receiving and delivering oracles was questioned. Herein lies the reason for the great output of pseudonymous literature.'[16] Guillaume goes on to argue that men who had a revelation from God could not speak in their own name, and consequently names like Jonah, Zechariah, Daniel, Baruch and others were attached to prophecies of which these long-deceased persons could have known nothing.

Once the custom had become established, it is argued, men like Jonah and Daniel, who were known to have been prophets in ancient times, were credited with definite written prophecies, and from that grew up a recognized literary convention. In short, pseudonymity is seen as one of the results of the suppression of prophecy. Others, on the analogy of probable additions to the works of Greek philosophers from the pen of disciples, argue that schools of prophets prophesied in the name of their master and sometimes added their words to his in writing. Whatever the rationale, the idea is widely accepted that the work of more than one prophet has been included in several of the prophetic books as we know them.

The book of Zechariah may perhaps be accepted as representative of this phenomenon of composite authorship. Without question there are distinct differences between chapters 1 – 8 and chapters 9 – 14 which to some scholars indicate a change of authorship. Some redivide the second part so as to suggest that three authors have contributed. Now it is true that the text presents new headings at 9:1 and 12:1 and that these subdivisions must feature in any analysis of the book, but to base a theory of multiple authorship on this evidence is another matter. Moreover, the number of contributors is commonly reckoned to be more than three because small sections tend to be seen as independent oracles.[17] In Zechariah, then, we have as good an example of alleged pseudonymity in the prophets as we should be likely to find.

In support of multiple authorship attention is drawn to the different character of chapters 9 – 14 as compared with 1 – 8: in the last six chapters no mention is made of the name Zechariah, and, moreover, it is impossible to recognize from historical allusions the period to which they belong. Indeed it is alleged that on three counts – style, vocabulary and contents – multiple authorship is indicated.[18] When the various arguments are backed up by historical settings as diverse as the pre-exilic and Maccabean periods (for despite the difficulty of the task this has been the standard approach), the case for several contributors to the Zechariah collection may seem to have been clinched.

The fact is, however, that the multiplicity of different dates given to the same material brings the historical method under suspicion. If Zechariah 9 – 14 can be understood only with reference to its original setting in life, then the honest course is to admit defeat and decline to attempt any exposition of it. There is, however, the possibility that when a section of a prophetic book is not specifically dated, there is another more appropriate clue to its meaning. In Zechariah 1 – 8, where the time note is important, three dates are given (1:1; 1:7; 7:1), but the headings in 9:1 and 12:1 include no date. May it not be that the author intends us to see that in what follows he is no longer tied to historic time, but is rather expressing theological truths related to God's future purpose?

That this is indeed his intention is borne out by the literary shape of his whole book. The visions (1:7 – 6:15), the messages prompted by the questions about fasting (7:1 – 8:19) and the two sections in part two of the book can be shown from the way the material is arranged to belong together.[19] Moreover, there is progression as the book moves from the establishment of the post-exilic community, with its rebuilt temple and recommissioned leaders and its understanding of the role of God's people among the nations (chapters 1 – 8) to the more eschatological perspective of chapters 9 – 14. Here the prophet rings the changes on the themes of jubilation, rebuke, mourning for a suffering shepherd and cataclysmic judgment, but according to the recognizable pattern which occurs in its simplest form in part one. The final note, the universal kingship of the Lord of Hosts (14:16–21), picks up the same theme from 6:15; 8:22 and 14:9, bringing it to a climax by laying stress on the removal of every obstacle to wholehearted worship of the Lord as King over all. Thus the book is a unity that progresses from historic time to end time, from the local to the universal.[20]

So closely knit is the fabric of the book that one mind must be responsible for its construction, and the simplest explanation is that the prophet Zechariah himself is the author of the total work that bears his name. Thus on internal evidence it can be shown that the theory of multiple authorship, together with the anonymity or pseudepigraphy that it entails, is not the only, nor even perhaps the best, explanation of the diversity within Zechariah. If this is the case here, why not in others? The fact that the prophetic books have come to us as entities provides the strongest evidence against attributing different parts to different authors, and the onus of proof lies on those who would assert that there have been pseudepigraphic additions.

Daniel

The book of Daniel, however, is in a category apart, not only because it is generally acknowledged to contain full-blown apocalyptic, but also because scholars are all but unanimous in judging that chapters 7 – 12, in which Daniel purports to write in the first person, are pseudepigraphical. The ground of such certainty is in the last analysis the content of those chapters which seem to foretell future stages of world history, and in particular chapter 11. These disclosures of the future are regularly classified as examples of *vaticinium ex eventu* or history written up as if it were a prophecy, and evidence in other ancient literatures is adduced for this phenomenon. If such a 'prophecy' is to carry conviction it must of necessity be put into the mouth of someone known to have lived at an earlier stage in history, and therefore it is essentially pseudepigraphical.[21] It follows that if this is the genre of Daniel 7 – 12 these chapters must be pseudonymous.

It may help to clarify the issue to spell out the difference the *ex eventu* theory makes to an understanding of the book of Daniel. The first two chapters claim to belong to the earliest period of Nebuchadrezzar's campaigns (Dan. 1:1; 2:1), before 600 BC, and the last date mentioned (10:1) refers to 537 BC. The impression given, therefore, is that the whole book comes from the sixth century, and increasingly scholars are tending to concede that the stories of chapters 1 – 6 belong earlier than the rest, and stem from the period of the exile. The visions of chapters 7 – 12, however, with their outline of future epochs (chapter 7) and their special interest in the Greek period (chapter 8) which focuses in chapter 11 on the reign of Antiochus Epiphanes (11:21ff.), reveal such detailed knowledge of the future that to reckon the visions prophetic seems to many inconceivable. According to John Goldingay, it is not so much that God could not but that he *would* not give such detailed information in advance.[22]

This is where the argument comes in that most of chapter 11, and by implication the other visions of future epochs, originated in the second century, and in that part of it which is dealt with in most detail in 11:21–35, namely the reign of Antiochus IV Epiphanes. The author had lived through the events he presented as prophecies of that reign. Previous centuries he knew from history. It follows that only a very small part of the visions relate to the future as it looked from the writer's standpoint. In reality he was summing up 350 years of history in the form of a prophecy about 165 BC, and was making a genuine prophecy only in 11:36–45 (or 40–45). In those verses he prophesied the way in which King Antiochus would meet his end.

The author proved to be a very second-rate prophet, however, because even that very short section of prophecy was proved by history to be incorrect! Antiochus did not die in the manner predicted. Moreover, the author made an even bigger mistake in implying that God would intervene in the immediate future by bringing history to an end. His third weak area was his knowledge of history. Many inaccuracies are alleged, some of them serious, but especially his conviction that there was a separate Median kingdom before that of the Persians. Now the book itself does not say that this was the author's interpretation of the four eras of chapters 2 and 7; indeed, 8:20 explicitly states that the Medo-Persian empire was a joint one. Though it is true that there is a focus on the second century in chapter 11 and that this was within the Greek period, the author was looking to a further empire under which God was going to intervene in an unprecedented way, namely the Roman empire, when the proclamation went out, 'the kingdom of God is at hand' (Mark 1:15). In short, the mistakes may be the fault of the interpreter rather than of the text.[23] Otherwise, how did the book ever qualify for inclusion in the canon of Scripture? Did none of the scribes who copied the manuscripts at Qumran, for example, spot the errors?[24]

Scholars who accept the *vaticinium ex eventu* theory, and some who do not explicitly mention it, go to some lengths to repudiate the idea that the pseudonymity involved is in any way fraudulent, or at least they argue that circumstances made it inevitable. Charles thought that the supremacy of the law made the revival of prophecy in the second century BC an impossibility, and Eva Osswald blamed the closure of the canon of revelation for the borrowing of the canonical name.[25] She saw two extra advantages of the pseudonym: added respect for the writing and possibly a means of saving the author from political danger. H. H. Rowley was of the opinion that pseudonymity could be recognized by the reader of the time;[26] Oesterley envisaged a long period of oral tradition preceding the written form of the work, which was attributed to the supposed initiator of the tradition,[27] while Russell contended that the writer thought of himself as an extension of the personality of the historic personage under whose name he wrote.[28]

Recently Klaus Koch has stated his position: 'association with a tradition confers legitimacy', and, 'since what is involved is not the conscious use of an inaccurate name, the designation "pseudonymous" should be used only with reservations'.[29] This reluctance to make use of the word 'pseudonymous' is significant. John Goldingay endeavours to show that pseudonymity is not incompatible with inspiration,[30] and Richard Bauckham argues that 'Pseudonymity is … a device expressing the apocalyptist's consciousness that the age of prophecy has passed: not in the sense that he fraudulently wishes to pass off his work as belonging to the age of prophecy, but in the sense that he thereby acknowledges his work to be mere interpretation of the· revelation given in the prophetic age.'[31] The use of *vaticinia ex eventu* was, according to this writer, in the interests of giving his contemporaries a relevant exposition of old prophecies.

It is true that in Daniel there is a comment on the seventy-year prophecy of Jeremiah, especially in chapter 9, but it is not possible to account for the other visions in this way, unless the dream image in chapter 2 is accepted as genuine ancient prophecy. Moreover, if the apocalyptist really was rewriting prophecies of the past to show how they had been fulfilled, why did he not write in his own name? Whatever the motivation behind his pseudonymity, he certainly succeeded in deceiving his readers, despite assertions to the contrary, as we have already shown. Jesus, according to the Gospel writers, and the early church Fathers, accepted the book as the work of Daniel, for it was not until Porphyry in the third century AD questioned the possibility of such accurate prediction that anyone doubted the genuineness of Danielic authorship.

This fact has, of course, always been put down to a pre-critical mentality, but, on the argument that the literary device of pseudonymity and *vaticinia ex eventu* deceived no-one, the Jewish expositors and the leaders of the early church should have been well aware of the true origin and intention of the 'prophecies', especially in view of the development of pseudonymous literature in the period between the Testaments. If, on the other hand, the author of Daniel did intend to deceive, he was entirely successful in doing so until the time of Porphyry. Had it been otherwise, the likelihood is that his work would have been excluded from the canon.

It will be noted that pseudepigraphy is said to fulfil functions which are mutually exclusive. On the one hand we are asked to believe that this was an accepted literary convention which deceived no-one, and on the other that the adoption of a pseudonym, which presumably went undetected, increased the acceptability and authority of a work. Those who contend that Daniel was written under a pseudonym cannot have it both ways.

While there are advantages in singling out a subject like pseudonymity for consideration in its own right, other factors, particularly date of writing, are bound up with it. If Daniel is a sixth-century work, the question of pseudonymity does not arise, whereas if it is a product of the second century BC a study of Hellenism and the literature in the world of that time becomes relevant. John J. Collins, in just such a study,[32] sees the undoubted rise in the number of pseudepigrapha during the Hellenistic period as one of a number of conspicuous phenomena resulting from the demise of national monarchies, loss of meaning and alienation. In a later article, however, having pointed out that the writer of Revelation eschewed pseudonymity, he gives the explanation: 'The lack of pseudonymity, then, reflects the heightened eschatological fervour of the early Christian community and its greater receptivity for apocalyptic revelations.'[33]

But if one era before Christ had to be selected as demonstrating the same kind of expectations, so far as the Jews were concerned the sixth century would take precedence over the second. Deprived of a king, deported, interned, they lost all hope to a degree that was never true of the later period. In their state of alienation, Ezekiel's visions of the great and holy Lord, who would reinstate the nation and so reveal his glory to the world, restored hope. Haggai and Zechariah ministered to the struggling community back in Judah. In that time of unrest and upheaval, apocalyptic imagery flourished, and these writers, by their skilful use of symbolic language and literary forms, brought reassurance of God's control in a chaotic world. On socio-historic grounds this is surely the period most likely to produce the book of Daniel.

As one who has endeavoured to write a commentary on Daniel I would claim that, whereas to postulate a second-century setting restricts the impact of the book's prophecies to that century because they are regarded as fulfilled in the time of the Maccabees, a sixth-century date of writing allows a more flexible interpretation based on the book's repeated claim to foretell the future. As Gordon Wenham points out, 'The idea that God declares his future purposes to his servants is at the heart of the book's theology.'[34] The expositor who fails to take this seriously fails to take the book seriously. The whole of chapter 10, for example, describing the experience of Daniel as he was being prepared to receive his final vision, becomes so much local colour in support of an elaborate fiction, for almost all that was to follow in chapter 11 was a recital of history, much of it recent. Similarly the prayer of chapter 9 and descriptions such as those of 8:15–19; 12:7–8 become so much padding to give the effect of reality.

Interpreted as history, the predictions have no further claim on the reader. Any interest is on a purely academic level. So to rob a book of its impact invites eccentric interpretations such as have come to be associated at a popular level with this book.

In conclusion, we contend that there is no clear proof of pseudonymity in the Old Testament and much evidence against it. When a writer made use of a literary convention, as in the case of Qoheleth, he made it abundantly plain that that was what he was doing. So far as the book of Daniel is concerned, there is no hint of such a thing, nor did the Old or New Testament church, which included the book in the canon, suspect it. If the historical setting provided by the text is accepted, there is no reason for postulating pseudonymity, and the task of proving that the book is in any part pseudonymous must rest with those who confidently make the claim.

Notes

1. As Helen Morgan, *What Price Glory?* (London: IVP, 1972); as Rhena Taylor, *Rough Edges* (Leicester: IVP, 1978).
2. See e.g. J. C. Fenton, 'Pseudonymity in the New Testament', *Theology* 58, 1953, pp. 51–56; K. Aland, 'The problem of anonymity and pseudonymity in Christian literature of the first two centuries', *JTS* 12 (1961), pp. 39–49; D. Guthrie, 'The development of the idea of canonical pseudepigrapha in New Testament criticism', *VoxEv* (1962), pp. 43–59; Bruce M. Metzger, 'Literary forgeries and canonical pseudepigrapha', *JBL* 91 (1972), pp. 3–24; John J. Collins, 'Pseudonymity, historical reviews and the genre of the Revelation of John', *CBQ* 39 (1977), pp. 329–343. Metzger and Collins touch on the Old Testament also.
3. 'The problem of pseudonymity', *JTS* 4 (1953), pp. 15–22.
4. 'A catalogue of texts and authors', *JCS* 16 (1962), pp. 59–76.
5. Ibid., p. 59.
6. Ibid., p. 73.
7. *The Expositor*, 4th series, 4 (1891), p. 94.
8. Metzger, 'Literary forgeries', pp. 5–6. He refers to Galen, *In Hipp. de nat. hominis* 1.42 (C. G. Kühn, *Medicorum graecorum opera* 15, p. 105).
9. Ibid., p. 11.
10. *Vaticinia ex eventu* and pseudonymity will be dealt with below in connection with Daniel.
11. For a recent commentary on Deuteronomy which argues for substantially Mosaic authorship see P. C. Craigie, *The Book of Deuteronomy*, New International Commentary on the Old Testament (Grand Rapids: Eerdmans; London: Hodder and Stoughton, 1976).
12. Derek Kidner, *A Time to Mourn, and a Time to Dance* (Leicester: IVP, 1976), p. 22.
13. *Judaism and Hellenism* 1 (London: SCM, 1974), pp. 129–130: Excursus 3: 'Koheleth and Solomon'.
14. J. Muilenburg, *BASOR* 135 (1954), pp. 23–24, on the basis of fragments of the book from Qumran Cave 4.
15. Solomonic authorship has been maintained by a few scholars, one of the most recent being G. L. Archer in *BETS* 12 (1969), pp. 167–181.
16. Alfred Guillaume, *Prophecy and Divination*, Bampton Lectures (London: Hodder and Stoughton,

1938), p. 163.

17. See e.g. O. Eissfeldt, *The Old Testament: An Introduction* (Oxford: Blackwell, 1965), pp. 438–440; G. Fohrer, *Introduction to the Old Testament* (London: SPCK, 1970), pp. 446–448.

18. A more detailed discussion of the subject may be found in the writer's *Haggai, Zechariah, Malachi* (London: IVP, 1972), pp. 60–70.

19. Ibid., pp. 8–86.

20. Ibid., pp. 74–81.

21. A study of *vaticinia ex eventu* in relation to Daniel is included in the Tyndale Old Testament Lecture 1978, by the present writer, published in *TB* 30 (1979), pp. 77–99.

22. *Themelios* 2.2 (January 1977), p. 49.

23. Robert J. M. Gurney, 'The Four Kingdoms of Daniel 2 and 7', *Themelios* 2.2, pp. 39–45, argues, however, that the four empires are indeed those of Babylon, Media, Persia, Greece, and that there is no historical mistake.

24. It is clear from the fragments of the book of Daniel found at Qumran and from other related texts that the book enjoyed great popularity there. See Joyce G. Baldwin, *Daniel*, Tyndale Old Testament Commentaries, (Leicester: IVP, 1978), introductory sections, viii and x (pp. 68–74).

25. R. H. Charles, *Apocrypha and Pseudepigrapha* 2, p. viii. Eva Osswald, 'Zum Problem der *Vaticinia ex eventu*', *ZAW* 75 (1963), pp. 27–44.

26. H. H. Rowley, *The Relevance of Apocalyptic* (London: Lutterworth, 1944), p. 39.

27. W. O. E. Oesterley, *The Jews and Judaism During the Greek Period* (London: SPCK, 1941), p. 74.

28. D. S. Russell, *The Method and Message of Jewish Apocalyptic* (London: SCM, 1964), pp. 127–139.

29. 'Pseudonymous writing', *Interpreter's Dictionary of the Bible: Supplementary Volume* (Nashville: Abingdon, 1976), p. 713.

30. *Themelios* 2.2 (January 1977), p. 49; *The Churchman* 90 (January–March 1976), pp. 6–23.

31. *Themelios* 3.2 (January 1978), p. 18 (= p. 50 of volume 3).

32. 'Jewish apocalyptic against its Hellenistic Near Eastern environment', *BASOR* 220 (1975), pp. 27–36.

33. *CBQ* 39 (1977), p. 332.

34. *Themelios* 2.2 (1977), p. 51. John Goldingay, on the other hand, finds a second-century dating more glorifying to God and more pastorally helpful (p. 49).

6

The Old Testament view of life after death

T. Desmond Alexander   Vol. 11.2 (1986)

Introduction

It is not uncommon to encounter statements which suggest that the Old Testament has almost nothing to say on the subject of life after death; and what little it does report is usually assessed in quite negative terms. Indeed, not a few writers give the distinct impression that for the Hebrews the afterlife was envisaged as a dull, dreary existence, lacking any of those pleasures which make this present life enjoyable and fulfilling. It was not until the late post-exilic period that immortality and resurrection became a part of Jewish thinking on life after death.

Yet, does this portrayal do justice to the contents of the Old Testament? Was this really the way in which the Hebrew patriarchs, prophets, priests and people perceived their future? Did the grave represent for them nothing more than an empty, joyless form of existence? Such queries readily prompt the basic question: what was the Old Testament view of life after death?

However, at the very outset we confront another problem: was there *an* Old Testament view of life after death? Does the Hebrew Bible present a single, uniform picture? Or ought we to look for a variety of positions reflecting, perhaps, different stages in the development of the Hebrew concept of the afterlife, or, alternatively, distinctions between 'official' and 'popular' views?

The general trend in recent writings has been to distinguish clearly between pre- and post-exilic developments in the Old Testament concept of the afterlife. The pre-exilic period is dominated by the belief that death, as a purely natural phenomenon, marked the end of life. The afterlife, if one can call it that, consisted of a silent existence in Sheol, the realm of the dead, where both righteous and wicked shared a common fate, isolated for eternity from God and the living. After the exile, the Hebrew view of the afterlife underwent various transformations due to the influence of other ideas. According to J. Jeremias, three significant changes occurred:[1] (a) the concept of resurrection gave rise to the idea that the dead would not remain in Sheol for ever; (b) Greek and Persian views on retribution after death resulted in the division of the underworld into different compartments for the righteous and the wicked; (c) the Greek concept of immortality led to the idea that the righteous went directly to heaven whereas the wicked descended to Sheol, which consequently was perceived as a place of punishment.

Although it is now widely accepted that the Old Testament concept of the afterlife developed, broadly speaking, along these lines, further considerations suggest that it may be necessary to modify this position somewhat.

The Old Testament view of death

Central to any discussion on the Old Testament view of the afterlife is the Hebrew understanding of *death*. How was death perceived? What actually happened to an individual when he died? Did it mean the end of existence? Or was there something beyond death?

Initially it is important to note that the Hebrew term for 'death', *māwet*, has a variety of connotations in the Old Testament. According to W. Brueggemann,[2] *māwet* is used in three distinctive ways: (a) *biologically*, indicating 'the end of historical life' (e.g. Gen. 21:16); (b) *mythologically*, 'as a power, agent or principle' (e.g. Job 18:13; Jer. 9:21);[3] and (c) *symbolically*, 'as the loss of rich, joyous existence as willed by God' (e.g. Deut. 30:15; Ps. 13:3–4). However, as these last two references reveal, it is not always possible to be completely certain when 'death' is being used in a symbolical or metaphorical sense; in both instances 'death' could be understood in its purely biological sense, 'the end of historical life'. A fourth possibility, not discussed by Brueggemann, is that 'death' refers to the place of existence after biological cessation (e.g. Job 38:17; Is. 28:15).[4] The fact that *māwet*, 'death', can convey a variety of meanings creates real difficulties in interpreting some passages. Not surprisingly, this can be a significant factor in attempting to appraise the Old Testament perception of the afterlife.

A 'good' death or a 'bad' death

In a recent monograph, *Death in the Literature of the Old Testament*, L. R. Bailey suggests that within the Hebrew Bible descriptions of biological death fall into two basic categories: an individual may experience either a 'good' death or a 'bad' death. The account of Abraham's decease in Genesis 25:8 (NIV)conveys a certain sense of comfort and reassurance: 'Then Abraham breathed his last and died at a good old age, an old man and full of years; and he was gathered to his people' (cf. Gen. 15:15). A similar appraisal of death occurs in the words of Eliphaz to Job about the fate of the righteous: 'You shall come to your grave in ripe old age, as a shock of grain comes up to the threshing floor in its season' (Job 5:26, RSV). Such descriptions, however, contrast sharply with those which refer to a 'bad' death. Jacob, for example, finds no comfort in the death of Joseph: 'Then Jacob tore his clothes, put on sackcloth and mourned for his son many days. All his sons and daughters came to comfort him, but he refused to be comforted. "No," he said, "in mourning will I go down to the grave [Sheol] to my son." So his father wept for him' (Gen. 37:34–35, NIV). Jacob's unwillingness to be comforted arose from the fact that Joseph had encountered a 'bad' death.

Given that the ancient Hebrews appear to have distinguished between a 'good' and a 'bad' death, what factors separated these two types of death? Bailey, for his part, suggests three conditions which characterize a 'bad' death: (1) if it is premature (e.g. 2 Sam. 18:32–33; Is. 38:1–12); (2) if it is violent (e.g. 1 Sam. 28:15–20; 1 Kgs. 2:28–33); (3) if there is no surviving heir (e.g. Gen. 15:2–3; 2 Sam. 18:18).[5] On the other hand, those who live to a good old age with children to succeed them have no reason to fear death (e.g. Gen. 25:8; 35:28–29).

While these factors certainly deserve consideration, it is the present writer's conviction that they do not *of themselves* explain why the Hebrews distinguished between a 'good' and a 'bad' death. The rationale for this distinction must be sought elsewhere. An initial reason for suggesting this is the fact that premature or violent deaths are not always viewed as 'bad'. Concerning premature death, we read in Isaiah 57:1–2, 'The righteous perish, and no-one ponders it in his heart; devout men are taken away, and no-one understands that the righteous are taken away to be spared from evil. Those who walk uprightly enter into peace; they find rest as they lie in death.' Here premature death is clearly envisaged as good, bringing deliverance from evil.[6] An actual case of this is King Josiah, who experienced not only a premature but also a violent death (2 Kgs. 23:29–30). Prior to his death he received the following divine assurance: 'I will gather you to your fathers, and you will be buried in peace. Your eyes will not see all the disaster I am going to bring on this place' (2 Kgs. 22:20; cf. 2 Chr. 35:24). Although these passages may prove to be exceptional, they do raise the possibility that the distinction between a 'good' and a 'bad' death may be due to factors other than those suggested by Bailey.

To appreciate fully Bailey's position it is essential to note that two important premises underlie his approach: (1) death in the Old Testament is viewed as a *natural* consequence of man's mortality; (2) after death a similar fate awaits both the righteous and the wicked. Let us examine both of these assumptions.

Death: natural or punitive

An important passage towards understanding the Old Testament perception of death is the account of its origin. Attention naturally focuses on the early chapters of Genesis where, in the garden of Eden narrative (Gen. 2:4 – 3:24), death is introduced for the very first time. Here discussions have tended to ask whether death is portrayed as *natural*, a consequence of man's mortality, or as *punitive*, a result of man's disobedience. On this issue modern scholarship seems to be almost equally divided.[7]

For his part Bailey follows the suggestion of E. Nielsen[8] that there are two different conceptions of death underlying the present account in Genesis 2 – 3: (i) 'a Paradise-hubris myth that looks upon death as a punishment for arrogance'; (ii) 'a Creation myth that regards death as the natural termination of created life'. Significantly, the first of these aetiologies, according to Bailey, 'had no influence upon subsequent Old Testament literature, although there is the related idea that human sin leads to *premature* death'.[9] However, the second aetiology, which portrays death as natural, represents 'the basic perspective of the Old Testament literature'.[10] Because death was natural, there was no need to fear it. 'Death … was not an irrational, intruding enemy but part of an ordered, controlled, harmonious creation. Biological life and death are not separate phenomena, as if the latter intruded to thwart the Creator's design. They are bound together as part of a singular divine will for his creatures. To accept one is to accept the other; to despise one is to despise the other.'[11] This being so, death was viewed as a natural consequence of human existence; it was only 'unnatural' when it occurred prematurely.

This proposal, however, that death was perceived by the Hebrews as natural, runs counter to much of the evidence. Bailey himself acknowledges that the account in Genesis 2 – 3 'can be read as a continuous story rather than as a combination of two earlier and conflicting folk accounts',[12] and, as Nielsen readily admits, these two accounts have been combined, with the result that 'death appears unambiguously as a punishment, for man's disobedience as well as for his arrogance'.[13] If, however, as Bailey suggests, 'the basic perspective of the Old Testament literature' was to view death as natural, would we not have expected this outlook to dominate the final form of the narrative in Genesis 2 – 3? Thus, although many writers suggest that death is viewed here as 'natural', there does seem to be a strong case, especially in the light of 2:17 and 3:3–4, for maintaining that death is portrayed as a divine punishment.[14]

Support for the opinion that all deaths were understood as *unnatural* can be deduced from various regulations in Leviticus and Numbers. In Numbers 19:16 we read: 'Anyone out in the open who touches someone who has been killed with a sword or someone who has died a natural death, or anyone who touches a human bone or a grave, will be unclean for seven days.' Thus corpses and objects closely associated with death defile an individual. This fact is underlined by the preceding verses of the same chapter: verses 11–13 describe the process of purification necessary after touching a corpse, and verses 14–15 indicate that one is defiled merely by entering a tent containing a dead body.[15] Stricter rules limiting contact with corpses are applied to priests (Lev. 21:2–3, 10–11) and Nazirites (Num. 6:6–12; cf. Judg. 14:8–9).[16] Finally, Leviticus 11 reveals that unless they have been ritually slaughtered, the carcasses of *all* animals are unclean.[17] That death is the decisive factor here is demonstrated by the fact that whereas a Hebrew might handle with impunity *living* unclean animals (e.g. camels, pigs), he would become temporarily unclean by touching the corpses of these same animals (vv. 8, 11, 24–28). In a similar fashion household objects or utensils were defiled when touched by the carcasses of certain small animals (vv. 29–38).

In all of these examples death is presented in negative terms: death, like sin, defiles and pollutes. If death was perceived by the Hebrews as entirely 'natural', is it not strange that they should have linked it with ritual defilement and uncleanness? Such a connection hardly supports the suggestion that death was 'part of an orderly, controlled, harmonious creation'. Thus Bailey's proposal that death in old age represented the divine intention in creation, and that only premature death was unnatural, is mistaken. On the contrary, the weight of evidence surely favours the view that death was indeed perceived by the Hebrews as a punishment for man's rebellion against God.

The Hebrew perception of 'Sheol'

The second major premiss underlying Bailey's position is that all men, irrespective of their moral character, share a similar destiny after death: all go down to Sheol.[18] On account of this any attempt to distinguish between a 'good' and a 'bad' death must be based on events prior to rather than after death. Thus Bailey focuses on the *circumstances* of death: whether it is premature, violent or childless.

The assumption, however, that the righteous and the wicked share the same fate in the afterlife rests upon a particular understanding of the Hebrew concept of Sheol: (a) that after death everyone, without exception, descends into the nether world, and (b) that in Sheol no distinction is drawn between the righteous and the wicked. However, as we shall presently observe, this portrayal of Sheol reflects only one of a number of possibilities.

Before considering these other possibilities we should note that efforts to determine the precise meaning of Sheol by appealing either to extrabiblical occurrences or to etymology have so far proved unsuccessful. Whereas the term Sheol occurs sixty-five times in the Old Testament, it is found only once in extrabiblical material, in the fifth-century Aramaic papyri of the Jewish inhabitants of Elephantine in Egypt,[19] and apart from the fact that it clearly refers to the place of the dead, little else can be gleaned from this particular reference. Regarding the etymology of Sheol, various suggestions have been made to explain its origin. F. Delitzsch proposed almost a century ago that it developed from an Accadian word, *šu'alû*, which he took to mean 'nether world'. More recently a number of scholars have followed the opinion that it is derived from the Accadian verb *š'l* (to 'ask' or 'enquire'; compare Hebrew *š'l);* initially Sheol denoted 'examination ordeal', but through time it came to mean 'nether world'. These proposed etymologies, unfortunately, are not without their difficulties and cannot be relied upon with complete certainty.[20] Since its exact meaning cannot be known from either extrabiblical references or etymology, we are left with no choice but to determine from each Old Testament context what Sheol was intended to denote. A number of possibilities exist.

Segregation within Sheol

One view with a long history, and which used to enjoy widespread support, is the idea that whereas everyone on dying actually descends into Sheol, once there the righteous and the wicked are segregated into different compartments. This idea is found, for example, in the *Hebrew and English Lexicon* of Brown, Driver and Briggs, where the Hebrew words *'ăbaddôn*, 'destruction', *bôr*, 'pit' and *šāḥat*, 'corruption' or 'pit', are taken to denote a 'place of ruin in She'ol for lost or ruined dead'.[21] It can, however, be traced back as far as the intertestamental book of *1 Enoch*, where it is now generally thought to reflect a later development in Jewish thinking on the afterlife. In *1 Enoch* 22:1–14 Sheol is divided into four sections: '(1) for the righteous – v. 9b; (2) for the wicked who have not been punished in this life – vv. 10f.; (3) for the martyred righteous – v. 12, cf. vv. 5–7; (4) for the wicked who have been punished in this life – v. 13'.[22] It has even been suggested that such a belief surfaces in a number of New Testament passages (e.g. Acts 2:27, 31; Eph. 4:9; 1 Pet. 3:19).[23]

While it is tempting to suggest, especially in the light of later Jewish thinking, that in Old Testament times Sheol was perceived as consisting of different regions, the biblical texts themselves do not support such a possibility. As has been clearly indicated by a number of scholars, the terms *'ăbaddôn*, *bôr* and *šāḥat* are merely synonyms for Sheol, and ought not to be viewed as designating a separate lower region within the nether world.[24] Similarly, we may reject all suggestions that certain New Testament passages allude to a compartmentalized nether world. When examined more closely it is quite apparent that they do not presuppose such a concept of Sheol.[25]

Sheol and the grave

More recently, a quite different approach has been suggested by R. L. Harris.[26] He argues that Sheol refers without exception to the grave, the place where the physical body is laid to rest. Significantly, this proposal is motivated by a desire to avoid a difficulty which arises if one accepts that the souls of all men coexist in Sheol: 'Does the Old Testament teach, in contradiction to the New Testament, that all men after death go to a dark and dismal place where the dead know nothing and are cut off from God?'[27] This theological problem disappears, however, if Sheol denotes merely the grave, the resting-place of the body but not of the soul. For the ultimate destiny of men's souls we must look elsewhere in the Scriptures (e.g. Exod. 3:6; Matt. 22:32).

Several factors, however, argue against this proposal. First, although Sheol comes sixty-five times in the Old Testament it never takes the definite article, suggesting that it may well have been used as a proper name denoting the nether world. Secondly, although Harris is correct in pointing out that some descriptions of Sheol resemble closely a Palestinian tomb (e.g. Ezek. 32:26–27), this may result from the fact that the Hebrews viewed Sheol as an extension of the grave. As O. Keel comments, 'As a land from which no one has ever yet returned (cf. Ps. 88:10; Jb. 7:9–10; 10:21; Akkadian *erṣet lā tari* "land of no return"), the actual realm of the dead is a speculative entity. Its concrete features are derived from empirical observation of the grave. Beyond that, very little can be said about the world of the dead. For that reason, it appears as a prototypical grave raised to gigantic proportions.'[28] Thus although Harris demonstrates that some descriptions of Sheol do resemble an ordinary grave, these same descriptions may also be equally appropriate for the nether world.

The nether world and the wicked

A third approach is that of A. Heidel, who proposes that the term Sheol exhibits a broad range of meanings. Whereas on occasions it clearly denotes the subterranean spirit world (e.g. Num. 16:30–33; Deut. 32:22), elsewhere it may refer to the grave (e.g. Is. 14:11; Ezek. 32:26–27), or even be 'used as a figure of speech to denote extreme misfortune, seemingly inescapable death, the brink of death, or the like (Pss. 30:4; 86:13; 88:4; Jonah 2:3 [= 2:2 in the English translation])'.[29] However, as well as suggesting that Sheol has a wide range of connotations, Heidel makes another observation of special relevance for our present discussion: 'As regards She'ol ... we have evidence that it, in the signification of the subterranean realm of the spirits, applies to the habitation of the souls of the wicked only.'[30] In saying this Heidel distinguishes clearly between the destiny of the righteous and the wicked in the afterlife; whereas the souls of the ungodly go down to Sheol, the souls of the pious ascend to heaven.

Although Heidel's thesis has the advantage of avoiding any theological difficulties created by the co-existence of the righteous and the wicked in the nether world, it may, however, be objected that he interprets the biblical evidence in a somewhat arbitrary manner. If a passage refers to the death of a righteous person, Sheol is taken invariably to mean 'grave' (e.g. Gen. 37:35; 42:38; Is. 38:10); but when the wicked are mentioned, Sheol usually means 'nether world' (e.g. Num. 16:30; Is. 14:13–15), although Heidel does allow that it can on occasions merely denote a grave (e.g. Is. 14:11; Ezek. 32:26–27). The question then arises: to what extent is Heidel's view on the fate of the righteous after death dependent upon his reading of Sheol as the 'grave'? Is his conclusion still viable if Sheol is understood to denote solely the 'nether world'?

Unfortunately, space does not permit us to discuss in detail every occurrence of 'Sheol'. We must therefore restrict ourselves to several summary observations. First, apart from a few references which are indecisive (e.g. Eccles. 9:10; Song 8:6), 'Sheol' always conveys negative overtones: for example, it is somewhere fearful and to be avoided (e.g. 2 Sam. 22:6; Pss. 16:10; 30:3; 86:13); it is the antithesis of heaven (e.g. Job 11:8; Ps. 139:8; Amos 9:2). Secondly, in a significant proportion of passages Sheol is linked unquestionably with evil-doers (e.g. Num. 16:30, 33; 1 Kgs. 2:6, 9; Job 24:19; Pss. 9:17; 31:17; 49:14; Prov. 5:5; 7:27; 9:18; Is. 5:14; 14:9, 11, 15; Ezek. 31:15–17; 32:21, 27). Taken together these observations would seem to indicate that Sheol does indeed denote the ultimate abode of the wicked alone.

There are, however, a few occurrences of Sheol which are generally thought to imply that the righteous were also to be found in the nether world. In mourning the untimely death of his son Joseph, Jacob laments, 'In mourning will I go down to the grave [Sheol] to my son' (Gen. 37:35). Similar comments come in Genesis 42:38 and 44:29, 31, this time motivated by Jacob's fear that his youngest son Benjamin will also be killed. Whereas Heidel takes Sheol to mean 'grave' in 37:35, Jacob's unwillingness to be comforted following the apparent killing of Joseph by a wild animal could suggest that he considers Joseph to have been divinely punished, and hence with the wicked in the nether world. This understanding of Sheol would certainly add weight to the expression of Jacob's grief for his son Joseph. A similar explanation would account for the use of Sheol in 42:38 and 44:29, 31.

Another passage which seems to imply that the righteous descend to Sheol is Isaiah chapter 38. After the prophet Isaiah predicts that king Hezekiah will suffer an early death, the king pleads that God may remember him. As a consequence he is granted a further fifteen years to live (vv. 1–8). In subsequently describing his feelings Hezekiah writes: 'I said, "In the prime of my life must I go through the gates of death [Sheol] and be robbed·of the rest of my years? ... Surely it was for my benefit that I suffered such anguish. In your love you kept me from the pit of destruction; you have put all my sins behind your back. For the grave [Sheol] cannot praise you, death cannot sing your praise; those who go down to the pit cannot hope for your faithfulness"' (vv. 10, 17–18). These comments are usually interpreted to mean that Hezekiah viewed the righteous as going to Sheol. However, in the light of Isaiah's prediction against him (v. 1) and the knowledge of his own sins (v. 17), Hezekiah may have had every reason to believe that he was doomed to join the wicked in the nether world. It is thus possible that both Hezekiah and Jacob understood Sheol to denote the final abode of the wicked.

Of the alternatives outlined above for understanding Sheol, we may now reject as improbable (i) the once popular view that Sheol consisted of different compartments, and (ii) the proposal of R. L. Harris that it denotes solely the grave. In choosing between the two remaining possibilities, we must decide whether or not the Hebrews believed that all men descended into the nether world, or only the wicked. As far as our investigation of the term 'Sheol' is concerned, it is difficult to reach a decisive conclusion, although the weight of evidence possibly favours Heidel's opinion that only the ungodly descended there. Moreover, there are a number of passages which seem to point in the same general direction.

First, the accounts of the translations of Enoch and Elijah suggest that not all men descend to Sheol (Gen. 5:24; 2 Kgs. 2:1–18). Whereas the reference to Enoch is brief, in the case of Elijah it is clearly stated that he was taken up by

God to heaven (2 Kgs. 2:1). In both instances it is implied that God has the power to take to himself those who enjoy an intimate relationship with him (cf. Ps. 73:24). Secondly, the author of Psalm 49, troubled by the prosperity and success of the wicked, finds comfort in the fact that any present imbalance between the fortunes of the godly and of the ungodly will be put to rights in the afterlife.[31] The psalmist clearly believes in different rewards in the life to come.

These two ideas, (a) the continuity beyond death of an intimate relationship with God, and (b) the redressing in the hereafter of inadequate temporal rewards and punishments, obviously reflect Hebrew thinking on the afterlife. Unfortunately, many scholars have tended to play down the significance of these and other passages, or have interpreted them in such a way as to remove any reference to the future life.[32] Such an approach, however, seems to be influenced more by the assumption that the concepts of immortality and resurrection were late developments in Jewish religion, than by a detailed study of the biblical texts in the light of other ancient near-eastern documents.[33]

The belief that Sheol was the final abode of the wicked is in keeping with the idea, discussed above, that the Hebrews perceived death as punitive rather than as natural. Since mankind was considered to be under divine condemnation, the normal consequence of dying was imprisonment in a dark, gloomy region from which no-one could ever escape. To go down to Sheol was to suffer a 'bad' death.

The righteous in the afterlife

Although the wicked encountered a 'bad' death, the righteous, in contrast, were perceived as experiencing a 'good' death. The question arises, however: what happened to the righteous after death?

Surprisingly, perhaps, the Old Testament contains no detailed account of the fate of the righteous immediately after death. As a result the best that one can do is piece together various snippets of information in the hope of producing a clear picture. One factor, however, which is especially significant in this regard is the concept of resurrection.

As noted earlier, many modern writers consider the concept of resurrection to be a relatively late development in Jewish thinking on the afterlife.[34] Two main arguments are forwarded in support of this position. First, those passages which refer explicitly to the resurrection of the dead can all be dated to the post-exilic period (i.e. Is. 26:19; Dan. 12:2).[35] Secondly, the Jewish concept of the resurrection appears to have been influenced by the Persian religion of Zoroastrianism, and this probably occurred during the early post-exilic period when the Jews and Persians were in close contact.

In a recent study, however, L. J. Greenspoon has challenged the view that the belief in a resurrection was a post-exilic development.[36] Rejecting the influence of both earlier Mesopotamian and Canaanite myths and rituals concerning 'dying and rising gods', and later Zoroastrian beliefs regarding the 'reconstitution of the body', he suggests that the Old Testament belief in bodily resurrection developed 'out of themes associated with YHWH as Divine Warrior'. In this capacity Yahweh is perceived as having the power to overcome death and release those under its control. Further, from a survey of relevant passages he concludes that the 'concept of bodily resurrection of the dead is expressed in biblical material that ranges in date of composition from the ninth to the second centuries B.C.E'.[37] Although Greenspoon's arguments are unlikely to reverse the present consensus favouring a late date for the introduction of the concept of resurrection into Jewish thinking on the afterlife, he does present reasonable grounds for believing that the idea of bodily resurrection can be traced back to the pre-exilic period.

An important implication of the doctrine of resurrection is that the righteous remain in the realm of the dead until divinely raised to life again.[38] This suggests that there must be some form of intermediate state between the time of death and resurrection. If, as many writers maintain, all men irrespective of their moral character descend to Sheol, then we must view the righteous as being resurrected from there. However, if Sheol is understood to be the abode of the wicked alone, then the righteous must have existed elsewhere prior to being raised to life again. Unfortunately, the Old Testament reveals little regarding the precise nature of the intermediate abode of the righteous.

One of the few indications of what became of the righteous after death is the expression 'to be gathered to one's people' (cf. Gen. 25:8, 17; 35:29; 49:33; Num. 27:13; 31:2; Deut. 32:50) or 'to be gathered to one's fathers' (cf. Judg. 2:10; 2 Kgs. 22:20; 2 Chr. 34:28). 'That these figures of speech do not refer to the interment in the grave of the fathers, or the ancestral tomb, as has been maintained, is clear from the fact that Abraham, Aaron and Moses were not united with their fathers in the grave. Nor do they have reference to burial in general, for in the stories of the "gathering" of Abraham and Isaac it is expressly added that they were buried (Gen. 25:8–9; 35:29); moreover, Jacob was "gathered to his people" (Gen. 49:33) several months before his body was committed to the ground (50:1–13).[39] Significantly, in their use of the expression 'to be gathered to one's fathers' (or 'people'), the biblical writers seem to convey a sense of optimism regarding death (cf. Gen. 15:15). Although death may separate an individual from his family and kin in this life, the righteous are reunited with those members of their families who have already died.

That death is sometimes described as falling asleep (e.g. Ps. 13:3; Dan. 12:2) and the resurrection as reawaking[40] (e.g. 2 Kgs. 4:31; Job 14:12; Is. 26:19; Dan. 12:2) suggests possibly that the intermediate state of the righteous is one of comparative tranquillity and peace. Even so, they are still perceived as being in the realm of the dead. Perhaps for this reason the Old Testament focuses attention not on the intermediate state of the righteous but rather on their eventual resurrection.

Taking these factors into account we may now be in a better position to appreciate the somewhat ambivalent attitude, noted above, of the Old Testament writers towards Sheol. Although all men may have been viewed as initially descending there on dying, the fact that the righteous would subsequently be resurrected, leaving behind the wicked, possibly explains why Sheol is generally presented in quite negative terms. Whereas the righteous would eventually enter into God's presence, the wicked continued to languish in the depths of Sheol. Thus, in spite of the temporary sojourn of the righteous there, Sheol represented for the Hebrews the ultimate and lasting abode of those who were excluded from the divine presence.

Conclusion

While some of the evidence is ambiguous, and questions remain to be answered, we are perhaps now in a position to clarify certain fundamental issues regarding the Old Testament perception of the afterlife. First, we may reject the currently popular belief that in the pre-exilic period death was viewed by the Hebrews as a natural legacy of man's mortality and that, as a consequence, little interest was shown in the afterlife. Secondly, it seems probable that the term Sheol frequently, if not always, designated the nether world, and that as such it represented the continuing abode of the ungodly. Thirdly, whereas the wicked were thought to remain in the dark, silent region of Sheol, the righteous lived in the hope that God would deliver them from the power of death and take them to himself (cf. Ps. 49:15).

Notes

1. J. Jeremias, 'hades', *Theological Dictionary of the New Testament* 1 (Grand Rapids: Eerdmans, 1964), p. 147. Various writers, however, question the extent of foreign influences upon Jewish thinking regarding the afterlife; cf. G. Nickelsburg, *Resurrection, Immortality, and Eternal Life in Intertestamental Judaism* (Harvard Theological Studies 26, Cambridge, MA: Harvard University Press, 1972); J. J. Collins, 'Apocalyptic eschatology as the transcendence of death', *CBQ* 36 (1974), pp. 21–43; W. Wifall, 'The status of "man" as resurrection', *ZAW* 90 (1978), pp. 382–394.
2. 'Death, theology of', *Interpreter's Dictionary of the Bible Supplement* (1976), pp. 219–220. This

threefold division is developed more fully by L. R. Bailey, *Biblical Perspectives on Death* (Philadelphia: Fortress, 1979), pp. 39–47.

3. Brueggemann comments, 'Israel's environment sustained a mythology which presented Death (Mot) as an active personal agent in combat with Yahweh' *(IDB Supplement*, pp. 219–220).

4. Cf. A. Heidel, *The Gilgamesh Epic and Old Testament Parallels* (Chicago: University of Chicago Press, 2nd edn 1949), p. 177; R. L. Harris, '*māwet*', *Theological Wordbook of the Old Testament* 1 (Chicago: Moody, 1980), p. 497.

5. Bailey, *Biblical Perspectives*, pp. 48–51.

6. Heidel, *The Gilgamesh Epic*, p. 150; cf. F. Delitzsch, *Isaiah* (Edinburgh: T. and T. Clark, 1873), pp. 368–369.

7. Cf. C. Westermann, *Genesis* 1 – 11 (London: SPCK, 1984), pp. 266–267.

8. 'Creation and the fall of man', *HUCA* 43 (1972), pp. 1–22.

9. *Biblical Perspectives*, p. 38.

10. Ibid.

11. Ibid., pp. 57–58; cf. J. B. Burns, 'The mythology of death in the Old Testament' *SJT* 26 (1973), pp. 327–340.

12. Ibid., p. 38; cf. U. Cassuto, *A Commentary on the Book of Genesis* 1 (Jerusalem: Magnes, 1961), pp. 92–94. Nielsen's proposal that two earlier and quite distinct accounts have been combined to form the present account is questionable: see S. T. Walsh, 'Genesis 2.4b – 3.24: a synchronic approach', *JBL* 96 (1977), pp. 161–177.

13. 'Creation', p. 17.

14. H. Blocher, *In the Beginning* (Leicester: IVP, 1984), pp. 184–187; cf. Rom. 5:12; 6:23.

15. G. J. Wenham, *The Book of Leviticus* (Grand Rapids: Eerdmans, 1979), pp. 290–291.

16. These indicate that death and holiness are incompatible; cf. Wenham, *Leviticus*, p. 20; E. Feldman, *Biblical and Post-Biblical Defilement and Mourning: Law as Theology* (New York: Ktav, 1977), pp. 13–30.

17. Wenham, *Leviticus*, pp. 176–177; cf. R. K. Harrison, *Leviticus* (Leicester: IVP), pp. 129–130.

18. Cf. T. H. Gaster, 'Dead, abode of the', *IDB* 1, pp. 787–788; A. Dagan, 'Olam Ha-ba', *Encyclopaedia Judaica* 12, p. 1356.

19. A. Cowley, *Aramaic Papyri of the Fifth Century BC* (Oxford: Clarendon, 1923), lxxi. 15.

20. Cf. R. Martin-Achard, *From Death to Life: A Study of the Development of the Doctrine of the Resurrection in the Old Testament* (Edinburgh: Oliver and Boyd, 1960), p. 37; J. Tromp, *Primitive Conceptions of Death and the Nether World in the Old Testament* (Rome: Pontifical Biblical Institute, 1969), pp. 21–23.

21. BDB, p. 2; cf. pp. 983, 1001; see also L. J. Afonso, 'Netherworld', *Encyclopaedia Judaica* 12, p. 996.

22. M. A. Knibb, *The Ethiopic Book of Enoch* 2 (Oxford: Clarendon, 1978), pp. 110–111; cf. Josephus, *Antiquities* XVIII:14.

23. Cf. J. Jeremias, 'hades', *TDNT* 1, p. 147; Martin-Achard, *From Death to Life*, p. 40.

24. Cf. E. F. Sutcliffe, *The Old Testament and the Future Life* (London: Burns Oates and Washbourne, 1946), pp. 43, 57–59; Heidel, *The Gilgamesh Epic*, p. 177; Tromp, *Primitive Conceptions*, pp. 66–71, 80–81.

25. For a detailed discussion of 1 Peter 3:19 see R. T. France, 'Exegesis in practice: two samples', in I. H. Marshall (ed.), *New Testament Interpretation* (Exeter: Paternoster, 1977), pp. 268–272. He concludes, 'Christ went to the prison of the fallen angels, not to the abode of the dead, and the two are never equated' (p. 271).

26. 'The meaning of the word *Sheol* as shown by parallels in poetic passages', *JETS* 4 (1961), pp. 129–135; cf. R. L. Harris, '*She'ôl*', *Theological Wordbook of the Old Testament*, pp. 892–893.

27. Ibid., p. 892. This position has been adopted in the NIV where Sheol is usually translated in the text by 'grave' or 'death', with a footnote referring to 'Sheol'.

28. O. Keel, *The Symbolism of the Biblical World* (London: SPCK, 1978), p. 63; cf. Martin-Achard, *From Death to Life*, p. 38: 'Sheol is, in fact, a sort of vast grave of which the individual tombs are merely particular manifestations'; W. H. Schmidt, *The Faith of the Old Testament* (Oxford: Blackwell, 1983), p. 270.

29. Heidel, *The Gilgamesh Epic*, p. 177. This would seem to be the view adopted by the translators of the AV: Sheol is translated 31 times 'hell', 31 times 'grave', 3 times 'pit'.

30. Ibid., p. 184.

31. Cf. ibid., pp. 184–186; Sutcliffe, *The Old Testament and the Future Life*, pp. 99–102; S. Woudstra,

'The Old Testament on the afterlife', *VoxR* 20 (1973), p. 13. Psalm 73 reveals a somewhat similar position. Balaam's comment, 'Let me die the death of the righteous, and may my end be like theirs' (Num. 23:10), also implies that there was a distinction between the death of the righteous and the wicked.

32. Sutcliffe, *The Old Testament and the Future Life*, pp. 81–108, sees them as having had a major influence in the formulation of the doctrines of immortality and resurrection in the last centuries of the pre-Christian era. Alternatively, however, these passages may presuppose the existence of such beliefs.

33. This point is forcefully made by M. Dahood, *Psalms* 3 (Garden City: Doubleday, 1970), pp. xli-lii; cf. E. Smick, 'The bearing of new philological data on the subjects of resurrection and immortality in the Old Testament', *WTJ* 31 (1968), pp. 12–21. However, note the response of, among others, B. Vawter, 'Intimations of immortality and the Old Testament', *JBL* 91(1972), pp. 158–171.

34. Cf. T. H. Gaster, 'Resurrection', *Interpreter's Dictionary of the Bible* 4 (New York: Abingdon, 1962), p. 39.

35. This assumes, however, a 2nd cent. BC date for Daniel and a late exilic or post-exilic date for the Isaiah Apocalypse (chs. 24 – 27).

36. 'The origin of the idea of resurrection', in B. Halpern and J. D. Levenson (eds.), *Traditions in Transformation: Turning Points in Biblical Faith* (Winona Lake: Eisenbrauns, 1981), pp. 247–321.

37. Ibid., p. 319.

38. In only one of the passages examined by Greenspoon is the concept of resurrection applied to the wicked (i.e. Dan. 12:2). Dating the book of Daniel to the 2nd cent. BC, Greenspoon considers this passage to be the very latest Old Testament reference to resurrection, and, significantly, it contains an important innovation: 'not only the righteous, but also the wicked are reawakened from the sleep of death' (p. 282). It may, however, be, as B. J. Alfring has suggested ('L'Idée de resurrection d'après Dan. XII, 1. 2', *Bib* 40 (1959), pp. 355–371), that v. 2 ought to be interpreted as saying, 'Many of those who sleep in the land of dust will reawake, these to everlasting life, those (who do not reawake) to disgrace and everlasting contempt.' Apart from bringing this verse into line with other Old Testament passages which restrict the resurrection of the dead to the righteous alone, this proposal also has the advantage of explaining why the first part of the verse restricts the scope of the resurrection to 'many'.

39. Heidel, *The Gilgamesh Epic*, pp. 187–188.

40. Cf. J. F. A. Sawyer, 'Hebrew words for the resurrection of the dead', *VT* 23 (1973), pp. 218–234.

Part 2
Hermeneutics

7

Hermeneutics and biblical authority

James Packer   Vol. 1.1 (1975)

The importance of my theme is obvious from the single consideration that biblical authority is an empty notion unless we know how to determine what the Bible means. This being so, I have been surprised to find how rare evangelical treatments of the relation between hermeneutics and biblical authority seem to be. Indeed, I do not know a single book or article by an evangelical writer that is directly addressed to this topic – though that may, of course, only indicate the narrowness of my reading! But my impression is that this is a subject on which fresh thought by evangelical Christians is very much needed; otherwise, we shall constantly be at a disadvantage, in at least two ways.

First, we shall be forced to remain (where we have long been!) on the edge of the modern Protestant debate about Holy Scripture; for in this debate the theme of my paper remains, as it always was, central. Since the age of rationalism in the eighteenth century, and of Schleiermacher in the nineteenth century, and more particularly since the work of Kähler, Barth, and Bultmann in the twentieth century, the relation between hermeneutics and biblical authority, and the meaning of each concept in the light of the other, have been constant preoccupations, and the mere mention, with Bultmann, of thinkers like Fuchs and Ebeling will assure us that this state of affairs is likely to continue for some time to come. Now, if we are going to join in this debate to any purpose, we must address ourselves seriously to the problem round which it revolves; otherwise, nothing we say will appear to be *ad rem*. One reason why the theology of men like Barth, Bultmann, and Tillich (to say nothing of J. A. T. Robinson!) has rung a bell in modern Protestant discussion, in a way no contemporary evangelical dogmatics has done, is that their systems are explicitly conceived and set forth as answers to the hermeneutical question – the question, that is, of how the real and essential message of the Bible may be grasped by the man of today. One reason why evangelical theology fails to impress other Protestants as having more than a tangential relevance to the ongoing theological debate of which we have spoken is that it does not appear to them to have tuned in on this wavelength of interest. That the interest itself is a proper one for evangelicals will not be denied, and it is not to our advantage when we appear to be neglecting it.

Then, second, in the absence of reflection on my present theme, we risk being contradicted in our own thinking by oversimplifications at more than one point. Let me set this out as I see it.

I am sure I need not spend time proving that oversimplification is a damaging form of mental self-indulgence, leading to shallow, distorted, and inhibited ways of thinking. I am sure that my evangelical readers have all had abundant experience of this particular evil. I am sure we have all had cause in our time to complain of oversimplifications which others have forced on us in the debate about Scripture – the facile antithesis, for instance, between revelation as propositional or as personal, when it has to be the first in order to be the second; or the false question as to whether the Bible is or becomes the Word of God, when both alternatives, rightly understood, are true; or the choice between the theory of mechanical dictation and the presence of human error in the Bible, when in fact we are not shut up to either option. I am sure we have all found how hard it is to explain the evangelical view of Scripture to persons whose minds have once embraced these oversimplifications as controlling concepts. Warned by these experiences, we shall be on our guard against allowing similarly cramping oversimplifications to establish themselves in our own thought.

The basic oversimplification that threatens us here, in my view, is that we should treat the relation between biblical authority and hermeneutics as a one-way relation, whereas in fact it is a two-way relation operating within a one-way system. Let me define my terms, and you will see what I mean.

Biblical authority

Biblical authority, as historically (and, in my judgment, rightly) understood by evangelicals, is a complex dogmatic construction made up of seven elements as follows.

The first is a view of *inspiration* as an activity whereby God, who in his providence overrules all human utterance, caused certain particular men to speak and write in such a way that their utterance was, and remains, his utterance through them, establishing norms of faith and practice. In the case of those written utterances which make up the canonical Scriptures, the effect of inspiration was to constitute them as norms, not merely for that limited group of people to whom God's messengers directly addressed their writings, but for all men at all times. This, I judge, is the precise notion expressed by Paul in 2 Timothy 3:16, where he describes 'all Scripture' as *theopneustos* (literally 'God-breathed'), and therefore 'profitable' as a standard of intellectual and moral perfection for anyone who would be a 'man of God'.

The theological basis of biblical inspiration is the gracious condescension of God, who, having made men capable of receiving, and responding to, communications from other rational beings, now deigns to send him verbal messages, and to address and instruct him in human language. The paradigm of biblical inspiration (not from the standpoint of its literal types or of its psychological modes, which were manifold, but simply from the standpoint of the identity which it effects between God's word and man's) is the prophetic sermon, with its introductory formula, 'Thus saith the Lord.' The significance of biblical inspiration lies in the fact that the inspired material stands for all time as the definitive expression of God's mind and will, his knowledge of reality, and his thoughts, wishes, and intentions regarding it. Inspiration thus produces the state of affairs which Warfield (echoing Augustine) summed up in the phrase: 'What Scripture says, God says.' Whatever Scripture is found to teach must be received as divine instruction. This is what is primarily meant by calling it the Word of God.

It is hardly possible to deny that what God says is true, any more than it is possible to deny that what he commands is binding. Scripture is thus authoritative as a standard of belief no less than of behaviour, and its authority in both realms, that of fact as well as that of obligation, is divine. By virtue of its inspiration the authority of Scripture resolves into, not the historical, ethical, or religious expertise of its human authors, however great this may be thought to have been, but the truthfulness and the moral claim of the speaking, preaching, teaching God himself.

The second element in the historic evangelical account of biblical authority is a view of the principle of *canonicity*, as being objectively the fact, and subjectively the recognition, of inspiration. This follows from what has just been said. All Scripture was given to be the profitable rule of faith and practice. It is not suggested that all the inspired writings that God ever gave were for the church's canon; the Scriptures themselves show that some books of prophetic oracles, and some church epistles of Paul (to look no further) have, in God's providence, perished. What is suggested is not that all inspired writings are canonical, but that all canonical writings are inspired, and that God causes his people to recognize them as such. Accounts of canonicity which distort, or discount, the reality of inspiration, and rest the claims of Scripture on some other footing than the fact that God speaks them, misrepresent both the true theological situation and the actual experience of Christians. This leads to our next point.

The third element in the evangelical position is a belief that the Scriptures *authenticate themselves* to Christian believers through the convincing work of the Holy Spirit, who enables us to recognize, and bow before, divine realities. It is he who enlightens us to receive the man Jesus as God's incarnate Son, and our Saviour; similarly, it is he who enlightens us to receive sixty-six pieces of human writing as God's inscripturated Word, given to make us 'wise unto salvation through faith which is in Christ Jesus' (2 Tim. 3:15, AV). In both cases, this enlightening is not a private revelation of something that has not been made public, but the opening of minds sinfully closed so that they receive evidence to which they were previously impervious. The evidence of divinity is there before us, in the words and works of Jesus in the one case and the words and qualities of Scripture in the other. It consists not of clues offered as a basis for discursive inference to those who are clever enough, as in a detective story, but in the unique force which, through the Spirit, the story of Jesus and the knowledge of Scripture always carry with them to strike everyone to whom they come. In neither case, however, do our sinful minds receive this evidence apart from the illumination of the Spirit. The church bears witness, but the Spirit produces conviction, and so, as against Rome, evangelicals insist that it is the witness of the Spirit, not that of the church, which authenticates the canon to us. So the fourth answer of the Westminster Larger Catechism declares: 'The Scriptures manifest themselves to be the Word of God, by their majesty and purity ... by their light and power to convince and convert sinners, to comfort and build up believers unto salvation: but the Spirit of God bearing witness by and with the Scriptures in the heart of man, is alone able fully to persuade it that they are the very Word of God.'

Fourthly, evangelicals maintain that the Scriptures are *sufficient* for the Christian and the church as a lamp for our feet and a light for our path – a guide, that is, as to what steps we should take at any time in the realms of belief and behaviour. It is not suggested that they tell us all that we would like to know about God and his ways, let alone about other matters, nor that they answer all the questions that it may occur to us to ask. The point of the affirmation is simply that, in the words of Article VI of the Church of England, 'Holy Scripture containeth all things necessary to salvation', and does not need to be supplemented from any other source (reason, experience, tradition, or other faiths, for example), but is itself a complete organism of truth for its own stated purpose. The grounds on which this position rests are, first, the sufficiency of Jesus Christ as Saviour; second, the demonstrable internal completeness of the biblical account of salvation in him; third, the impossibility of validating any non-scriptural tradition or speculation relating to Christ by appeal to an inspired source.

Fifthly, evangelicals affirm that the Scriptures are *clear*, and interpret themselves from within; and consequently, in their character as 'God's word written' (Article XX), are able to stand above both the church and the Christian in corrective judgment and health-giving instruction. With this goes the conviction that the ministry of the Spirit as the church's teacher is precisely to cause the Scriptures to fulfil this ministry toward the church, and so to reform it, and its traditions, according to the biblical pattern. It is also held that the ministry of the Spirit as interpreter guarantees that no Christian who uses the appointed means of grace for understanding the Bible (including worship and instruction, both formal and informal, in the church – there is no atomic individualism here) can fail to learn all that he needs to know for his spiritual welfare. Not that the Christian or the church will ever know everything that Scripture contains, or solve all biblical problems, while here on earth; the point is simply that God's people will always know enough to lead them to heaven, starting from where they are.

Sixthly, evangelicals stress that Scripture is a *mystery* in a sense parallel to that in which the incarnation is a mystery – that is, that the identifying of the human and the divine words in the one case, like the taking of manhood into God in the other, was a unique creative divine act of which we cannot fully grasp either the nature or the mode or the dynamic implications. Scripture is as genuinely and fully human as it is divine. It is more than Jewish-Christian religious literature, but not less, just as Jesus was more than a Jewish rabbi, but not less. There is a true analogy between the written word and the incarnate Word. In both cases, the divine coincides with the form of the human, and the absolute appears in the form of the relative. In both cases, as we say, the divine in the human manifests and evidences itself by the light and power that it puts forth, yet is missed and overlooked by all save those whom the Holy Ghost enlightens. In both cases, it is no discredit to the believer, nor reason for rejecting his faith, when he has to confess that there are problems about this unique divine-human reality that he cannot solve, questions about it that he cannot answer, and aspects of it (phenomena) which do not seem to fit comfortably with other aspects, or with basic categories in terms of which it asks to be explained as a whole (sinlessness, for instance, in the case of Jesus; truthfulness, for instance, in the case of Scripture). When you are dealing with divine mysteries you must be prepared for this sort of thing; and when it happens, you must be quick to recognize that the cause lies in the weakness of your own understanding, not in any failure on God's part to conform to his own specifications.

Seventhly, evangelicals hold that the obedience of both the Christian individually, and the church corporately, consists precisely in *conscious submission*, both intellectual and ethical, to the teaching of Holy Scripture, as interpreted by itself and applied by the Spirit according to the principles stated above. Subjection to the rule of Christ involves – indeed, from one standpoint, consists in, subjection to the rule of Scripture. His authority is its, and its is his.

Hermeneutics

Such is biblical authority; what, now, is hermeneutics? Hermeneutics, as commonly understood, is the theory of biblical interpretation. Interpretation has been defined as the way of reading an old book that brings out its relevance for modern man. Biblical hermeneutics is the study of the theoretical principles involved in bringing out to this and every age the relevance of the Bible and its message. Evangelical practice over the centuries has reflected a view of the process of interpretation as involving three stages: exegesis, synthesis, and application. *Exegesis* means bringing out of the text all that it contains of the thoughts, attitudes, assumptions, and so forth – in short, the whole expressed mind – of the human writer. This is the 'literal' sense, in the name of which the Reformers rejected the allegorical senses beloved of medieval exegetes. We would call it the 'natural' sense, the writer's 'intended meaning'. The so-called 'grammatico-historical method', whereby the exegete seeks to put himself in the writer's linguistic, cultural, historical, and religious shoes, has been the historic evangelical method of exegesis, followed with more or less consistency and success since the Reformers' time. This exegetical process assumes the full humanity of the inspired writings.

Synthesis means here the process of gathering up, and surveying in historically integrated form, the fruits of exegesis – a process which is sometimes, from one standpoint, and at one level, called 'biblical theology' in the classroom, and at other times, from another standpoint, and at another level, called 'exposition' in the pulpit. This synthetic process assumes the organic character of Scripture.

Application means seeking to answer the question: 'If God said and did what the text tells us he did in the circumstances recorded, what would he say and do to us in our circumstances?' This applicatory process assumes the consistency of God from one age to another, and the fact that 'Jesus Christ is the same yesterday and today, yea and for ever' (Heb. 13:8, RV).

Now, it is already clear from what has been said that the principle of biblical authority underlies and controls evangelical hermeneutics. The nature of this control can conveniently be shown by adapting Bultmann's concept of the 'exegetical circle' – a concept springing from recognition of the truth (for truth it is) that exegesis presupposes a hermeneutic which in its turn is drawn from an overall theology, which theology in its turn rests on exegesis. This circle is not, of course, logically vicious; it is not the circle of presupposing what you ought to prove, but the circle of successive approximation, a basic method in every science. Without concerning ourselves with Bultmann's use of this concept of the 'exegetical circle', we may at once adapt it to make plain the evangelical theologian's method of attaining his hermeneutic. First, he goes to the text of Scripture to learn from it the doctrine of Scripture. At this stage, he takes with him what Bultmann would call a 'pre-understanding' – not, like Bultmann, a Heideggerian anthropology, but a general view of Christian truth, and of the way to approach the Bible, which he has gained from the creeds, confessions, preaching, and corporate life of the church, and from his own earlier experiments in exegesis and theology. So he goes to Scripture, and by the light of this pre-understanding discerns in it material for constructing an integrated doctrine of the nature, place, and use of the Bible. From this doctrine of the Bible and its authority he next derives, by strict theological analysis, a set of hermeneutical principles; and then, armed with this hermeneutic, he returns to the text of Scripture itself, to expound it more scientifically than he could before. Thus he travels round the exegetical circle. If his exegetical procedure is challenged, he defends it from his hermeneutic; if his hermeneutic is challenged, he defends it from his doctrine of biblical authority; and if his doctrine of biblical authority is challenged, he defends it from the texts. The circle thus appears as a one-way system: from texts to doctrine, from doctrine to hermeneutic, from hermeneutic to texts again.

What control does the hermeneutic which derives from the evangelical doctrine of Scripture place upon one's exegesis? First, it binds us to continue using the grammatico-historical method; second, it obliges us to observe the principle of harmony. We will say a word about each of these, though brief formal discussion of them (which is all that our space allows) can scarcely give an idea of how far-reaching they really are.

The grammatico-historical method of approaching texts is dictated, not merely by common sense, but by the doctrine of inspiration, which tells us that God has put his words into the mouths, and caused them to be written in the writings, of men whose individuality, as men of their time, was in no way lessened by the fact of their inspiration, and who spoke and wrote to be understood by their contemporaries. Since God has effected an identity between their words and his, the way for us to get into his mind, if we may thus phrase it, is via theirs. Their thoughts and speech about God constitute God's own self-testimony. If, as in one sense is invariably the case, God's meaning and message through each passage, when set in its total biblical context, exceeds what the human writer had in mind, that further meaning is only an extension and development of his, a drawing of implications and an establishing of relationships between his words and other, perhaps later, biblical declarations in a way that the writer himself, in the nature of the case, could not do. Think, for example, how messianic prophecy is declared to have been fulfilled in the New Testament, or how the sacrificial system of Leviticus is explained as typical in Hebrews. The point here is that the *sensus plenior* which texts acquire in their wider biblical context remains an extrapolation on the grammatico-historical plane, not a new projection on to the plane of allegory. And, though God may have more to say to us from each text than its human writer had in mind, God's meaning is never less than his. What he means, God means. So the first responsibility of the exegete is to seek to get into the human writer's mind, by grammatico-historical exegesis of the most thoroughgoing and disciplined kind – always remembering, as Calvin so wisely did, that the biblical writer cannot be assumed to have had before his mind the exegete's own theological system!

As for the principle of harmony, this also is dictated by the doctrine of inspiration, which tells us that the Scriptures are the products of a single divine mind. There are really three principles involved here. The first is that Scripture should be interpreted by Scripture, just as one part of a human teacher's message may and should be interpreted by appeal to the rest. *Scriptura scripturae interpres!* This does not, of course, imply that the meaning of all texts can be ascertained simply by comparing them with other texts, without regard for their own literary, cultural, and historical background, and without regard for our extrabiblical knowledge bearing on the matters with which they deal. For instance, one cannot get the full point of 'Thou shall not seethe a kid in his mother's milk' (Exod. 23:19; 34:26; Deut. 14:21) till one knows that this was part of a Canaanitish fertility rite, and this one learns, not from comparison with other texts, but from archaeology. Similarly, this principle gives no warrant for reading the Bible 'in the flat' without any sense of the historical advance of both revelation and religion, and the difference of background and outlook between one biblical author and another. Such lapses would show failure to grasp what grammatico-historical exegesis really involves. But the principle that Scripture interprets Scripture does require us to treat the Bible organically and to look always for its internal links – which are there in profusion, if only we have eyes to see them.

The second principle is that Scripture should not be set against Scripture. The church, says Article XX of the Church of England, may not 'so expound one place of Scripture, that it be repugnant to another' – nor should the individual expositor. The basis for this principle is the expectation that the teaching of the God of truth will prove to be consistent with itself.

The third principle is that what appears to be secondary and obscure in the Scripture should be studied in the light of what appears primary and plain. This principle obliges us to echo the main emphases of the New Testament and to develop a Christocentric, covenantal, and kerygmatic exegesis of both Testaments; also it obliges us to preserve a studied sense of proportion regarding what are confessedly minutiae, and not to let them overshadow what God has indicated to be the weightier matters.

These three principles together constitute what the Reformers called *analogia Scripturae*, and what we have termed the principle of harmony. It is a principle which makes an integrative aim in interpretation mandatory at every point. To have such an aim is, of course, no guarantee that the interpreter will always succeed in achieving what he aims at, but at least it keeps him facing in the right direction and asking some of the right questions.

Here, then, are two hermeneutical axioms which we may call 'deductive' principles, though, as we have seen, they derive from an exegetical induction in the first instance. They are presuppositions, gained through exegesis of some texts, which demand to control the exegesis of all texts. They are historically, and in my view rightly, basic to evangelical interpretation of Scripture.

Oversimplification

Now it is just here, as it seems to me, that the dangers of oversimplification threaten. I am not now thinking of the popular pietistic oversimplification of supposing that if one approaches Scripture by the light of these evangelical axioms, then interpretations will become magically easy and one's exegesis will be infallibly right. Such ideas do not demand discussion here; we know better than to expect interpretation ever to be easy, and we know there are no infallible interpreters, certainly not ourselves. No; the oversimplifications I have in view are other than this.

The first and basic oversimplification consists simply of forgetting that, as our concept of biblical authority determines our hermeneutic in the manner described, so that concept itself is always, and necessarily, open to challenge from the biblical texts on which we bring our hermeneutics to bear. For our concept of biblical authority is a theological construct, or theory, one of a number which make up our dogmatics; and theological theories, like the theories of natural science, have to be tested by seeing whether they fit all the relevant biblical data. (Think, for instance, of the doctrine of the Trinity, which is an example of a successful theological theory.) If the data seem not to fit the theory, then the relation between them should be thought of as one of reciprocal interrogation: each calls the other in question. So, if particular texts, despite our exegetical coaxing, still appear to be out of accord with each other in some significant way, or to assert what is untrue, methodologically the first thing we have to do is to re-examine our concepts of biblical authority, and of the hermeneutic which we drew from it. But we must do this by appeal to the proper evidence, that is, the statements of Scripture about itself, not the phenomena which have prompted the check-up. A mistake in method at this point would be disastrous, as the following comments by Dr Roger Nicole on one of the theses of Dr Dewey Beegle's book *The Inspiration of Scripture* will show.

Dr Beegle very vigorously contends that a proper approach to the doctrine of inspiration is to start with induction from what he calls 'the phenomena of Scripture' rather than with deduction from certain biblical statements about the Scripture ... This particular point needs to be controverted. If the Bible does make certain express statements about itself, these manifestly must have a priority in our attempt to formulate a doctrine of Scripture. Quite obviously, induction from Bible phenomena will also have its due place, for it may tend to correct certain inaccuracies which might take place in the deductive process. The statements of Scripture, however, are always primary. To apply the method advocated by Dr Beegle in other areas would quite probably lead to seriously erroneous results. For instance, if we attempted to construct our view of the relation of Christ to sin merely in terms of the concrete data given us in the Gospels about His life, and without regard to certain express statements found in the New Testament about His sinlessness, we might mistakenly conclude that Christ was not sinless. If we sought to develop our doctrines of creation merely by induction from the facts of nature and without regard to the statements of Scripture, we would be left in a quandary. The present remark is not meant to disallow induction as a legitimate factor, but it is meant to deny it the priority in religious matters. First must come the statements of revelation, and then induction may be introduced as a legitimate confirmation, and, in some cases, as a corrective in areas where our interpretation of these statements and their implications may be at fault.[1]

When we check our concept of the nature and authority of Scripture by the appropriate biblical evidence, in the light of the specific questions raised by the hard texts, we may find that our previous interpretation of the evidence needs to be modified; or we may not. In the latter case, methodologically we are now bound to embrace as our working hypothesis that the inconsistency of the phenomena with the biblical doctrine is apparent, not real. However, the embracing of the hypothesis is not itself a solution of the problem, and a real tension between our deductive principles and the phenomena remains. When, as in most if not all cases, the puzzling phenomena are minutiae, the principle of *analogia Scripturae*, as we saw, would counsel us not to get them out of proportion. But as long as they are there, they continue to present a challenge to us to check and re-check our doctrine of Scripture, and the hermeneutical principles which we derive from it, just as our doctrine of Scripture challenges us to seek harmonistic explanations of puzzling phenomena. it would be a potentially serious oversimplification, as it seems to me, to ignore the fact that we may need to go round the one-way system of the exegetical circle very many times, reviewing our doctrine of Scripture and our hermeneutics again and again in the light of the various queries about both that the different classes of phenomena raise. The point can be illustrated and, perhaps, given some application by citing from two evangelical documents which have had some currency in recent years, and whose overall thrust is in each case admirable. On page 49 of his *Introduction to Systematic Theology*, Louis Berkhof states boldly, as Warfield did before him, that part of the interpreter's task is to 'adjust the phenomena of Scripture to the biblical doctrine of inspiration'. A memorandum for theological students produced under the auspices of the International Fellowship of Evangelical Students in 1961 closed with a summons to 'development of a truly biblical, i.e. biblically determined, hermeneutic' and 'derivation from this hermeneutic of a proper understanding of the nature of biblical authority'. My present point is simply that to say either of these things without the other would be to oversimplify. The first statement is no more than a half-truth, until it is added that our apprehension of 'the biblical doctrine of inspiration' itself must be constantly checked against the queries concerning it which the phenomena themselves raise. The second statement is no more than a half-truth, until it is added that some pre-understanding of the nature of Scripture and its authority is necessarily involved in any attempt to develop a 'biblically determined hermeneutic'. (After all, even Bultmann would claim, on the basis of his own pre-understanding at this point, that his own hermeneutic was 'truly biblical, i.e. biblically determined'! It is at the point of this pre-understanding that the ways divide.) The truth is that neither our doctrine of Scripture nor our exegesis can be in a healthy state unless they constantly interact, and each undergoes constant refinement in the light of the other.

If, therefore, we allowed ourselves to treat a prepackaged, deep-frozen formula labelled 'the evangelical doctrine of Scripture' as a kind of untouchable sacred cow, we should not only be showing ourselves more concerned about our own tradition than about God's truth (and you do not need me to remind you how dangerous that would be); we should also be jeopardizing our own prospects in the realm of biblical exposition. If, however, we recognize and accept the principles just stated, it will keep vividly before us the element of *mystery* that confronts us in the Scriptures, the *audacity* of our confession of the doctrine of biblical authority, with so many problems, albeit small ones, yet unsolved, and the need to make this confession in great *humility* and utter dependence upon God; and this will undoubtedly be good both for us and for our handling of the sacred text.

The modern debate

I want now to glance at the modern hermeneutical debate, and to consider how far evangelicals are equipped to enter into it.

The debate has sprung from felt perplexities at three points. First, there are perplexities about the Word of God. Since Barth, the Bible has been re-acknowledged as the medium of God's self-communication to man; but the question presses, how can this be, when (*ex hypothesi*) the Bible, regarded as a human book, is both fallible and fallacious? How does God communicate himself through the Bible? What is the real nature of the Word of God? What is its relation to the words of the book?

Then, second, there are questions about the New Testament. Modern scholars, preoccupied with the complexities of its contemporary setting, and working in disregard of the notion of revealed truth, feel it to be a most elusive book. What is its real nature? What is its real relation to the Old Testament? What is the significance of its intractable eschatology? What must one do to it to make plain its message for our own time?

Then, third, linked with this are problems about preaching. The New Testament is *kerygmatic*: it consists of proclamation of Christ; but the world to which it proclaims him is a very different world from ours. What transpositions of the form of the message are needed to enable us to preach it today?

To these questions various answers are given. Let us briefly remind ourselves of three of the main ones.

1. Karl Barth holds that God communicates with man through the Scriptures by freely choosing to use them to make Jesus Christ, the true Word

of God, known. The statement that Scripture is the Word of God means simply that God constantly uses it in this way. Christ is the reality to which all Scripture, when thus used by God, bears witness. Barth's hermeneutical method, therefore, is to apply the 'Christological method' of his *Dogmatics*, asking all texts one question only – what have you to say of Jesus Christ? According to Barth's ontology, it is only when one is reading Christ out of texts that they tell us anything about either God or man. This at first sounds promising to evangelical ears; however, what we find is that Barth's ontology, which goes off at a tangent from what the biblical writers were concerned to say about God and his world, imposes on his thought a cramping preoccupation with problems of theoretical knowledge, and the dogmatic arbitrariness of his 'Christomonism', as Althaus called it, according to which all truth about creation and the created order is swallowed up into the doctrine of Christ, leads him to conceptions of election, reprobation, and redemption, which systematically distort both his exegesis and any preaching that may be based on it.

2. The 'biblical theology' and *Heilsgeschichte* movements tell us that God has revealed himself through a sequence of redemptive events which came to its climax in the life, death, and resurrection of Jesus Christ. To this historical sequence Scripture is man's interpretative witness. Scripture is the product of illumination and insight, but not of inspiration as we earlier defined it, and there is no identity of God's word with man's. The hermeneutical method of these movements, therefore, is to ask the texts what witness they bear to the acts of God, and to integrate their testimony into a complex Christocentric whole by means of the organizing categories of prospect and fulfilment. ('Prospect' is a better word than 'promise' here; the God of 'biblical theology' does not speak, and so cannot make promises.) One odd result is that theologians of this type seem a good deal more sure that this pattern as a whole corresponds to the acts of God as a whole than they are about the truth of any single part of it! This is particularly noticeable in such a writer as Alan Richardson. The preaching that springs from this movement is a summons to trust in the God, and the Christ, of this whole story, which is good so far; but since this teaching affords no basis for a direct correlation between faith and Scripture in general, or the biblical promises in particular (since it is not held that God has ever actually used words to talk to man), the preaching is necessarily inadequate.

3. Bultmann holds that God acts in man's consciousness through the myths of the New Testament *kerygma* (which myths, he says, we may now cere-monially debunk, and replace, in order to show modern man that they are nothing more than myths!). His action consists of bringing about in

experience the dynamic event of the 'word of God'. This 'word of God' is a summons and a decision to live in openness to the future, not bound by the past: which is the whole of Bultmann's understanding of faith. Nothing depends for Bultmann on the fact that the Christ of the myths has no basis in the facts concerning the historical Jesus: 'faith' for him is not correlated to particular historical facts, any more than it is to particular divine words. His hermeneutical method is to ask how the texts disclose the human situation according to Heidegger, and how they summon us to the decision of faith, as described above.

Our enumeration need not go further; these three positions are, between them, the fountain-heads of all the main hermeneutical trends of our time. (The so-called 'new hermeneutic' is new only in the sense of being an extended development of the third approach.) They all appear as products of Christian thought deflected, more or less, from the historical biblical road by the Kantian and post-Kantian heritage in western philosophy. Kant's 'Copernican revolution' in the philosophy of mind and nature, carried through at just the critical moment when Europe was recoiling from Rationalism into Romanticism, diverted interest from the known world to the knowing subject, ruled out the possibility of God addressing man in words, and let loose the bogey of sceptical and nihilistic solipsism to plague his successors. Idealism, positivism, and existentialism, the three main philosophical developments since Kant's time, should be seen as a series of attempts to banish the bogey by new answers to the problem of the knowing subject; and similarly the three types of hermeneutic sketched out above should be seen as so many attempts to banish the same bogey by vindicating the proposition that Christians really know God, even though he does not really talk to us. But this is precisely what the God of the Bible does – and the first point to be made as we approach the modern hermeneutical debate is that, to the extent to which an expositor denies or discounts the reality of divine talk, to that extent he neither opens the Scriptures nor confesses their God, but wrests the former and denies the latter.

In none of the positions described is the testimony of Scripture to a speaking God, and to itself as his organic revealed Word, taken with full seriousness. Each of them effectively breaks loose from the authority of the Bible by declining fully to accept either its account of its own nature or the hermeneutic that is bound up with that account. Each, in consequence, fails satisfactorily to answer the questions from which it starts. Arbitrariness of this kind brings its own penalty of instability, not to say untruth. In fact, the true key to solving the problems which sparked off the modern hermeneutical debate is to take the Bible's self-testimony perfectly seriously, and to give full weight to the truth that, to put it as vividly as I can, *God has talked*, and Holy Scripture is his own recorded utterance, and what he said in Scripture long ago he says still, in application to ourselves.

It is sometimes said that this view of revelation is itself arbitrary, since the texts on which we rely do not really affirm so much; but Warfield answered that thesis two generations ago, and nothing since his day has in my judgment affected the conclusiveness of his answer. It is also said that this position is rationalistic. That word is, of course, a dreadful missile, but what does it signify in this context? 'Rationalistic' in theology may mean (1) reducing reality, both God and his world, to the limits of an exhaustively intelligible scheme, so ruling out all recognition of the partial character of knowledge of God in this world, as compared with that which is to come (1 Cor. 13:13); or (2) going against Scripture at some particular point at the dictates of reason; or (3) speculating beyond biblical limits; or (4) seeking to ground on logical or historical proof truths about God which should be received by faith, simply on the ground that God has told us of them. In which of these senses, now, can the evangelical revelation-claim be called rationalistic? In none! The truth is that it is not rationalistic at all, but simply *rational*. It is a confession of faith in a rational God who has talked rationally to creatures whom he made rational, and whom he declines to treat as anything other than rational.

And the evangelical hermeneutic is a rational hermeneutic, based on the recognition that the affirmations of the biblical writers are the authoritative affirmations of God himself, and seeking to extract them by exegesis in order that they may he applied afresh to men and their problems in our own day, so that God's message to us may be made plain. Traditionally, when formulating our hermeneutics, we evangelicals have limited the subject to questions of exegesis and synthesis (see any textbook, Berkhof's *Principles of Biblical Interpretation*, or Ramm's *Protestant Biblical Interpretation*, for example, for proof of this) and have left questions of the application of truth to be dealt with under the rubrics of homiletics and practical theology; but it is much to be wished that we might restate our hermeneutics in explicit correlation to the concept of God *communicating*, God speaking in a way that terminates on man. This would involve a final section in the textbooks and lecture courses on the possibility, purpose, and modes of God's address to men through the Bible, and the discussion would cover topics like the *imago Dei* in man as the presupposition of communication; sin, which makes man deaf to God, and grace, which unstops his ears; the whole complex of relations that exists between the revealing Spirit and the revealed Word; preaching as the Word of God; and the church as the community that listens to God's Word, and lives by it.

The concept of God active in communication is certainly the focus of hermeneutical interest and the field of hermeneutical debate, in modern theology, and when one observes the encroaching shadows of post-Kantian nihilism one sees why this should be so. But this does not mean that there is anything wrong with the concept itself. The truth is rather the reverse. Is not the thought of God active in communication the central, and organizing, hermeneutical concept to which the Bible itself would lead us? If so – and I think it is – then our traditional presentation of hermeneutics ought to be rethought and re-angled so as to express this fact. Until we have shown ourselves to be tackling this task in good earnest, we are hardly ready to take part in current hermeneutical discussions; for not only shall we not be on its 'wavelength', we shall be making it plain to all the world that we have not yet learned, in the theological sense, to take our own hermeneutical principles quite seriously. Books like Gustav Wingren's *The Living Word* and Alan Stibbs' unpretentious and untechnical, yet extraordinarily seminal, little paperback *Understanding God's Word* give some of the leads that are in point here.

Inerrancy

It is sometimes supposed that evangelical hermeneutics are necessarily vitiated by evangelical adherence to the concept of biblical inerrancy. For some reason which, to say the least, is not obvious, this adherence is thought to betray an anachronistic resolve to make the Bible teach science, in the modern sense and with modern precision, and thus to mark a departure from the grammatico-historical method which cannot but distort interpretation radically. It is also thought to betray confidence of 'having the answer' to all seeming contradictions and difficulties in the biblical text. In view of these mistaken impressions, it is well to round off this paper by sketching out what inerrancy does and does not mean.

Inerrancy is a word that has been in common use only since the last century, though the idea itself goes back through seventeenth-century orthodoxy, the Reformers, and the Schoolmen, to the Fathers and, behind them, to our Lord's own statements, 'the scripture cannot be broken', 'thy word is truth' (John 10:35; 17:17). The word has a negative form and a positive function. It is comparable with the four negative adverbs with which the Chalcedonian definition fenced the truth of the incarnation. Its function, like theirs, was not to explain anything in a positive way, but to safeguard a mystery by excluding current mistakes about it. It, like them, has obvious meaning only in the context of the particular controversy that caused it to be used; apart from that context it, like them, may well seem esoteric and unhelpful. Logically, its function has been to express a double commitment: first, an advance commitment to receive as truth from God all that Scripture is found on inspection actually to teach; second, a methodological commitment to interpret Scripture according to the principle of harmony which we analysed above. It thus represented not so much a lapse into rationalism as a bulwark against rationalism – namely, that kind of rationalism which throws overboard the principle of harmony. It thus expressed also, not an irreligious pre-occupation with scientific accuracy, as some have suggested, but an attitude of reverence for the sacred text which some were irreverently expounding as if it were in places self-contradictory and false.

Whether evangelicals continue to speak of biblical inerrancy or not will depend on whether we think that the gain of having a verbal pointer to this double commitment outweighs the disadvantage of being lumbered with a term that is regularly, though mistakenly, taken to imply a blanket claim to know solutions for all apparent biblical discrepancies. The prevalence of this misconception is really rather disastrous, for scholarly advance in biblical study, as in all other realms of science, has the effect, not only of extending broad areas of certainty, but also of increasing the number of questions of detail which at any single moment have to be regarded as open, pending further enquiry or the discovery of more evidence – some of these, inevitably, being questions to which earlier generations thought they knew the answer; and if we evangelicals are thought to be making a claim which shows, not merely unawareness of this fact, but a dogmatic interest in denying it, we shall have a hard time convincing others that our approach to Scripture is not fundamentally unscientific and unsound. This might be thought a strong argument for eschewing the word wherever possible. But whether or not we use the word is not the most important issue. What matters is that in our exegetical practice we should abide by the principle of harmony; in other words, that we should be agreed at the methodological level. If, on the one hand, we actually agree to receive as truth from God all that Scripture writers are found actually to assert, and, on the other hand, we are agreed in continuing to look for convincing harmonizations of the hard places and declining to cut the knot by saying flatly that the Bible errs, it will not matter whether we talk of inerrancy or not. What matters is never the word, this or any other, but the thing for which it stands.

What I am saying assumes that the scope of each biblical passage, its literary genre, and the range and content of the actual assertions made, must be determined entirely inductively, by grammatico-historical exegesis. It is necessary to insist constantly that the concept of inerrancy gives no direct help in determining such questions as these. It is not – repeat, *not* – an exegetical short cut. No doubt we shall all find that many particular exegetical and harmonistic problems, arising from puzzling biblical phenomena, will have to be left open at every stage in our pilgrimage of biblical study. What significance has this fact? I would suggest that it has no significance that need alarm us. It is stimulating for continued exegetical enquiry; it is unimportant, so far as I can see, for dogmatics, except insofar as it stimulates closer reflection on the doctrine of Scripture; and it is unmanageable for apologetics only if one's apologetic method is rationalistic in type, requiring one to have all the answers to the problems in a particular area before one dare make positive assertions in that area, even when those positive assertions would simply be echoing God's own, set forth in Scripture. But it might be worth asking whether it is not perhaps a blessing to be warned off apologetics of that kind.

Notes

1. *Gordon Review*, Winter 1964–5, p. 106.

© James Packer 1975

8

Did Jesus and his followers preach the right doctrine from the wrong texts?

An examination of the presuppositions of
Jesus' and the apostles' exegetical method

G. K. Beale   Vol. 14.3 (1989)

Introduction

The degree of continuity and discontinuity in both theology and interpretative method between Christianity and its Jewish environment has been a point of much debate in New Testament studies. This has especially been the case with the issue of the use of the Old Testament in Judaism and in the New Testament.

One widely held position is that Jesus and the writers of the New Testament used non-contextual and atomistic hermeneutical methods such as were used by their Jewish contemporaries. We today would regard such methods as illegitimate. But, we are assured, they were guided in their interpretation by the example of Christ and by the Spirit, and so, although we cannot imitate their methods today, we can trust their conclusions and believe their doctrine.[1] This article is intended to raise questions about this approach and to o er a possible alternative.

The issue of non-contextual exegesis in post-biblical Judaism and its relation to the New Testament methodology

Our starting-point is to observe that it is not at all clear that non-contextual midrashic exegesis was as central to earlier Pharisaic and Qumran exegesis as is suggested by scholars favouring the approach we have described. First, it may not be appropriate to speak of a non-contextual *rabbinic* method in the pre-AD 70 setting, since most examples come from after AD 70, and those which can be dated with probability before that do not appear to reflect such an atomistic approach.[2] Secondly, concern for contextual exegesis is found not uncharacteristically both in Qumran and in Jewish apocalyptic.[3] This analysis has far-reaching implications for the argument of those who believe that early Christian exegetes were influenced by a prevalent atomistic Jewish hermeneutic.

But even this assumption of influence may be questioned. It sounds *a priori* plausible that the exegetical procedures of the New Testament would resemble those of contemporary Judaism. And yet, since early Christianity had a unique perspective in comparison with early Judaism, one should not assume that Jewish and Christian hermeneutical approaches will necessarily have been identical in every way.[4] It is necessary to look at the New Testament itself, without prejudice about methodological continuity or discontinuity, in order to assess the issue.

It is often claimed that an inductive study of the New Testament reveals a predominantly non-contextual exegetical method. But, in fact, of all the many Old Testament citations and allusions found in the New Testament, only a very few plausible examples of non-contextual usage have been noted by critics. These include:[5]

1. *ad hominem* argumentation: the role of angels revealing the law in Galatians 3:19; the Exodus 'veil' theme in 2 Corinthians 3:13–18;

2. non-contextual midrashic treatments: the understanding of baptism and the 'following rock' in 1 Corinthians 10:1–4; Deuteronomy 30:12–14 in Romans 10:6–8; Genesis 12:7ff. in Galatians 3:16; Psalm 68:18 in Ephesians 4:8.

3. allegorical interpretations: Deuteronomy 25:4 in 1 Corinthians 9:9; the use of the Old Testament in Galatians 4:24; Genesis 14 in Hebrews 7;

4. atomistic interpretation: Isaiah 40:6–8 in 1 Peter 1:24ff.

Two things need to be said about such examples. First, it is by no means certain that even these examples are actually non-contextual. A number of scholars have offered viable and even persuasive explanations of how they could well be cases of contextual exegesis.[6] But, second, even if it is granted that they are convincing examples of non-contextual hermeneutics, it does not necessarily follow that they are truly representative of a wider hermeneutical pattern in the New Testament.[7] They may be exceptional rather than typical.

The contribution of C. H. Dodd

A substantial and often neglected argument against the view that the New Testament uses the Old Testament atomistically is C. H. Dodd's classic work,

According to the Scriptures (London: Nisbet, 1952). In brief, Dodd observed that throughout the New Testament there are numerous and scattered quotations that derive from the same few Old Testament contexts. He asks the question why, given that the same segment of the Old Testament is in view, there are so few identical quotations of the same verse, and secondly, why it is that different verses are cited from the same segments of the Old Testament. He concludes that this phenomenon indicates that New Testament authors were aware of broad Old Testament contexts and did not focus merely on single verses independent of the segment from which they were drawn. Single verses and phrases are merely signposts to the overall Old Testament context from which they were cited. Furthermore, he concludes that this was a *unique hermeneutical phenomenon* of the day. He goes on to assert that since this hermeneutical phenomenon can be found in the very earliest strata of the New Testament traditions, and since such innovations are not characteristic of committees, then Christ was the most likely source of this original, creative hermeneutic and it was from him that the New Testament writers learned their method.[8]

Some disagree with Dodd; indeed, many scholars in this field affirm that the New Testament writers often employ a non-contextual exegetical method.[9] Nevertheless, others have supported Dodd's thesis about the New Testament's unique and consistent respect for the Old Testament context, rightly in our opinion.[10]

(To accept Dodd's view is not to deny that New Testament authors display varying degrees of awareness of literary context, as well as perhaps of historical context. Those texts with a low degree of correspondence with the Old Testament literary context can be referred to as semi-contextual, since they seem to fall between the poles of what we ordinarily call 'contextual' and 'non-contextual' usages.[11] Indeed, there are instances where New Testament writers handle Old Testament texts in a diametrically opposite manner to that in which they appear to function in their original contexts. Often, upon closer examination, such uses reveal an ironic or polemical intention.[12] In such examples it would be wrong to conclude that an Old Testament reference has been interpreted non-contextually. Indeed, awareness of context must be presupposed in making such interpretations of Old Testament texts. On the other hand, non-contextual uses of the Old Testament may be expected to occur where there is unintentional or unconscious allusion. Caution should be exercised in labelling Old Testament usages merely either as contextual or non-contextual, since other more precisely descriptive interpretative categories may be better.

The distinctive presuppositions of the apostles' exegetical method

But neither Dodd nor his followers have enquired deeply enough into the more fundamental issue concerning the reason why the New Testament is different from Judaism in its contextual approach (assuming for the sake of argument that a non-contextual method was an inherent trait of Jewish exegesis, a position we have tentatively questioned). Therefore, what were the presuppositions which inspired what Dodd and others believe to be a unique, consistent contextual approach to the Old Testament?

The answer which makes most sense of the data is that Jesus and the apostles had an unparalleled redemptive-historical perspective on the Old Testament in relation to their own situation. (There are some parallels with Qumran, but there is not space to discuss the reasons for its methodological differences with the New Testament, except to note the following assumptions of the New Testament writers.) This perspective involved a framework of five hermeneutical and theological presuppositions:

1. the assumption of *corporate solidarity* or *representation*;[13]

2. that Christ is viewed as representing the *true Israel* of the Old Testament and true Israel, the church, in the New Testament;[14]

3. that *history is unified by* a wise and sovereign plan so that the earlier parts are designed to correspond and point to the latter parts (cf. Matt. 11:13f.);[15]

4. that the age of *eschatological fulfilment* has come in Christ.[16]

5. As a consequence of (3) and (4), the fifth presupposition affirms that the latter parts of biblical history function as the broader context to interpret earlier parts because they all have the same, ultimate divine author who inspires the various human authors, and one deduction from this premiss is that Christ as the centre of history is the *key to interpreting the earlier portions of the Old Testament and its promises.*[17]

It is only in the light of this fifth presupposition that we may legitimately speak of a *sensus plenior* of Scripture, although it is probably best not to use this phrase since it is not often understood in this precise manner (*sensus plenior* is typically defined as the full meaning of Scripture of which an author was probably not cognizant; there is a wealth of literature discussing the legitimacy of seeing such meanings).[18] On this view it is quite possible that the Old Testament authors did not exhaustively understand the meaning, implications and possible applications of all that they wrote. Subsequently, New Testament Scripture interprets the Old Testament Scripture by expanding its meaning, seeing new implications in it and giving it new applications.[19]

I believe, however, that it can be demonstrated that this expansion does not contravene the integrity of the earlier texts but rather develops them in a way which is consistent with the Old Testament author's understanding of the way in which God interacts with his people – which is the unifying factor between the Testaments. Therefore, the canon interprets the canon; later parts of the canon draw out and explain more clearly the earlier parts.[20]

LaSor has explained well the fifth presupposition of canonical contextual interpretation:

> In one sense, it [the sensus plenior or fuller meaning] lies outside and beyond the historical situation of the prophet, and therefore it cannot be derived by grammatico-historical exegesis. But in another sense, it is part of the history of redemption, and therefore it can be controlled by the study of Scripture taken in its entirety.
>
> Perhaps an illustration will make [this] clear ... An ordinary seed contains in itself everything that will develop in the plant or tree to which it is organically related: every branch, every leaf, every flower. Yet no amount of examination by available scientific methods will disclose to us what is in that seed. However, once the seed has developed to its fullness, we can see how the seed has been fulfilled ... [and] we have sufficient revelation in the Scriptures to keep our interpretations of *sensus plenior* from becoming totally subjective.[21]

The biblical basis for each of these presuppositions needs more elaboration than the limits of this essay allow. Nevertheless, it is within this framework that we are to understand why the early church believed that through identification with Christ it was the continuation of the true Israel, living in the inauguration of the latter days. As such it was beginning to fulfil the Old Testament prophecies and promises about eschatological Israel.

It is within this framework too that the whole Old Testament was perceived as pointing to this eschatological age both via direct prophecy and the indirect prophetic adumbration of Israel's history. This latter point is especially significant. Old Testament history was understood as containing historical patterns which foreshadowed the period of the eschaton. Consequently, the nation Israel, its kings, prophets, priests and its significant redemptive episodes, composed the essential ingredients of this sacred history. This is what scholars sometimes call 'typology', which is often defined as the study of correspondences between earlier and later events, persons, institutions, etc., within the historical framework of biblical revelation, and which from a retrospective viewpoint are perceived to have a prophetic function. Ideal or even enigmatic depictions in the Old Testament became 'ideal' candidates to select for descriptions of features in the eschatological period which had finally arrived. These came to be considered as typical or ideal prophetic portraits.

I would argue that this broad redemptive-historical perspective was the dominant framework within which Jesus and the New Testament writers thought, serving as an ever-present heuristic guide to the Old Testament. In fact, it is this framework which should be seen as the wider literary context within which the New Testament authors interpreted Old Testament passages. Consideration of the immediate literary context of Old Testament verses, which is what most exegetes affirm as an essential part of the historical-grammatical method, should therefore be supplemented with the canonical literary context.

But when these five presuppositions are related closely to the New Testament's exegetical method, they provide the best explanation for Dodd's observations and conclusions, especially why the New Testament does not focus on verses independent of their contexts. Their selection of Old Testament texts was determined by this wider, overriding perspective, which viewed redemptive history as unified by an omnipotent and wise design. Throughout this plan are expressed the unchanging principles of faith in God, God's faithfulness in fulfilling promises, the rebellion of the unbelieving, God's judgment of them and his glory. Therefore, there was an emphatic concern for more overarching historical patterns or for significant persons (e.g. prophets, priests and kings), institutions and events which were essential constituents of such patterns. Such an emphasis was probably facilitated by the belief that Christ and the church now represented the true Israel, so that it would have been attractive to see various segments and patterns of Israel's history from the Old Testament as recapitulated in the New Testament. This then was a holistic perspective guiding them away from concentrating on exegetically or theologically insignificant minutiae in passages and quoting individual references as signposts to the broad redemptive-historical theme(s) from the immediate and larger Old Testament context of which they were a part. Is not this the most likely explanation for the phenomenon in the New Testament of so few identical quotations but different citations from the same segments of the Old Testament?

One reason why many see the New Testament typically interpreting the Old Testament non-contextually is often because the New Testament applies the Old Testament to new situations, problems and people which were not in the minds of the Old Testament authors. Interestingly, many of the cases where such misuse is cited are passages where what was intended for Israel (or leaders or righteous individuals in Israel) in the Old Testament is now applied often by a typological method to either Christ or the church.[22] One aspect of this is that many see typology as an arbitrary method which typically involves allegory, and therefore it is also viewed as a good example of non-contextual exegesis. But most scholars today agree that typology is not allegory because it is based on the actual historical events of the Old Testament passage being dealt with and because it essentially consists of a real, historical correspondence between the Old Testament and New Testament event. Typological interpretation involves an extended reference to the original meaning of an Old Testament text which develops it but does not contradict it. Put another way, it does not *read into* the text a different or higher sense, but *draws* out from it a different or higher application of the same sense.[23] Indeed, the five presuppositions of early Christian exegesis cited earlier undergird the typological method and distinguish it from allegory which not only disregards historical context but reads in a new, unrelated meaning to passages.[24]

Typology is also faulted for being non-contextual because it sometimes refers to purely historical events as being prophetically fulfilled (cf. the introductory *plēroō* formula) when they are clearly not intended as prophecies from the Old Testament author's perspective. This occurs mostly in Matthew but appears as well in the other Gospels. But, as we have discussed above, this is partly explicable on the basis of the early Christian community's presupposition that Christ and the church (believing Jews and Gentiles) now represented true Israel, so that the various characteristic segments and patterns of God's interaction in Israel's history now apply to Christ and the church as the new people of God in the New Testament. Alternatively, such an approach is understandable because of its foundational assumption that history is an interrelated unity and that God had designed the earlier parts to correspond and point to the latter parts, especially to those events which have happened in the age of *eschatological fulfilment* in Christ. Consequently, the concept of prophetic fulfilment must not be limited to fulfilment of direct verbal prophecies in the Old Testament, but broadened to include also an indication of the 'redemptive-historical relationship of the new, climactic revelation of God in Christ to the preparatory, incomplete revelation to and through Israel'.[25]

Typology therefore indicates fulfilment of the indirect prophetic adumbration of events, people and institutions from the Old Testament in Christ who now is the final, climactic expression of all that God ideally intended through these things in the Old Testament (e.g. the law, the temple cultus, the commissions of prophets, judges, priests and kings). Everything which these things lacked by way of imperfections was prophetically 'filled up' by Christ, so that even what was imperfect in the Old Testament pointed beyond itself to Jesus.[26] Romans 5:12–21 is a classic example of this, where Christ is not only contrasted with Adam but is said to have accomplished what Adam failed to do, i.e. to obey righteously. This is why Adam is called a *typos* in Romans 5:14. Therefore, it is a too narrow hermeneutic which concludes that New Testament writers are being non-contextual when they understand passages from historical or overtly non-prophetic genre as typologically prophetic.[27]

In addition, changed applications of the Old Testament in general, whether or not typology is involved, do not necessitate the conclusion that these passages have been misinterpreted. For example, Matthew applies to Jesus what the Old Testament intended for Israel (e.g. Matt. 2:4–22)[28] and Paul does the same thing with respect to the church (e.g. Rom. 9:24–26). What should be challenged is not their interpretation of the Old Testament but the validity of the above-mentioned framework through which they interpreted the Old Testament, especially the assumption that Christ corporately represented true Israel and that all who identify with him by faith are considered part of true Israel. If the validity of these presuppositions be granted, then the viability of their interpretation of the Old Testament must also be viewed as plausible. Of course, many do not grant the legitimacy of these assumptions and consequently view the New Testament as distorting the original intention of the Old Testament. But whatever conclusion one reaches, it is not based only on raw exegetical considerations but on the theological presupposition of the individual interpreter! For example, Hanson affirms that modern interpreters cannot reproduce the typological exegesis of the New Testament writers because essential to such exegesis was belief in the actual historicity of the events of the Old Testament texts being referred to, a belief purportedly no longer tenable to post-critical thinking.[29]

Further, changes of application need not mean a *disregard* for Old Testament context. Given the viability of the presuppositions, although the new applications are technically different, they nevertheless stay within the conceptual bounds of the Old Testament contextual meaning, so that what results often is an extended reference to or application of a principle which is inherent to the Old Testament text.[30] Of course, it would be possible to hold these presuppositions and still interpret the Old Testament non-contextually, but the point we are attempting to make here is that when a case-by-case study is made, our recognition of such presuppositions among the New Testament writers nevertheless helps us to see *how* their interpretations could have been contextual from their particular perspective and *why* they would have been more sensitive to respecting contexts.[31]

Even when there is use of the Old Testament with no apparent interest in prophetic fulfilment, there appears to be a redemptive-historical rationale at work behind the scenes. For example, when an Old Testament reference is utilized only for the perceptible purpose of making an analogy, a key idea in the Old Testament context is usually in mind as the primary characteristic or principle applied to the New Testament situation. These comparisons almost always broadly retain an essential association with the Old Testament context and convey principles of continuity between Old Testament and New Testament even though they are handled with creative freedom. This is true even in the Apocalypse,[32] which is often seen as creatively handling the Old Testament in a hermeneutically uncontrolled manner.[33]

In the light of our overall discussion, the proposal of many that the New Testament's exegetical approach to the Old Testament is characteristically non-contextual is a substantial overstatement. It would take more space than allowed in this article to discuss all the relevant cases where the Old Testament is used in the New Testament, but the present aim has been to focus on methodological and presuppositional issues which often influence the exegetical task itself. I remain convinced that once the hermeneutical and theological presuppositions of the New Testament writers are considered, there are no clear examples where they have developed a meaning from the Old Testament which is inconsistent or contradictory to some aspect of the original Old Testament intention.[34] However, there will probably always remain some enigmatic passages that are hard to understand under any reading.

The 'normative versus descriptive' debate

The conclusion of those who see the New Testament use of the Old Testament as non-contextual is that twentieth-century Christians should not attempt to reproduce the exegetical method of the New Testament writers, except when it corresponds to our grammatical-historical method.[35] There are usually two major reasons given for this assertion. First, we do not have the revelatory inspiration which the New Testament writers had in their *pesher* (and other non-contextual) interpretations (direct prophetic fulfilment and typological fulfilment are typically included as sub-categories of the *pesher* method, which can be defined as an *inspired application*).[36] But it is not necessary to claim that we have to have such inspiration to reproduce their method or their conclusions. The fact that we do not have the same 'revelatory stance' as the New Testament writers only means that we cannot have the same epistemological certainty about our interpretive conclusions and applications as they had. *Exegetical method* should not be confused with *certainty* about the conclusions of such a method, since the two are quite distinct.

One reason for discouraging imitation of the New Testament's exegesis is a justified fear of an uncontrollable typological exegesis, since typology has been misused throughout church history. How can we today look at the apparently non-prophetic portions of the Old Testament and try to make the same kind of correspondences between them and the New Testament which the inspired authors were able to make? However, the wrong use of a method should not lead to the conclusion that the method itself is wrong, but only that great caution should be exercised in using it. Yet should not such care be taken with all the methods we employ in interpreting the Bible, since it is God's Word? Although we cannot reproduce the certainty the biblical authors had about their conclusions, should we not try to interpret the Old Testament in the same way as they did, as long as we keep in mind the presuppositions which guided their approach to the Old Testament and as long as we are ever cautious, in the light of the way such a method has been misused in past church history?[37]

Uppermost among the presuppositions to be aware of is the concern for broad historical patterns or significant individuals (prophets, priests, kings, etc.), institutions and events which integrally formed a part of such patterns.[38] Such a perspective should steer us away from illegitimately focusing on minutiae as typological foreshadowings (like the scarlet thread which Rahab hung out of her window in Josh. 2 being a type of Christ's blood, or the trees which Israel cut down in the promised land as a type of Satan whom Christ would slay).

Therefore, typology by nature does not necessitate a non-contextual approach (although like any method it can be misused in that way), but it is an attempted identification of Old Testament contextual features with similar escalated New Testament correspondences (many evangelical scholars would want to restrict the identification of what Old Testament texts are typological only to those so referred to by New Testament writers, yet, on the other hand, they would not be willing to acknowledge these as non-contextual uses of the Old Testament). Whether or not we have made a legitimate connection is a matter of interpretive possibility or probability. One may not reply that this is an inappropriate method on the basis that the authorial intention of Old Testament writers, especially of historical narratives, would never have included such New Testament identifications. This is because we are also concerned with divine intention discernible from a retrospective viewpoint, which is fuller than the original human intention but does not contradict its contextual meaning. The larger context of canonical, redemptive history reveals how such narrow human intentions are legitimately and consistently developed by other biblical writers (and ultimately by the divine author) to include wider meaning, so that the whole canon of Scripture becomes the ultimate context for interpreting any particular passage.[39] Other controlling, heuristic guides helpful for typological exegesis may also be suggested. Repeated historical events, phrases or pictures may provide hints of typological correspondences both within the Old Testament and between the Testaments.[40] Nevertheless, these are only general parameters and will not be infallible guards against misuse and misinterpretation. We must also remember that the conclusions of all biblical exegesis are a matter of degrees of possibility and probability, and the conclusions of typology must be viewed in the same way.

Some dispute that typology should be referred to as a method of exegesis since exegesis is concerned with deriving a human author's original intention and meaning from a text.[41] But this question is also bound up with the prior question of whether or not typology is prophetic.[42] If typology is classified as partially prophetic, then it can be viewed as an exegetical method since the New Testament correspondence would be drawing out retrospectively the fuller prophetic meaning of the Old Testament type which was originally included by the divine author. One's presuppositions also can determine how typology is classified. For example, if we concede that God is also the author of Old Testament Scripture, then we are not concerned only with discerning the intention of the human author but also with the ultimate divine intent of what was written in the Old Testament, which could well transcend that of the immediate consciousness of the writer.[43] The attempt to draw out the divine intention of a text is certainly part of the exegetical task. And above all, if we assume the legitimacy of an inspired canon, then we should seek to interpret any part of that canon within its overall canonical context (given that one divine mind stands behind it all and expresses its thoughts in logical fashion).

In this regard, typology can be called contextual exegesis within the framework of the canon, since it primarily involves the interpretation and elucidation of the meaning of earlier parts of Scripture by latter parts. If one wants to refer to such canonical contextual exegesis instead as the doing of biblical or systematic theology, or even as scriptural application, it would seem to be but a purely semantic distinction. Rather than exegeting a text only in the light of its immediate literary context within a book, we are now merely exegeting the passage in view of the wider canonical context. The canonical extension of the context of a passage being exegeted does not by itself transform the exegetical procedure into a non-exegetical one. Put another way, the extension of the data base being exegeted does not mean we are no longer exegeting but only that we are doing so with a larger block of material. Even those rejecting typology as exegesis employ exegetical language to describe typology.[44]

The plausibility of the suggestion that typological interpretation is normative and that we may seek for more Old Testament types than the New Testament actually states for us is pointed to by the observation that this method is not unique to the New Testament writers but pervades the Old Testament.[45] The fact that later Old Testament writers understand earlier Old Testament texts typologically also dilutes the claim that the New Testament writers' typological method was unique because of their special charismatic stance.[46] It is nevertheless still true that we today cannot reproduce the inspired *certainty* of our typological interpretations as either the Old or New Testament writers could, but the consistent use of such a method by biblical authors throughout hundreds of years of sacred history suggests strongly that it is a viable method for all saints to employ today.

A second reason given for rejecting the normativity of New Testament exegetical method is their supposed non-contextual use of the Old Testament.[47] But we have already seen reason to question whether such use was characteristic of the New Testament writers. According to some scholars, the New Testament writers' methods were wrong according to twentieth-century standards, but their conclusions from this method were right because they were inspired. Of course, if this assessment about the New Testament approach is correct, one is forced to conclude that we should not imitate their methods. However, if an inductive study of the New Testament yields the results that the New Testament method is contextual, then we may imitate their approach. This is the answer to the question sometimes posed about 'how those exegetical procedures [of the New Testament] should be considered normative and exactly how they should be worked out'.[48]

I am prepared to accept the possibility of non-contextual, Jewish *ad hominem* argumentation used polemically by New Testament writers, although I am unconvinced that this occurs anywhere in the New Testament. If it did occur, it might best be understood as the author's intention not to exegete the Old Testament but to beat the Jews at their own game. This would not be imitated by us as a method of exegeting the Old Testament, since it plausibly would not have been originally intended as a method of exegesis but as a manner of polemicizing. This is not to say that the New Testament writers were not influenced by Jewish exegetical methods, interpretations and theology. Indeed, such influence pervades the New Testament but the influential methods consist of varieties of contextual approaches (which include *degrees* of contextual consideration) and the interpretive and theological traditions upon which they relied can be seen viably as consistent though quite creative developments of the Old Testament.

A possible response to part of what has here been said is that it is incorrect to label the New Testament's (or the Jewish) interpretive method as 'wrong' according to twentieth-century criteria of logic, since first-century Judaism thought more holistically and employed less analytical and logical ways of thinking. We may only say that what applied in that culture and time no longer applies to ours, which can appear equivalent to saying that methodology is culturally determined and therefore relative (the same argument is sometimes appealed to in the biblical-authority debate). But this response is a philosophical one (part of which James Barr in his studies on semantics has rightly criticized), arguing that our laws of logic underlying our evaluative standards were not the same laws of thought governing ancient, Semitic writers. The inductive historical evidence for this is negligible and, therefore, the assertion takes the form of a presupposition (although some have proposed that the purported presence of 'error' in biblical literature supports the contention, a proposal which itself has met with much response in recent discussions concerning the nature of scriptural inspiration). Moreover, it is unlikely that it is logically legitimate to separate method in this instance from conclusions derived from the method.

Finally, the significance of this discussion should not be limited to exegetical method because it also has a bearing on theology and theological method, since the use of the Old Testament in the New is the key to the theological relation of the Testaments, which many scholars have acknowledged.[49] If we are limited to understanding this relation only by the explicit conclusions concerning particular Old Testament passages given by New Testament writers, vast portions of the Old Testament are lost to us. We can use the 'contextual method' of interpreting these portions, but we have to remember, according to some scholars, that this was not the dominant hermeneutical approach of the New Testament writers. Therefore, a hiatus remains between the way they linked the Testaments both exegetically *and* theologically and the way we should. If the contemporary church cannot exegete and do theology the way the apostles did, how can it feel corporately at one with them in the theological process? If a radical hiatus exists between the interpretive method of the New Testament and ours today, then the study of the relationship of the Old Testament and the New Testament from the apostolic perspective is something to which the church has little access. Furthermore, if Jesus and the apostles were impoverished in their exegetical and theological method and only divine inspiration salvaged their conclusions, then the intellectual and apologetic foundation of our faith is seriously eroded. What kind of intellectual or apologetic foundation for our faith is this? M. Silva is likely correct when he states that 'if we refuse to pattern our exegesis after that of the apostles, we are in practice denying the authoritative character of their scriptural interpretation – and to do so is to strike at the very heart of the Christian faith'.[50] Indeed, the polemical and apologetic atmosphere of early Christian interpretation also points to an intense concern for correctly interpreting the Old Testament (e.g. Acts 17:2; 18:24–28; 1 Tim. 1:6–10; 2 Tim. 2:15).

Thus, I believe a positive answer can and must be given to the question 'Can we reproduce the exegesis of the New Testament?' True, we must be careful in distinguishing between the normative and descriptive (and this is an area in which there is disagreement in many areas among evangelicals in general), but in the case of the New Testament's method of interpreting the Old Testament the burden of proof rests upon those attempting to deny its normativity.

Notes

1. For a lucid and sympathetic presentation of this sort of view see, for example, the writings of Richard Longenecker, including his recent article '"Who is the prophet talking about?" Some reflections on the New Testament's use of the Old', *Themelios* 13.1 (1987), pp. 4–8.
2. On this latter point D. Instone Brewer has identified all the exegetical examples representing this early period (approx. 100) of purported pre-AD 70 proto-rabbinic exegesis. He has attempted to demonstrate that every example shows that, while these Jewish exegetes may not have always succeeded, they attempted to interpret the Old Testament according to its context, and they never supplanted the primary meaning by a secondary or allegorical one. Even if his conclusions are judged to be overstated, they nevertheless reveal an early concern for context to varying significant degrees which previously has not been sufficiently acknowledged (see his *The Hermeneutical Method of Early Judaism and Paul*, PhD dissertation, Cambridge University, 1989).
3. In Qumran, e.g. 1QM1; 1QS A 1; in Jewish apocalyptic, e.g. *Enoch* 36 – 72; *4 Ezra*; *2 Baruch*; *The Testaments of the Twelve Patriarchs*. See my own *The Use of Daniel in Jewish Apocalyptic Literature and in the Revelation of St John* (Lanham: University Press, 1984); L. Hartman, *Prophecy Interpreted* (Lund: C. W. K. Gleerup, 1966).
4. E.g., as Longenecker surprisingly assumes ('"Who is the prophet talking about?"', p. 7), since he points out the same kind of presuppositional fallacy on the part of others (ibid., p. 1).
5. Here I am using Longenecker's examples from his 'Can we reproduce the exegesis of the New Testament?', *TB* 21 (1970), pp. 3–38, and *Biblical Exegesis in the Apostolic Period* (Grand Rapids: Eerdmans, 1975).
6. On 1 Cor. 10 and Gal. 3 – 4 see E. E. Ellis, *Paul's Use of the Old Testament* (Grand Rapids: Baker, 1957), pp. 51–54, 66–73; R. M. Davidson, *Typology in Scripture* (Berrien Springs, MI: Andrews University, 1981), pp. 193–297, and D. A. Hagner, 'The Old Testament in the New Testament', in *Interpreting the Word of God, Festschrift* in honour of S. Barabas, ed. S. J. Schultz and M. A. Inch (Chicago: Moody, 1976), pp. 101–102, who sees a broad, contextual and typological approach in these texts.

   On 2 Cor. 3 see W. J. Dumbrell, *The Beginning of the End* (Homebush West, Australia: Lancer, 1985), pp. 107–113, 121–128, and S. Hafemann's work on 2 Cor. 3:13–18 in *Review and Expositor* 86, pp. 325–344.

   On 1 Cor. 9:9 cf. A. T. Hanson, *Studies in Paul's Technique and Theology* (London: SPCK, 1974), pp. 161–166; S. L. Johnson, *The Old Testament in the New* (Grand Rapids: Zondervan, 1980), pp. 39–51; D. J. Moo, 'The problem of sensus plenior', in *Hermeneutics, Authority and Canon*, ed. D. A. Carson and J. D. Woodbridge (Grand Rapids: Zondervan, 1986), pp. 179–211.

   On Rom. 10, cf. M. A. Seifrid, 'Paul's Approach to the Old Testament in Romans 10:6–8', *TJ* 6 (1985), pp. 3–37, who sees a contextual and typological use.

7. But Longenecker has most recently contended that among New Testament writers there can be found only 'some literalist, straightforward exegesis of biblical texts', that the *pesher* method (which he defines as an atomistic approach and which includes typology) 'dominates' Matt., John and the early chapters of Acts and 1 Pet., and that midrashic interpretation (which he also views as a non-contextual method) 'characterizes' Paul and Heb. ('"Who is the prophet talking about?"', pp. 6–8; cf. his *Biblical Exegesis*, pp. 218–219). He does qualify this by saying that New Testament authors employed a 'controlled atomistic exegesis' *(*ibid., p. 7), but this is unclear and he never explains what he means by this.

8. Dodd, *According to the Scriptures*, pp. 110, 126–127.

9. E.g. A. C. Sundberg, 'On Testimonies', *NovT* 3 (1959), pp. 268–281; B. Lindars, *New Testament Apologetic* (London: SCM, 1961); S. V. McCasland, 'Matthew twists the Scripture', *JBL* 80 (1961), pp. 143–148; S. L. Edgar, 'Respect for context in quotations from the Old Testament', *NTS* 9 (1962–3), pp. 56–59; A. T. Hanson, *The Living Utterances* of God (London: Darton, Longman and Todd, 1983), pp. 184–190; M. D. Hooker, 'Beyond the things that are written? St Paul's use of Scripture', *NTS* 27 (1981–2), pp. 295–309; B. Lindars, 'The place of the Old Testament in the formation of New Testament theology', *NTS* 23 (1977), pp. 59–66; for other references in this respect consult Longenecker's bibliography in *Biblical Exegesis*, pp. 223–230.

10. In addition to the sources cited above in this regard, see also, e.g., S. Kistemaker, *The Psalm Citations in the Epistle to the Hebrews* (Amsterdam: Van Soest, 1961); R. Rendell, 'Quotation in Scripture as an index of wider reference', *EQ* 36 (1964), pp. 214–221; Hartman, *Prophecy Interpreted*; R. T. France, *Jesus and the Old Testament* (Grand Rapids: Baker, 1971); idem, 'The formula-quotations of Matthew 2 and the problem of communication', *NTS* 27 (1980–81), pp. 233–251; D. Seccombe, 'Luke and Isaiah', *NTS* 27 (1980–81), pp. 252–259; Johnson, *The Old Testament in the New*; D. Moo, *The Old Testament in the Passion Narratives*; W. C. Kaiser, *The Uses of the Old Testament in the New* (Chicago: Moody, 1985); Moo, 'The problem of sensus plenior'; G. Beale, *The Influence of Daniel Upon the Structure and Theology of John's Apocalypse*, *JETS* 27 (1984), pp. 413–423; idem, 'The use of the Old Testament in Revelation', in *It is Written: Scripture Citing Scripture*, Festschrift for B. Lindars, ed. D. A. Carson and H. Williamson (Cambridge: Cambridge University Press, 1988), pp. 318–336; idem, 'The Old Testament background of reconciliation in 2 Cor. 5 – 7 and its bearing on the literary problem of 2 Cor. 6:14 – 7:1', *NTS* 35 (1989), pp. 550–581. I. H. Marshall, 'An assessment of recent developments' in *It is Written: Scripture Citing Scripture*, pp. 1–21. Although more nuanced than Dodd, see also Richard B. Hays, *Echoes of Scripture in the Letters of Paul* (New Haven: Yale University Press, 1989).

11. Cf. Beale, 'The use of the OT in Revelation'.

12. Cf. Beale, 'The use of the OT in Revelation', pp. 330–332.

13. E.g. H. W. Robinson, *Corporate Personality in Ancient Israel* (Philadelphia: Fortress, 1964; as qualified by later critics) and his bibliography; E. E. Ellis, *Prophecy and Hermeneutic in Early Christianity* (Grand Rapids: Eerdmans, 1978), pp. 170–171.

14. E.g. Is. 49:3–6 and the use of 49:6 in Luke 2:32, Acts 13:47 and Acts 26:23; note how Christ and the church fulfil what is prophesied of Israel in the Old Testament; see also France, *Jesus and the Old Testament*, pp. 50–60, 75; N. T. Wright, 'The Paul of history and the apostle of faith', *TB* 29 (1978), pp. 66–71, 87; H. K. LaRondelle, *The Israel of God in Prophecy* (Berrien Springs: Andrews University, 1983); Beale, 'The Old Testament background of reconciliation'.

15. Dodd, *According to the Scriptures*, pp. 128, 133; and F. Foulkes, *The Acts of God* (London: Tyndale, 1958); cf. the significance of the temporal merisms applied to God's – and Christ's – relation to history in Eccles. 3:1–11; Is. 46:9–11; Rev. 1:8, 17; 21:6; 22:13; see likewise Rev. 1:4; 4:8; cf. Eph. 1:11.

16. E.g. Mark 1:15; Acts 2:17; Gal.4:4; 1 Cor. 10:11; 1 Tim. 4:1; 2 Tim. 3:1; Heb. 1:2; 9:26; 1 Pet. 1:20; 2 Pet. 3:3; 1 John 2:18; Jude 18. Longenecker has a brief discussion of these first four presuppositions but he does not relate them to the issue of contextual exegesis (cf. *Biblical Exegesis*, pp. 93–95, and '"Who is the prophet talking about?"', pp. 4–5). Likewise, see the brief article by E. E. Ellis, 'Biblical interpretation in the New Testament church', in *Mikra, Text, Translation and Interpretation of the Hebrew Bible in Ancient Judaism and Early Christianity* (Minneapolis: Augsberg Fortress, 1989).

17. Cf. 2 Cor. 1:10–21; Matt. 5:17; 13:11, 16–17; Luke 24:25–27, 32, 44–45; John 5:39; 20:9; Rom. 10:4.

18. For one of the most recent surveys of significant literature discussing *sensus plenior* see

G. Reventlow, *Problems of Biblical Theology in the Twentieth Century* (London: SCM, 1986), pp. 37–47.

19. For a partial exegetical demonstration of this, see the representative literature in favour of a contextual interpretation of the Old Testament in the New Testament cited throughout the present article.

20. So also Moo, 'The problem of sensus plenior', pp. 204–211; V. S. Poythress, 'Divine Meaning of Scripture', *WTJ* 48 (1986), pp. 241–279; W. S. LaSor, 'Prophecy, inspiration, and sensus plenior', *TB* 29 (1978), pp. 54–60; idem, 'The "sensus plenior" and biblical interpretation', *Scripture, Tradition and Interpretation, Festschrift* for B. F. Harrison, ed. W. W. Gasque and W. S. LaSor (Grand Rapids: Eerdmans, 1978), pp. 272–276; D. A. Carson, *Matthew*, in *The Expositor's Bible Commentary* 8 (Grand Rapids: Zondervan, 1984), pp. 92–93; J. I. Packer, 'Infallible Scripture and the role of hermeneutics', *Scripture and Truth*, ed. D. A. Carson and J. D. Woodbridge (Grand Rapids: Zondervan, 1983), p. 350; see Moo and LaSor for examples of how this method can be applied.

21. 'Prophecy, inspiration and sensus plenior', pp. 55–56.

22. Cf. the typical examples noted by McCasland, 'Matthew twists the Scripture'; Edgar, 'Respect for context in quotations from the Old Testament', pp. 56–59.

23. P. Fairbairn, *The Typology of Scripture* 1 (Edinburgh: T. and T. Clark, 1876), p. 19.

24. This is an important distinction which cannot be developed further here, but for more discussion in agreement with our distinction see e.g. L. Goppelt, *Typos* (Grand Rapids: Eerdmans, 1982); Hanson, *Studies in Paul's Technique and Theology*, p. 186; Foulkes, *Acts of God*, e.g. p. 35; O. Cullmann, *Salvation in History* (London: SCM, 1967), pp. 132–133.

25. Moo, 'The problem of sensus plenior', p. 191, who cites others such as Moule, Banks, Metzger, Meier and Carson in support.

26. On this point see G. von Rad, *Old Testament Theology* 2 (New York: Harper and Row, 1965), pp. 372–373.

27. Cf., however, France, *Jesus and the Old Testament*, pp. 38–40, and D. Baker, 'Typology and the Christian use of the Old Testament', *SJT* 29 (1976), p. 149, who do not conclude that typology includes a prophetic aspect. But the *plēroō* formulas prefixed to citations from formally non-prophetic Old Testament passages in the Gospels decisively argue against this. See in general agreement Fairbairn, *The Typology of Scripture* 1, p. 46; Johnson, *The Old Testament in the New*, pp. 55–57; Goppelt, *Typos*, pp. 18, 130, passim; Davidson, *Typology in Scripture*, passim; Moo, 'The problem of sensus plenior', pp. 196–198; Foulkes, *Acts of God*, pp. 35–40, although he is sometimes cited wrongly as not holding this position.

28. Cf. France's good discussion of this context in 'The formula-quotations of Matthew 2'.

29. *Studies in Paul's Technique and Theology*, pp. 229–235.

30. For examples of these kinds of changes of application see France, *Jesus*; Beale, 'The use of the OT in Revelation'; idem, 'The Old Testament background of reconciliation'; for further discussion of the legitimacy of this principle of extension see the section below entitled 'The normative versus descriptive debate'.

31. Again, for numerous examples of inductive case studies where this can be argued see the literature supporting a contextual approach cited throughout this article.

32. For examples of this see Beale, 'The use of the OT in Revelation', pp. 321–332; J. Cambier, 'Les images de l'Ancien Testament dans l'Apocalypse de saint Jean', *NRB* (1955), pp. 114–121; A. Vanhoye, 'L'utilisation du livre d'Ezéchiel dans l'Apocalypse', *Bib* 43 (1962), pp. 462–467; 'L'utilizzazione del Deutero-Isaia nell'Apocalisse di Giovanni', *Euntes Docete* 27 (1974), pp. 322–339.

33. E.g. see L. A. Vos, *The Synoptic Traditions in the Apocalypse* (Kampen: J. H. Kok, 1965), pp. 21–37, 41.

34. This conclusion is corroborated by the articles of Moo, 'The problem of sensus plenior'; R. Nicole, 'The New Testament use of the Old Testament', in *Revelation and the Bible*, ed. C. F. H. Henry (Grand Rapids: Baker, 1958), pp. 135–151, and idem, 'The Old Testament in the New Testament', in *The Expositor's Bible Commentary* 1, ed. F. E. Gaebelein (Grand Rapids: Zondervan, 1979), pp. 617–628.

35. E.g. see Longenecker, 'Can we reproduce the exegesis of the New Testament?', *TB* 21 (1970), p. 38.

36. Longenecker, *Biblical Exegesis*, pp. 99–100.

37. See likewise Moo, 'The problem of sensus plenior', pp. 197, 206–210; Fairbairn, *Typology* 1, 42–

44; M. Silva, 'The New Testament use of the Old Testament: text form and authority', *Scripture and Truth*, pp. 162–163; Johnson, *The Old Testament in the New*, pp. 23, 67, 77–79, who generally hold that it is plausible to attempt to discern with caution Old Testament types beyond those mentioned in the New Testament.

38. For one of the most recent surveys of significant literature discussing typology, see G. Reventlow, *Problems of Biblical Theology in the Twentieth Century*, pp. 14–37.

39. See on this point the above discussion of the fifth presupposition of early Christian exegesis of the Old Testament.

40. E.g. see Foulkes, *Acts of God*.

41. France, *Jesus and the Old Testament*, pp. 40–41, and Baker, 'Typology', p. 149.

42. France, ibid.

43. On the fallacy of equating meaning exhaustively with authorial intention, see P. B. Payne, 'The fallacy of equating meaning with the human author's intention', *JETS* 20 (1977), pp. 243–252, in contrast to the more extreme position of W. Kaiser, 'The eschatological hermeneutics of "evangelicalism": promise theology', *JETS* 13 (1970), pp. 94–95; 'The present state of Old Testament studies', *JETS* 18 (1975), pp. 71–72, who thinks that discerning only the human author's intention exhausts the *full meaning* of an Old Testament text and that the New Testament provides no fuller meaning of Old Testament texts than the Old Testament authors would not also have been completely cognizant of; the unusual interpretations which result from this view can be seen in Kaiser's *The Uses of the Old Testament in the New Testament* (Chicago: Moody, 1985).

44. E.g. Baker, 'Typology', p. 155, says that 'although it is not a method of exegesis, typology supplements exegesis by throwing further light on the text in question'; cf. Goppelt, *Typos*, pp. 152, 198, who, although referring to typology as not 'a systematic exposition of Scripture, but as a spiritual approach', says it 'is the method of interpreting Scripture that is predominant in the New Testament'.

45. So Foulkes, *Acts of God*, passim; e.g. p. 40.

46. In addition to Foulkes, *Acts of God*, cf. M. Fishbane, *Biblical Interpretation in Ancient Israel* (Oxford: Clarendon, 1985), pp. 350–379, and sources cited therein for discussion of such typological exegesis within the Old Testament itself; see likewise H. G. Reventlow, *Problems of Biblical Theology in the Twentieth Century*, pp. 28–29; H. D. Hummel, 'The Old Testament basis of typological interpretation', *BR* 9 (1964), pp. 38–50.

47. E.g. Longenecker refers to their 'atomistic manipulations of midrash … the circumstantial or [Jewish] *ad hominem'* polemical argumentation ('"Who is the prophet talking about?"', p. 8) and 'their allegorical explications' (*Biblical Exegesis*, p. 218).

48. Longenecker, '"Who is the prophet talking about?"', p. 7.

49. E.g. see G. Hasel, *Current Issues in New Testament Theology: Basic Issues in the Current Debate* (Grand Rapids: Eerdmans, 1978); D. L. Baker, *Two Testaments, One Bible: A Study of Some Modern Solutions to the Theological Problem of the Relationship between the Old and New Testaments* (Leicester and Downers Grove: IVP, 1977); Reventlow, *Problems of Biblical Theology in the Twentieth Century*. So also Longenecker, '"Who is the prophet talking about?"', p. 1.

50. 'The New Testament use of the Old Testament', p. 164, although he does slightly qualify this assertion; so likewise Johnson, *The Old Testament in the New*, p. 67.

9

How far do readers make sense?

Interpreting biblical narrative

John Goldingay   Vol. 18.2 (1993)

Over the past thirty years, the study of biblical narrative has kept changing its focus; as has often happened over the millennia, it has followed changing fashions in secular literary criticism, even if keeping a few years behind (though a decreasing few). During the 1960s, interpreting biblical narrative meant discovering who wrote it and what historical events it referred to. That study remains of fundamental significance because biblical narrative relates a gospel, and the factuality of the gospel is crucial to its being a story we can base our lives on. The historical 'having happened-ness' of the biblical story matters.

During the 1970s, however, many interpreters of narrative turned from questions about its origin and historical reference to renewed study of the narrative itself. What are its structure and plot? Who are its characters? From what points of view is it told? Anyone who believes that the actual text of these biblical narratives is 'given by inspiration of God' will be enthusiastic about the stimulus and the help we can receive from such renewed study of the text of Scripture itself, which is a powerful aid to our being grasped by its message.

During the 1980s, in turn, many of the interpreters who had enthused over the approaches of the 'new criticism' moved on from those questions, too, to the readers of the text. What audience is presupposed by it? How does it communicate with them? How do they go about making sense of it? Do texts have meaning at all, or are they only dots on paper which readers provide with their meaning?

Each of these three sorts of question promises a different set of insights as well as presenting a different set of questions for someone who believes that the Bible tells God's story and who wants to hear the biblical text speak in God's name. My concern here is with the last of these approaches, reader-centred ones, the developing current fashion in biblical interpretation.

The audience implied by the story

Stories themselves presuppose certain sorts of hearers, and sometimes indicate what sort of audience can hear them aright. Reader-oriented approaches to interpretation ask questions about the nature of the readers presupposed by a story and what a story is designed to do to them. It is appropriate to think at least as much in terms of audiences and hearers as of readers. In the ancient world, as far as we can tell, the normal way to attend to Scripture would not be reading it silently; few people would have access to a personal copy of a biblical scroll in order to read it for themselves. It would be hearing it read. For Jews, of course, even the private reading of the Torah is a spoken act. If scriptural authors had in mind a means of the dissemination of their work, then, it would have been its reading to a congregation or a group. This has implications for the interpretation of it.[1] 'In the beginning was the word,' Martin Buber was fond of pointing out – the spoken word. The reading of a story is a speech-act.[2]

Although the human authors of a story are all-important to its existence, the form of a story enables them to hide; we are invited to collude with them in acting as if the story came into existence of itself and is its own authority. In the same way, the audience of a story is not usually directly addressed by it, as it is in some other forms of speech, but it is thereby the more compellingly manipulated. Although formally absent from the story, the audience is substantially omnipresent in so far as stories are created not just for their own sake but in order to do something to some people. A story has 'implied readers' – people who are in a position to make the proper response to it.[3] It is told in such a way as to work for an audience, e.g. by means of the order in which it relates events (commonly not the chronological one) and the rate at which it releases information. It tantalizes, teases, challenges, upsets, makes the audience think, forces it to come inside the story and involve itself with it if it is to understand.[4]

In Luke-Acts and John, the implied audience of the narrative sometimes becomes visible as the narrative addresses it directly, just as the narrators themselves also occasionally become visible and speak about their purpose. But the narratives indirectly offer further clues regarding the audience which they envisage and which will be able to 'make sense' of them. The language of all four Gospels, for instance, identifies their audience as Greek-speaking and thus probably urban communities, people living in the theological space between Jesus' resurrection and his final appearing.

In the case of Matthew, J. D. Kingsbury collects references which suggest that his audience is a firmly established and well-to-do Christian community living after the fall of Jerusalem, one with a substantial Jewish element, though (to judge from the Gospel's Gentile bias) also with a Gentile element. They stand outside the orbit of official Judaism but in close proximity to both Jews and Gentiles and under pressure from both. They are also under pressure from within, from miracle-working false prophets and from people who wish to impose a more hierarchical leadership pattern.[5] Matthew's audience thus differs quite markedly from that presupposed by Luke, with its famous stress on the poor. Such differences in slant hint at and reflect differences in audience. There is material here for consideration as interpreters seek to take account of Jesus' 'bias to the poor' and to discover what attitude he would take to the not-so-poor.

Given that we are not the originally envisaged audience of any biblical story, we are invited to an act of imagination which takes us inside the concerns of such an audience. The fact that we cannot precisely locate these hearers geographically or chronologically (the concern of the historical approach to the Gospels) need not matter because it is the concerns that the stories themselves express that we seek to share. We are invited to listen to them as people for whom such stories were told, to listen to them from the inside. Interpretation of biblical stories is not a matter of untrammelled imagination but one which involves close attention to the particularities of *this* text. At the same time it is not merely an analytic and intellectual affair, but one which involves being willing to be drawn into stories; with regard to their interpretation, 'a man without an imagination is more of an invalid than one who lacks a leg'.[6]

We cannot live our real lives inside these stories. We have to live them in our own context, confronted by its questions, needs and pressures. If the stories are to do to us what they were designed to do to their original hearers, a further act of imagination is needed, one which sets some of our questions, needs and pressures alongside those which the stories directly addressed, in a way which is open to seeing how they address these, so that we may respond to them by telling our story in a way which links it on to the biblical stories – as Acts already does in adding the church's story on to Jesus'.

These two acts of imagination can be clearly distinguished conceptually. In their operation they are likely to interpenetrate each other. Grasping the biblical stories' significance may enable us to see how to tell our story; bringing our story to the biblical stories may also fill out our grasp of their own significance. Interpretation involves the whole person – feelings, attitudes and wills, as well as minds; it also involves *us*, not merely people 2,500 years ago.

Specifically, there are religious and person-involving aspects to biblical stories, and in themselves literary methods are no more designed to handle these than are historical approaches. They, too, can encourage interpreters to distance themselves from the text. To avoid imposing our own questions on it is not yet to let it press its questions on us, only to overhear it talking to itself. Interpreting biblical narratives involves more than merely understanding a text as an object over against me of which I seek to gain a rational, objective grasp. The stories were written to do something to people, and our interpretative approach needs to be able to handle – or to be handled by – this aspect of them. It involves the possibility of there happening to us that which the story had the power to make happen to its audience.

The role of ambiguity and openness in stories

One of the ways in which stories do things to an audience is by leaving questions and ambiguities for their audience to answer or to resolve. We have to recognize and accept the presence of such ambiguity in texts rather than work on the assumption that if only we had all the right information, everything would be clear. Sometimes authors do not make themselves clear, either by accident or on purpose. Whichever is the case, ambiguity is then a fact to be acknowledged and made the most of. It can be creatively provocative, evidently part of God's purpose.

Beyond this kind of special deliberate or accidental ambiguity, no story can tell us everything that happens in the course of the events it relates, or everything about its characters. 'There is something more to the reception of the meaning of a literary work than simply its decoding by means of universally held, deep structures. What is in need of decoding by the reader is not entirely determined … The structure itself involves potentialities. Gaps that occur in the text are deliberate and essential.' As a result, the same story can be actualized in a variety of ways by different readers.[7]

Traditional biblical interpretation has difficulty tolerating ambiguity and openness; it assumes that the author aimed at clarity and precision, and it brings all the resources of historical and linguistic scholarship to bear on the elucidating of the text's clear meaning. If texts seem ambiguous, we assume this derives from our not sharing the conventions and assumptions that author and first audience shared. Literary interpretation, too, seeks by means of its close study of the objective data provided by a biblical text to discover its inherent meaning and provide a check on our intuitions as to its meaning. But there are aspects of the intrinsic meaning of biblical stories on which such data seem to be missing. An audience-oriented approach to interpretation presupposes that ambiguity may be inherent in a story, and asks what its opennesses do to an audience, or what it does with them, aware that it is precisely in its ambiguity at such points that the story can challenge an audience regarding its own attitude. We have to 'fill in the blanks' in the story.[8] We do not do that once and for all; the openness of the story means we have to keep coming back to it, 'brooding over gaps in the information provided'.[9] In this sense, the meaning of a story is something which its audience provides; 'readers make sense'.[10]

There are irresolvable ambiguities in the portraits of characters such as Moses or Saul or David, which prohibit simple understandings of their stories. Is David raised up by God to be Israel's king, or does he emerge as an epic hero? Is he the man who does the right thing and the man with God's blessing, or is he the man with an eye to the main chance and the man who always manages to fall on his feet? What are we to make of the two accounts of his introduction to Saul?[11] When Moses strikes out at the sight of an Egyptian beating an Israelite (Exod. 2:11–15), is he using the wrong method to reach the right end, or manifesting the qualities of spirit worthy of one who is to be the means of Yahweh's smiting Pharaoh? There are hints in the passage pointing both ways, so that it brings out rather than resolves the ambiguities in the act of violence.[12]

Alter suggests that the 'indeterminacy of meaning' characteristic of much biblical narrative, with its 'complex moral and psychological realism', reflects an implicit theology. 'God's purposes are always entrammeled in history, dependent on the acts of individual men and women for their continuing realization. To scrutinize biblical personages as fictional characters is to see them more sharply in the multi-faceted, contradictory aspects of their human individuality, which is the biblical God's chosen medium for his experiment with Israel and history.'[13] This links with the disinclination of biblical narrative to pronounce on people's inner thoughts: leaving the gaps leaves room for the 'conjectures of grace' and 'the mystery of God-with-us'.[14] To seek to understand them in the way we seek to understand the fictional characters in a novel, of course, is not to presuppose that they *are* merely fictional characters, but rather to use approaches appropriate to fictional narrative as heuristic tools.

Pannenberg makes a parallel point when he urges the historian to focus on the particularities of history and not to rush into speculating about God's providence, because it is through human activity that God works in the world

– indirectly, though as its Lord.[15] Allusiveness regarding the character of human actors both honours them and highlights the importance of the divine director of the story. It offers an indirect witness to the God who is the story's ultimate subject. It invites an act of faith in God, not in God's human agents, on whom the narrative is content to be unclear. The story of Job implies that allusiveness and ambiguity in portraying biblical characters do not stop short of the character of God. That means that the stories offer true witness to the complexity and mystery of God's character; it also highlights the fact that 'a coherent reading of the biblical narratives' is as much an act of faith as a ground for faith.[16]

What we bring to stories

If understanding stories inevitably involves *us* as whole people, it involves us hearing them with the advantages and disadvantages of our background, experience and commitments. Historical and literary approaches are often treated as if they were objective and positivist rather than hermeneutical in their own nature. They are not.

Literary interpretative methods that claim to be objective and analytical can be very fruitful in enabling a modern audience to be drawn into the text itself and addressed by it. On the other hand, they do not always bear this fruit; they can seem to be a matter of dry word-count. In having these two capacities, they parallel other methods of exegesis, and illustrate how exegetical method and hermeneutics may not be as separate in practice as we may assume they are in theory. This phenomenon is not confined to the application of literary-critical methods to *biblical* material. Literary criticism itself is both a would-be objective, scientific affair, *and* an enterprise which hopes to discover and unveil truth about the world and about what it means to be human. Even literary reading of stories will be influenced in what it looks for, or limited in what it perceives, by the historical and social position of its practitioners. Paying close attention to the text does not in itself solve the question of how stories in their foreignness are grasped by people and grasp them.[17]

Many stories are rich in theme and defy simple analysis in terms of their 'intention' or 'message'; different audiences (or the same audience at different times) perceive different aspects of this richness. These differences do not indicate that only one or another theme belongs to the story; they reflect the differences among the audiences and the different ways in which the story of their own life resonates with that of the story they are listening to, at the point it has at a given moment reached. It is sometimes asked whether there is point in the continuing production of new works of interpretation.[18] One aspect of its rationale is that interpretations in their variety give testimony to the richness of their texts as they are read out of different contexts.

Liberation and feminist hermeneutics illustrate the way in which audiences with particular backgrounds are able to perceive, articulate, and respond to aspects of texts which audiences with other backgrounds may miss and be missed by, even though they also illustrate how the same audiences (like all audiences) are also by virtue of their background liable to mishear the text in other respects. Both can be seen as instances of reader-response approaches to Scripture, ones which use their particular initial horizons or pre-understandings as their ways into the text's concerns, and both make it clear that what we are able to see reflects not merely our intellectual pre-understanding but our practical pre-commitment. Interpretation is shaped by the way we live. This has been so with slavism, racism, sexism, homophobia and capitalism (which has discounted the Hebrew Bible's proscription on usury).[19] It has also been so with their antonyms.[20]

In practice, some of the most interesting or suggestive or illuminating or life-changing exercises in narrative interpretation integrate one of the more text-centred approaches with one of the more self-consciously committed approaches. Liberation or feminist approaches may combine with deconstructive criticism.[21] Materialist understandings may combine a structuralist approach to understanding the actual text with Marxist insights into the relationship between literature (and our interpretation of it) on the one hand and social contexts on the other. There is no necessary implication that the aesthetic and the socially functional aspects of the text are reducible to one another.[22] Russian formalism and Marxism might seem a natural pairing (Vladimir Propp was actually a student at the time of the 1917 revolution), though the Russian formalists of the 1920s were too interested in literary study for its own sake for the liking of Marxist critics; this fact lies behind the neglect of Propp's work until after the Second World War.[23]

Alongside liberationist interpretation, feminist interpretation also illustrates the way in which illuminating or life-transforming exercises in narrative interpretation may combine a self-consciously committed approach with one of the more text-centred literary methods. This is so with Phyllis Trible's work on some agreeable texts in the opening chapters of Genesis, Ruth and the Song of Songs, and some more terrifying ones later in Genesis, Judges and 2 Samuel, with Mieke Bal's deconstructionist work, and with Elizabeth Schüssler Fiorenza's historical-critical study.

The admission that one is using historical-critical method with a 'bias' may seem scandalous, but it is becoming clear that historical-critical history regularly functions ideologically in respect of the concerns and presuppositions which it allows to determine what counts as history.[24] Since historical-critical exegesis is the ruling method in professional biblical study, one purpose of its exercise is now to legitimate the scholarly guild in their position of power.[25] Thus there is a feminist challenge to the 'objectivist-factual' pretension of traditional critical scholarship and its failure to acknowledge the (e.g. male) 'interests' it serves, which urges that recognition of bias and enthusiasm about looking at questions in the light of a different set of biases will lead to new historical discoveries.[26]

Of course, no prior commitment is immune from leading to misreadings or incomplete readings. Feminist interpreters have found Trible too unequivocal in her reading of Genesis 2 – 3, the Song of Songs and Ruth.[27] David Clines regards the whole enterprise of a feminist reading of a passage such as the Genesis creation story anachronistic if it pretends to be exegesis, and sees it as rather an (in principle) entirely appropriate readerly approach to the text; as such it is no more anachronistic than nineteenth-century concern to relate Genesis 1 – 11 to scientific study or to Middle Eastern creation and flood stories.[28] Those who pretend to be objective and critical and who then find their own concerns in the texts they study – whether these be Enlightenment or existentialist or feminist or Reformed concerns – need to take a dose of self-suspicion.[29]

Every audience comes to a story with different prior commitments. Our hearing of it is never exclusively objective. Both historical and literary study is undertaken by interpreters who belong in particular contexts and do their work out of particular commitments. That is ground for (self-)suspicion and a longing to test my reading of stories by readings from other commitments.

What we read into stories

There is another sense in which the objectivity of literary interpretation may be questioned. It might seem that analyses of the structure of texts were objective and easy to agree on, but this does not seem to be so. The theory was that literary approaches should enable us to discover something of the stories' own burden. By taking their own structural, rhetorical and linguistic features as the key to identifying their central concerns, we should be able to concentrate attention on questions raised by the chapters themselves rather than ones extrinsic to them.

The conviction that there is some objectivity about these matters is subverted by the fact that reports of chiasms, for instance, have a habit of appearing more objective than they may seem when one subsequently checks them by the text.[30] Even the process of 'positing various structures' in works may be seen as part of 'the activity of the reader' in interpretation.[31] Chiasms apart, different scholars often give different accounts of the structure of a story. While some stories give objective markers regarding their structure, many do not. The structure of a story may thus be difficult to identify and interpreters may differ in the way they understand it, as is the case with the Gospels and with Genesis.[32] This may mean that no one analysis is exclusively 'right' and that different aspects of the story's meaning emerge from various analyses of its structure. Perhaps structure lies in the eyes of the beholder – it is something we as readers of a narrative find helpful. Even the analytic aspect to interpretation cannot be claimed to be wholly objective.

There is a real distinction between literary-critical approaches which focus on the text itself and approaches which focus more on the process of reading and the contribution of the reader; but it is readers who undertake readings. Like fact and interpretation (of which they are actually a version), questions about the text and questions about readers can be distinguished but not ultimately kept apart. Structuralism, indeed, is often described as a theory of reading rather than a theory about writing.[33] To emphasize this interweaving is not to collapse the distinction; it perhaps makes it more important. The fact that we read with the advantages and disadvantages of our background and commitments is reason for doing so reflectively and self-critically rather than unthinkingly, if we want to have a chance of seeing what is actually there in the text. 'No close reading of a work is ever close enough', in that it involves trying to make sense of it, and thus 'inevitably, we ignore, leave out, suppress' elements from it in the light of our background and prejudices.[34] There is always more to discover.

Is it audiences who make sense of stories?

When we move away from objective-looking questions such as structures to questions regarding the broader meanings of works, the question whether stories have objective meaning becomes yet more difficult. Does Jonah tell a story to bring home the love of God for all peoples, or to dramatize how not to be a prophet, or to invite Israel itself to return to Yahweh? According to the Genesis creation story, do men and women have equal authority and responsibility, or are men given authority over women? Are Ruth, Naomi and Boaz all selfless, enlightened and honourable people, or self-centred and ambiguous like the rest of us? If the very nature of narrative works such as the Gospels is to have many meanings and to be open to many understandings,[35] do such questions have answers, or does everything depend on the hearers of the stories? Do texts have determinate meaning at all? The observation that 'readers make sense'[36] can be understood more radically than we have allowed above; the meaning of a story is always provided by its audience. A text is only a matter of marks on a piece of paper. Despite exegetes' continuing attempts to state the objective meaning of texts, 'criticism is an ineluctably creative activity. Prior to the interpretive act, there is nothing definitive in the text to be discovered.'[37]

There are a number of difficulties with this view. When we speak of 'making sense' of a statement, we usually mean 'discovering the sense which must somehow be there', not creating sense in something which lacks it. We presume that the statement was an attempt at communication, and we wish to receive the communication. Thus in general authors, too, surely write to say something of determinate meaning, readers read (or audiences listen) reckoning to discover what that is, and then share their understanding of this with other people in the expectation that they can be understood and can carry conviction; and the same is surely true with regard to Scripture.[38] A standard introduction to audience-oriented criticism begins by discussing the literary text as a form of communication between author and reader.[39] And without the assumption that texts have determinate meaning, interpretation as a cognitive activity becomes logically impossible.[40] If the meaning of texts is created by their readers, no readerly-inclined interpreter could talk of misreading the text; but Nolan Fewell, at least, does.[41]

The view that narratives have different meanings in different contexts or for different audiences offers openness and scope to interpreters, but it does threaten arbitrariness and relativism. It perhaps reflects and shares the strengths and the dangers of cultural and moral pluralism in society.[42] An emphasis on objective meaning can admittedly conversely be an ideological concern designed to support the status quo and can be self-deceived regarding its own subjectivity.[43] But to abandon it may be to submit oneself to something just as ideological.

Stanley Fish, a key theorist of this approach to interpretation, suggests that right interpretation is interpretation which accords with the conventions of a particular interpretative community, and sees this as the safeguard of objectivity in interpretation.[44] But such a way of attempting to handle this question only serves to underline the problem. An interpretative community may be a safeguard against individual oddity, but otherwise it merely replaces individual subjectivism by communal subjectivism or relativism.[45] Perhaps it rather institutionalizes an already existent communal subjectivism, for readers inevitably read out of the corporate context in which they are embedded, not as independent, individual selves.[46]

It is often the case that 'arguments over method are fundamentally differences in assumptions or beliefs'.[47] It is for this reason that Christians have taken a long time to come to terms with historical-critical method. Ironically, when that venture may be largely over, another replaces it. 'As the challenge was once to come to terms with the modernist Bible, so now the challenge is to come to terms with its postmodern successor.'[48] As with the older challenge, we have to live through a period in which we do not yet entirely know how to come to terms with it – but in the light of the earlier experience we may live through that period reckoning that we will eventually do so.

Hirsch argues that it is worth betting on the reality of determinate meaning because – as with Pascal's wager – if it is indeed real, we have gained, whereas if it is not, we have lost nothing.[49] Further, the wager is, like Pascal's, at least open to verification at the End.[50] If our discussion takes place within the context of the view that God is there, the odds in the wager may seem stacked Pascal's way. As we may believe that it is more likely that God would have ensured that an adequate witness to the Christ event would have survived than that it would have been allowed to disappear, so we may believe that the texts' witness to that event has meaning of its own rather than only having meaning when we provide it.

Theological and philosophical, as well as personal, factors thus enter into the judgment whether determinate meaning is possible or important.[51] It is perhaps for this reason that the acrimony and contentiousness of literary-critical debate sometimes appear also in biblical studies.[52] In my view, all three factors just noted (theological, philosophical, personal) point to attempting to hold on to a both-and rather than submit to an either-or. Audiences contribute to the identification of meaning, but their contributions are subject to the meaning of the text, not creative of it.

Textual criticism proceeds as if it were possible to reach a 100% correct version of the text. This is only theoretically possible – indeed, perhaps not even theoretically possible. Yet as an aim it fulfils an important function. In a parallel way we will never attain a 100% correct understanding of a text, or of anything else. Yet the impossibility of total understanding does not negate the worth of attempting whatever degree of understanding will turn out to be possible. The attempt is likely to be more successful if we behave as if total understanding were possible. If you aim at the moon, you may hit the lamp-post. The notion of determinate meaning has functional efficacy.[53]

Why is there diversity in the way people understand texts?

Works on biblical interpretation have often given the impression that the central question in hermeneutics is how we decide between conflicting interpretations of texts, how we avoid misinterpretation.[54] The more dominant recent view is that this misconceives the central concern of hermeneutics. That concern is how interpretation can happen at all, how our eyes and ears can be opened to what texts have to say. Nevertheless, it may be argued that 'the diversity of readings is *the* fact to be explained by any literary theory'.[55] If we resist the idea that there is no such thing as determinate meaning, what explanation do we offer?

The question might first be countered by another. If meaning is indeterminate, why is there so much overlap between interpretations? Our concentration on differences and disagreements on interpretation may mask the degree of commonality. Why does no-one take up the theoretical possibility of understanding as adverbs all words which have henceforth been taken as verbs? Formally, the answer may be that the interpretative community has a tacit agreement on grammar, but that agreement surely includes a presupposition that this understanding of grammar corresponds to something inherent in the text, which establishes objective constraints within which anything which is to count as interpretation takes place. It is difficult to know whether Genesis begins 'In the beginning God created ...' or 'In the beginning when God created ...', but there is no doubt that it excludes 'In the beginning the world came into being by accident or by the activity of Marduk'. The ways in which a text can be understood are finite in number, and some understandings of them can be said to be wrong.

Interpretation has traditionally sought to safeguard the importance of objectivity in interpretation by seeing its goal as the ascertaining of the original meaning of the text, its meaning in the context in which it was written. One may affirm this principle but still recognize that different people can come to different interpretations of a story. There is in fact a variety of explanations of diversity in readings, some already hinted at in this article; different ones will apply to different texts.

First, all texts have some degree of openness; if every point in them were to be made explicit, the story would never finish. Our assumption in writing and reading, in speaking and hearing, is that enough is said to make communication possible, but their inevitable allusiveness means that more than one understanding of aspects of them can co-exist.

Second, there are texts which achieve part of their effect by leaving an extra degree of ambiguity and openness. The fact that the stories of Saul and David attract widely varying interpretations[56] is an indication that they are texts of this kind, not that all texts are.

Third, many stories are rich and complex. We do not have to argue about whether the stories in Daniel are really about the significance of imperial kingship as opposed to the possibility of being a successful but faithful Jewish politician – really about the kings or the Jewish sages – because both can be true. The reason why different people may offer varying legitimate interpretations of some stories is that a story's meaning may have a number of facets.[57] Its meaning is an objective matter, something there in the text, but it may nevertheless be a quite complex matter. Part of the greatness of some stories is a richness that cannot be encapsulated in a simple formula ('this story is about *x*'). It is in this sense that the question 'Which is the right interpretation of the text?' is as inappropriate to the Bible as it is to Shakespeare: the question about interpreting *Hamlet* is: 'How we can feed on such a rich work?'[58]

This is not to imply that there is no such thing as a wrong understanding of a work such as *Hamlet*, only that concern with this possibility misses the point. Missing right understanding is a more threatening danger than arriving at a wrong understanding. Reading from the perspective of the oppressed uncovers in the parable about the workers in the vineyard a message about human solidarity to add to its message about the grace of God.[59] Polyvalency involves a story having many facets; it does not mean that questions about meaning are inherently arbitrary, or even that such analytic models 'provide meaning *to* the text rather than discovering meaning *in* the text'.[60] One can grant that there are many aspects to a story's meaning but still reckon that there are limits to what can be read out of a story, and it may be that interpreters can agree on meanings which do not belong to a story – not so much because author or audience could or would not have envisaged them but because they are not a natural understanding of this actual story.

Indeed, one aspect of the problem in this discussion is the very notion of the meaning of a story. The meaning of a story cannot really be abstracted from the story itself, as if a summary of the principles it illustrates could adequately represent the story itself. In the case of Hamlet, or Ruth, or a parable, the story *is* the meaning or the message. An author discovers what to say only through saying it, and an audience understands it only through hearing it.[61] What it says in a detailed and concrete way by means of a portrayal of events, characters and conversations, achieves something for both parties which an abstract cannot. It may not convey new information, but it may convey new knowledge.[62]

Fourth, texts may have one intrinsic meaning (even a complex and rich one) but many significances or applications, or one sense but many references. Many diversities of interpretation are differences over the way the story applies to different people or in different contexts rather than differences about its inherent meaning.[63] It is this which makes it of inexhaustible significance and needing to be grasped by every age in its own terms, which may be different from those of its authors.[64] Statements of the text's significance may also be mutually incompatible in a way that statements of the text's actual meaning may not.[65]

When an account of an event is put into writing, there is a sense in which this definitively determines the event's meaning; yet paradoxically the narrative's coming into being as an independent object simultaneously opens it up to a multiplicity of new readings.[66] When people speak, what they mean by their words largely dominates the way their words are heard; words in written form can more easily be heard independently of their author's purpose and meaning. 'Writing is central to the hermeneutical phenomenon, insofar as its detachment both from the writer or author and from a specifically addressed recipient or reader has given it a life of its own.'[67] The ironic reading of biblical stories instances this difficulty. L. R. Klein's interpretation of Judges, for instance, sees it as a systematically ironic book. On what basis can we evaluate that understanding? We cannot ask the authors whether they intended the book ironically. We can only ask ourselves whether that understanding corresponds best to the nature of the book that we have, or whether an ironic understanding of the book, starting from our inability to take seriously a more straightforward understanding of it, is the only way we can 'make sense' of it. We may be unconsciously finding *significance* in it rather than its own *meaning*. Similar questions arise from David Gunn's ironic reading of 1 Kings' comment on Solomon, its 'innocuous "only"' (he obeyed God *except for* sacrificing at the high places, 1 Kgs. 3:3; cf. the 'only' in 15:5; 2 Kgs. 14:4; 15:4), and his identifying an irony in the portrayal of David in 2 Samuel 21 – 24.[68]

Howard Marshall began the symposium *New Testament Interpretation* with a consideration of John 4, and noted that the story has been seen as an example of Jesus' pastoral dealings with people which provides an example for his followers. That understanding is hardly at the centre of its intrinsic significance. It might be a secondary aspect of the story's own meaning, part of its richness as a story; it might be an implication of the story, given the Gospel's conviction that Jesus' disciples are sent by the Father as he was (John 20:21); it might be not part of the story's meaning but an aspect of its significance for hearers involved in pastoral ministry, justified by the general New Testament assumption that Jesus is a model for ministry. Which is correct makes little difference, as is often the case with arguments about right and wrong interpretations, though there is a point of more importance in the reminder that whichever is right, the story centrally concerns how Jesus revealed himself rather than what disciples should be.

One might draw a parallel with the grassroots communities' Bible study such as that collected by E. Cardenal in *Love in Practice: The Gospel in Solentiname.*[69] This begins, for instance, with a transcript of a discussion of John 1:1 which understands the declaration that Christ is the Word to signify that God expresses himself through Christ to denounce oppression. That is hardly an example of 'liberating *exegesis*', the title of a book on the Bible study of the grassroots communities by Christopher Rowland and Mark Corner, but it is indeed an example of liberating exposition. It discerns not the meaning of the text, but its significance for these audiences. *Love in Practice*'s subsequent discussion of throwing pearls to pigs further illustrates the application of the text to a context rather than insight into the inherent meaning of the text out of a context. That difference remains worth preserving. On the other hand, the fact that fifty preachers might produce a dozen different sermon angles from the same text[70] is not necessarily cause for concern. The opposite phenomenon might be more worrying.

What readers discover from Scripture is that its being God's inspired Word makes it a rich treasure whose potential we have hardly begun to mine.

Notes

1. S. D. Moore, *Literary Criticism and the Gospels* (New Haven and London: Yale University Press, 1989), pp. 76–77, 84–88.
2. S. Talmon, 'Martin Buber's ways of interpreting the Bible', in *JJS* 27 (1976), pp. 202–203.
3. W. J. Iser, *The Implied Reader* (Baltimore and London: Johns Hopkins University Press, 1974); see also W. C. Booth, *The Rhetoric of Fiction* (Chicago and London: University of Chicago Press, 1961, 2nd edn 1983).
4. T. J. Keegan, *Interpreting the Bible* (Mahwah, NJ: Paulist Press, 1985), pp. 84–85.
5. J. D. Kingsbury, *Matthew as Story* (Philadelphia: Fortress, 1986), pp. 120–133; cf. R. A. Culpepper, *Anatomy of the Fourth Gospel* (Philadelphia: Fortress, 1983), pp. 204–227, on the 'implied reader' in John.
6. K. Barth, *Church Dogmatics* (ET Edinburgh: T. and T. Clark; New York: Scribner's, 1936–), III/1, p. 91.
7. Keegan, pp. 80, 103–104, summarizing Iser.
8. So e.g. P. D. Miscall, *The Workings of Old Testament Narrative* (Philadelphia: Fortress, 1983).
9. R. Alter, *The Art of Biblical Narrative* (New York: Basic; London: Allen and Unwin, 1981), p. 12.
10. E. V. McKnight, *The Bible and the Reader* (Philadelphia: Fortress, 1985), p. 133 and often.
11. See Alter, pp. 147–153.
12. So B. S. Childs, *The Book of Exodus* (Philadelphia: Westminster, 1974) = *Exodus* (London: SCM, 1974), p. 46.
13. Alter, p. 12; cf. pp. 22, 33; also pp. 114–130 on David.
14. D. Buttrick, *Homiletic* (Philadelphia: Fortress; London: SCM, 1987), p. 334.
15. W. Pannenberg, *Basic Questions in Theology* (ET London: SCM; Philadelphia: Westminster, vol. 1, 1970, vol. 2, 1971), 1, p. 79.
16. R. F. Thiemann, 'Radiance and obscurity in biblical narrative', in G. Green (ed.), *Scriptural Authority and Narrative Interpretation* (Hans Frei *Festschrift*, Philadelphia: Fortress, 1987), p. 30.
17. L. M. Poland, *Literary Criticism and Biblical Hermeneutics* (Chico, CA: Scholars, 1985); cf. M. Gerhart, 'The restoration of biblical narrative', in M. Amihai et al. (eds.), *Narrative Research on*

the Hebrew Bible, *Semeia* 46 (1989), pp. 13–29.

18. Cf. J. Culler, *The Pursuit of Signs* (Ithaca, NY: Cornell University Press; London: Routledge, 1981), p. ix.

19. K. G. Cannon and E. Schüssler Fiorenza (eds.), *Interpretation for Liberation, Semeia* 47 (1989).

20. See W. M. Swartley, *Slavery, Sabbath, War, and Women* (Scottdale, PA: Herald, 1983).

21. D. Jobling, 'Writing the wrongs of the world', in G. A. Phillips (ed.), *Poststructural Criticism and the Bible, Semeia* 51 (1990), pp. 81–118.

22. See K. Füssel, 'Materialist readings of the Bible', in W. Schottroff and W. Stegemann (eds.), *God of the Lowly* (ET Maryknoll, NY: Orbis, 1984), pp.13–25.

23. See P. J. Milne, *Vladimir Propp and the Study of Structure in Hebrew Biblical Narrative* (Sheffield: Sheffield Academic Press, 1988), pp. 19–32.

24. See e.g. W. Breuggemann, *Abiding Astonishment: Psalms, Modernity, and the Making of History* (Louisville: Westminster John Knox, 1991), pp. 37–46.

25. Füssel, p. 15.

26. E. Schüssler Fiorenza, *Bread not Stone* (Boston: Beacon, 1984; Edinburgh: T. and T. Clark, 1990), pp. 141–147.

27. D. Nolan Fewell, 'Feminist reading of the Hebrew Bible', in *JSOT* 39 (1987), pp. 80–82; E. Fuchs, 'Who is hiding the truth?', in A. Yarbro Collins (ed.), *Feminist Perspectives on Biblical Scholarship* (Chico, CA: Scholars, 1985), pp. 137–144; S. S. Lanser, '(Feminist) criticism in the garden: inferring Genesis 2 – 3', in H. C. White (ed.), *Speech Act Theory and Biblical Criticism, Semeia* 41 (1988), p. 79.

28. D. J. A. Clines, *What Does Eve Do to Help? and Other Readerly Questions to the Old Testament* (London, SCM, 1974), pp. 25–48; J. Rogerson, *Genesis 1 – 11* (Sheffield: Sheffield Academic Press, 1991), pp. 11–17.

29. R. Lundin et al., *The Responsibility of Hermeneutics* (Grand Rapids: Eerdmans; Exeter: Paternoster, 1985), p. 23.

30. Cf. J. L. Kugel, 'On the Bible and literary criticism', in *Prooftexts* 1 (1981), pp. 224–225, and the debate between Wenham and Emerton on Gen. 6 – 8.

31. Cf. Culler, *Pursuit*, p. 121, summarizing S. Fish, *Is There a Text in this Class?* (Cambridge, MA, and London: Harvard University Press, 1980).

32. For contrasting opinions, see M. Amihai et al. (eds.), *Narrative Research on the Hebrew Bible, Semeia* 46 (1989), pp. 31–50, and J. Goldingay, 'The patriarchs in Scripture and history', in A. R. Millard and D. J. Wiseman (eds.), *Essays on the Patriarchal Narratives* (Leicester: IVP, 1980; Winona Lake, IN: Eisenbrauns, 1983), ch. 1.

33. E.g. J. Barton, *Reading the Old Testament* (London: Darton, Longman and Todd; Philadelphia, Westminster, 1984), p. 126.

34. Nolan Fewell, 'Feminist reading', p. 79–80, paraphrasing P. de Man, 'Introduction', *Studies in Romanticism* 18 (1979), pp. 495–499.

35. F. Kermode, *The Genesis Secrecy* (Cambridge, MA, and London, Harvard University Press, 1979), e.g. p. 145.

36. McKnight, p. 133; cf. D. M. Gunn, 'New directions in the study of biblical Hebrew narrative', in *JSOT* 39 (1987), pp. 68–69.

37. Moore, p. 121.

38. M. H. Abrams, 'The deconstructive angel', in *Critical Inquiry* 3 (1977), p. 426; Keegan, p. 10.

39. S. R. Suleiman and I. Crossman (eds.), *The Reader in the Text* (Princeton and Oxford: Princeton University Press, 1980), p. 7.

40. F. Lentricchia, *After the New Criticism* (Chicago: University of Chicago Press; London: Athlone, 1980), p. 190.

41. D. Nolan Fewell, *Circle of Sovereignty: A Story of Stories in Daniel 1 – 6* (Sheffield: Sheffield Academic Press, 1988), pp. 17–18.

42. Thiemann, pp. 22–24.

43. K. M. Craig and M. A. Kristjansson, 'Woman reading as men/women reading as women', in G. A. Phillips (ed.), *Poststructural Criticism and the Bible, Semeia* 51 (1990), pp. 121–122.

44. Fish, p. 14.

45. W. G. Jeanrond, *Text and Interpretation* (ET Dublin: Gill and Macmillan, 1988; New York: Crossroad, 1991), p. 113.

46. Keegan, p. 88.

47. E. L. Greenstein, 'Theory and argument in biblical criticism', *HAR* 10 (1986), p. 90, as quoted by R. Polzin, '1 Samuel', *RSR* 15 (1989), p. 305.
48. Moore, pp. 129–130.
49. E. D. Hirsch, 'The politics of theories of interpretation', *Critical Inquiry* 9 (1982), pp. 243–244.
50. K. C. Boone, *The Bible Tells Them So* (Albany, NY: SUNY, 1989; London: SCM, 1990), pp. 67–68.
51. Cf. Boone, p. 67.
52. See J. Culler, *On Deconstruction* (Ithaca, NY: Cornell University Press, 1982; London: Routledge, 1983), p. 17; for examples, see D. Nolan Fewell and D. Gunn, 'Is Coxon a scold?', *JSOT* 45 (1989), pp. 39–43; and J. Barr, *Fundamentalism* (London: SCM; Philadelphia: Westminster, 1977, rev. edn 1981).
53. Against A. K. M. Adam, 'The sign of Jonah', in G. A. Phillips (ed.), *Poststructural Criticism and the Bible, Semeia* 51 (1990), p. 179.
54. Cf. E. D. Hirsch, *Validity in Interpretation* (New Haven and London: Yale University Press, 1967).
55. F. W. Burnett, 'Postmodern biblical exegesis', in G. A. Phillips (ed.), *Poststructural Criticism and the Bible, Semeia* 51 (1990), p. 59.
56. Cf. D. M. Gunn, 'Reading right', in D. Clines et al. (eds.), *The Bible in Three Dimensions* (Sheffield: Sheffield Academic Press, 1990), pp. 62–63.
57. Hirsch, *Validity*, p. 128.
58. G. Josipovici, *The Book of God* (New Haven and London: Yale University Press, 1988), p. 5.
59. L. Schottroff, 'Human solidarity and the goodness of God', in W. Schottroff and W. Stegemann (eds.), *God of the Lowly* (ET Maryknoll, NY: Orbis, 1984).
60. Against S. Wittig, 'A theory of multiple meanings', in J. D. Crossan (ed.), *Polyvalent Narration, Semeia* 9 (1977), p. 90.
61. Moore, pp. 64–65.
62. R. Bambrough, *Reason, Truth and God* (London: Methuen; New York: Harper, 1969), pp. 119–125; cf. D. F. Ford, *Barth and God's Story* (Frankfurt: Lang, 1981, 2nd edn 1985), p. 48.
63. So Hirsch, *Validity*, pp. 8, 140.
64. So H.-G. Gadamer, *Truth and Method* (ET New York: Seabury; London: Sheed and Ward, 1975; rev. edn New York: Crossroad, 1989), e.g. pp. 265–266, 280.
65. Hirsch, *Validity*, pp. 227–230.
66. J. S. Croatto, *Biblical Hermeneutics* (ET Maryknoll, NY: Orbis, 1987), pp. 16–20, 41, following P. Ricoeur, *Interpretation Theory* (Fort Worth: Texas Christian University Press, 1976).
67. Gadamer, p. 353.
68. Gunn, 'New directions', pp. 70–72.
69. ET Marknoll, NY: Orbis, 1976; London: Search, 1977, e.g. pp. 1–2, 238–239.
70. Buttrick, pp. 242–243.

Additional bibliography

K. G. Cannon and E. Schüssler Fiorenza (eds.), *Interpretation for Liberation, Semeia* 47 (1989).

R. Detweiler (ed.), *Reader-Response Approaches to Biblical and Secular Texts, Semeia* 31 (1985).

J. A. Emerton, 'An examination of some attempts to defend the unity of the flood narrative in Genesis', Part ii, *VT* 38 (1988), pp. 1–21.

J. Goldingay, *Approaches to Old Testament Interpretation* (Leicester and Downers Grove, IL: IVP, 1981, rev. edn 1990).

W. J. Iser, *The Act of Reading* (Baltimore and London: Johns Hopkins University Press, 1978).

I. H. Marshall (ed.), *New Testament Interpretation* (Exeter: Paternoster; Grand Rapids: Eerdmans, 1977).

C. Rowland and M. Corner, *Liberating Exegesis* (London: SPCK; Louisville: Westminster John Knox, 1990).

L. M. Russell (ed.), *Feminist Interpretation of the Bible* (Philadelphia: Westminster; Oxford: Blackwell, 1985).

E. Schüssler Fiorenza, *In Memory of Her* (New York: Crossroad, London: SCM, 1983).

M. A. Tolbert (ed.), *The Bible and Feminist Hermeneutics, Semeia* 28 (1983).

P. Trible, *God and the Rhetoric of Sexuality* (Philadelphia: Fortress, 1978; London: SCM, 1991).

————, *Texts of Terror* (Philadelphia: Fortress, 1984; London: SCM, 1991).

G. J. Wenham, 'The coherence of the flood narrative', *VT* 28 (1978), pp. 336–348.

T. R. Wright, *Theology and Literature* (Oxford and New York: Blackwell, 1988).

Part 3
Systematic and historical theology

10

Can we dispense with Chalcedon?

Gerald E. Bray   Vol. 3.2 (1978)

The problem stated

It should come as no surprise to discover that the Chalcedonian Definition, and in particular its relevance both to the teaching of Scripture and contemporary thought, occupies a large place in modern Christological discussion. A confession which has been the touchstone of orthodoxy for fifteen centuries cannot lightly be ignored or abandoned. Yet increasingly there are voices raised calling for either a complete overhaul of the traditional formula, with the object of devising a new statement more in line with current theological ideas, or – more frequently – a recognition of a theological pluralism in the area of Christology in which no one statement of faith could be claimed as definitive. Recently, these voices, which are often backed by an impressive biblical and theological scholarship, have extended the debate to the church at large, and it would now seem that a thorough reassessment of Chalcedon's significance for the life of the church, possibly leading to a downward revision in its status, will not be long delayed.

If the Chalcedonian Definition is to be defended, one must begin with a consideration of its relationship to Scripture.

From the purely historical point of view, it is clear that the framers of the Definition believed themselves to be standing in a tradition of exegesis going back to the apostles themselves. The accusations of philosophizing which are levelled against them today are by no means new, however. Throughout the fourth and fifth centuries, the orthodox party had to contend with an opposition which accused it of deserting the plain words of Scripture in favour of a semi-Platonic construction. Philosophical influences were present, of course, but they were not nearly as decisive as is generally assumed. Great care was taken to find scriptural support for every statement, and although there was often a tendency to allegorize, there is little or nothing in the Definition which cannot be supported, even now, from a biblical text. Even its most vehement detractors usually accuse the Definition only of selective exegesis and conceptual or presuppositional error; given the assumptions of the council, even they will usually agree that it was a masterpiece of dogmatic definition.[1] The real force of modern objections lies elsewhere.

First, it is claimed that Chalcedon endorsed a formula which is *untrue to the meaning of Scripture.* At the heart of this argument lies the contention that Chalcedon thought in ontological terms, whereas the New Testament picture of Christ is largely or even exclusively functional. There is widespread agreement here that the transition from functionalism to ontology was made in the passage from a Palestinian Jewish to a Hellenistic milieu; the chief problem is to determine when this took place. Oscar Cullmann has argued that it was a post-biblical development, an idea now widely shared, in England at least; but R. H. Fuller traces the shift to the New Testament itself,[2] and Martin Hengel puts it back to the very earliest period of Christianity.[3]

Functional Christology rests on a number of presuppositions which give it its validity in the eyes of its exponents. First of these is that the New Testament is the record of the divine plan of salvation (*Heilsgeschichte*) of which Jesus was the divinely appointed agent. Some functionalists see this in a basically orthodox light, and speak of the Son's pre-existence and so on; others do not. In any case, it does not really matter. What counts is what Jesus did, not who he was. Functionalists assume that the work of Christ – whatever may be its relationship to empirical history – was the culmination and fulfilment of Old Testament prophecy and Jewish messianism. The exegetical key (which Chalcedon, of course, ignored) lies in the titles given to Jesus. By examining their significance, and the way in which the New Testament writers selected and conflated them, we may arrive at some understanding of what the Christ-event means for salvation.

On this view, all talk of the person and natures of Christ is beside the point, whether or not it is true. The Chalcedonian fathers arrived at their conclusions because they looked at texts from an ontological standpoint. But many passages, it is claimed, present a picture of Christ which is more accurately called 'subordinationist' or 'adoptionist'. At Chalcedon these were either reinterpreted or ignored, with the result that the council cannot justly claim to have faithfully transcribed all that the New Testament says about Christ. Furthermore, the eclipse of Jewish apocalypticism, at least in the Hellenistic world, deprived the Christian theologians of the knowledge necessary to appreciate the background and meaning of the New Testament. With their essentially non-historical and non-relativistic approach, it is only natural that the framers of the Definition should have read the Bible as if it were a contemporary document, and read all their own presuppositions into it.

A *second* objection, which overlaps with functionalism, but is not identical with it, is the contention that Chalcedon betrays a *confusion of thought-categories*. This means that the Definition draws no clear distinction between the physical-historical frame of reference on the one hand and the metaphysical-mythological frame of reference on the other.[4] Of itself, this confusion does not make Chalcedon unbiblical, of course, since the Scriptures are themselves confused at this point. But while Scripture, as the record of *Heilsgeschichte*, is necessarily mythological, Chalcedon is mistakenly so. According to this line of thinking, the fathers of the council were concerned to present a rationally justifiable account of the Christ-event, but made the mistake of treating New Testament myths, like the story of the virgin birth, as straightforward historical fact. Chalcedon began with the premiss that all Christology must inevitably begin 'from above', with God. Because of this, the Definition necessarily stressed the divinity of Christ as essential to his nature and tacked on the impersonal humanity, if not quite as an afterthought, then at least as a secondary matter of lesser importance. The equilibrium between God and man which the Definition claimed in theory was thus compromised in practice, and made orthodox Christology incurably docetic at its root.

As long as most men were prepared to believe in a world in which supernatural beings were more real and powerful than natural ones, Chalcedonian Christology, though imperfect, was nevertheless an effective instrument for conveying the church's faith. The explosion of the traditional worldview, however, has destroyed its usefulness and it ought now to be scrapped as out of date.

But is it really necessary to revise our estimate of Chalcedon in the light of intellectual developments in the past two centuries? Is it true that the Definition reinterprets Scripture from an alien philosophical perspective with the result that it has produced a narrow, one-sided and docetic Christology? Where does the ontological understanding of Christ come from? It is the answers to these questions which will determine the future course of our Christology in the light of modern philosophical developments.

The appeal to Scripture

As we have already indicated, the authority of the Chalcedonian Definition rests ultimately on its claim to be a comprehensive analysis of biblical teaching. By 'comprehensive' we do not of course mean that it claims to be an exhaustive statement of everything Jesus did and taught – even the Gospels do not claim that much – but rather that it is inclusive of every factor necessary to do justice to the New Testament picture of Christ. It must also be said that the validity of our enterprise depends on the assumption that there is fundamentally only one picture of Jesus in the New Testament, whatever the diversity of approaches. This of course is precisely what is *not* agreed today, but without it, Chalcedon's own claim to rest on the consensus of Scripture ought probably to be ruled out as invalid from the start.

It may however be argued that this is an extreme view, that in fact the different currents in Scripture are logically connected and led to the ontological development of Chalcedon either by a random (but nevertheless understandable) choice of alternatives or by an inner logic present in the kerygma from the beginning. It should not be forgotten, however, that from a purely Chalcedonian standpoint, both these views, however much they may differ from one another, are equally insufficient to do justice to its position with regard to the New Testament evidence. No doubt a Chalcedonian would prefer Martin Hengel's belief that the transition from a functional to an ontological Christology occurred in the wake of the Easter-event to Oscar Cullmann's insistence that such a transition is not to be found in the New Testament at all. But it must also be remembered that even Hengel's view inevitably drives a wedge between the teaching of Jesus and the thought of the early church, an idea which is basically foreign to Chalcedon. Hengel tries to make the wedge as thin as possible, and insists that the theological reflection of the pre-Pauline church was both necessary and inevitable, but we are still some distance from the Chalcedonian position.

The main reasons for this, I would submit, are presuppositional and concern questions of general critical method. Nowadays virtually all students of Christology begin with the assumption that Jesus of Nazareth was a man who had, or thought he had, a special mission from God. What that mission was is hard to say, but it conflicted with contemporary secular and religious authority and he was eventually crucified. From this bare historical minimum some scholars have built up more or less conservative positions, including a belief in the resurrection as an historical event, and even, in a few cases, an acceptance of the incarnation as the ultimate affirmation of Christology.[5] But even the most conservative of these thinkers makes such a development necessarily post-resurrectional. Jesus himself may have said and done any number of things which would act as a catalyst in this process, but whoever arrived at the conclusion that Jesus was God did so by putting two and two together. Whether one thinks the final answer they got was three, four or five then becomes a matter of scholarly opinion, and immaterial from the Chalcedonian standpoint.

Modern reductionist tendencies, the so-called 'Christology from below', together with a reluctance to pronounce any of Jesus' sayings as incontrovertibly genuine, have produced an intellectual climate in which the Chalcedonian Definition has no logical place. But were the fathers of the council therefore wrong in their assumptions and theological method? Does the New Testament really support modern critical theories in the way that their defenders claim? Here the crucial question is whether the New Testament shows signs of theological development into an ontological position. The Chalcedonian fathers might have agreed that it does, but they would have located this in the teaching of Jesus himself. It was Jesus who made the fundamental change from a functional to an ontological Christology, not his disciples or the early church. The apostles, on this view, were the transmitters of a teaching which they had received from Jesus; they were not creative theologians in their own right.

Now it would be hard to deny that the *prima facie* New Testament evidence lends support to this second view. Not everyone would agree, of course, but as long as considerable allowance is made for theological developments within the early church colouring the narrative, it is probable that the majority of scholars would be prepared to grant this much. Many indeed would go a good deal farther and grant that the historical Jesus claimed for himself such divine prerogatives as the power to forgive sins, while leaving open the question of his claim to ontological divinity.[6]

Traditionally, research of this kind has concentrated on the synoptic Gospels, because of widespread doubts as to the historical reliability of John. These doubts have now diminished considerably, although it is probably still true to say that most scholars believe that the ontological bias of the fourth Gospel represents a modification of the original tradition.[7] If this is true, then Chalcedonian Christology, which relies heavily on the fourth Gospel, is derivative and does not represent Jesus' self-understanding.

Ontology in the Gospel of John

I should like to begin an investigation of this Gospel's evidence with some words of Barnabas Lindars: 'John, with his unerring capacity to pierce through to the inner meaning of the primitive logia, has the unique distinction of bringing to expression on the basis of them the deepest and most compelling interpretation of Jesus' self-understanding before God.'[8] This statement represents perhaps the most conservative scholarly opinion today. But is it really tenable? Are not many of the 'primitive logia' themselves so shot through with ontological assumptions that it is inconceivable for them to have existed otherwise?

Let us take, for example, *the story of Nicodemus*. In spite of many difficulties there would appear to be little reason to doubt the essentially authentic character of this story – the awareness of a time before hostility between Jesus and the Pharisees had polarized into open warfare, the use of characteristic Semitic sayings like 'Amen, amen, I say unto you,' the intense Jewishness of the argument and Jesus' description of himself as Son of man all tell in its favour. Nicodemus perceived Jesus to be 'a teacher come from God' (John 3:2, RSV), which in effect meant that Jesus was a man of the same class as himself (cf. verse 10) but with special power to perform miracles. This is not good enough for Jesus, however, who promptly begins a long discourse on ontology, first in general terms and then, with increasing concentration, focusing on himself. Nicodemus is led on by stages, but the final result is never in doubt. The whole story anticipates the conclusion in such a way that it does not seem possible that it could be a modification of anything. There is in fact nothing very extraordinary about it before verse 13, but it would be strange if this verse is a later addition put in by John, since it is the logical climax to the whole story. There is no question of a progression from a functional to an ontological Christology, but only from a universal ontology to a particular one. Yet such a 'Greek' idea would hardly have been intruded into a conversation with a Pharisee! From the start, moreover, Jesus was busily scrapping Nicodemus' presuppositions, not building on them – a fact which only confused him, and contributed further to the general incomprehension surrounding Jesus and his teaching.

The possibility that John constructed the Nicodemus story according to a preconceived plan is diminished when we look at the story of *the woman at the well*, which is completely different in every way except for the ontological implications of Jesus' words. The woman, struck by Jesus' willingness to speak to her, enquires of him the reason for such unusual behaviour. Jesus sidesteps the question, as usual, and tries to focus her mind on his person (verse 10). When she misunderstands him completely, Jesus shifts his ground to the woman herself, by putting his finger on her past life. Now the woman is truly shaken, but she does no more than call Jesus a prophet, and asks him the most awkward – and at the same time the most obvious – theological question she can think of. Again, Jesus leads her into an ontological consideration – God is spirit and therefore desires spiritual worship. The woman, however, has still not got beyond the fact that Jesus knew her past life. But, in her understanding, the man who would reveal such things was the Messiah – could this be Jesus?

Even after Jesus admits this, however, she is still only half-convinced, and has seen nothing beyond the aspect of Jesus' teaching which directly affected her. The villagers, however, pursued the matter further, and eventually arrived at the confession that Jesus was the saviour of the world. Many would no doubt agree with Cullmann that this is still a functional, not an ontological confession, but on what was this based? Certainly not on post-Easter reflection, but on Jesus' teaching which, if it bore any relation at all to what he said to the woman, was essentially directed towards an ontological understanding. It seems probable, in fact, that the villagers confessed Jesus the saviour as a person, without any very clear idea – and certainly no experience – of what this would mean in practice. The absence of an explanation just where one would most expect it only confirms this view.

The story of the woman shows us clearly that *Christological titles*, although Jesus was prepared to accept them, could not adequately convey the full extent of his message because of the limitations of the thought-pattern in which they were embedded. This is a theme which recurs later in the Gospel (e.g. 7:25–31). As we see from chapter 1, there were many people who were only too ready to slap a messianic label on an unusual figure, and this ties in well with what Josephus and others tell us of this period in Palestine. Thus Jesus could publicize his claim only with caution – a feature of his ministry which is amply confirmed in the synoptic tradition, and in Mark in particular.

Jesus' attitude to Christological titles was therefore hesitant, but this is still a very long way from *the attitude of John the Baptist*, who not only refused to apply them to himself, but refused to use them in his descriptions of the coming one as well – an indication that John did not regard them as suitable for him either. Instead, John describes his mission at length in ways which indicate that he was expecting someone more than the popular version of the Messiah; indeed, that the one expected was none other than God himself (1:23). Later, anthropomorphic terms become more prominent, but there is still much to indicate that we are not to think of a man in the ordinary sense (1:30). It is only when Jesus appears that the connection becomes clear, but the build-up cannot fail to raise questions which go far beyond the range of a functional Christology.

The appearance of Jesus at this point in the Gospel turns our attention once more to his role. Both here and throughout the Gospel we are reminded of his favourite self-description, *Son of man*, and most would agree that this is an authentic touch. Our problem is to discover whether it is functional or ontological in meaning. Considered as a title, *huios tou anthrōpou* is vague and obscure, the more so because it was not developed by the early church. Lindars claims that John was unique in this respect, but while he talks freely of his bringing out the inner meaning, etc., he stops short of crediting John with an ontological understanding of the term. This hesitation would seem to be unnecessary, however, from a consideration of John 5:25–27. Here the Son of God is identified with the Son of man in a way which Lindars claims makes it necessary to understand the latter as the figure of Daniel 7:13. If this is correct, then it is testimony of the greatest importance. The Danielic Son of man was a heavenly figure whose functions on earth were extensions of his heavenly being; they were not its cause or justification (e.g. through obedience). The same point is made in John 3:13–16, with even greater clarity.

Furthermore, this understanding of Son of man cannot have been a purely Johannine insight. The independent witness of the synoptic Gospels makes the connection with Daniel explicit at the trial of Jesus (Matt. 26:64; Mark 14:62; Luke 22:69). The priests clearly understood Jesus' remarks as blasphemy, and it is well known how difficult it is to account for Jesus' condemnation if this is disregarded. If this is so, however, we have two independent witnesses to the fact that Jesus himself claimed to be the divine Son of man and that this was meant to be understood ontologically and not merely functionally.

Ontology – Hebrew or Greek?

The scandal and incomprehension which greeted Jesus' remarks can in fact be understood only on the basis of Hebraic ontology. It is doubtless true that the Jewish concept of the Messiah was essentially functional, at least in mainstream Judaism, and this was inevitable given their concept of God. It is surely not necessary to remind ourselves that at least from the time of Moses, Hebrew religion had had a strong ontological base – not only was God the Absolute Existent, but there was a radical and unbridgeable separation between him and man in their respective natures. This did not preclude a certain functional unity, of course – God was frequently portrayed in the Old Testament in anthropomorphic terms, and his voice spoke through human agents – but never was there any suggestion that God and man might or could be one. This rigid separation, moreover, carried through to all the many phases and branches of Judaism and nowhere, as far as I know, is any earthly figure apotheosized. Even those who come closest, like Enoch and Elijah, are carefully distinguished from God in his essence.

Now, had Jesus been content to fit into this pattern, he might well have evoked scribal curiosity, after the manner of John the Baptist, but he would hardly have attracted the ontological interest which they evidently had in him. The root of the problem seems to have been that Jesus called God his father.

There is no reason to doubt the historical accuracy of this and, in a sense, it is true that the Old Testament portrays the relationship of Israel to God as that of a son to his father. There is therefore no *a priori* reason why Cullmann should not be right to say that Jesus innovated only in individualizing this concept and applying it to himself.[10] Unfortunately, this possibility recedes dramatically when we look at the reaction Jesus provoked. No-one valued the special position of Israel more than the scribes and Pharisees, and if this was what Jesus meant, no-one was in a better position than they to appreciate it. It is quite untrue to Scripture to suggest that their opposition to Jesus was from the beginning so intense that they were incapable of seeing so obvious a point.

It is quite clear, however, from the sequence of events in John 5:14–18 that this is not the kind of sonship Jesus had in mind. His was a sonship not of legal inheritance, but of essence – a familiar Semitic idiom, strange only in the context of a man claiming to be related to God in this way. The following verses make the intimacy of the relationship even plainer. However much these verses may lend themselves to a functional interpretation, I would submit that verse 21 is decisive for an ontological viewpoint. Here the construction 'As the Father ... so also the Son ...' establishes identity of action; what is true of the Father is equally true of the Son. But the phrase 'to whom he will' makes it plain that the Son is both equal to the Father *and autonomous* – an impossibility unless he is also God. Moreover, this is not a theological construction grafted on to Jesus' original words – it is implicit in his whole concept of Sonship from the beginning.

It was when they realized this fundamental difference about Jesus' claims that the Jewish leaders had him arrested and put to death. This was their solution to the ontological problem of Jesus – no man could be God, therefore he was a blasphemer. The early Christians, however, were faced with a problem scarcely less serious. For how could one accept a Hebraic concept of deity and yet still affirm that the man Jesus was God? At one extreme was the possibility that Jesus was not a man at all, but God in a borrowed body. At the other extreme was the view that Jesus was not really God, but merely some kind of divine man. Both these views were put forward in antiquity, but neither one, in its pure form at least, was the basis of any major heresy. The reason for this was that the problem for Greek minds lay elsewhere.

Jewish Christians had trouble accommodating a God-man, but their difficulties were as nothing compared with those of the Greeks. The Jews, after all, began with the right concept of ontological divinity, an idea which was largely missing in the Greek world. Greek Christians in fact were fighting two battles at once – on the one hand, they had to fight for a Hebraic conception of God; on the other, they had to keep the God-man Jesus intact.

Greek paganism, it is true, had no difficulty with divine-human intermediaries. Greek mythology and philosophy were both rooted in an ontological hierarchy of beings graded from top to bottom and shading into one another rather like a vertical rainbow. So god-men existed quite happily in the intermediate zone, but in principle divinization was possible for anyone, and the philosophical practice of Apathy, for instance, was designed to hasten the process.

The Hebrew God, however, did not fit this chain of being at all. (Marcion disagreed, but he was a unique case.) But many Greeks refused, or were unable, to abandon their philosophical ideas. So, the Hebrew God was put at one end of the chain, with an absolute barrier between his essence and any created thing. But because God was unique, he was alone at the head of the chain, with all creation lower down; because of his absolute separation, he could not communicate directly with this creation, but needed a mediator (*mesitēs*). This mediator was like him in every way, except that he was created. As such he could move down the scale, make himself a little lower than the angels and become man, in order to raise man again to the number two spot in the hierarchy. This, essentially, was the philosophical background of Arius, which led to his peculiar form of subordinationism. As a heresy it was very subtle, especially since there were many biblical texts which appeared to support his subordinationist position.

Arianism was by no means the only ancient heresy, of course, but it was the one which proved most difficult to refute. Not only did the orthodox party have to maintain the complete ontological otherness of God, which Arius was so concerned to assert; it also had to argue for the full divinity of the man Jesus in a way which would command full biblical support. They did this by relying heavily on the Gospels, especially John. The prologue to the fourth Gospel showed that there was more than one hypostasis in God. We cannot pause to examine the logic of trinitarian doctrine, but eventually equilibrium was established between the unity and the diversity within the Godhead in a way which avoided any suggestion of Platonic emanation. This was sufficient to condemn the subordinationism of Arius, but it left open the problem of the hypostatic union.

The Chalcedonian solution

Given that the second person of the Trinity was a pre-existent divine hypostasis, how could he be the man Jesus at the same time? Everyone agreed that God and man had come together in Christ, but it was impossible to agree as to how this had occurred. Every solution proposed seemed to lead either to dualism, in which God and man came together (*synchōrēsis*) without actually uniting, or to a *tertium quid*, in which the fusion of God and man produced a being who was neither the one nor the other but contained elements of both. The former solution safeguarded the distinction of the natures while sacrificing the unity of the person; the latter held up the unity of the person but compromised the separation of the natures. The first of these views was propounded by Nestorius, the second by Apollinarius, and later, in a somewhat different form, by the Monophysites of Alexandria.

The Chalcedonian solution to this dilemma was as follows. The divine and human natures were distinct and could not be confused in any way. Each nature was complete in itself and obeyed its own internal laws. The divine nature was eternal, the human nature assumed in the incarnation. Jesus, who was only one person, was therefore divine. On the other hand, his humanity was not a veil covering this divinity, in the way that ancient philosophy imagined the flesh to be covering the soul. All such dualism was ruled out by the virginal conception – usually called, mistakenly, the virgin birth – by which the divine hypostasis became man in the womb of the virgin Mary. Mary was therefore of necessity the *Theotokos*, or God-bearer. Nestorius had protested against this on the ground that Mary was not the mother of Christ's divinity, but although this was certainly agreed to in principle, Nestorius' preference of the title *Christotokos* for Mary could not be admitted because of its implied dualism. The union between God and man was such as to preclude the independent existence of the manhood – which is the meaning of Leo's phrase 'impersonal humanity'.

Furthermore, the two natures, though united, continued to possess the characteristics proper to them, which is why Jesus was portrayed in the Gospels as experiencing human suffering yet at the same time raising men from the dead, or walking on water. No attempt was made to explain this further – Chalcedon contented itself with the mystery that Jesus was one person 'made known in two natures'. R. V. Sellers has pointed out the significance of this *gnōrizomenos* ('made known') for understanding the true meaning of the Definition, and claims that it goes a long way towards answering many modern objections to the doctrine.[11] Chalcedon did not claim to know how the hypostatic union occurred in terms of biology or genetics – such knowledge was in any case beyond human understanding. What it did claim was that the empirical, historical Jesus was a God-man, and that it had established, in the light of Scripture, the boundaries within which this perfect union must be seen in order to avoid compromising the evidence.

Chalcedon today

Is this solution still valid today? If so, is it still necessary? This is the question which most modern theologians, even those who are prepared to accept Chalcedon in its context, are now raising. Let us examine some of these objections to see whether they are in fact as cogent as their proponents claim.

1. Probably the most damaging modern objection to the Definition is the charge *that it is fundamentally docetic.* According to this way of thinking, it is impossible to be fully a man and yet God at the same time. Chalcedon tried to give equal weight to both, but in fact erred on the side of the divine nature. The Chalcedonian Christ is accused of being less than fully human because (a) he is sinless; (b) he is genetically absurd; (c) he lacks a human personality.

These objections arise, however, because their proponents have a defective understanding of what human nature is. In fact, it is precisely because of this defective ontology of man that a functional Christology has seemed to be necessary. Those who take this line define humanity empirically – what I am, man is. But that is not the biblical view of man at all. In the Bible, sin, for example, is not a part of human nature but a corruption of it; its present universality is the result of inheritance by common descent, but it is not inherent in man's nature. It is true that solidarity with the human race requires descent from Adam, but Jesus had this through his mother. We all know what problems the church has had over the question of Mary's sinfulness, but I would suggest that this was adequately nullified by the word *Theotokos* in the Definition and by the almost contemporary statement in the Athanasian Creed which speaks of the hypostatic union 'not by conversion of the Godhead into flesh, but by taking of the Manhood into God'. The power of the greater assumed and consequently overcame the weakness of the lesser substance. This is not docetism, as is so often alleged, but the very opposite. Christ was not a freak, but the firstborn of a new creation, the prototype of the perfection to which every Christian aspires. The Chalcedonians did not take themselves as the norm of humanity, but Christ, the second Adam. Their concern was not to make him 'one of them', but to make themselves some of his.

The genetic argument is more difficult, particularly as the council was quite unaware of modern biology. Nevertheless, they clearly believed that the virgin birth was a miracle and that it did not impair Jesus' humanity. Adam, after all, had not come into being by the procreative process, nor had Eve. Natural procreation may be normal in our experience, but it is not necessary for humanity. Nor should we forget his uniqueness – Jesus was fully man, but he was certainly not *merely* man. One might possibly draw the analogy of dual nationality, where a man might have two distinct identities and yet remain the same person. When he is with us, we may assimilate him to ourselves, even to the point where we are surprised if we discover that the same person speaks a different language and carries within him a completely different set of cultural references. Such a man, of course, is neither a schizophrenic nor an impossibility; it is merely that we have failed to grasp the complete situation. So it is, on a different level, with Jesus. The fact that his Father is 'foreign' in some sense to us does not exclude him from full participation in our life as one of us; it means rather that we must broaden our horizons to accommodate someone who is both like us and different at the same time.

The argument that the Chalcedonian Christ lacks a human personality is sheer misunderstanding. Leo the Great described Christ's humanity as 'impersonal' simply in order to emphasize that Jesus was never a *mere* man – in other words, that as God and man together, he was not a split personality. Of course, we must also pay attention to the meaning of the word 'person', which means simply an 'autonomous individuality', within which there is a wide range of variable characteristics composing the personality. These can and do change – sometimes quite drastically – without, however, compromising the objective existence of the individual concerned. Jesus' personality was provided for by the insistence that he had a human soul and a human will – though this second point was not clarified until later.

The failure of a Christology based on principles like these may be seen from the case of John Robinson. Robinson is as insistent as anyone could be in stressing the humanity of Jesus in empirical terms. For him, Jesus is not God incarnate but a God-filled human personality. Nevertheless, Jesus is still unique. Why? Because it is through him that we perceive God. As Robinson has written: 'It is in Jesus, and Jesus alone, that there is nothing of self to be seen, but solely the ultimate, unconditional love of God. It is as he emptied himself utterly of himself that he became the carrier of the "name which is above every other name".'[12] But this is thoroughly docetic. Why? Because a functional Christology like Robinson's finds itself invariably in an ontological impasse. It tries to re-emphasize the humanity of Jesus by stripping him of his Chalcedonian divinity, but at the same time it wants to reassert that Jesus revealed God as no other man has ever done. In practice, of course, this is possible only by overcoming the humanity, which can only be a barrier to the perception of God. The more perfect the divine revelation is, the more the humanity is superseded, until it vanishes entirely. The Chalcedonian position is nothing like this – Jesus' humanity in orthodox thought is not a barrier but a means to the perception of God.

Those who take Robinson's line, if they are consistent, must eventually see that Jesus' humanity does not and cannot disappear, from which they conclude that he was not unique as a revealer of God, since other great men have achieved remarkable degrees of self-abnegation. This line, recently propounded by John Hick and Dennis Nineham, among others, makes Jesus but one more extraordinary man, and is the end of Christianity as a distinctive, coherent religion. Yet it must be remembered that *The Myth of God Incarnate* is not a freak development, but the logical outcome of a functionalist Christology.

2. The second major objection to Chalcedon concerns *its supposed out-of-date Hellenism*. According to this argument, the Definition was a fine thing in its day, but now with new philosophies and new cultures we need a new statement of faith.

Superficially this sounds very plausible – it is all a question of translation, we are told, of the need to find dynamic equivalents for ideas which are no longer current. Unfortunately, this point of view ignores the fact that the Definition presents us with a thought-world which claims eternal validity and relevance. We are too ready to assume that modern equivalents can be found for terms like 'person', 'nature' and 'substance'. We forget that the early Christians did not just slide into Platonism – on the contrary, they were all too acutely aware of the dangers of doing just that and fought to keep as close to the Bible as possible in their terminology and expressions. It is true, of course, that words like *ousia*, *physis* and *hypostasis* were used in Greek philosophy, but not in the same way. Likewise other terms simply had to be invented, like *homoousios*, or borrowed from quite different disciplines, like *prosōpon*. Christian dogmatic concepts may have been expressed in words taken from the surrounding culture, but they do not depend on it.

We have already argued that the ontological quest of the early church arose from an Old Testament view of God. In the same way, the need to express the reality of the incarnate Christ arose from, and was governed by, New Testament requirements. Chalcedon did not adopt philosophy; it took some basic philosophical words and forged a theology based on Scripture. Its logic is a systematization of the logic inherent in Scripture, not a philosophical corruption of primitive texts. For that reason, although it may be simplified for mass consumption, it can never be replaced. Ontological Christology is part of the biblical revelation which cannot and must not be compromised in the name of historical and/or cultural relativism.

Conversion to Christ today can only mean what it meant to our ancestors – that we must put on a new mind and a new heart as men and women transformed by the transcendent power of the Christian gospel. This is the reality which is enshrined in the Chalcedonian Definition which will stand unchanged and unsurpassed as long as Christian faith endures.

Notes

1. Thus Maurice Wiles, 'Does Christology rest on a mistake?' in S. W. Sykes and J. P. Clayton (eds.), *Christ, Faith and History* (Cambridge, 1972), pp. 3–12.
2. *The Foundations of New Testament Christology* (London, 1965).
3. *The Son of God* (London, 1976).
4. One of Wiles's key points, op. cit.
5. E.g. W. Pannenberg, *Jesus, God and Man* (London, 1964).
6. So H. Schlier, 'Amen', in *Theological Dictionary of the New Testament*; B. Fuchs, *Studies of the Historical Jesus* (London, 1964), p. 36; G. Bornkamm, *Jesus of Nazareth* (London, 1960), p. 57, etc.
7. I. H. Marshall, *The Origins of New Testament Christology* (Leicester, 1977).
8. B. Lindars, in B. Lindars and S. S. Smalley (eds.), *Christ and Spirit in the New Testament* (Cambridge, 1973), p. 60.
9. See H. Schlier, op. cit.
10. *The Christology of the New Testament* (London, 1959), pp. 275–290.
11. *The Council of Chalcedon* (London, 1953), pp. 216ff.
12. *Honest to God* (London, 1963), p. 74.

11

James Barr on 'fundamentalism'

A review article

David F. Wright   Vol. 3.3 (1978)

It is surely remarkable that a prominent biblical scholar who has taught in Scotland, the USA and England should have to embark on a programme of research in order to write about one of the major currents of Christian life in Britain, conservative evangelicalism. Such is the ignorance of the movement that prevails in other sectors of the church and theology. The reasons for this fact are no doubt complex, but this much is obvious, that Barr will have had no difficulty finding out about his subject, for his analysis is largely based on literature freely available in the bookshops. His work is to be welcomed as a serious attempt to correct a major defect in the internal ecumenism of British Christianity. It may at least be hoped that as a consequence conservative evangelicals will find themselves better understood by other Christians.

As a pioneer Barr perhaps deserves special consideration from a reviewer. It must nevertheless be pointed out that his research displays grave limitations. His familiarity with the works of leading evangelical scholars like John Stott, F. F. Bruce, Earle Ellis, Ralph Martin, G. W. Bromiley and Howard Marshall is severely restricted and rarely up to date. By ignoring G. C. Berkouwer altogether, Barr manages to extend Van Til's almost total rejection of Karl Barth to evangelicals in general (p. 220). He never mentions Tyndale House and its library or the Tyndale Fellowship or Latimer House, and he appears to be unacquainted with evangelical periodicals. The National Assemblies of Evangelicals in Britain in recent years, the National Evangelical Anglican Congress at Keele in 1967 and the Lausanne Congress of 1974, seem to lie beyond Barr's ken, so that he remains unaware of important developments in evangelical thought, including the element of self-criticism he failed to find in

Britain (pp. 222, 353). On one point, evangelical attitudes to evolution, the dated quality of Barr's work has left him ignorant of a recent anti-evolutionist reaction (p. 92).

It would have been helpful if Barr had identified the other critical observers of conservative evangelicalism he refers to from time to time, and also been more open about his own fundamentalist past which he hints at once or twice. One can understand but not condone his disingenuousness about his earlier involvement with a variety of Christianity he now patently detests. A quarter of a century ago he was president of the Christian Union at Edinburgh University. This may be thought to give him a peculiar authority to write on this subject, but its significance is probably to be found more in the old-fashioned flavour of some of his material and in the fact that he directs his fire chiefly against the British IVF (now UCCF) and IVP publications. Augustine of Hippo spent most of his twenties in the ranks of Manichaeism, which after his catholic conversion he proceeded to assail with both the insight and the vehemence of an ex-Manichaean. Barr is no Augustine, but the parallel may still hold.

Some explanation is certainly needed why a book which sets out to analyse and understand (p. 9) becomes a hatchet job. Like a child with the pile of wooden bricks on the cover, Barr is bent on demolishing evangelicalism. A sympathetic reviewer in *The Scotsman* called him 'ruthless', and so he is. It will be no surprise if the book embitters relations between different kinds of Christians. Time and again I found my own taste soured by the harsh caricatures, exaggerations and even scurrilities of Barr's arguments (e.g. pp. 98, 99, 101, 120, 164, 172, 247). The tone is set on the very first page which selects three negative features (biblical inerrancy, hostility to modern theology and biblical criticism, rejection of non-evangelicals as not true Christians) as 'the most pronounced characteristics' of conservative evangelicalism.

One of the most perceptive contributions to the 1955–56 debate on fundamentalism was entitled *The Many Fundamentalisms* (by Cyril Bowles, then Principal of Ridley Hall, Cambridge, and now Bishop of Derby). Barr shows some of the symptoms of the fundamentalism of the biblical critic. This may explain why he conceives of evangelicalism chiefly as anti-criticism (pp. 208, 344), and why he endeavours to contrast Reformation and evangelical theologies on the wholly tautological grounds that 'theology in the pre-critical period was not animated by the anti-critical animus and passion of modern conservative theology' (p. 174). While poking fun at the extravagances of conservative scholars, he shows little awareness of the follies and excesses of liberal criticism. I cannot forget the day when a lecturer at Cambridge tried to convince us that Matthew was so obsessed with Old Testament proof texts that he actually believed Jesus rode into Jerusalem on *both* a donkey *and* a donkey's colt *at the same time* (Matt. 21:1–8)! Barr would have helped evangelicals to come to terms with biblical criticism, as indeed very many have done, if he had directed some of his fire against those practitioners who have brought it into so much discredit.

But then Barr's book as a whole seems so ill-suited to educate conservative Christians that it is doubtful whether it was written with them in mind at all. He expects an unfavourable reception from evangelical readers, and is really intent on addressing to outsiders a dissuasive from 'fundamentalism'. He is not at all sure that conservative evangelicals should be tolerated in the churches (pp. 343–344). Such a posture is nothing new, although it may not be entirely accidental that it coincides with other signs of renewed pressure against evangelicals.

Barr's critical-fundamentalist cast of mind is probably linked to his antipathy to theology and often theologians (as distinct from biblical and historical scholarship and scholars), which is well known from some of his earlier writings. 'Biblical theology' and neo-orthodoxy come under attack again here, sometimes when Barr is overtly attacking only conservatives. His own theological convictions remain unclear, except that they are subservient to the currents of liberal criticism (pp. 185, 186). The chapter on 'Fundamentalism and Theology' is the most lamentable in the book. Exaggerations abound (e.g. 'In fundamentalism all relations with non-conservative theology are purely polemical', p. 163), even absurdities ('If you ask what is the reason why one should be a conservative evangelical, rather than some other sort of Christian, the answer will very likely be: because of sin', p. 177), while his attempt to show that the line of continuity from Luther and Calvin runs down to, let us say, *The Myth of God Incarnate*, rather than to evangelicalism, is myopic. Barr is clearly not at home in historical theology; he discounts an Athanasian Christology (p. 171), and twice misconstrues the Westminster Confession (pp. 261ff., 294). Above all, Barr's distaste for theology may be responsible for his fastening on the formally negative, technical concept of inerrancy as the most significant feature of the evangelical view of Scripture. In reality, the divine authority of the Bible, which is a positive theological principle, is of far greater importance.

One of Barr's tactics is the age-old policy of divide and conquer. He arrays against conservative evangelicalism not only modern theology (undefined – Barth or Tillich?) but also the Reformation, the Westminster Confession and in important respects the Princeton theology of the Hodges and Warfield. More interestingly, he finds popular evangelicalism less objectionable than scholarly evangelicalism. It is almost as if he is afraid of the increasing prominence of evangelicals in professional biblical circles. He is anxious to assure his readers that biblical criticism is not on the wane (pp. 132–133), which is undoubtedly true. But it remains a half-truth unless one adds that a growing number of biblical critics remain 'fundamentalists', which Barr cannot stomach. For Barr, a conservative evangelical has no business engaging in biblical criticism unless he allows the latter to overthrow his evangelicalism. He is in fact a very difficult man to please. When evangelicals learn from others, they are hanging on their coat-tails (p. 232), when they quote non-evangelical writers, it implies no lessening of hostility towards them (p. 233). When evangelicals are politically and socially conservative, it is the fault of their conservative evangelicalism, but when they are more to the left, their socialism has nothing to do with their evangelical faith (p. 108).

It is partly the limitations of Barr's research which have led him seriously to underestimate the diversity of British evangelicalism (e.g. he has missed the Reformed evangelical's pursuit of a Christian society, p. 100). At the same time, on a host of issues he is unaware of the strong winds of change blowing through the movement. But the neat, static quality of the picture he paints is also integral to his campaign of isolation and demolition. If he encounters a writer or a viewpoint which does not fit in with his schematic presentation, he discounts them as 'not really conservative' (p. 233).

A number of Barr's criticisms fail to take into account the minority-outsider position that evangelicalism has had to occupy until relatively recent times. This helps to explain, for example, why evangelicals have often excluded non-evangelicals from their platforms. Things are changing here too, now that evangelicals do not always have to fight for the right to be heard. But when Barr alleges that it is 'fundamentalist policy' to reject non-conservative arguments unheard, the boot is really on the other foot, at any rate in the world of biblical and theological study. A brief perusal of the bookshelves of conservatives and non-conservatives would rapidly have robbed Barr of this complaint.

In fact, I repeatedly felt that Barr's arguments could be stood completely on their head. He accuses evangelicalism of being parasitic on non-evangelical Christianity, whereas in reality the ranks of ecclesiastical and theological leaders in Britain would be much thinner without those won to the Christian faith by evangelicals and later wooed to more respectable brands of Christianity. When Barr discovers a kind of evangelical anticlericalism echoing 'the typical secularistic reaction of irreligious man' (p. 101), I am less convinced than I was by John Robinson's earlier highlighting of a strong clericalist streak among evangelicals in the major churches.

The general flavour and gross simplifications of the book are regrettable for the further supremely important reason that they may hinder evangelicals from taking to heart its *many* valid criticisms of evangelicalism. Some of these merit special mention.

1. Evangelicals generally lack a satisfactory understanding of doctrinal development. As a consequence, theology is rarely seen as a constructive and creative task (p. 223), and the most overtly developed Christian doctrine, that of the Trinity, enjoys little more than formal recognition in much evangelicalism (pp. 176–177). As so often, however, Barr spoils a sound point by blatant misrepresentation (the traditional faith of the church and the Fathers count so little for evangelicals that on these grounds they would just as readily be unitarians as Trinitarians – p. 177), which he has earlier directly contradicted ('true fundamentalism' has no role for theology other than the conservation and reiteration of tradition – p. 162).

2. One of our most urgent unfinished tasks is the elaboration of a satisfactory doctrine of Scripture for an era of biblical criticism. The development of critical, i.e. literary and historical, study of the Bible constitutes one of the great divides in Christian history; there can be no turning the clock back. We cannot afford to rest on Warfield's laurels, but must meet the challenges of today. In particular, we have to work out what it means to be faithful at *one and the same time both* to the doctrinal approach to Scripture as the Word of God *and* to the historical treatment of Scripture as the words of men. It is at this point that Barr's strictures are most acute and accurate – and it is a crucially central point.

3. We must be careful not to appear to usurp the divine prerogative in our use of terms like 'a Christian'. Unnecessary offence has clearly been given by statements like 'He is not a Christian', when what is meant is 'He is not an evangelical (Christian)'. The former may have its place in an evangelistic context, but not in the setting of differences among professing Christians. God alone knows those who are his.

4. We must dare to be more self-critical of false structures of thought and practice within our own ranks. Barr's target here is dispensationalism, whose prevalence I feel he considerably exaggerates, partly because his evidence is out of date, and whose appeal and significance he surrounds with considerable speculation. Nevertheless he carries conviction in claiming that we have been soft on such internal evangelical excesses.

5. Evangelicals' economic, political and social attitudes have often been unthinkingly conformist and complacent. Barr is again woefully behind the times (the Shaftesbury Project, for instance, is unmentioned) and blind to the increasing diversity of evangelical viewpoints. Yet we do well to heed his comments.

6. Barr repeatedly claims to have detected a rationalistic streak in

evangelical writings. Some of his examples suggest that a lack of confidence in accepting the miraculous has fostered a rationalizing outlook at times. But big questions arise here, for example, of the relation between historical evidence and acts of God, which Barr is in no position to settle. His argument in the chapter on 'Miracles and the Supernatural' is open to objection at several points. There is no necessary inconsistency, as Barr assumes (seeking to divide J. N. D. Anderson and G. E. Ladd and conquer), between an apologetic appeal to the evidence for the resurrection and the recognition that the raising of Jesus from the dead is an act of God *sui generis*. And it is frankly incredible, at least for those of us who know and read liberal biblical critics, that their beliefs about miracles or the supernatural do not influence their historico-literary study of the Bible (p. 236). It simply begs the whole issue (or sells the pass) to assert that 'even where miracles and supernatural events are related, the historical and literary questions can be and should be treated as a matter of normal human relations' (p. 237).

Barr has produced a book of remarkable ingenuity and industry which is liable to mislead many of its readers. Very few indeed outside the ranks of evangelicals will be sufficiently well read to assess his accuracy. Indeed, 'Barr' is likely to become a substitute for first-hand familiarity with conservative evangelicalism and to be quoted authoritatively in the judgments of the ignorant. In so far as he hoped to teach evangelicals a better way, he has only himself to blame if he misses the mark. We owe it to ourselves, if not to him, to see that he does not.

James Barr's Fundamentalism *is published by SCM Press, London, 1977 (379 pp.).*

© David F. Wright 1978

12

A taproot of radicalism

Paul Helm   Vol. 11.1 (1985)

Biblical theologians are sometimes puzzled by the radical attacks made by assumedly Christian theologians upon the evidential value of the words and work of Jesus presented in the New Testament. While they can readily appreciate the views of those who argue, on textual and historical grounds, that this or that particular miracle story is unauthentic, even though they may not share those views, they find it almost incredible that scholars should refuse to take the New Testament documents seriously, at face value. For it seems as if such scholars are flying in the face of a lot of evidence. If the New Testament contained an account of only one miracle, or of one event which ought reasonably to be interpreted as a miracle, one could understand a certain scepticism. But who could responsibly reject all the data?

Facts and interpretations

Various theories have been offered to explain this state of affairs by people who deplore it. For some it is a conspiracy to subvert the faith. For others it is the result of baseless speculation. For others still it is the latest slither down the slippery slope, a slide which began a century or more ago, while for others it is a case of theologians trying to snatch the headlines. For any of these claims to be persuasive it would be necessary to produce some facts which only they account for. But are there such facts? Is there any evidence, for instance, that in the last hundred years first one tenet of the faith and then another has been denied because the first has been denied, with cumulative effect?

Even if there were such confirmatory evidence, it would still rather miss the point, just as it misses the point to say that such radicalism is 'out of date'. For the question is not whether radical theologians have *motives* for their radicalism, but whether they have *reasons* for it, reasons that will stand up to scrutiny and that will constrain objective enquirers to join them. Whether the radical is reluctant or eager, whether he works with ill-will or goodwill – these are irrelevant considerations for someone who wants to know whether or not he ought to be a radical.

So the attitude which rejects radicalism because it allegedly flies in the face of the evidence of the New Testament, though widespread, is naïve.

It is understandable that a Christian theological student, immersed in the details of his study of the New Testament, should not be able to see much beyond these details. But he is wrong not to do so, and particularly wrong if what he is ultimately trying to do is to integrate the fruits of his study into responsible Christian confession and witness.

In terms of a familiar distinction, between *data* and *theory*, or between *facts* and *interpretation*, the narratives of the Gospels may be thought of as the *data* or *facts*. (Of course, these facts, because they are in the form of words and clauses and sentences, are the result of lexical and grammatical interpretation, but this can be taken for granted in what follows.) The theological student's bewilderment at the wholesale dismissal of the miraculous in the New Testament by theologians and others may arise from a failure to see that this rejection is not simply a denial of the factual character of certain events on the grounds, say, that there are discrepant accounts of them, but a denial of certain facts *because of certain theories about such facts which are already held.*

Suppose that Mrs Smith is accused of witchcraft or sorcery. Some may wonder whether or not the evidence to support this accusation is good. What exactly did she do? Who saw her? What effect did her actions have? But another might say: Mrs Smith could not have been a witch because there are no witches. He might agree that she acted like one, and thought she was one, and that her actions had serious effects. But how could she have been a witch, since there are none? (Compare the defence by the town-clerk of Ephesus of Diana-worship in Acts 19:35–36.) The objection here is not on the grounds that the facts are inadequate to support the conclusion, but to the very idea of such a conclusion.

To say that facts are interpreted in the light of theories is not at all to suggest that those who hold the theories have no reasons for holding them, that it is a leap of faith. Unfortunately the impression is sometimes given that these matters are always a matter of blind faith by a careless use of the word 'presupposition'. 'It's all a matter of their presuppositions,' as though 'presuppositions' are mysterious, secret, unchallengeable things.

To simplify somewhat, it can be said that there are three main theories of the miraculous in the New Testament. The first theory holds that such events, divine acts in history, unprecedented acts of the Creator upon and within his creation, are possible and that the only question for the responsible New Testament scholar to answer is whether they in fact occurred. The second theory holds that such events could have occurred but that the evidence that they did not is always greater than the evidence that they did. The third theory is that such events could not have occurred.

It is the third theory which is important here. Clearly, if a person holds such a theory, then, faced with the New Testament narratives, he *must* interpret them non-miraculously. But why should anyone hold such a theory?

Kantian theology

There is one dominant pattern of argument in western culture for the conclusion that miracles cannot happen. The argument has the following form:

1. Miracles are, by definition, acts of God.

2. To suppose that God acts is to suppose something which no human mind could know.

3. Therefore no person can know that an event is a miraculous act of God.

The reason for this conclusion is not that there is not enough evidence to conclude that a miracle has occurred. If it were a matter of not having enough evidence, then perhaps more could be gained, or at least there could be dispute over whether the existing evidence is sufficient. Rather, the reasoning has to do with the limits of the human mind, limits which, it is claimed, cannot in the very nature of the case be overcome.

What are those alleged limits? Chiefly, that any individual thing about which people claim to know anything must be a possible object of our experience, and anything which is a possible object of experience lies within the boundaries of space and time. Hence we can never properly think of (form concepts of) God, since to do so would take us beyond the necessary boundaries of our experience. To put the point slightly differently, the only kind of God conceivable by us is one falling within space and time, a purely anthropomorphic God. But God is by definition not in space or time. He is therefore 'beyond all the knowledge which we can attain within the world'.

This is Immanuel Kant's argument. The whole basis of Kant's philosophy is a criticism of metaphysics, of the idea that through reason, or revelation, it is possible to gain some knowledge of the nature of things. Metaphysical enquiry, according to Kant, generates antinomies, sets of conflicting arguments which all seem equally valid. Thus, for instance, our intellectual enquiries require us to think that the universe has a beginning in time and is a bounded space, and at the same time that the universe is infinite in time and space. Such antinomies are generated because the human mind is so structured as to be capable of experiencing things only in terms of their appearances, never as things-in-themselves. We are required by our experience to *postulate* things-in-themselves, but they are never *known* in experience. The idea that we might know things-in-themselves is an illusion of thought through which we mistake the regulative requirements of our thinking for objects of knowledge.

Kant applies this to human thought about God. God is unknowable and yet his existence is required, particularly (according to Kant) by the nature of morality. The moral law (which is not, for Kant, the law of God but a law which rational, autonomous agents 'legislate', i.e. will, for themselves) requires the idea of God as the rewarder of virtue and the punisher of vice. Only on such a supposition is morality made intelligible, for only God could ensure the connection between virtue and happiness. Thus, though human beings cannot know God, they are required by the nature of morality to postulate his existence.

Kant's book *Religion Within the Limits of Reason Alone* (1792–3) is in essence the application of this critical philosophy to Christianity considered as a historical religion. According to Christianity, God makes himself known and makes known what he requires of men and what he has done for men through Scripture. Kant turns this claim upside down. For him, morality is in no sense derived from religion or theology; rather, morality (understood in purely secular terms) requires that theology, and the theological texts of Christianity, especially the New Testament, are to be interpreted, or rather reinterpreted, in the light of Kant's critical philosophy and rational morality. As John Kemp has put it, Kant

> has no use for such Christian concepts as grace, salvation, and the service of God except in so far as they are given a moral interpretation: the service of God consists in leading a morally good life, not in rites and observances, and grace and salvation are earned by moral goodness and nothing else – Kant will have no truck with the doctrine of justification by faith.[1]

It is not that Kant thinks the New Testament does not teach the doctrine of justification by faith. Rather, since that doctrine is based upon unacceptable epistemological and moral assumptions, it cannot be the truth.

The influence of Kant's view upon subsequent theology, particularly continental Protestant theology, can hardly be exaggerated. It had two major consequences. One was to make impossible or irrelevant the programme of natural theology, that of proving the existence of God from reason or nature. The other was to make impossible the idea that any source whatever – Bible or miracle – could provide us with revelation, with the knowledge of God.

So much for the negative and destructive side of Kant's proposal. But Kant was not an atheist. What did he propose? Although God cannot be known, and hence nothing can be a revelation of him, yet God's existence can and must be *postulated*, for God's existence is a requirement of morality. Without the idea of a *summum bonum*, the idea of God as the rewarder of virtue and the punisher of vice, there could be no morality.

These two ideas, that there can be no knowledge of God but that the idea of God is *regulative*, have set the agenda for subsequent Protestant theology. Religion is not the bounden allegiance to God arising from his self-disclosure, as in orthodox Christian theology, rather it is (for example) the feeling of absolute dependence (Schleiermacher), or it is a life of service embodying the ethics of the kingdom of God to be realized here on earth (Ritschl), or it is the following of Christ whose character is understood exclusively in this-worldly moral terms (Bonhoeffer).[2]

But what has Kant's philosophy to do with the study of the New Testament, and particularly the interpretation of the miracles? It is of central importance, for however these accounts are to be interpreted they *cannot* be interpreted as they stand, as recording the acts of God. Some other way *must* be found to interpret them, or they must be abandoned altogether.

Furthermore, according to Kant there is something improper or unbecoming about a religion which depends upon miracles. This point can be vividly illustrated from the work of Kant himself. In *Religion Within the Limits of Reason Alone* Kant offers a reconstruction of Christianity in line both with his negative attitude to the knowledge of God which has been sketched above, and with the supreme importance he attaches to the morality of duty in accordance with what he calls the moral law. Some samples of his exegesis of the New Testament might be of interest.

First, Kant's general attitude to Scripture. The interpreter must bring to its interpretation a supreme moral criterion.

> The final purpose even of reading these holy scriptures, or of investigating their content, is to make men better; the historical element, which contributes nothing to this end, is something which is in itself quite indifferent, and we can do with it what we like.[3]

Kant distinguishes between an empirical faith (Christianity, in his case) and moral faith (faith understood in accordance with his own ideas of autonomous reason).

> If such an empirical faith, which chance, it would seem, has tossed into our hands, is to be united with the basis of a moral faith (be the first an end or merely a means), an exposition of the revelation which has come into our possession is required, that is, a thorough-going interpretation of it in a sense agreeing with the universal practical rules of a religion of pure reason. For the theoretical part of ecclesiastical faith cannot interest us morally if it does not conduce to the performance of all human duties as divine commands (that which constitutes the essence of all religion). Frequently this interpretation may, in the light of the text (of the revelation), appear forced – it may often really be forced; and yet if the text can possibly support it, it must be preferred to a literal interpretation which either contains nothing at all (helpful) to morality or else actually works counter to moral incentives.[4]

What Kant is in effect proposing here is a hermeneutic of Scripture which is in accordance with his view of what religion is, whether or not that hermeneutic does violence to the actual meaning of Scripture. 'Reason has freed itself, in matters which by their nature ought to be moral and soul-improving, from the weight of a faith forever dependent upon the arbitrary will of the expositors.'[5] So Kant affirms as a basic principle of his exegesis that the attempt must be made 'to discover in Scripture that sense which harmonizes with the *most holy* teachings of reason'.[6]

> There is therefore no norm of ecclesiastical faith other than Scripture, and no expositor thereof other than pure *religion of reason* and *Scriptural scholarship* (which deals with the historical aspect of that religion). Of these, the first alone is *authentic* and valid for the whole world; the second is *merely doctrinal*, having as its end the transformation of ecclesiastical faith for a given people at a given time into a definite and enduring system.[7]

It is not surprising to find Kant reconstructing traditional Christian doctrine to suit the ends of pure moral religion. Writing about the virgin birth he says:

Yet of what use is all this theory pro or con when it suffices for practical purposes to place before us as a pattern this idea taken as a symbol of mankind raising itself above temptation to evil (and withstanding it victoriously)?[8]

Since Kant wrote this, the application of his basic approach to the critical study of the New Testament has taken one of two different forms, which may be called the *blanket* and the *filter* applications. The first treats the New Testament as a seamless whole which, since it contains reports of miraculous occurrences and purports to be a revelation of God, is to be reinterpreted wholesale, the whole corpus of the documents being regarded as (for instance) the product of the faith of the early church having a historical basis which is now totally indiscernible. Alternatively, attempts have been made (notably in successive 'quests' for the historical Jesus) to filter out of the New Testament writings (particularly the Gospels) those elements which are regarded as mythological or legendary accretions in order to regain what must (it is thought) have been the true, original, unadorned *facts* of the matter: the career of Jesus the moral teacher, the victim of Pharisaic hypocrisy and of Roman callousness and indifference.

The details of these various programmes do not matter here. What is important is to see that this Kantian philosophical outlook enables the one who holds to it to treat the New Testament, perfectly consistently, in what would otherwise seem to be a dogmatically arbitrary manner. While such an attitude to the New Testament is not dogmatic, it is certainly *a priori* in that the Kantian interpreter brings to the text of the New Testament definite views both about the limits of human knowledge and about the nature of religion as being the embodiment or expression of certain moral and social ideas.

Kantianism and the radicals

The recognition that such a general outlook is widespread in Protestantism, not only on the continent but also in the British Isles, serves to render the views of theologians such as Don Cupitt and the Bishop of Durham [David Jenkins] more intelligible. When the Bishop spoke, on a notorious occasion, of 'conjuring tricks with bones' in connection with the idea of Jesus' physical body being raised, he was not being facetious or attempting merely to capture the headlines. He was being consistently Kantian, consistent at least to the extent of saying, with Kant, that the true meaning, or value, or import of the resurrection has essentially nothing to do with a physical body come alive again (because that is contingent, historical and uncertain, and in any case a miracle), but that its true meaning or value is moral or ideal.

While it would be too much to say that the Kantian framework is the only or dominant motif in Bishop Jenkins' ideas, nevertheless there are key expressions which are characteristic of a Kantian theologian. For instance, in the much-publicized *Credo* programme on British television (29 April 1984) the emphasis falls on

> telling miraculous stories because you've already had a wonderful belief and I think the virgin birth is like that ... The virgin birth, I'm pretty clear, is a story told after the event in order to express and symbolize a faith that this Jesus was a unique event from God ... What seems to me to have happened is that there was a series of experiences which gradually convinced a growing number of apostles that Jesus had certainly been dead, certainly buried and he wasn't finished but he was raised up, that is to say, the very life and power and purpose and personality which was [sic] in him was actually continuing and was continuing both in the sphere of God and in the sphere of history so that he was a risen and living presence and possibility.

This reading of the text is one that only Kant's critical philosophy makes possible, yet the centre of gravity for Bishop Jenkins (perhaps not altogether consistently) lies in his unconcern with the miracle stories as historical events (though not with a historical figure called Jesus) rather than in a purely moral faith bereft of any essential historical connections with Jesus. His is a filter, rather than a blanket, approach to the New Testament.

The Kantian influence is more marked in the case of the radical theological views expressed by Don Cupitt:

> Theology may be subjectively impossible in that our cognitive powers are limited by the bounds of sense and God must be outside their scope, as Kant taught.[9]

In a later book, *Taking Leave of God*,[10] Cupitt appears to have moved from a position which stresses negative theology (the idea that it is possible to say only what God is not, not what he is) to one which regards most if not all questions about the objective reality of God as wholly unimportant, if not quite misplaced – misplaced because they treat the issue of whether or not God exists as one which can arise outside the context of human spirituality. Nevertheless, the influence of Kant is manifest in the way in which a strong version of the idea of personal moral autonomy governs all else in theology, in

Cupitt's view of spirituality, with its emphasis on disinterestedness and its non-theological, purely formal character, and in the way in which Cupitt attempts to 'decode' the divine attributes as aspirations of human spirituality. As part of this project, Cupitt emphasizes the bounds of human experience,[11] and hence the idea that God forms a part of transcendent reality about which we can say nothing,[12] for God is 'altogether unspecifiable'[13] and the idea of God is a projection of the human consciousness,[14] though not, strangely, as a postulate in strict Kantian fashion.[15] Cupitt's proposals here come within a whisker of theological reductionism, though he would probably reject the charge as being yet another attempt to make concern about God 'objective', thus taking that concern out of the context of human religion.

In his latest book, *Only Human*,[16] the framework of negative theology is abandoned, for 'all dogmatic theological beliefs as such, belong to a world that is gone, and now can no more be put to effective use in our own world than can the myths of some exotic tribe'. But the Kantian idea that the world is bounded by our experience 'and outside it there is nothing at all, not even nothingness', remains, even though the postulated God of Kant is no more. The result is an attempt to provide a humanistic spirituality.

In so far as Cupitt's earlier negative attitude to the knowledge of God has roots in Anglican theology it can be traced to H. L. Mansel[17] (1820–71). Besides being influenced by continental neo-Kantianism, Mansel himself is in the line of earlier Anglicans such as Archbishop King (1650–1729) and Bishop Peter Browne (d. 1735), whose views were rejected by Bishop Berkeley in his *Alciphron* (1732). While men of this school spoke of human ignorance of God's faculties as they are 'in themselves', their emphasis on the language of theology being regulative rather than cognitive was grounded more in the doctrine of the incomprehensibility of God rather than, as with Kant, based on the necessary limitations of the human mind in gaining knowledge of anything. The words of Scripture were treated by them as wholly metaphorical, not as truths but as symbols. But what the language of theology was meant to regulate were the conventional ideas of 'practical religion' of eighteenth-century Anglicanism.

Some conclusions

So far, it has been argued that much of the current attitude to the miraculous in the New Testament, that which is at the heart of the Christian gospel, can be illuminatingly explained not as carelessness or unconcern over the evidence of the New Testament, but as a conclusion drawn from a set of Kantian premisses about the limits of human knowledge and thus the priority of the moral over the metaphysical in doctrinal constructions or reconstructions of the Christian faith. From this analysis it is possible to draw some conclusions for those who strive to maintain the orthodox Christian view of the gospel in the current theological scene.

It was noted earlier that attitudes to the miraculous in the New Testament are a matter of 'presupposition'. From the point of view of argument, presuppositions are premises from which certain conclusions – in this case conclusions about the reports of the miraculous in the New Testament – are drawn. But such premises are not self-evidently true. The fact that they function as premises does not give them a status which renders them immune to criticism.[18] Not being self-evident, such premises may be rejected, or regarded as conclusions of other arguments with other premises. There is no process of 'pure logic' by means of which the Kantian conclusions which lie at the root of characteristically modern attitudes to the New Testament are inevitably arrived at. The premises of such conclusions are themselves conclusions which require premises. Perhaps the pattern of reasoning from premises to conclusion does not continue indefinitely, but every step in the reasoning can be argued over.

Another conclusion to be drawn from the previous discussion is that basic issues in the interpretation of the New Testament are *theological* issues (or perhaps, better, metaphysical issues). It is possible to engage in a 'surface' interpretation of the New Testament, the philological and grammatical construing of the text. But if the results of such interpretation are to gain purchase as truth, then, necessary as such work is, it is not sufficient. It has to be possible to move outside the circle of such interpretations and counter-interpretations and to use the results to make truth-claims about God binding upon the intellect and the conscience. So for someone to say, 'I'm not interested in all this theology. Let's get back to the text of the New Testament', displays considerable naïvity.

What makes such an attitude naïve is that it supposes that the present situation is one in which the New Testament is barnacled over with theology and that the interpreter must somehow remove or avoid the barnacles and get at the ringing metal of the text. There have been situations in the history of the church when, by and large, this was the correct procedure. It was the correct procedure at the time of the Reformation when, as the Reformers correctly argued, the text of Scripture was hidden by encrustations of tradition. Hence the need for the plain, unvarnished exposition of the text of Scripture. And behind this procedure at the time of the Reformation stands Christ's procedure with the Pharisees.

But this is not the position at present, not at least in those circles heavily influenced by the work of academic theologians in the universities. Here the status of the text itself is an issue, or rather it is an issue which has been very largely settled by a consensus in favour of the Kantian position. It is therefore necessary that anyone who wishes to be properly equipped for the business of using the New Testament theologically, who wishes to answer the question 'What truth does the New Testament teach today?', should be equipped not only with the necessary skills in grammatical, philological and literary analysis, but should also be aware of the metaphysical setting in which he is endeavouring to research and write.

A third consequence which arises concerns the question of the direction of the education of theological students, particularly those who wish to devote themselves to understanding and propagating of the historical Christian faith today. One's impression is that students of the text of Scripture are by and large people who have had a training in modern languages or classics, very rarely in philosophy. And those who do have a taste for theological construction tend very often to gravitate towards historical theology or the history of doctrine, the Reformation perhaps, or Puritanism. As a consequence, very few who have a training in philosophy or in a course which has required some philosophy then move into Christian theology, the theology of today, either New Testament theology or systematic theology, *and stay there*. These are of course only impressions, but are they so inaccurate?

A possible response to radicalism

So far, an attempt has been made to offer a way of understanding contemporary 'radical' theology, analysing it in terms of the assumptions of Kantianism which have been so prevalent in Protestantism, particularly on the continent, but from time to time, and certainly recently, in the British Isles. Understanding the background of such radicalism is of course important, and such understanding may go a long way to remove the mystique which seems presently to surround writers like Don Cupitt.

But how, it might reasonably be asked, can such an approach be answered? A number of steps must be taken. As regards the Kantian framework of the theology, the weaknesses of Kant's theory of knowledge need to be explored, both in general, and more particularly as they affect the whole question of the knowability of God. Christian theology has always recognized elements of metaphor and analogy in our talk of God, but has claimed with equal emphasis that it is possible to speak of God with literal sense.[19] If that is so, then there can be no *a priori* objection to the idea of God working miracles or to his acts being known. Thus the *a priori* objection to the miraculous may be neutralized by counter-arguments.

Is it possible to be more positive than this and to provide a philosophical underpinning of the Christian faith that is superior to the Kantian framework? It is a mistake to attempt to offer a philosophical defence of one's faith. This way lies rationalism, the constraining of faith into a 'reasonable' *a priori* framework. The alternative is to deploy a positive argument for both the historical meaning and truth of Scripture at two levels. It is classically understood that Scripture has held authority over two thousand years of Christianity; this understanding has brought peace with God, new hope and moral vision, comfort in bereavement and in approaching dissolution. It has borne the weight of the collective experience of the church. Of course, this could be massive collective deception, but is there any reason to think so?

The second level is more individual and personal. The 'bottom line' as regards our attitude to the New Testament, whether as 'professional' theologians or as ordinary, unprofessional believers, is whether that New Testament, understood as conveying the historic message of deliverance from sin through the work of the divine Saviour, bears the weight of *our* experience: not whether it 'speaks to us' in some vague way, but whether its detailed message enables us to make sense of our lives.[20]

A note on books on the philosophy of Kant

Perhaps the best way of gaining an entry into Kant's philosophy is through two short introductory works with fearsome titles, *Prolegomena to Any Future Metaphysics* (1783) and *Groundwork of the Metaphysic of Morals* (1785). (The best and most accessible translation of the *Groundwork*, by H. J. Paton, is called *The Moral Law*.) Only then ought one to graduate to the two *Critiques*, the *Critique of Pure Reason* (1781) and the *Critique of Practical Reason* (1788). *Religion Within the Limits of Reason Alone* is required reading for intending theologians. Of numerous books on Kant's philosophy, those by John Kemp, *The Philosophy of Kant* (Oxford, 1968) and Roger Scruton, *Kant* (Oxford, 1982), are recommended as introductory treatments. *Kant's Analytic* (1966) and *Kant's Synthetic* (1974), both by Jonathan Bennett, are standard modern critical treatments of Kant's philosophy from an empiricist standpoint. *Kant's Moral Religion* by Allen Wood (1970) is a useful exposition of Kant's philosophy of religion.

Notes

1. *The Philosophy of Kant* (1968), p. 95.
2. The Kantian framework of Bonhoeffer's Christology is stressed by Stewart Sutherland in *God, Jesus and Belief* (Oxford, 1984), pp. 114–120.
3. *Religion Within the Limits of Reason Alone*, trans. T. M. Green and H. H. Hudson (New York, 1960), p. 102.
4. Ibid., pp. 100–101.
5. Ibid., p. 122.
6. Ibid., p. 78.
7. Ibid., p. 105.
8. Ibid., p. 75 (footnote).
9. *Christ and the Hiddenness of God* (London, 1971), p. 29.
10. London, 1980.
11. Ibid., p. 73.
12. Ibid., p. 96.
13. Ibid., p. 13.
14. Ibid., p. 14.
15. Ibid., p. 80.
16. London, 1985.
17. D. Cupitt, 'Mansel's theory of regulative truth', *JTS* (April 1967). See also Part One of *Christ and the Hiddenness of God*, 'The limits of thought about God'.
18. As an example of such a criticism, Dr Joe Houston has argued that if the Gospels are regarded as being made-up stories to justify the disciples' experiences and originally understood as such, they could not have had, nor have, a legitimizing function any more than there can be a commonly accepted practice of telling lies. One can appeal to the past to legitimize the present only if one appeals not to a fictitious past but to the past as one believes it to have been. See his 'Objectivity and the Gospels', in P. Helm (ed.), *Objective Knowledge: A Christian Perspective* (Leicester: IVP, 1987), pp. 149–165.
19. One piece of evidence that this is possible is the rich and varied treatment of the attributes of God in current analytic philosophy of religion (e.g. Richard Swinburne's *The Coherence of Theism*) – work which Cupitt regards as being irrelevant because 'unhistorical'.
20. I have tried to argue for this at greater length than is possible here in 'Faith, evidence and the Scriptures', in *Scripture and Truth*, ed. D. A. Carson and J. D. Woodbridge (Grand Rapids: Zondervan, 1983).

Part 4
Application

13

Secularization
The fate of faith in modern society
David Lyon   Vol. 10.1 (1984)

It is a commonplace that western society – and other parts of the world influenced by the West – is secular society. Many people routinely assume that modern society tends to squeeze out religion. In fact, some think religion is so irrelevant that it could never again have the influence on society that it is said to have once had. Modernity sounds religion's death-knell. Both in popular speech and in more academic discourse such assumptions hold sway. But much confusion reigns as soon as one attempts to unpack these taken-for-granted ideas. Yet the effort is worthwhile, for much hangs on an understanding of secularization. The term points to a crucially significant aspect of our social context in the so-called advanced societies.

This essay focuses on the debate over secularization as it has appeared in the literature of the past twenty years. We shall comment first upon attempts to clarify the meanings of the term. Then, as some of the sociological disputes have their origin in theological statement, we shall take a specific look at the 'theology' of secularization. Needless to say, the implications of this topic for theology are tremendous. Thirdly, we describe what I call the 'strong secularization thesis', the idea that religion declines with the onset of modernity, and then consider the various forms that criticism of the 'strong thesis' have taken. We conclude by tracing some 'new directions' in secularization studies. My emphasis falls mainly on the social analysis of secularization, but part of my message is that *theological* understanding tends to be embedded in sociological explanation.

Clarifying the concept

There is little doubt that Larry Shiner's article 'The concept of secularization in empirical research'[1] is the best-known attempt to unravel and disentangle secularization's diverse threads. He argues that five different meanings of the term may be distinguished. They are as follows. First, secularization may be defined as 'the decline of religion'. 'The previously accepted symbols, doctrines and institutions lose their prestige and influence.' On this argument, one would end up with a religionless society. The difficulties with this definition are twofold: when was society *really* religious anyway, and how does one measure such a decline? The second definition of secularization is 'conformity with this world'. In this case attention is said to turn from the supernatural and towards an exclusive concern with 'this world'. Eventually, the 'pragmatic tasks of the present' would become paramount and religion would cease to have any distinguishing identity. Again, the problem with this, says Shiner, is the ambiguity involved in measuring such secularization. Are not theological definitions intruding into social science? Who is to say that concern for this world is not the authentic culmination of faith?

A third, more specific understanding of secularization is the 'disengagement of society from religion'. Society increasingly distances itself from religion, especially in political life, but also in spheres such as education and welfare. Religion is relegated to the private domain, having no effect on public life. Take, for example, Luther's doctrine of the calling. He argued that all, not only priests, work in 'callings'. Does this apparent demotion of priests to the level of everyman count as an instance of secularization? Talcott Parsons, who prefers the term 'differentiation' to 'disengagement', thinks not. Rather, secular life is being endowed with religious legitimation. That is, the opposite of secularization is occurring. Clearly, secularization is more subtle than it appears at first sight.

'The transposition of religious belief and institutions' is Shiner's fourth definition. Obvious examples of this include seeing a Marxist revolutionary vision as a 'secular transposition' of Jewish-Christian eschatology. 'Obvious' it may be to some, but this example highlights the main difficulties of secularization as transposition. How does one prove that some functional parallels are really related to one another in a causal fashion? Shiner is confident that he has sniffed out another illegitimate theological assumption here.

Shiner's fifth definition of secularization is 'the desacralization of the world'. He takes as his key example the work of Max Weber, who argued that the increasing rationalization characteristic of modern society spelled its 'disenchantment' (*Entzauberung*).[2] The gradual loss of a sense of the sacred (as Mircea Eliade puts it)[3] is closely related to the matter-of-fact approach to the world associated especially with the rise of modern science. Of course, one immediately has to make qualifications about this definition. For instance, was it not the very desacralizing tendencies within Protestantism (in asserting that nature is not itself infused with magic or mystery) which helped foster the early development of modern science?[4] Of these five definitions, Shiner says (and I largely agree) that the ideas of disengagement, disenchantment, and transposition are the most helpful. They are complementary to one another, and also have the advantage of referring to society in general, not just to the church. Although the two are connected, it makes sense to distinguish secularization of society from the inner secularization of the churches.

Several notable attempts have been made by others to refine the definition(s) of secularization. Mention might be made of David Martin's *The Religious and the Secular*,[5] Peter Glasner's *The Sociology of Secularization*[6] and Karel Dobbelaere's *Secularization: A Multi-dimensional Concept*.[7] Martin alerted us to the use of secularization by 'counter-religious ideologies'. The term has been wielded as a weapon in a war against religion on more than one occasion. This raises again the question of how 'neutral' the word can ever be. Exploring such issues is of perennial importance for social science. Peter Glasner's contribution takes Martin's suggestion somewhat further, showing that secularization may have the status of a 'social myth' by which people come to understand the world. (This theme is echoed in a slightly different way by the more recent book by Harry Ausmus, *The Polite Escape*.[8]) Glasner's demolition work is more useful than his constructive efforts, however, and his book ends in what, for many, is a blind alley. He says that we cannot comment, sociologically, on the effects of the social process of secularization on religious vitality today.

This situation is redeemed to some extent by Dobbelaere, whose teasing out of the 'dimensions' of secularization is not dissimilar to Shiner's. Dobbelaere places together 'disengagement, desacralization and transposition' and refers to them collectively as 'laicization'. So society becomes progressively split off from religion, and as this happens, 'secular' functions of religion are taken over by society. Thus a process of 'disenchantment' (or desacralization) spells an ever-increasing social reliance on technology and calculation. Dobbelaere proposes further refinement by distinguishing between other dimensions of secularization; namely 'religious involvement' and 'religious change'. The former (roughly parallel with Shiner's 'decline of religion' or 'de-christianization') focuses on the extent to which people really take seriously and live out the beliefs, morals, and so on, of religious groups. The latter (roughly paralleling 'conformity with this world') expresses changes occurring in the posture of religious organizations. For a current example, many churches are moving from unconcern to awareness or involvement over issues such as the world rich–poor gap, or the nuclear debate.

What then are we left with, by way of a definition of 'secularization'? Patently, we are left with problems, especially those relating to the inter-pretation of history, and the nature of 'religion'. There is also the issue of social-scientific 'neutrality'. Then there are clearly several distinguishable dimensions of secularization, so single, blanket definitions are unobtainable. That secularization acts as a bridging concept between religion and society is true, but does not take us very far. That it might have to do with 'temporality' (as recently suggested by Richard Fenn)[9] takes us further, but still leaves loose ends.

In Fenn's view, secularization could be thought of as the process in which greater concern with the 'passing age' is evidenced. There are several gains to make from this, some of which carry us another step further than where Dobbelaere leaves us. For example, 'conformity with the world' still leaves open the question: what is the 'world'? From a Christian perspective, an ambiguity lurks here. Concern with the world as 'created order' is mandatory, but when such a concern lacks a transcendent dimension – that is, failing to see it as *God's* world – it is a seductive concern, to be resisted.

Enough of the definitional problem for the present. The concept of secularization on its own explains nothing. The term is a 'problematic', in Philip Abrams' sense of 'a rudimentary organisation of a field of phenomena which yields problems for investigation'.[10] The agenda for investigation is, I believe, clarified by the work of Shiner, Martin, Dobbelaere and Fenn, but the issues raised by them and others are by no means dead. They emerge especially in the work of Bryan Wilson, to which we turn in a moment. Before that, however, we must note one other muddying of the waters achieved by the 'theology of secularization'.

The theology of secularization

Rather like the sociological debate, the theological debate over secularization appears at first glance to be passé, out of fashion. But the similarity continues, in that the assumptions surrounding the debate are still invoked, implicitly or explicitly, nearly a quarter of a century after the debates began. Although the most spectacular moments for secular theology were probably the publication of John Robinson's *Honest to God* and Harvey Cox's *The Secular City*,[11] it could well be argued that books like Don Cupitt's *Taking Leave of God* and some productions of the liberation theology school follow the same trail.[12] Each of these, in its way, represents an attempt to come to terms with modernity, with the social conditions of the mid- and later twentieth century. Perceiving the possible benefits of some aspects of secularization, they try to recast Christianity in this mould. Even secularism may become, in this view, a truly Christian option.

It must be quickly conceded that, at base, some of this secular theology had a good point. Friedrich Gogarten, for instance, argues that secularization in the sense of humans taking responsibility for the world (rather than just being in bondage to it) is the goal of the biblical tradition.[13] There was a 'secularizing tendency' within the Puritanism which insisted that nature is not imbued with magical forces. But it is clear that Gogarten and friends wished to travel a very different road from the Puritans!

In 'taking responsibility' for life, human beings were frequently said to be 'coming of age'. Possessing the technological means to control nature seemed to mean that an older reference to the transcendent God of traditional religion could happily be jettisoned. *Homo religiosus* was dead. He died when he realized that prayer would not mend the spindle or repair the computer. Many secular theologians took the work of Dietrich Bonhoeffer as their starting-point. He it was who had popularized the phrase 'religionless Christianity'.[14] His objection was to various aspects of Christian 'religion' which seemed to him (and to most Christians, one would imagine) inimical to Christianity. In particular, he singles out individualism, the concern with the metaphysical, the putting of religion in a separated 'compartment' of life, and the idea of a God who steps in to rescue, rather than always being at the centre of life. But Bonhoeffer wished to assert that *no* religion of any sort need be involved in Christianity. As Leon Morris points out in his sensible evangelical critique of 'religionless Christianity', however much his admirers wish to deny that Bonhoeffer meant what he said at certain points, it is difficult to resist the conclusion that what begins as a useful attack on Christian deficiency ends as a repudiation of some basic Christian truths.[15]

Hence it comes as no surprise that Robinson, who frequently refers to Bonhoeffer, takes religionless Christianity to what many felt to be an atheistic conclusion. Robinson mistook Paul Tillich and Bonhoeffer to be saying more or less the same thing, which was that 'secular man' has no need of God, as traditionally conceived, and that Christianity must adapt itself accordingly. To use our earlier terminology, Robinson was trying to hasten 'religious change'. Such secularization was desirable, as far as Robinson was concerned.

But secularization was also seen in a rosy hue by Harvey Cox, who wrote in praise of *The Secular City*. He began in much more sociological vein than

Robinson: 'The rise of urban civilization and the collapse of traditional religion are the two main hallmarks of our era ...'[16] But Cox and Robinson shared the same mentor, Bonhoeffer. Only for Cox, 'man comes of age' in the 'secular metropolis'. He takes 'secular' to mean 'temporality', but rather than seeing this in terms of the difficulties it raises, as Fenn does, Cox applauds it. Religion has been outgrown: 'Secularization is man turning his attention away from the worlds beyond and towards this world and this time.'[17] Cox discerns a (progressive?) shift through history, first through 'tribal' and then through 'town' stages. He announces the arrival of a third stage, 'technopolis', and devotes the book to an examination of this theme. Of course, the processes of urbanization and secularization are closely linked together, although the nature of the relationship is a matter for debate and empirical study.[18]

In a sense, as I suggested, there is a connection between a Robinson and a Cupitt; between Cox and some liberation theology. On the one hand there is the idea that in a scientific world there is no room for a 'traditional' image of a creating and providential God. On the other, and partly as its mirror image, is the view that the world is very much in human hands. Although this is by no means the theme of all liberation theology, the notion that we take matters into our own hands – the self-liberation of the poor, for instance – echoes the tones of Cox's secular theology. It comes as little surprise then, when an Edward Norman launches a critical campaign against what he sees as the 'politicization' of faith, or when James Childress and David Harned ask, 'Is secularization really as hospitable to Christian faith as Christian faith seems hospitable to secularization?'[19]

Of course, the answers to such critiques and queries must be ambiguous. Aspects of secularization, as we have seen, are important for the survival of authentic Christianity. Others may be inimical to it. Again, political awareness and responsibility are an aspect of New Testament Christian discipleship; *exclusive* concern with the temporal, the political, is the denial of discipleship. Peter Berger put his finger on an important point when he described the 1960s trends as the *product* of secularization; this was the 'secularization of theology'.[20] That is, theological development clearly does not take place in a social vacuum. Rather, said Berger, secular theology has to be seen against the backdrop of wider social processes such as the decline of Christendom, the competition offered to Christian faith by 'imported' alternatives from other cultures, increased geographical and social movement, and the pervasive influence of the mass media.

Berger is here engaging in one of his favourite sports: 'relativizing the relativizers'. For if the voguish theologians' declarations of the redundance of religion could be seen as being in part a reflection of their peculiar historical-social milieu, then in time their declarations might themselves prove redundant. Of course, this could also be seen as a tail-chasing exercise, but it does highlight a crucial issue: is secularization primarily an intellectual or a social process – or both? If intellectual, then the mere 'history of ideas' approach is sufficient; if social, then presumably a discipline like sociology should be able to grapple successfully with it.[21]

Christian apologetes, raised within a western mindset, have often operated as if the intellectual problem is the key. The defence of the faith may be seen in exclusively cognitive terms. For all his fine contributions, a person like Francis Schaeffer[22] sometimes leaves the impression that social changes tend always to follow intellectual ones rather than *vice versa*.[23] But the study of secularization has given fresh impetus to those who long suspected that *social* factors might be rather significant. For example, it provides a leading motif to the work of two authors who tried in the 1970s to initiate a dialogue between theology and sociology: Robin Gill and Gregory Baum.[24] Gill, an Anglican, argued in *The Social Context of Theology* that effective Christian communication with the 'outside world' is severely hampered without some grasp of the social dimension of secularization. Baum, a Catholic, similarly uses the debate over secularization as a bridge for discussing the interaction between theology and society. In more popular vein, Os Guinness has articulated for an evangelical audience another version of the same conviction. In *The Gravedigger File*[25] he warns against the social subversion (and unwitting churchly collusion in this) of Christianity.

All this returns us to where we began, the *social analysis* of secularization. For all the optimism of the secular theologians, can Christianity really survive in a secular society? This is the issue addressed in the 'strong secularization thesis' encapsulated in the writings of Oxford sociologist Bryan Wilson.

The strong secularization thesis

The strong secularization thesis is that the modern world pushes traditional religion to the margins of society, leaving it no role to play at the centre of social life. It is a process, says Bryan Wilson, 'by which religious institutions, actions and consciousness, lose their social significance'.[26] (He has stuck with more or less this definition since his mid-1960s work, *Religion in Secular Society*.[27]) A calculating rationality, concerned for the best means rather than the best ends, has corroded old beliefs and morality, not just in an intellectual sense, but by becoming the very basis of society. Who now needs a religious legitimation of the power of the state, when democracy is the order of the day? And who needs personal morality when 'electronic eyes and data-retrieval systems have largely supplanted interpersonal concern and the deeply implanted virtues of honesty, industry, goodwill, responsibility and so on'?[28]

This strong thesis is derived above all from the work of Max Weber, on 'rationalization'. In *The Protestant Ethic and the Spirit of Capitalism*[29] he tried to show not only how Puritanism had an indirect connection with early capitalism, but also how the values embodied in that Puritanism became submerged in the process of capitalist development. The 'fate of the times', he lamented, is to live in a society characterized by 'mechanized petrification'. Weber gave us the image of a rationalized society as an 'iron cage' to picture what the spread of science, bureaucracy and capitalism was doing to people in the modern world. Weber also agonized over the encroachment of 'rationalization and disenchantment' in a speech to students in 1918. One aspect of this can be traced to the rapid rise of double-entry accounting in the fourteenth and fifteenth centuries. Numbers and quantitive thinking displaced qualitative, aesthetic and moral values, according to Weber. As he said, 'precisely the ultimate and most sublime values have retreated from public life ...'[30] He saw little hope of their revival.

Wilson catches Weber's wistfulness. He clearly regrets the passing of a kind of society in which the 'salt of the earth' is still able to 'sustain the social order'. But equally clearly, he believes that such a society is virtually irretrievable.[31] The cityscape of an earlier era does teach us something about the dominance of religion, in the soaring spires which cast their shadow over home and workplace. Not that this necessarily means that all *believed*. Rather, religion was socially significant in a deep way. Nor does Wilson ignore massive regional variation in the modern societies once touched by Christianity. The indicators may be different from place to place, and the pace may be sudden or slow.[32]

But however it has happened, according to Wilson, something he calls 'societalization' has occurred. Communities, as local, persisting, face-to-face groups, have fragmented or disappeared. Human life is lived in a *societal* (especially the nation-state) context rather than communally. As religion had its strength in the local group, decline in the latter means decline in the former. Whereas once upon a time the processes of production, consumption, co-ordination, control, and knowledge (possession and dissemination) were under religious direction, now this is patently not the case. Religion is consigned to socially irrelevant private spaces, away from where 'real' life is lived. Thus for Wilson, loss of community is loss of religion. Local points of reference are no longer germane, he insists, in industrial society.

Wilson sees religion in terms of its contribution to social morality. Hence his stress on factors like the quest for personal gain as the symbol of what dominates modern life. We now live in a technical, not a moral, order. The transmission of moral values to each succeeding generation is rendered obsolete in the transitory world of commuting, migrating, and the separation of home and work. The emphasis is on individual liberty to do one's own thing, the only checks on which are (rationally negotiated) laws. What with natural explanations of events, technical control of everyday life (traffic lights to conveyor belts), and with existence geared to individual advantage, no space is left for any conception of ultimate salvation. Nor is there any guarantee of social cohesion and continuity (and it is this which seems to be the bigger worry for Wilson). Even those revivals of traditional religion, or the flowering of new religious movements, are powerless in the face of societalization and secularization. What is left is religion reduced to a residual remnant, a reminder of a world we have lost.

Needless to say, there are other versions of a 'strong secularization thesis'. Early sociologist Emile Durkheim believed that religion declined in social significance in industrial society. The separating out of different spheres of life rendered religion less able to maintain its overarching legitimacy.[33] Durkheim, however, saw new social forms of religion emerging within industrial society, a possibility about which Wilson is less than convinced. Wilson prefers to think of religion in more conventional terms. Karl Marx was another who perceived the demise of traditional religion. The secularizing effects of the progression of capitalism had, he believed, 'drowned the most heavenly ecstasies of religious fervour, of chivalrous enthusiasm, of philistine sentimentalism, in the icy waters of egoistic calculation'.[34] Although debate continues on Marx's own stance towards religion,[35] his followers have done much to promote the impression that secularization should be seen as a positive policy strategy, as well as a feature of the modern world.

I shall limit myself to brief comment on two contemporary secularization theorists who also follow a fairly 'strong' thesis, but from very different standpoints. Vernon Pratt, in his *Religion and Secularization*,[36] is sure that religion has had its day, and that this is no bad thing. Modern people have 'lost a concept of the supernatural' and, in a scientific milieu, such loss is permanent. He discusses sociologists, theologians, and philosophers to make a case for what might be called a 'secularist' interpretation of secularization. It amounts to secularization with no regret.

Sabino Acquaviva sticks more closely to empirical evidence about church-related activity (mainly) in continental Europe in his *The Decline of the Sacred in Industrial Society*.[37] He accepts that industrialization does bring about a crisis of faith, from which there appears to be precious little exemption. As he sadly concludes, 'From the religious point of view, humanity has entered a long night that will become darker and darker with the passing of the generations, and of which no end can yet be seen. It is a night in which there seems to be no place for a conception of God, or for a sense of the sacred, and ancient ways of giving significance to our own existence, of confronting life and death, are becoming increasingly untenable.'[38] This is secularization with regrets.

A third theorist who deserves mention at this point is Peter Berger. His immensely stimulating studies of religion and secularization have served to orient a generation of students in the sociology of religion. He sees secularization as a product of modernization[39] and thus as a process which affects people in contemporarily industrializing societies in similar ways to those which are already 'advanced'.[40] But Berger cannot neatly be slotted into the strong thesis camp, not least because his view of secularization has been changing over the last decade.[41] His view is in fact softening to the point at which he is drawing attention not only to the 'crisis of religion' in the modern world, but also to the 'crisis of secularity'.

We can see that the strong secularization thesis may be held both by those sympathetic to religion and by those who for some reason may wish to hasten the decline of religion or some aspect of it. It is generally stated in terms of the *disengagement* of religion and society, and of *desacralization* or *disenchantment*, the supposed concomitant of rationalization. The fragmentation of society into different spheres as industrialism expands accounts for the former, while the rise of science, capitalism, and a rational-calculating approach to life is the social background to the latter. The process of secularization, according to the 'strong' theorists, seems to lead only in one direction, and in an apparently irreversible fashion. Without for a moment wishing to cast doubt on the notion that the social setting of industrial capitalism (in its state and its market form) *does* make a difference to the way that religion may be practised, we now must turn to an examination of some of the main forms of criticism which may be brought against the strong thesis.

Criticizing the strong thesis

The main trouble with the strong thesis is that it is too simple. Its strength is in fact its weakness. The view that in time past people were somehow more religious, and that modernity systematically rots religion, is spurious. In what follows we shall give only the flavour of the discussion, and direct the reader to some relevant sources.

Probably the most devastating critique comes from anthropologist Mary Douglas, who berates students of religion for having their eyes 'glued to those conditions of modern life identified by Max Weber as antipathetic to religion'.[42] Mary Douglas herself works out of a predominantly Durkheimian tradition which, it must be said, frequently seems to explain (away?) religious belief in terms of its supposed social function.[43] However, Douglas targets a key assumption which appears false to her. She fears that too many theorists have assumed that religion is 'good for you' (even if it is not in some sense 'true'). Definitions of religion laden with good values reflect this, and, since modernization is bad for religion, we are in an unprecedented cultural crisis.[44] Douglas is unhappy with such bias towards the assumed 'goodness' of 'religion' on several counts, but most generally because blanket definitions obscure rather than clarify both what religion does for people (integrate them into society?) and what religion most people actually hold (superstition, luck?).

The most celebrated version of the latter objection, that the definition of religion is too narrow, comes from Thomas Luckmann.[45] Conventional religion may well have receded from the centre of modern life, but are there not new social forms of religion which have taken over some of the traditional functions of religion? Such 'invisible religions' could be seen in today's family-centredness, sexuality, or individualism. Christian authors, writing more popularly, have come right out and argued that we are really talking about modern forms of idolatry.[46] The gradual collapse of Christendom is an undisputed historical fact, they would say, but it is a mistake to confuse this with the decline of religion as such. Christian instincts may favour this approach, certainly over against that which suggests that humans may be somehow quite devoid of religious inclination.[47] It also makes mandatory what Douglas calls for, namely an evaluation of the different claims and effects of different religions: they are not all the same. Biblically distinctions are often made between sham religions and pure ones. But at the same time it must be said that for the purposes of discussing secularization as *disengagement*, a more conventional institutional definition is required. Above all, this criticism shows that it is imperative to be clear about what is included under the 'religion' rubric.[48]

So secularization has been a Procrustean bed. A sociological theory has been imposed on historical data in a very contrived fashion. For example, many (who should know better) have fallen into the trap of imagining that once upon a time society was 'really' religious.[49] Such a moment is taken to be the baseline from which secularization begins. Most secularization theorists have to concede that they are referring to a time when ecclesiastical power and political power were closely linked.[50] This could then in fact be seen as a distortion of Christian faith (whose 'kingdom is not of this world'), thus putting this kind of secularization in a more favourable light.

The related idea that moderns are utterly different from everyone else because of modernization is also attacked by Mary Douglas. This, she says, is a case of tribal myopia. Have science, technology and bureaucracy really 'quenched the sources of religious feeling and undermined religious authority'? Douglas doubts it. The marvels of modern science are at least as awe-inspiring as discoveries of a previous era. And the vast impersonal bureaucratic machine may indeed provoke crises of identity, but are such not the very stuff of the religious quest, since time immemorial? She wishes to show that many 'primitive' groups are and have been just as 'secular' as moderns; secularity is not a phenomenon peculiar to the post-Victorian epoch.

The historical issue has several other dimensions. Secularization studies have in the past ridden roughshod over historical specifics in different societies. David Martin is the champion of historical carefulness at this point. His *General Theory of Secularization* examines the variety of patterns which secularization takes in different settings. He shows how the situation in the USA is quite different from, say, Scandinavia, because of the different church–state relations obtaining before modernization. It comes as little surprise to him that Sweden, which still has a state church, should in fact have very low attendance, whereas the opposite situation is found in the USA. In fact, too many secularization theorists have been naïve with regard to historical data. The welcome publication of specific historical studies can only benefit attempts to theorize secularization. One major advantage conferred by such studies is that the role of human action is brought more clearly into the scene than in many standard sociologies of secularization (which tended to be weighted towards 'the massive social force' view).[51] The result of a proper integration of history and sociology of secularization should be that notions that secularization is irreversibly one-directional are jettisoned. History is much messier; the tide of secularization ebbs and flows.

This leads to another criticism of the strong secularization thesis, which is that it fails properly to account for evidence which seems to call the theory in question. The so-called new religious movements which have blossomed since the mid-century, for example, even if they have no direct effect on the running of society, can scarcely be written off as being of no religious significance.[52] The resurgence of traditional Christian religion (especially evangelicalism in the USA, but also its persistence in the UK)[53] is as yet unarticulated within a modest secularization theory. This would not necessarily have to go to the lengths of Andrew Greeley's blunderbuss defence of *Unsecular Man.*[54] Rather, what is required is a sober assessment of what is actually happening in the contemporary world, without special pleading on behalf of either religious persistence or decline.

Secularization as a concept is unlikely to be abandoned because of the various criticisms just mentioned. The strong, or perhaps simplistic, version of secularization, though taken for granted by some, is used only with great caution by others. As a problematic, it still serves the useful purpose of alerting us to a cluster of issues which deserve serious investigation in our day, issues at the crossroads between religion and society. The process of rethinking secularization[55] should yield positive benefits for clarification of the present religious situation in societies which do evidence 'disengagement' and 'rationalization'. But it is appropriate to conclude with a few observations on possible new directions discernible in current research.

New directions in secularization studies

An obvious implication of the critique of the strong secularization story is that more care must be taken to ensure that the 'fit' between the 'facts' and the 'theory' is good. The confident assumption (whether coming from 'theologians' or 'sociologists') that we are entering a 'religionless society' will not stand up. So theory requires modification, in the light of rigorously sifted data. But those data, which give us the empirical constraint required, still need a theory to hold them together.

Specific studies, such as some of those already mentioned, help fill out the picture of religion in society. One might also refer, as an example, to Hugh McLeod's recent work on *Religion and the People of Western Europe*.[56] He has paid special attention to religion among the working classes. Investigations like these can eventually lead to new insights into the secularization process. For instance, it has often been argued that there is a basic incompatibility between the work of David Martin and that of Bryan Wilson. The latter suggests that religion was once socially dominant, whereas the former maintains that there has always been a strong and widespread rejection of official religion in favour of folk or common religion and superstition in Europe. Bryan Turner now proposes that both are right, in a limited way, but they are focusing on different class levels. A social élite may well at times use religion to legitimate its position, but that does not mean that those in more lowly social echelons are in any strong sense affected by the supposedly dominant religion.[57]

In fact, the whole question of where authority resides in modern societies is an important one for secularization studies. Richard Fenn has followed a significant trail in examining the way in which the courtroom may become the place of 'ultimate authority', sometimes overruling that of sincere religious conviction. (One of his most interesting examples is of a Catholic woman whose wish to have her life-support machine switched off was discounted by the court.)[58] Scientific authority is another area of interest, and again I shall refer readers to just one fascinating study. Eileen Barker has shown how, despite the diversity of theological persuasion, persons involved in cosmological debates (over 'origins') all appeal to *scientific* authority to make their case.[59] It seems to me that important work could be done in relating the current growth and diffusion of information technology to secularization. Is it possible, for example, that we are further abandoning the authority of properly formed human judgment in favour of mere 'calculation'?[60] Or will computers be treated only as *aids* to decision-making, rather than as somehow possessing that capacity?

Another new direction, if it may be so termed, is to find clues about secularization outside of the sociology of religion. Following the work of Michel Foucault, for example, it has been proposed that in the secularization process, various forms of moral restraint, asceticism, and so on, are replaced by secular practices such as dietary control.[61] Again, increased concern with cultural symbols also enhances our understanding of how phenomena – such as rock music – may be symptomatic of a secularizing tendency.[62] (Moves like this also serve to help put religion back on the sociological map after what some might have interpreted as the disciplinary suicide of being obsessed with a concept – secularization – which seemed to bid farewell to the subject-matter of the sociology of religion!)

The theological response to secularization must clearly become more sophisticated than that exhibited in the excesses of the 1960s secular theology fad. To talk in bland blanket terms about 'secular society' is not on. Thankfully, some hopeful signs are emerging, which demonstrate an awareness of the complexity and ambiguity of 'secularization'.[63] For instance, the secularization of thought, regretfully documented by various Christian commentators, ought not to be confused (though the connections should be displayed) with social secularization or 'disengagement'. An aspect of the secularization of thought is what is often called the 'loss of a Christian mind'. From a Christian viewpoint this is properly deplorable, in a way that, for example, the prising apart of church and state is not. The latter may not be such a bad thing for the church, which now has to find its feet in a situation of greater cultural confrontation, rather than enjoying the dubious privilege of state support. In such a context certain New Testament passages about Christian 'citizenship' take on a fresh significance!

One last note. I am in no way implying that careful empirical study will sort out all the problems connected with this slippery secularization concept. Indeed, I see no way in which 'theological' assumptions can finally be eradicated from definitions of religion and secularization. The point is to be clear as to what we do mean, and as to what the implications of this view seem to be. For historical sociology (which is where secularization concepts are properly located and assessed) is ever a matter of rhetoric.[64] That is, we are engaged in the task of constructing an argument, in this case, to explain some of the relationships between religion and society, by using a suitably qualified concept. Theology may actually contribute insights to this argument, for instance as we test out whether the biblically derived notion of 'temporality' is illuminating for secularization studies. There is no excuse for allowing secularization studies themselves to become a secular pursuit by default.

So does 'secularization' tell us anything about the 'fate of faith in the modern world'? The answer I have given is yes; in a limited way it helpfully alerts us to some significant dimensions of the religion-and-society problem. It raises some important questions, rather than explaining anything as such. It indicates some connections between modern life and religious practice, although in itself it tells us little about related notions such as 'pluralism', the retreat of religion to the private sphere, or the rise of 'surrogate religions'.

But the concept of secularization is inevitably bound up with questions which no sociology can resolve on its own. For they are also theological questions, in the sense that one's understanding of 'religion' or of 'historical interpretation' is reflected in the kind of secularization theory produced. So the onus is on those who care about relating social science to a Christian world-view (as distinct from some other) to enter the socio-theological dialogue in the quest of better understanding in both areas.[65]

The result of such dialogue will probably lead well beyond 'secularization' itself, away from the narrower ecclesiastically based definition of religion, into wider cultural analysis. The trend to be welcomed, in my view, is that which treats our own society as anthropologists have treated 'alien' societies. This is much more likely to provide a realistic picture of the 'signs of the times' – including those forms of symbol to which people really refer as guides to life. Coupled with new opportunities in social science to be explicit about one's presuppositions, such understanding could yet become the vitally needed complement to responsible Christian mission in the modern world.

Notes

1. Larry Shiner, 'The concept of secularisation in empirical research', *JSSR* 6 (1967), pp. 207–220.
2. Max Weber, 'Science as a vocation', in H. Gerth and C. Wright Mills (eds.), *From Max Weber: Essays on Sociology* (London and Boston: Routledge and Kegan Paul, 1948).
3. Mircea Eliade, *The Sacred and the Profane* (New York: Harper and Row, 1961).
4. The sixth definition of secularization, referring as it does to a general process of social change, is not relevant to our present discussion.
5. David Martin, *The Religious and the Secular* (London: Routledge and Kegan Paul, 1969).

6. Peter Glasner, *The Sociology of Secularization: The Critique of a Concept* (London: Routledge and Kegan Paul).
7. Karel Dobbelaere, *Secularization: A Multi-dimensional Concept* (*Current Sociology* [Monograph] 29:2, Summer 1981).
8. Harry Ausmus, *The Polite Escape: The Myth of Secularization* (Athens, Ohio: Ohio University Press, 1982).
9. Richard Fenn, *Liturgies and Trials: The Secularization of Religious Language* (Oxford: Blackwell, 1982), p. 8.
10. Philip Abrams, *Historical Sociology* (Shepton Mallet: Open Books, 1982), p. xv.
11. J. A. T. Robinson, *Honest to God* (London: SCM, 1963); Harvey Cox, *The Secular City* (London: SCM, 1965).
12. Don Cupitt, *Taking Leave of God* (London: SCM, 1980).
13. Friedrich Gogarten, *The Reality of Faith* (Philadelphia: Westminster, 1959).
14. Dietrich Bonhoeffer, *Letters and Papers from Prison* (London: Fontana, 1959).
15. Leon Morris, *The Abolition of Religion* (London: IVF, 1964).
16. Harvey Cox, op. cit., p. 1.
17. Ibid., p. 2.
18. See the rather different treatment of, e.g., Richard Sennett, *The Fall of Public Man* (New York: Vintage Books, 1976).
19. E. R. Norman, *Christianity and World Order* (Oxford: Oxford University Press, 1978); James Childress and David Harned (eds.), *Secularization and the Protestant Prospect* (Philadelphia: Westminster, 1970), p. 19. Bryan Wilson, whose work is examined in the next section, sees secularization as systematically excluding Christian faith.
20. Peter Berger, 'A sociological view of the secularization of theology', *JSSR* 6 (1969), pp. 3–16.
21. See e.g. Owen Chadwick's important *The Secularization of the European Mind in the Nineteenth Century* (Cambridge: Cambridge University Press, 1975) and David Lyon, 'Secular minds and secular societies', *Fides et Historia* (forthcoming).
22. This comes across in many of his writings. See, e.g., *How Should We Then Live?* (Old Tappan: Revell, 1976).
23. The contrary view is explored interestingly by Alasdair MacIntyre in *Secularization and Moral Change* (Oxford: Oxford University Press, 1967).
24. Robin Gill, *The Social Context of Theology* (Oxford: Mowbrays, 1975), Gregory Baum, *Religion and Alienation: A Theological Reading of Sociology* (New York: Paulist, 1975).
25. Os Guinness, *The Gravedigger File* (London: Hodder and Stoughton, 1983).
26. Bryan Wilson, *Religion in Sociological Perspective* (Oxford and New York: Oxford University Press, 1982), p. 149.
27. Bryan Wilson, *Religion in Secular Society* (London: Watts, 1966) p. 149.
28. Wilson, *Religion in Sociological Perspective*, p. 42.
29. Max Weber, *The Protestant Ethic and the Spirit of Capitalism* (New York: Scribners, 1976).
30. Max Weber, in Gerth and Wright Mills (eds.), op. cit., p. 155. See also the comments in David Lyon, *Sociology and the Human Image* (Leicester and Downers Grove: IVP, 1983), pp. 74–77.
31. Ernst Gellner is quite convinced there can be no return or revival. See his *The Legitimation of Belief* (Cambridge: Cambridge University Press, 1974), especially the final chapter.
32. He refers to David Martin, *A General Theory of Secularization* (Oxford: Blackwell, 1978) on this. See below for further comment.
33. Emile Durkheim, *The Division of Labour in Society* (New York: Free Press, 1964).
34. Karl Marx and Frederick Engels, *The Communist Manifesto* (Harmondsworth: Penguin).
35. The most recent evidence is in José Miranda, *Marx against the Marxists* (London: SCM, 1980). It is probably true that Marx was less virulently anti-Christian in *practical policy* than many of his followers, but it is doubtful that 'enforced secularization' is inconsistent with Marx's position.
36. Vernon Pratt, *Religion and Secularization* (London: Macmillan, 1970).
37. S. S. Acquaviva, *The Decline of the Sacred in Industrial Society* (Oxford: Blackwell, 1979).
38. Ibid., p. 202.
39. Peter Berger, *The Sacred Canopy* (New York: Anchor, 1967) (UK: *The Social Reality of Religion*, Harmondsworth: Allen Lane).
40. Peter Berger et al., *The Homeless Mind* (Harmondsworth: Penguin, 1974). See also David Lyon, 'Secularization and sociology: the history of an idea', *Fides et Historia* 13.2 (1981), pp. 38–52.

41. Peter Berger, *The Heretical Imperative* (New York: Anchor, 1979).

42. Mary Douglas summarizes her views in 'The effects of modernization on religious change', *Daedalus* 111:1 (1982), pp. 1–19.

43. Of course, the dividing line between 'explaining' and 'explaining away' is a thin one. Douglas' work is highly suggestive and helpful, e.g., in trying to explain Old Testament food prohibitions. See e.g. R. K. Harrison's comments in *Leviticus* (Leicester: IVP, 1980), pp. 27–29.

44. Mary Douglas, 'The effects of modernization', p. 6.

45. Thomas Luckmann, *The Invisible Religion* (New York: Macmillan, 1967).

46. Jacques Ellul, *The New Demons* (Oxford: Mowbray, 1975); J. A. Walter, *A Long Way from Home* (Exeter: Paternoster, 1980) (USA: *Sacred Cows*, Grand Rapids: Zondervan).

47. This was Bonhoeffer's position, it seems. He could conceive of moderns as religionless.

48. See Robert Towler, *Homo Religiosus* (London: Constable, 1974), chapter 8. Other candidates for inclusion as 'religion' include 'common' or 'folk' religion which is that constellation of beliefs and practices associated with luck, magic, and superstition. These are on occasions combined with (or grow in symbiotic relation with) official religion. David Martin picturesquely refers to 'subterranean theologies' (in *A Sociology of English Religion*, London: Heinemann, 1967). Beyond this is 'civil religion', a term made famous by Robert Bellah, and referring to the association of certain religious themes with nationality and civic identity. (See his *The Broken Covenant*, New York: Seabury, 1975.) References to God in American presidential speeches are the classic example of this. Yet another possible evidence that religion is not altogether dead is perceived by some in the persistence of ritual in advanced societies, be they capitalist (Robert Bocock, *Ritual in Industrial Society*, London: Allen and Unwin, 1974) or (officially atheistic) state socialist (Christal Lane). Harry Ausmus (op. cit.) has brought the argument about secularization round full circle by proposing that 'secularization' is *itself* a form of 'religious' explanation of the world, a 'theodicy' to which people cling.

49. Martin Goodridge, 'Ages of Faith: Romance or Reality?' in *Sociological Review* 23.2 (1975), pp. 381–396, or George Marsden, 'America's "Christian origins": Puritan New England as a case study', in S. Reid (ed.), *The Influence of John Calvin on History* (Grand Rapids. Eerdmans, 1983).

50. Recent examples include: Jeffrey Cox, *The English Churches in a Secular Society* (New York: Oxford University Press, 1982), Alan Gilbert, *The Making of Post-Christian Britain* (London: Longmans, 1980), or George Marsden, *Fundamentalism and American Culture* (New York: Oxford University Press, 1980).

51. Richard Penn's *Toward a Theory of Secularization* (Storrs, CT: University of Connecticut, 1978) makes this point well.

52. For a survey from several different perspectives see Eileen Barker (ed.), *New Religious Movements* (New York: Edwin Mellen, 1982).

53. On the UK see Steven Bruce, 'The persistence of religion', *Sociological Review* (1983).

54. Andrew Greeley, *Unsecular Man* (New York: Dell, 1974).

55. See further comments on this in David Lyon, 'Rethinking secularization: retrospect and prospect', *Review of Religious Research* 26.3 (1985), pp. 228–243.

56. Hugh McLeod, *Religion and the People of Western Europe* (New York: Oxford University Press, 1982).

57. Bryan Turner, *Religion and Social Theory* (London: Heinemann; New York: Humanities Press, 1983). Such theorizing also has implications for some liberation theologians who blithely assume that religion can represent a 'dominant ideology'.

58. Richard Fenn, *Liturgies and Trials: The Secularization of Religious Language* (Oxford: Blackwell, 1982).

59. Eileen Barker, 'In the beginning: the battle of creationist science against evolution', in R. Wallis (ed.), *On the Margins of Science* (*Sociological Review* Monograph 27).

60. See e.g. Joseph Weizenbaum, *Computer Power and Human Reason: from Judgement to Calculation* (Cambridge, MA: MIT, 1976; Harmondsworth: Penguin, 1984).

61. See Turner, op. cit., p. 133.

62. See e.g. Bernice Martin, 'The socialisation of disorder: symbolism in rock music', *Sociological Analysis* 40:2 (1977), pp. 87–124.

63. E.g. Os Guinness, op. cit., and Williamson and Perrota (eds.), *Christianity Confronts Modernity* (Ann Arbor: Servant, 1981).

64. See David Bebbington, *Patterns in History* (Leicester and Downers Grove: IVP, 1979), and David Lyon, 'Valuing in social theory: postempiricism and some Christian objections', *CSR* XII.4, (1983), pp. 324–338.
65. On this, see David Lyon, *Sociology and the Human Image* (Leicester and Downers Grove: IVP, 1983), especially chapter 2.

14

The concept of relationship as a key to the comparative understanding of Christianity and Islam

Ida Glaser   Vol. 11.2 (1986)

Religion concerns the interaction of finite and infinite: the relationship of parties that are essentially other. Sometimes the otherness may be stressed, and sometimes the relationship. The balance between the two is, I would suggest, a determinant of a system.

Where the idea of otherness is submerged, there are two possible outcomes. We may find an infinite that is almost human, or that can be apprehended by human reason, as in the ancient Greek or modern liberal systems. Alternatively, we may find that humanity is absorbed into the infinite, as in Hinduism or Buddhism.

Where the idea of relationship is weak, we may find that the infinite recedes so far from man as to be inaccessible and unknowable. It is towards this end of the scale that orthodox Islam lies[1] – although by no means at its extreme. The Christian faith, on the other hand, lies somewhere in the middle. It is clear that God and man are other, but it also offers close relationship between them. The ideas of otherness and relationship are not considered mutually exclusive; and in this I suppose it to be unique. It is therefore a helpful basis on which to build a comparative understanding of other religions.

In this paper we shall seek to compare Christianity and Islam. Beginning with the nature of God himself, we shall see that the notion of relationship runs through a number of major areas of Christian doctrine, and that a weakening of this notion will produce doctrines that come close to an Islamic understanding. We shall go on to see how these differing ideas of relationship make some key areas of the Christian faith unacceptable to Muslims. The discussion will include a number of statements that appear rather simplistic and in need of qualification. This is necessary for brevity, and for clarity in comparison of emphases in the two systems.

The nature of God

The Christian doctrine of the nature of God is that of the Trinity: three persons in one God from eternity. It is also that of a God with certain characteristics, notably holiness and love.

All this implies relationship. For what do we mean by a person? The great characteristic of a person is that he relates to others. He communicates, chooses, acts in relationship to other persons. To say that God is three persons is to imply that those persons relate. It is relationship that unites persons, so at least one way of understanding the unity of the three is as a unity of relationship.

What is holiness? It implies otherness, but it also implies morality. The Trinity is set apart from us by its moral purity. Yet I would ask how we can understand moral purity apart from relationship. Can one be good in a vacuum? I doubt it! Goodness is a quality, as is faithfulness, but we can see it only when it is applied in the context of some sort of relationship, just as we can be aware of light only when it enters our eyes. To say that a person is good without reference to anything but himself may be true, but his goodness can be seen – and hence known – only with reference to its results relative to others.

What about love? Love makes no sense without an object, for love has essentially to do with relationship. God is love from eternity not because he might potentially love, but because he does in fact love. There is love – and therefore relationship – between the persons of the Trinity.

So at the centre of the Christian idea of God we see the relationship of persons that are other. God is three – he is three persons who exist over against each other. But he is also one, for the three are united in a relationship of holiness and love.

If we remove the concept of relationship, what have we left? If we have the one, we cannot have the three. We can have the holiness, but not the love, and the moral dimension of holiness must be changed. This moves us towards the Islamic idea of God. There is no plurality in him: his essential characteristic is that of unity. He is not plural in himself, and he is to be associated with no other. He is not, therefore, in relationship in eternity, for there is no other with whom he might relate.

The characteristics of holiness and love are not absent from the Islamic concept of God. Both are predicated of him: but I would suggest that the words do not have the same content as they do in a Christian context. Thus God's holiness sets him apart, and makes him the judge, but it does not tie him down to morality. In fact, nothing can tie him down. He is free to will as he wishes, and powerful to carry out his will. He can therefore be tied down by no law, not even one that he has made.[2] In this sense, his moral character is secondary. It is subject to his will.

God's love may cause him to have mercy on his creatures, even to the extent of communicating with them; but it is a love that condescends in benificence rather than a love that shares in relationship. God may love us if he so chooses, but his relationship with the objects of his love is very different from that envisaged in the Christian faith.

In Islam, God is certainly other than man. He is high and exalted, and powerful to do and will as he pleases. These are his fundamental character-istics, which can supersede both justice and love as the Christian would understand them. Both will and power are predicated of God himself, without necessary reference to anyone else, for God in eternity is not in relationship. The relationship characteristics of justice and love are secondary.

In Christianity, on the other hand, love and justice are primary. God is all-powerful, and can will as he pleases, but his character of faithfulness ensures that he does not act apart from his love and justice. His power and will are in that sense limited. He is in relationship from eternity, and the relationship characteristics come first.

The nature of man

The fundamental difference between the relating-in-eternity God of Chris-tianity and the purely-one God of Islam is reflected in other areas of religious understanding. Most importantly it is reflected in understandings of the nature of man.

In the Christian scheme we see man as a creature over against God and other than him. Yet he is made 'in the image of God': there is a likeness between creature and creator. This likeness includes the quality of person-hood: the essential characteristic of God that implies the ability to relate is present in man also.

This does not only mean that man can relate with his fellow men. The biblical picture indicates that the likeness between creature and creator is sufficient to make possible between them the mutual love, pain and communication of relationship. Man can relate with God himself: indeed, it is for this relationship that he is made. He is to relate with his maker in mutual love as a son relates with his father.

The Islamic picture is different. Man is, as in Christianity, a spiritual as well as a physical being.[3] He is able, and responsible, to receive God's revelation and to act with reference to him. But the idea that he is made in the image of God is absent. Man cannot be said to be 'like God' – the very suggestion is considered blasphemous, since there is none like him.[4] The absence of likeness immediately removes the dimension of mutuality in any relationship between man and God. In particular, man cannot affect God, since this would detract from his power and self-sufficiency. As the Hadith says,

'O my servants, you can neither do Me any harm nor can you do Me any good.'

Not the combined races of men and jinn can in any way conspire to augment or reduce the power of God.[5]

The Christian would largely agree with this, but the Muslim would push the idea to the conclusion that man cannot affect God *in any way*. He cannot cause him grief or joy. Thus, although God has deigned to communicate with his creatures, and even to love them, the relationship cannot be mutual since man's response can make no difference to God. We read in the Qur'an:

'I created the jinn and humankind only that they might worship Me.
I seek no livelihood from them, nor do I ask that they should feed Me.
Lo! Allah! He it is that giveth livelihood, the Lord of unbreakable might.[6]

The relationship becomes more like that between potentate and subject than that between father and son, since man is made primarily for worship rather than relationship. There is relationship between God and man, but it is not that of mutual love pictured in the Bible.[7]

Khurshid Ahmad describes 'realization of man's relation to Allah' in terms of the saying of Muhammad, 'You should worship Allah as if you are seeing him, for he sees you though you do not see him.' He tells us:

It means that all action should be performed with Allah in your vision. If that is not possible you must realize that Allah is seeing you. This realization is regarded as the basis of true devotion. It signifies that man has identified his will with the Will of God and has brought it, at least as far as he is concerned, completely in tune with the Divine Will ... Man comes nearest to God by excelling in this process of identification of man's will with the Divine Will.[8]

Closeness between man and God is described in terms of knowledge rather than likeness, and the ultimate in relationship is willing submission rather than interaction.

The nature of sin

The fundamental question concerning the nature of sin is not so much what constitutes sin as what sin does, for the latter determines the former.

In the Christian scheme, the dreadful thing about sin is that it breaks relationship between God and man. This has an effect on the sinner – it cuts him off from God's presence, makes him deaf to God's communication, and puts him under judgment. However, since the relationship is mutual, sin also affects God. It offends him and grieves him so that he longs to restore the sinner, although his character of holiness means that he will not overlook the sin.

In Islam, on the other hand, we have seen that God cannot be grieved or offended by anything that man does. Sin can affect only man and not God. In our relationship picture, since there was no mutual relationship in the first place there is no relationship to be broken. After sin, man is still the subject of the potentate as he was before. The difference is that sin makes him liable to punishment in the hereafter, and to all the consequences of not following the path that God has declared to be best in the present. When he sins, man may injure himself and his people, but not God.[9]

This difference in the effects of sin is reflected in what constitutes sin in the two systems. In Islam, sin is essentially a violation of the law, of God-given instructions concerning religious duties and moral and social obligations. In Christianity, on the other hand, sin is often described in relationship terms: grieving the Holy Spirit, spurning the Son, being at enmity with the Heavenly Father. In Romans 6, for example, Paul speaks of men being in sin and under the dominion of sin: fundamentally, sin is a state of separation from God rather than a series of violations of his regulations.

Yet there is some overlap here: the Bible also describes sin as transgression of the law or wrongdoing.[10] Does this imply that the biblical and Qur'anic understandings of sin are closer than I have suggested? I think not, for the biblical and Qur'anic understandings of law are widely separated.

The differences can again be understood in terms of relationship. In the biblical system even the Old Testament law is given in the context of relationship. It is significant that Abraham comes before Moses: the law is given to those who are already God's covenant people. The regulations are given in the context of covenant relationship and are expressive of it. The New

Testament has the same emphasis: it is as God's chosen ones, those who are in relationship with him, that we are to act in accordance with his will. We are to be perfect because we are children of the Heavenly Father.[11] That is why disobedience spoils relationship: it defies the one with whom we ought to relate.

In Islam, the order is reversed. It is not that we become God's people, and therefore act in a particular way, but that we act in a particular way and are therefore God's people. The practices, the obedience to regulations, are of primary importance. It is by keeping these that the believer pleases God and draws near to him, and that he receives the best in this life and in the next. That is why violation of the commandments deprives him of the good that comes through acting according to what God has said.

Sin for the Christian, then, is anything that offends God and therefore breaks relationship with him, while sin for the Muslim is a wandering from God's laws that results in judgment.

These fundamental differences in understanding of God, man and sin result in many mutual misunderstandings. In particular, Christian doctrines about salvation and about the Lord Jesus Christ may appear unnecessary, nonsensical and even blasphemous to the Muslim. It is to these doctrines that we now turn.

The doctrine of salvation

In his book *Salvation of the Soul and Islamic Devotions* (Kegan Paul International, 1983, pp. 28–29), Muhamed Abul Quasem recognizes that, in the Christian faith, 'salvation is primarily deliverance from sin'. 'Such deliverance', he says of Christianity, 'is possible here and now. When it is made actual a new spiritual life is achieved through which the interrupted communion or fellowship with God is restored.' Such is not the case with Islam:

> Islamic teaching is that sin stands between man and God no doubt, but he is not dead in it; so no new birth of the spirit is needed; he must, however, repent. Man is not by nature in a position from which he needs to be redeemed. He commits sin from which he must repent; his repentance is not salvation, but only a means to it; salvation is safety from punishment from sin in the life after death (p. 29).

Quasem is clear here on the differences between the Christian and Islamic ideas of salvation. The Christian seeks salvation from the state of sin itself, and the Muslim from punishment for sin. This, of course, reflects the ideas of sin discussed above. The Christian wants to be saved from the state of sin because that state is one of being cut off from relationship with God. The Muslim does not see the need for such a salvation, since he does not believe that he has fallen out of relationship. Indeed, he does not believe this relationship to be possible. He sees man as he is – fallen, out of relationship with God – and assumes that to be his natural state. He may therefore seek to approach closer to God, and to know more of him, but he will not seek the restoration of a relationship which he does not believe ever existed. Salvation for him, if we can rightly use the word in this context, can imply only an escape from judgment and an entry into paradise.

Since the nature of salvation in the two systems is different, the means of attaining it is also different. The Christian believes that God's primary holiness requires judgment on all sin, and that something must be done to remake the broken relationship, hence the need for the work of Jesus Christ. The Muslim, however, would reject both of these ideas. First, since there is no broken relationship, nothing need be done to restore it. Secondly, since God's holiness is subject to his will, there is no necessity that sin should be judged. The Qur'anic idea of justice differs from that in the Bible:

> The idea of transference of the punishment of sins or vicarious punishment is not accepted by the Qur'an. But it must be noticed that, according to the Qur'an, the punishment is not the necessary and unavoidable consequence of sin. If there is repentance then any sin, however grave it may be, can be forgiven by the mercy of God. God is not bound to punish. Contrary to Augustinian understanding of justice, Divine justice in the Qur'an means that God does not punish anyone without reason, or beyond that which is necessary. Justice also means that no good of man is left by God unrecognized and unrewarded. It does not mean that God is not allowed to leave any sin unpunished.[12]

God, then, is free to forgive, to show mercy, on whom he wills. Nothing has been broken by sin so nothing needs to be mended. Nothing needs to be done in expiation for sin: sacrifice is unnecessary.

What, then, is necessary for salvation – escape from judgment – in Islam? From God, the Muslim needs not an act of salvation but an act of revelation. He needs guidance as to what he should do, and mercy to help him to do it. The guidance is available in the Qur'an and in the Hadith – the words revealed to the Prophet Muhammad and the records of his life. The believer's response is to be twofold. He is to believe in God and in his messenger and message, and he is to act as the message directs. This will lead him both to the best in this life, and to paradise after death.

For the Muslim, therefore, the Christian means to salvation are quite simply unnecessary. God can forgive sin without sacrifice or mediator,[13] and no restoration is required. At the same time Christianity is seen as lacking in what is really needed for salvation – the details of actions that will please God. The Bible, and particularly the New Testament, is singularly lacking in regulations about both religious and social duties, since it primarily records the history of relationship between God and man, and seeks to lead man back into that relationship. The Muslim seeks law that will lead him into salvation; biblical law makes sense only in the context of relationship – of salvation already achieved.

The doctrine of Jesus Christ

For the Muslim, there is simply no need for anyone to be sent from God in other than a prophetic capacity.[14] Since guidance and warning are the ultimate needs of man, there can be no higher calling than that of bringing him the needed message. Since the biblical idea of the work of Christ is unnecessary within the Islamic framework, Christian doctrines about his person are also superfluous.

More than that, the Christian doctrine of Jesus is rooted in the idea of relationship between God and man. The essential work of Christ is to restore relationship, but there is more to it than that. The very idea that God can appear in human form implies a certain likeness, and therefore a possible relationship, between God and man. In Jesus, God himself comes among his creatures and relates with them. Not only does he speak to them, guide them and judge them: he also touches them, weeps with them, rejoices with them and eats with them. If there is no likeness between God and man, this cannot be. The very thought of it is blasphemy.

When we consider the nature of Jesus himself, we find a problem not unlike that of the Trinity: we have a plurality in unity. There, three persons in one God; here, two natures in one person. Again, a possible key is relationship. If God and man can relate, we can conceive of both being perfectly present in Christ. If not, if their essential otherness dominates, incarnation is nonsense, and the suggestion that a man might be God becomes unthinkable blasphemy. Even the notion of Jesus as Son of God does not help. For one not used to thinking in terms of relationship, this would imply a physical sonship – an idea as abhorrent to Christians as to Muslims.

Conclusion

It is therefore not surprising if Muslims vehemently deny biblical ideas about Jesus and the salvation that he brings. At best these ideas are considered unnecessary and nonsensical; at worst, blasphemous. We need to understand that such reactions may not be the results of ignorance of Christian doctrines, nor of hostility towards them, nor even of spiritual blindness. They are the expected consequences of belief in a system that is fundamentally different from Christianity in its understanding of God and of his creatures. If Muslims and Christians are to understand each other, these differences must be recognized.

Notes

1. This paper deals with mainstream, Sunni Islam, although much of it is also relevant to other forms of Islam. An exception is Sufism, the esoteric, mystical branch of Islam. Sufis often use vocabulary that implies relationship ideas similar to those in Christianity, or even a pantheistic view. It is worth noting here that even such vocabulary must be interpreted within the Muslim understanding of the overwhelming transcendence of God. Thus the famous statement of Hallaj, 'I am God', implies, according to some interpreters, not the absorption of man into God but the negation of man in relationship to the one God who is all. See for example Rumi, Discourse 11.
2. Commenting on Surah 87, The Most High, v. 7: 'We shall teach you to read and you shall not forget save what Allah wills', Sayyid Qutb writes: 'Every time the Qur'an states a definite promise or a constant law, it follows it with a statement implying that the Divine will is free of all limitations and restrictions, even those based on a promise from Allah or a law of His. For His will is absolute beyond any promise or law.' (*In the Shade of the Qur'an*, vol. 30, p. 140, MWH, London.)
3. See Surah 15, Al-Hijr, vv. 26ff.
4. See Surah 117, The Unity, but note again the divergence with Sufism where the tradition that 'God made Adam in his image' is often quoted, although not necessarily with the same content as in Christianity.
5. Sahih Muslim, Al-Birr (ch. 1115 in Abdul Hamid Siddiqi's translation, Kitab Bhavan, India, 1979).
6. Surah 51, The Winnowing Winds, vv. 56–58, translation from M. M. Pickthall, *The Meaning of the Glorious Qur'an* (Mentor).
7. Again we note the expressions of mutual love between God and man in Sufism. It is of interest, however, that the picture of father and son is seldom used to illustrate this love. Even when the analogy is that of lover and beloved, God is usually the beloved who is sought rather than the lover who seeks.
8. In *Islam – Its Meaning and Message* (Islamic Council of Europe, 1975), p. 24.
9. See the description of the sin of Adam, Surah 7, The Heights, v. 23.
10. E.g. Jas. 2: 9–10; 1 John. 3:4; 5:17; etc.
11. E.g. Matt. 5:48; Col. 3:12ff.; etc.
12. Muzammil Husain Siddiqi, 'The doctrine of redemption: a critical study', in K. Ahmad and Z. I. Ansari (eds.), *Islamic Perspectives* (Islamic Foundation, 1979), pp. 99–100.
13. There are traditions about the intercession of Muhammad as a means to entering paradise, and some look to 'Ali or to other saints as intercessors. However, there is still no idea of one person bearing another's sin.
14. The prophetic capacity here includes personal example, as is recorded in the case of Muhammad in the Hadith.

© Ida Glaser 1986

15

Methods and perspectives in understanding the New Age

John W. Drane   Vol. 23.2 (1998)

In the early 1990s, British tabloid newspapers created an image of New Agers as gangs of unkempt, drug-crazed travellers living in old buses parked illegally on other people's property, in the vicinity of places like Stonehenge and other ancient 'spiritual' sites. In the USA, on the other hand, the New Age will forever be linked with Hollywood actress Shirley MacLaine and her TV mini-series, *Out on a Limb*, which portrayed the New Age not as a concern of social drop-outs, but as the playground of the rich and the famous, searching for a spiritual dimension to life because they already had everything else. Younger members of the British Royal Family have also been known to connect with this kind of spiritual search – and there is not a major city anywhere in the world which does not host a regular exhibition related to 'mind, body and spirit'. Here, the makers of witches' broomsticks rub shoulders with the saffron-robed devotees of ISKCON, while crystal healers stand alongside students of ancient Coptic gnostic texts, tarot-card readers, specialists in past-life recall, Kirlian photographers, channellers of spirit guides, aficionados of extraterrestrial intelligence, and therapists of every conceivable variety – to mention only a tiny sample of what is typically on offer. Nor are these things confined to large urban centres, for most small communities boast their psychic fairs, while one of the surprising growth industries of the last two decades has been the unprecedented spread of metaphysical bookstores.

Definitions

It is easy enough to describe and document all this activity. But what makes these things 'new age'? In her history of the Findhorn Community, Carol Riddell describes life there as 'a spiritual supermarket, with all kinds of different "products" on the shelves to sample'.[1] She provides a bewildering list of what these 'products' might include: Buddhism, Hatha Yoga, Ta'i Chi, Sufism, Transcendental Meditation, organic food, past-life therapy, *A Course in Miracles*, as well as various elements from the Christian tradition. She goes on to indicate that 'all this makes up what has been described as the "new age" movement'.[2] What she describes is a mere drop in the ocean compared with what is more widely on offer. Indeed, the sheer diversity of all this led one recent writer to conclude that the New Age is 'a cluster of related ideas, teachings and groups, not altogether coherent, most of which would identify with this title'.[3]

Such a description is so vague as to be almost worthless, which is why others question whether the New Age really is an identifiable entity at all. Just to complicate the picture even further, some of those who once happily used the term would now prefer to discard it. Carol Riddell again is typical:

> We are now a little wary of this description, which was once eagerly embraced by the Findhorn Community, because in popular thought it has become connected with the sensation seekers ... whose interest lies less in seeking spiritual transformation than in dabbling in the occult, or in practising classical capitalist entrepreneurship on the naive.[4]

Among scholars, some regard it as the outcome of eastern religions being adapted into western culture. Others trace it back to the counter-culture of the 1960s, transposed into a different key as hippies reach mid-life. For yet others it is part of a revivalist movement within the traditional western esoteric circles inspired by people like Swedenborg, the Transcendentalists, or Helena Blavatsky and the Theosophical Society.[5] All these understandings contain elements of truth. But none of them alone can explain the amazing rise to prominence of the New Age; and it is in any case far more eclectic and more all-embracing than any or all of its apparent forerunners. Part of the difficulty of definition is related to the analytical categories within which western scholarship has traditionally operated. We do not find it easy to imagine how anything so apparently diffuse and disorganized could also be so successful. But the truth is that there is no central organization behind the New Age, there is nothing to join, and no one way of actually being a New Ager. The movement has been variously described as a 'metanetwork', or a network of networks,[6] or a SPIN (segmented polycentric integrated network),[7] while Wittgenstein's notion of 'family resemblance' can also be invoked.[8] Just to make things even more complex, the New Age is also very definitely a 'movement', in the quite literal sense that it is always on the move. Things are constantly changing, as spiritual searchers keep looking in new places, which means that almost any definition we might produce can, with perfectly good reason, be challenged by others whose experience of the phenomenon has been different. Diversity is one of the key identifying factors of the New Age, and for that reason alone the search for a single theological perspective that will be shared by all New Agers is doomed to failure.

Cultural change

In reality, the various threads that go to make up the New Age tapestry are held together not by a common ideology, but by a shared perception of the nature of contemporary cultural change. In essence, the New Age is a form of postmodernity, and as such it is part of the questioning and redefining of the values and methods inherited from the European Enlightenment that has swept through all areas of intellectual reflection in the last twenty years or so.[9] The New Age's answer to the dislocation and collapse now facing the world is that the only way forward will be through a massive transformational shift in consciousness, of cosmic proportions. As with many critiques of modernity (including Christian ones), the New Age is itself a product of the same worldview with which it expresses dissatisfaction, though unlike other critiques it also unashamedly searches for solutions in what can only be described as a 'pre-modern' worldview, based on a pre-scientific, essentially mythological epistemology.[10]

There are many ways of articulating this understanding, but something along the following lines would be typical:

Our present predicament can be traced mostly to mistakes made by western thinkers in the course of the last 500 years, which in turn was rooted in the west's love affair with the rationality of the Greeks. This philosophy has led to the marginalization of human and spiritual values, and an unhealthy preoccupation with a mechanistic, rationalist, reductionist worldview. There has been a profound loss of spiritual perception, and to resolve the present crisis that trend needs to be reversed. The recovery of spirituality must be a top priority. Traditional western sources of spiritual guidance will, however, be of little help in this process: the Christian church is inextricably bound up with the old cultural establishment, so much so that the defective Enlightenment worldview was, in effect, little more than the logical outcome of classical Christian beliefs and values.

The relationship between Christianity, Enlightenment and western culture is not quite that simple, of course.[11] But in the New Age, as in postmodernism more generally, image and perception are everything, and once something is believed by a sufficient number of people, it becomes irrelevant whether or not it is historically accurate or literally true. For better or worse, therefore, Christianity (in its classical western form) is increasingly perceived as part of the problem, and for that reason it cannot also be part of the solution: if spirituality is to be restored to today's world, it will have to come from somewhere else.

New Age reference points

It is pointless to try to construct a detailed route map that will guide us through all the intricacies of New Age spirituality. As we will see, the New Age can hold together beliefs and practices that, on conventional definitions of rationality, would be regarded as incompatible, logically contradictory and mutually exclusive. Nevertheless, it is perfectly feasible to identify some fundamental compass points that can provide a general sense of direction through the New Age maze, without being prescriptive about the actual path that any given New Ager might actually follow. My proposal is that there are four dominant polarities through which transformational philosophies and experiences are presently being pursued within the New Age.[12]

Non-western worldviews

That is, the traditional worldviews of eastern religions. An attractive, if superficial, view states that, if the cause of our present predicament rests in things that are modern and western, then the way to resolve it will be to seek solutions in things that are ancient and eastern (or at least, non-western in the traditional sense). On this basis, many western people are committing themselves to eastern spiritual paths, particularly – but not exclusively – Buddhism, albeit in a westernized form. Shirley MacLaine expresses a popular opinion when she comments that this New Age is the time when the intuitive beliefs of the East and the scientific thinking of the West could meet and join – the twain wed at last.[13]

First-nation beliefs

Long before white westerners settled in the Americas, or Australasia, these lands – and others like them – were home to ancient nations. The environmentally friendly lifestyles of these people were brutally suppressed, and their spirituality was devalued by western imperialists who labelled it 'primitive' and 'unscientific'. But with the benefit of hindsight, it seems that western people could have learned much from the traditional lifestyles of aboriginal peoples. Could it therefore be that by reaffirming these values that were previously discarded, the world's peoples together might find new ways to take us forward into the future? In the process, white westerners might also expiate some of the guilt they now feel for the behaviour of their forebears. This has become a major concern within the New Age.

Creation-centredness

Long before the spread of classical 'western' values, articulated through the categories of Greek philosophy and spread by the power of Christendom, Europe itself was home to a different, arguably more spiritual, worldview. Should western people not therefore be looking for answers within their own heritage, by the rediscovery and appropriation of the kind of worldview that inspired and motivated their own distant ancestors? This concern accounts for the burgeoning interest in neo-paganism in its many forms, which is one of the fastest-growing aspects of New Age spirituality in northern Europe today.[14]

Person-centredness

Many of those who today are searching for new ways of being have no interest at all in anything that could be called 'religion'. The development of psychotherapies of various kinds – not least the rise of transpersonal psychology – is providing this kind of 'secular' person with access to the same kind of transformational experiences as mystical religious traditions offer, without the initially unwelcome baggage of religious dogma.[15] Hence the popularity of transformational video and audio tapes, bodywork and other therapies – often supported by claims that modern physics and mathematics are somehow 'proving' the value of all this in some kind of scientific sense.

The unique forms of New Age spirituality emerge from the interweaving of these different and ostensibly unrelated threads. But while diversity is a key empirical hallmark of the New Age, not all New Agers are equally supportive of the attempt to construct an eclectic worldview from such widely assorted materials. David Spangler and William Irwin Thomson are typical of those who welcome the self-conscious merging of different traditions:

> ... This new planetary sensibility or culture will be less a thing and more a process that nourishes our creativity and wholeness and provides sustenance for building the bodies of tomorrow ... we are reimagining our world. We are taking hunks of ecology and slices of science, pieces of politics and a sprinkle of economics, a pinch of religion and a dash of philosophy, and we are reimagining these and a host of other ingredients into something new: a New Age, a re-imagination of the world ... [16]

Others are less convinced by this approach. Starhawk writes disdainfully of people who are spiritually starved in their own culture and 'unwittingly become spiritual strip miners damaging other cultures in superficial attempts to uncover their mystical treasures'.[17] Carol Riddell sounds a similar warning:

> It is as if we were in a market place with many stalls offering goods. Some people go to one stall to buy, others go to another. We support each other constantly, *but the path of inner transformation is ultimately a personal one. However much we may share with others, each of us has a unique path to the Self.*[18]

Wider connections

It is not necessary here to consider every possible connection there may be between aspects of New Age thinking and the wider world of spirituality. Rather, I wish to single out two examples to show how the New Age deals with those spiritual traditions it embraces, and then to make some comments about issues of power and its wider sociological significance.

Observers with a sense of Christian history will instinctively think of gnosticism when they encounter the New Age. As part of the wider spiritual renaissance, there is indeed a revival of gnostic ideas today, and even the emergence of self-consciously gnostic 'churches'.[19] Carl Gustav Jung, whose insights are highly valued in many New Age circles, himself owed a debt to his study of ancient gnosticism,[20] and one of the leading New Age journals is called simply *Gnosis*. Observing all this, Ted Peters describes the New Age as 'perennial gnosticism', because 'The new age is reminiscent of gnosticism in the ancient Roman Empire both in what it teaches and in its competitive position *vis-à-vis* Christian orthodoxy'.[21]

There are indeed some sections of the New Age which adopt what is in effect a gnostic worldview. Sir George Trevelyan, the 'father' of the British New Age, makes this connection explicit and traces his own spiritual lineage back to ancient gnosticism, as mediated through the Knights Templar, the Cathars and Albigenses, Rosicrucianism and freemasonry. Moreover, he invokes the familiar gnostic notion of spiritual hierarchies, and sees no hope for humankind apart from a final escape from material existence into the world of spirit.[22] Those New Agers who specialize in channelling messages from spirit guides and extraterrestrials, and speculating about the lost continents of Lemuria and Atlantis or legends of Arthurian Britain, would also share this highly dualistic outlook, in which salvation can be found only through the intervention of beings from other worlds.

Because of its frequently bizarre manifestations, this dualistic New Age has often attracted media attention. But it is only one part of the whole movement, and arguably not the largest or most significant part. Many other New Agers reject such dualism, and instead adopt a monistic worldview, in which there is an essential unity between all things, both spiritual and physical. They might share a starting-point with gnosticism (human alienation as a result of people being trapped in some form of existence which inhibits the full expression of their true nature), but their answer to it is quite different. Gnostics adopted a Platonic view, seeing the human predicament as a metaphysical imprisonment of the spirit, whereas to monistic New Agers Platonism is the root cause of the problem, and enlightenment comes not through escape from this material world, but very much within it, as people attune themselves to the spiritual powers that are all around them, and of which they are already themselves a part. Far from being world-denying in an anti-materialistic sense (like gnosticism), this part of the New Age is strongly world-affirming. Here, dualism is not the answer to the human predicament, but a part of the problem, as it sets up confrontations between people and the environment, between women and men, between different races, and so on. On this view, the West's basic problem is its love affair with dualism, and the sooner it is discarded, the better.

Shirley MacLaine, who is representative of this monistic side of the New Age, highlights the dynamic of what is going on here, when she claims that in ancient times 'Christian Gnostics operated with New Age knowledge and thinking'.[23] In other words, the New Age provides the controlling agenda, arising from its essential character as a product of modernity, in particular its spin on the western doctrines that materialism is a good thing, and that individual freedom and choice are the best ways to exploit material existence. In so far as ancient gnosticism shared some aspects of that, it can be claimed as an ally providing an ancient image to what is a contemporary movement.

Much the same comment may be made about the way the New Age appears to promote ideas drawn from eastern spirituality. For example, reincarnation is popular in many New Age circles, but it would be a mistake to see this as evidence that the New Age is a form of Indian philosophy transferred to the West. For the nature of New Age reincarnation has little in common with either Indian metaphysics or ethics. In the New Age, even reincarnation can be presented as a matter of individual human choice. People are here in the form they now have because they have chosen it in accordance with their own cosmic intentions, and for their ultimate spiritual development. In the words of J. L. Simmons:

> ... the decision to be reborn is self-determined by each being ... The rebirth is planned ... Such plans include the circumstances of birth and a blueprint outline of the life to follow, so that certain experiences might provide the opportunity to learn certain lessons.[24]

Opinions like this have nothing at all to do with traditional eastern spirituality: they are the product of the culture of modernity, with its emphasis on personal responsibility, individual choice, and the underlying philosophy which projects an unrealistically optimistic view of human nature with no limits at all to human potential.[25]

As we approach the millennium, it is obvious that the New Age is the product of competing western worldviews, and whenever materials from other traditions are utilized, they are consistently cut loose from their original contexts and ransacked for whatever spiritual insights they may seem to offer. For that very reason, there is also a sociological side to the rise of the New Age which will help to identify other reasons for its current popularity. One of the most unexpected places where it is taken seriously is in the training of top business executives. A management course written by two professors at Stanford University describes its rationale as follows:

> We look within to find our own individual self and universal source. That source has been called the inner self, the Self, the hidden mind, the divine spark, the Divine Ego, the Great I Am, God, and Essence. Some say that the very purpose of human existence is to get acquainted with your own essential qualities and express them in your daily activities. Whether it is the purpose of life or not, it is a fine definition of personal creativity: living every moment from your essence.[26]

These authors then proceed to offer advice about assorted spiritual techniques and therapies that, they claim, will put modern executives in touch with spiritual realities, including overt instructions on how to contact disembodied spirits allegedly from other worlds. Nor is this an isolated example: the phenomenon of New Age business courses has been well documented elsewhere.[27] So what do ambitious business executives, homeless New Age travellers, high-profile members of the British aristocracy, and countless multitudes of visitors to New Age festivals have in common? The answer, perhaps, is deceptively simple: they are all struggling with the discontinuities of western life at the end of the twentieth century, the loss of power by westerners in general, and the loss of power by significant minorities in particular. In his book *The Interruption of Eternity*, Carl Raschke observed that throughout history such forms of esoteric spirituality have arisen in response to a loss of social power and prestige. In this context, the disinherited (at both ends of the social spectrum) retreat into

> ... a self-enforced pariah mentality, expressed in both their contempt for legitimate authority and their creation of a closed symbolic universe which only those with the proper credentials can penetrate ... the safekeeping of magical lore reflects a vicarious exercise of power which in reality has slipped away from them.[28]

This is why there are superficial resemblances between the New Age and earlier movements like gnosticism: both may be understood as responses to the breakdown of the prevailing culture, which in this case was the same culture. Ancient gnosticism arose as a response to the collapse of the Greek worldview as it had been applied and exploited by the pragmatism of Rome; the New Age is a reaction to the collapse of the same essential worldview, this time mediated through the Renaissance, Reformation, Enlightenment, and the imperialistic expansion of western nations. More than fifty years ago, Aldous Huxley argued that when material revelation becomes problematic there has been throughout the history of the West a tendency to revert to what he called 'the perennial philosophy' and search instead for an essentialist, idealist (and therefore timeless) way of understanding the meaning of life.[29] When combined with further traumas for western culture related to rapid globalization, the spoiling of the environment, and the manifest failure of the Enlightenment vision, we can see that the New Age has always been a movement just waiting to happen.

Christian responses

Finally, we come to a brief survey of some Christian responses to the New Age. Considering the way in which the New Age has opened up the whole subject of spirituality and placed it firmly on the popular agenda, it is remarkable how few Christians have engaged with it at all. And when they have done so, they have frequently made two mistakes that have tended to undermine, rather than enhance, the Christian case.

First has been the tendency to adopt an uncritical approach which assumes that the New Age is some kind of monolithic movement that can be categorized rather easily. This undifferentiated approach has led some to suppose that lurking behind the New Age is a conspiratorial attempt to undermine western civilization as we know it.[30]

But if western civilization is collapsing, it is because of inherent flaws in its own philosophical base, not as a result of any New Age conspiracy against it. Indeed, the New Age – however inadequately – is trying to ask where we go from here, given that the western Enlightenment vision is no longer viable. As far as I can see, there is absolutely no evidence of any New Age conspiracy to undermine democracy or whatever, and on those occasions when New Age people do use triumphalist language they are to be viewed in the same light as Christians, who similarly claim from time to time that they will 'revolutionize the world with the gospel'.

Allied to this is the tendency of Christians to fail to take account of the different nuances that undoubtedly exist within the New Age. For example, it is widely taken for granted that the New Age has a monistic worldview, whereas in reality it quite clearly has at least two worldviews, one monistic and the other strongly dualistic.[31] These two strands do not share the same heritage: the one has historical connections to a creation-based spirituality which is either pantheistic or panentheistic and can be traced through Romantic poets such as Shelley, Blake and Wordsworth, while the other has more in common with the movements associated with people like Swedenborg, Mesmer, Blavatsky, Bailey and Cayce. To the outsider they might easily look like two entirely unrelated movements. There is certainly a significant discontinuity between them. This has been a major reason why some commentators dismiss the New Age as irrational and nonsensical. But a more productive under-standing will locate these apparent contradictions in the New Age's foundational understanding of the nature of human alienation. For the experienced alienation of western people today is not, on the whole, a cosmological or metaphysical phenomenon, but a cultural alienation. In this context, the ultimate expression of spiritual ignorance is critical scientific thinking, and it is from this that the human spirit must be set free.

This brings us to our second mistake and highlights a further weakness in many Christian responses to the New Age, which have tended to tackle it on a rational, analytical level.[32] It is not that the New Age ought not to be subjected to such criticism, and, in the face of an increasingly irrational intellectual Establishment, one of the things that Christians need to bear witness to today is the fact that we are creatures of reason, and that, notwithstanding all the mistakes that our forebears have undoubtedly made, the capacity for rational understanding is one of the fundamental marks of being fully human. But to engage with the New Age at this level only is a serious mistake, for, to most New Agers, this methodology is one of the key contributory factors to the crisis in western culture. Using the tools of modernity to address the New Age will get nowhere, for it is by definition immune to rational criticism. Indeed, having the courage to transcend the boundaries of conventional linear western forms of perception and to discard the narrow confines of an over-reliance on rationalism is, for many, the ultimate expression of the kind of spirituality that will take us forward into the next century. Psychology professor Marilyn Ferguson expresses it eloquently:

> We live what we know. If we believe the universe and ourselves to be mechanical, we will live mechanically. On the other hand, if we know that we are part of an open universe, and that our minds are a matrix of reality, we will live more creatively and powerfully.[33]

We are on surer ground when we draw attention to the moral relativism of much that is in the New Age. But in the process of making an honest assessment of the flaws in the New Age, Christians also need to be prepared to face up to the weaknesses of the church itself. The simple fact is that, while many aspects of the New Age prescription for the ailments of today's world may be nonsensical and meaningless, its diagnosis of the disease is too accurate for comfort. Dean W. R. Inge (1860–1954) is reputed to have observed that 'A church that is married to the spirit of its age will find itself widowed in the next', and that just about sums up where Christians today find themselves. Christian beliefs, spirituality and lifestyles have become almost exclusively focused on rational systems of thinking, with a consequent marginalization of the intuitional, the emotional, the relational and the spiritual.[34] There is a need to recognize those things that are right about the New Age analysis. But beyond that, there is also a requirement for a missiological engagement with the New Age that will effectively challenge some of its conclusions. It would take another article to begin to unpack specifically what this might involve. But it would certainly take seriously scriptural models such as that provided by Acts 17:16–34 (Paul in Athens), as well as basing itself on the 'style' adopted by Jesus. Identifying 'the unknown god' in today's burgeoning spiritual market-place will be challenging for many Christians, and probably threatening, because it requires a confidence to move well beyond the safe boundaries of current church perceptions, which in turn is likely to open those who do it to criticism from others within the Christian community. Australians Ross Clifford and Philip Johnson are among the few genuine trail-blazers in this direction, and their book *Sacred Quest* deserves to be more widely known than it is, pointing the way forward to effective engagement with the New Age, and at the same time posing hard questions for the church that could yet lead to the emergence of a way of being Christian that will be so attuned to the realities of contemporary culture that there will be no need for New Age spiritual searchers to look any further. For it is a simple fact that I have never yet met a New Ager who could not potentially be a Christian, if the gospel were presented in a way that they were able to hear.[35]

Notes

1. Carol Riddell, *The Findhorn Community: Creating a Human Destiny for the 21st Century* (Findhorn: Findhorn Press, 1990), p. 222. Findhorn is on the Moray Firth in north-east Scotland, and is arguably one of the most important New Age centres anywhere in the world.
2. Ibid., p. 63.
3. Denise Cush, 'British Buddhism and the New Age', *Journal of Contemporary Religion* 11.2 (1996), p. 196.
4. Riddell, *Findhorn Community*, p. 64. Others wish to distance the serious New Age search for a new paradigm of reality from the populist or 'glamour' New Age, which concerns itself with things like the channelling of spirit guides, crystal healing, and similar phenomena. Cf. David Spangler, *The Rebirth of the Sacred* (London: Gateway, 1984), p. 79.
5. 'New thought and the New Age', in *Perspectives on the New Age*, ed. J. R. Lewis and J. G. Melton (Albany, NY: State University of New York Press, 1992), pp. 15–29.
6. Elliot Miller, *A Crash Course on the New Age Movement* (Grand Rapids: Baker, 1989), p. 14.
7. Cf. Marilyn Ferguson, *The Aquarian Conspiracy* (London: Paladin, 1982), pp. 231–241; Michael York, *The Emerging Network* (Lanham, MD: Rowman and Littlefield, 1995), pp. 324–334; Michael York, 'The New Age in Britain today', *RT* 9.3 (1994), pp. 14–21.
8. L. Wittgenstein, *Philosophical Reflections* (Oxford: Blackwell, 1968), pp. 65–78.
9. On postmodernity more generally, see Walter Truett Anderson, *Reality Isn't What it Used to Be* (San Francisco: Harper and Row, 1990); David S. Dockery, *The Challenge of Postmodernism: An Evangelical Engagement* (Wheaton, IL: Bridgepoint, 1995); David Harvey, *The Condition of Postmodernity* (Oxford: Blackwell, 1989).
10. Cf. Paul Heelas, 'The New Age in cultural context: the pre-modern, the modern and the post-modern', *Religion* 23.2 (1993), pp. 103–116.
11. Though there is more than a grain of truth in the New Age analysis. *Cf.* the comment of David Bebbington: 'It is extremely hard to resist the conclusion that the early evangelicals were immersed in the Enlightenment. They were participating fully in the progressive thought of their age' ('The Enlightenment and evangelicalism', in *The Gospel in the Modern World*, ed. M. Eden and D. F. Wells, Leicester: IVP, 1991, p. 76).
12. See my 'Christian theology, New Agers and the spiritual search of western culture', in *RJCM* (1 Jan. 1994), pp. 20–25; 'Christians, New Agers, and changing cultural paradigms', *ExpT* 106.6

(1994–5), pp. 172–176, reprinted in *MFAR* 4 (1996), pp. 13–21.

13. Shirley MacLaine, *Going Within* (London: Bantam, 1990), p. 99, a view put forward with some vigour (and scientific insight) by Fritjof Capra, *The Turning Point* (New York: Simon and Schuster, 1982); Fritjof Capra, *The Web of Life* (London: HarperCollins, 1996).

14. For an informed account of neo-paganism, see Graham Harvey, *Listening People, Speaking Earth: Contemporary Paganism* (London: Hurst and Co., 1997). There is a good deal of debate as to whether this really is a rediscovery of the past, or whether it is not an imposition on the past of a modern agenda. See, for example, discussions of the allegation that Christianity (= 'patriarchy') displaced an original goddess-centred matriarchal culture: Mary Jo Weaver, 'Who is the goddess and where does she get us?', *JFSR* 5.1 (1989), pp. 49–64; Sally Binford, 'Are goddesses and matriarchies merely figments of feminist imagination?', in *The Politics of Women's Spirituality*, ed. Charlene Spretnak (Garden City, NY: Doubleday, 1982): pp. 541–549.

15. Though there is a great deal of religious baggage associated with transpersonal psychology: *cf.* R. S. Valle, 'The emergence of transpersonal psychology', in R. S. Valle and S. Halling (eds.), *Existential-Phenomenological Perspectives in Psychology* (New York: Plenum Press, 1989), pp. 257–268.

16. David Spangler and William Irwin Thomson, *Reimagination of the World* (Santa Fe: Bear and Co., 1991), p. xvi.

17. Starhawk, *The Spiral Dance* (San Francisco: Harper and Row, 1989), p. 214.

18. Riddell, *Findhorn Community*, p. 63, italics mine.

19. On gnostic 'churches', cf. my *What is the New Age Saying to the Church?* (London: HarperCollins, 1991), pp. 86–94. For wider connections, cf. R. A. Segal (ed.), *The Allure of Gnosticism* (Chicago: Open Court, 1995).

20. Cf. June Singer, *Seeing Through the Visible World: Jung, Gnosis and Chaos* (San Francisco: Harper and Row, 1990); R. A. Segal, *The Gnostic Jung* (Princeton, NJ: Princeton University Press, 1992).

21. Ted Peters, *The Cosmic Self* (San Francisco: HarperCollins, 1991), pp. 55–56.

22. George Trevelyan, *Operation Redemption: A Vision of Hope in an Age of Turmoil* (Walpole, NH: Stillpoint Publishing, 1985).

23. MacLaine, *Going Within*, p. 30.

24. J. L. Simmons, *The Emerging New Age* (Santa Fe: Bear and Co., 1990), pp. 69–70.

25. This understanding of reincarnation also raises some frightening moral spectres: cf. my *What is the New Age Saying to the Church?*, pp. 127–134.

26. Michael Ray and Rochelle Myers, *Creativity in Business* (New York: Doubleday, 1986), p. 9.

27. Cf. Rachel Storm, 'Disciples of the New Age', *International Management* (March 1991), pp. 42–45; Richard Roberts, 'Power and empowerment: New Age managers and the dialectics of modernity/postmodernity', *RT* 9.3 (1994), pp. 3–13; and my *What is the New Age Saying to the Church?*, pp. 168–201.

28. C. A. Raschke, *The Interruption of Eternity* (Chicago: Nelson-Hall, 1980), p. 42.

29. A. Huxley, *The Perennial Philosophy* (New York: Harper, 1944).

30. For examples of this approach, see Constance Cumbey, *The Hidden Dangers of the Rainbow* (Lafayette, LA: Huntington House, 1983); Alan Morrison, *The Serpent and the Cross* (Birmingham: K. and M. Books, 1994).

31. I myself failed to note this distinction in my 1991 study of the New Age, and assumed that monism was one of its universal characteristics (see *What is the New Age Saying to the Church?*). For a corrective, see Paul Greer, 'The Aquarian confusion: conflicting theologies of the New Age', *JCR* 10.2 (1995), pp. 151–166. The same is true of the propensity of Christians to see the New Age as an occult movement. While some traditionally occult practices are undoubtedly followed by some New Agers, this is a tiny proportion of the entire movement (I would estimate that less than 10% of it falls into this category).

32. An example of this approach would be Douglas Groothuis, *Unmasking the New Age* (Downers Grove, IL, and Leicester: IVP, 1986), and *Confronting the New Age* (Downers Grove, IL, and Leicester: IVP, 1988).

33. Ferguson, *The Aquarian Conspiracy*, p. 146.

34. For more on this, see my *Faith in a Changing Culture* (London: HarperCollins, 1997).

35. Ross Clifford and Philip Johnson, *Sacred Quest* (Sutherland, NSW: Albatross, 1995). Though some have labelled him a 'New Ager', I would personally place the work of Matthew Fox in this category too. He lacks the prophetic edge of Clifford and Johnson, and has a wholly inadequate sense of

Christian history, but he is genuinely searching for a way of articulating Christian faith that will meet the needs of postmodern culture: cf. Matthew Fox, *Confessions* (San Francisco: Harper-Collins, 1996); *Original Blessing* (Santa Fe: Bear and Co., 1983); 'Spirituality for a new era', in Duncan S. Ferguson (ed.), *New Age Spirituality* (Louisville, KY: Westminster/John Knox, 1993), pp. 196–219. For a critical assessment, see Richard J. Bauckham, 'The New Age theology of Matthew Fox: a Christian theological response', *Anvil* 13/2 (1996), pp. 115–126; also my article 'Matthew Fox', in *The Dictionary of Historical Theology*, ed. Trevor A. Hart (Carlisle: Paternoster, 1997). The debate about 'post-evangelicalism' inaugurated by Dave Tomlinson is also wrestling with some of the same fundamental issues: cf. D. Tomlinson, *The Post-Evangelical* (London: Triangle, 1995); Graham Cray et al., *The Post Evangelical Debate* (London: Triangle, 1997); and David Hilborn, *Picking up the Pieces: Can Evangelicals Adapt to Contemporary Culture?* (London: Hodder and Stoughton, 1997).

16

The Bible and homosexuality

J. Glen Taylor   Vol. 21.1 (1995)

Preamble

The role of the Bible in addressing the modern question of the place of the homosexual in the church is complex. The nature of a biblical perspective will invariably be affected by the questions posed of the Bible, by the particular hermeneutic employed, and by the unavoidable perspective which every student (or scholar) brings to his or her reading of the Bible. In writing this essay, I hope to ask some of the right questions and to be fair to the views of others concerning this important issue which is pressing hard on the church and on the consciences of Christian people in various parts of the world.

Clarifications

First, the term 'homosexuality' (and 'homosexual') will be avoided in the biblical portion of this essay in preference for a more awkward cluster of words like 'homosexual relations'. This odd change in terminology is necessary because, as P. D. M. Turner notes, the term 'homosexuality' does not match well with the way in which the Bible itself addresses the issue.[1] Turner's point is that 'homosexuality' can refer to a condition or inclination apart from the acting-out of sexual relations, whereas the Bible does not recognize this distinction but normally speaks rather in terms of actual same-sex sexual relations.[2]

Second, in view of the danger to which the church has often succumbed, that of showing insensitivity towards chaste persons of homosexual orientation,[3] it is important to clarify that the issue for the Christian is *not* whether persons with homosexual orientation should be welcomed into the fellowship of the church – let us never forget that Christ died for all – but whether sexual relations between homosexuals are ever appropriate and, if so, on what terms. Because conduct and not orientation is the real issue, the purpose of this essay is to ask whether the Bible considers homosexual relations to be sinful. If the answer suggested by biblical reflection is 'yes', even when the case of covenanted Christians of homosexual orientation is considered, then the homosexual person accepted by God in Christ could no more engage in this activity than any other faithful Christian could in other forms of sin. The perspective of the Bible – indisputably authoritative in matters of Christian faith and practice – is thus crucial; it plays a primary role in determining the context and terms within which Christ is calling the church to minister faithfully to persons of homosexual orientation.

Because the Bible nowhere directly answers the question concerning the modern phenomenon of a person with homosexual orientation seeking to be involved in a covenanted relationship, we must first ask what the Bible says in response to questions raised about homosexual relations in ancient times, and then we must ask how what the Bible says may be applied to the modern situation. We begin, however, with a brief consideration of the background against which these questions must be raised, the general tenor of Scripture as a whole.

The general tenor of Scripture

The issue of homosexual relations and the Bible cannot simply be addressed with reference to the half-dozen or so passages that have at least traditionally been understood as condemning homosexual intercourse; otherwise, we might be guilty of 'proof-texting'. Rather, we must ask: in which direction *on the whole* do the biblical winds blow with respect to appropriate sexual expression between persons? By virtually any notion of the 'literal sense' of the Bible, these winds blow in the direction of heterosexual marriage, with affirmation being given to celibacy alone as an alternative. This is so from Genesis to the Song of Songs to Revelation, through well over a millennium of Scripture writing and in both the Old and New Testaments. The rapidly evolving dominance of heterosexual relations within the context of a monogamous nuclear family is unmistakable; quite simply, heterosexual relations (or, in their place, celibacy) are the only options which appear to receive approval in the Bible. Thus, unlike the ministry of women or the notion of freedom from slavery, no biblical winds blow in the direction of same-sex relations that similarly invite re-evaluation of passages traditionally considered a problem for such a view. (It is nonetheless important to re-examine the traditional passages to see if they are indeed condemnatory of homosexual relations as has traditionally been thought, a point to which we shall return.)

The account of creation is a prime example of the predominant biblical affirmation of heterosexual marriage. In Genesis 1:27–28, humanity in the form of both male and female is created in the 'image of God'. In Genesis 2 the Lord creates woman, God's specially selected emotional and physical counterpart to the man, and the two – the *'iš* and the *'iššâ* – become 'one flesh'. Within the canonical context of the preceding chapter, this 'wedding' is not just a union, but a reunion of humanity created in the image of God. Just as Genesis 1 ends with a declaration that the order of creation involving the creation of man and woman is 'very good', Genesis 2 ends with the climactic statement that the woman is the reason why a man leaves his own father and mother, to become 'one flesh' with his wife (Gen. 2:24).[4] If the powerful affirmation of heterosexual relations as the carefully planned order of creation in these two introductory chapters of the Bible is not striking to the modern Christian reader, it certainly was to the writer(s) of the Holiness Code and·to St Paul (Lev. 18:22; 20:13; Rom. 1:26–27); indeed, the doctrine of creation articulated in these early chapters of Genesis seems to be at the heart of the Bible's uniformly negative attitude towards same-sex sexual relations.

Some scholars have suggested that a few passages in Scripture constitute an important exception to the idea that heterosexual relations alone are appropriate in the Bible. For example, Tom Horner maintains that David and Jonathan and Naomi and Ruth respectively had possible homosexual relations, and he even goes so far as to suggest that Jesus and Paul had homosexual traits.[5] Leaving aside the Christological issue that the suggested case of Christ would present, V. P. Furnish is almost certainly correct that 'our sources simply do not provide the data to support such ideas'.[6] Similarly, the relative infrequency with which the Bible mentions homosexual relationships, and the possible silence of Jesus on the issue,[7] do not suggest that these relationships were relatively unimportant to biblical writers or to Jesus, as is sometimes maintained.[8] Rather, the phenomenon of relative silence probably reflects the fact that homosexual relations were not a major issue in the early church, most likely because it shared the perspective of Hellenistic Judaism that sexual relations of this kind were sinful. In sum, one searches the Bible in vain for the suggestion that homosexual relations were a viable option for the faithful.

With this general perspective in mind, we now turn to consider the passages which specifically make reference or allusion to homosexual sex. Our approach will be to survey a range of exegetical options (both traditional and revisionist), and to assess the feasibility of the various options offered.

Passages traditionally considered to condemn homosexual relationships

The Old Testament

Genesis 19; Judges 19

These well-known stories recount incidents in which the male citizenry of a town (Sodom and Gibeah respectively) proposes to have intercourse with a male visitor (or, in Gen. 19, visitors).

D. S. Bailey's attempt to interpret the verb 'know' in Genesis 19:5 as meaning something other than sexual knowledge[9] is untenable in light of verse 7, in which Lot's daughters are offered as an alternative to the men.[10] Homosexual relations are clearly in view here and they are almost certainly construed negatively. The *type* of homosexual union negatively construed, however, is far from what is typical today (it is homosexual *gang rape*, which is no less abhorrent to most modern-day homosexuals than to heterosexuals), and the broader context which concerns a breach of eastern hospitality is at least partly involved in the negative construal.[11]

A few considerations from the broader context are also relevant. Because Genesis 19 has parallels with Genesis 6:1–4, which concerns 'unnatural' relations between angels and humans, it is probably important for the story that the sexual sins of Sodom also be understood as unnatural; they are, in fact, doubly so, since the sexual relations proposed are with visitors who are both men and angels. Moreover, as Gordon Wenham notes, just as the story of unnatural relations between angels and humans in Genesis 6 is followed by a judgment involving destruction (the flood), so too the unnatural relations proposed in Genesis 19 are followed by a parallel judgment involving destruction (the downpouring of fire and brimstone).[12] In sum, although set within a particularly abhorrent context, the homosexual nature of the relations proposed forms part of the basis upon which the judgment is made that the people of Sodom were 'wicked, great sinners before the Lord' (Gen. 13:13), and thus deserving of destruction.

As an important corrective to those who might judge the sin of Sodom to be homosexual relations alone, Bailey and others rightly point out that the Bible on the whole interprets the sin of Sodom very broadly to include things other than homosexual intercourse, such as pride and insensitivity to the poor (Ezek. 16:49–50; cf. Is. 3:9). This does not mean, however, that the sexual dimension (i.e. involving unnatural relations) is ignored in the biblical witness; important here is Jude 7, which refers to Sodom's indulgence in 'unnatural lusts', and 2 Peter 2:6–7 which mentions Lot's oppression by the 'sensual conduct of unprincipled men'.[13] Of course, only at a later period does Sodom become a byword specifically for homosexual (or bestial) relations.

Leviticus 18:22 and 20:13

As Wenham notes, because Leviticus 18:22 uses the very general term *zākûr*, 'male', the passage clearly prohibits every kind of male–male intercourse (were the word *na'ar*, 'youth', used instead, presumably only pederasty would be condemned).[14] These homosexual relations are further described by the very strong word *tô'ēbâ*, 'abomination'.[15] In Leviticus 20:13 the penalty for offenders is death, putting the offence on a par with adultery (20:10) or the worst cases of incest (20:11, 12).[16] Moreover, three factors make it clear that the sexual relationship here condemned involved mutual consent between two males: (1) both parties are punished; (2) the verb used is simply 'lie' (as opposed to, say, 'seize and lie' which would imply rape); and (3) the further comment is made, 'their blood be upon their own heads', which suggests an awareness of the action and its consequences.[17] Thus, unlike Egypt, where only pederasty was condemned, or Mesopotamia, where apparently only forcible homosexual relations were forbidden, Old Testament law appears to forbid *all forms* of homosexual relations.[18] Wenham's explanation is probably correct that 'it therefore seems most likely that Israel's repudiation of homosexual intercourse arises out of its doctrine of creation'.[19]

Some scholars cast these passages from Leviticus in a very different light, however. For example, it is sometimes maintained that the context for the homosexuality referred to in Leviticus is cultic prostitution within a pagan Canaanite shrine and that the biblical writer is thus concerned more with idolatry than with homosexuality.[20] In support of this view it is sometimes claimed that the term *tô'ēbâ*, 'abomination', is a highly specific word that points toward a religious concern for cultic purity in relation to the other nations and their gods.[21] What is in view, so the argument goes, is cultic prostitution in which the participants attempt to procure fertility and fecundity by sympathetic magic through ritual sex acts, as is thought to have taken place in Canaanite culture. In short, the problem is not homosexual relations but their pagan, often idolatrous context(s).[22] Which of these perspectives is correct?

The weight of evidence at present seems clearly to favour the former construal. Recent Old Testament scholarship questions seriously the extent to which the traditional model for understanding cultic prostitution was in evidence at all either in Canaan or in Israel.[23] Moreover, it is clear from the use of the term 'abomination' elsewhere in the Bible and in other literature that an abomination could refer generally to various things abhorrent to God and that it could even refer to practices of the Gentiles, in which case the word cannot be limited to a specific concern within Hebrew religion for purity in relation to other nations.[24] Thus, given the uncertainties concerning this narrower understanding of the context and the clear generality of the condemnation of men lying with men, the view of Wenham that all forms of homosexual relations are condemned seems preferable.

A problem still possibly remains with these passages, namely their applicability to a setting in the New Testament and beyond to our own day. For example, on what grounds should the law concerning homosexuality be upheld and the law concerning intercourse with a woman during menstruation, mentioned in the same context, be dismissed?[25] Though alien to the Old Testament itself and difficult to sustain, the theological distinction between moral laws which are binding, and ceremonial, ritual, and civil laws which are not, has long been upheld in Christian tradition (note for example Article VII of the Thirty-Nine Articles of Religion).[26] The problem in the present case is nonetheless mitigated significantly by the fact that the Old Testament attitude to homosexuality is picked up and carried into the New Testament, which clearly has binding authority for Christians.[27] Certainly, early Christian writers considered the levitical laws concerning homosexual intercourse to be relevant to the issue of sexual behaviour in their own day, a point denied by Boswell but convincingly reaffirmed by Wright.[28]

Summary

To summarize, the attitude towards male homosexual relations in the Old Testament is uniformly negative. Contrary to some current thinking, the relevant passages in Leviticus do not appear to condemn homosexual relations for their associations with prostitution within the context of an idolatrous heathen cult.[29] Thus, unlike in other societies in the Ancient Near East, this negative construal within Hebrew society seems to apply to all forms of homosexual intercourse. Homosexual sex between men was termed an 'abomination' (something abhorrent to God), for which the prescribed legal penalty was so severe as to function as a strong deterrent. The explanation for this apparently blanket condemnation of homosexual unions is almost certainly to be found in the Hebrew understanding of creation, according to which the divinely ordained context for human sexuality takes place between a man and his wife. Together, the male and the female reflect the image of God, and their union, alone deemed natural in the created order, ensures procreation and the formation of a nuclear family.

The New Testament

Romans 1:26–27

Romans 1:26–27 is clearly the most important passage on homosexual intercourse in the New Testament. The broad context is summarized succinctly by Robin Scroggs: 'Since the entire world, both Jew and Gentile, is guilty of sin, grace (salvation) is entirely God's gift and extends equally to Jew and Gentile.'[30]

The more immediate context is Paul's story of how the world came to be guilty of sin; it is Paul's 'story of the universal fall'.[31] Paul argues that humanity committed the primal sin of rebellion against God by failing to acknowledge God as creator and instead turned to idolatry, the worship of created things. As a consequence of or punishment for the sin of abandoning the worship of God in favour of the worship of things in nature, 'God handed them [humanity] over in the lusts of their hearts to impurity, to the dishonouring of their bodies among themselves …' (Rom. 1:24–25).

How do the depravities in verses 24–31, including specific mention of homosexual relations in verses 26–27, contribute to Paul's argument? According to the exhaustive treatment of Hays, the depravities function in two ways: (a) 'First of all, when the text is read with literal precision, these various forms of "base mind" and "improper conduct" are seen to be *manifestations* (not provocations) of the wrath of God, punishments inflicted upon rebellious humanity … rather like the plagues visited upon the Egyptians in Exodus'; and (b) 'At the same time, the heaping-up of depravities also serves to warrant Paul's evaluation of humanity as deeply implicated in "ungodliness and wickedness" (1:18b).'[32] The depravities point to the conclusion that 'the refusal to acknowledge God as creator ends in blind distortion of the creation'.[33]

It is probably safe to say that no New Testament scholar denies that the passage presents homosexual relations as an obvious sinful distortion of God's original intention for creation.[34] Moreover, a majority of these scholars maintain that the reference to homosexual relations in Romans 1:26–27 is not to homosexual cultic prostitution, but rather to homosexual (including lesbian) sex in general; as even Boswell admits at one point, 'it is clear that the sexual behavior itself is objectionable to Paul, not merely its [cultic] associations'.[35] However, as Hays has conclusively demonstrated in his lengthy rebuttal of the late Yale historian, Boswell is far from correct in going on to conclude (a) that Paul's words are not applicable to persons of homosexual orientation (Boswell, McNeill, and others maintain that Paul refers to heterosexual people unnaturally 'exchanging' heterosexual[36] for homosexual unions), and (b) that 'contrary to nature' means not immoral but merely 'unexpected, unusual, or different from what would occur in the normal order of things'.[37] Contrary to Boswell, the 'exchange', for Paul, is between the natural course of things such as worshipping God instead of idols, and heterosexual union instead of homosexual union, and *para physin* means not simply 'unusual', but 'contrary to nature'. Hays puts Paul's concept bluntly: 'those who indulge in sexual practices *para physin* are defying the creator and demonstrating their own alienation from him'.[38]

Nevertheless, in much contemporary reflection upon Romans 1, scholars differ about the abiding hermeneutical significance of Paul's argument that homosexual acts are 'contrary to nature'. For example, because Paul's argument is not original, but is in fact closely paralleled in the Graeco-Roman philosophers and in literary texts, Furnish seems to imply that Paul's assumption that homosexual relations are 'contrary to nature' is not of abiding significance but reflects simply the common (Stoic) wisdom of the day which is subject to reinterpretation in our own day.[39] However, although Furnish is right that Paul's teaching here has clear parallels, Furnish does not emphasize sufficiently well an important aspect of the discussion, namely that Hellenistic Jewish writers such as Philo and Josephus – and, significantly, Paul – recognized a parallel between the secular Hellenistic notion that what was 'unnatural' was wrong and the *Old Testament teaching* of the law of Moses in which all forms of intercourse between males were 'unnatural' because they were contrary to the order of the world as designed by God the creator (see the discussion of Lev. 20:13; 18:22 above). Significantly then, only when the reference to God as creator and the clear allusions to the creation story in Genesis 1 – 3 are ignored or significantly downplayed (as in the works of William Countryman, Scroggs and Furnish, for example)[40] can Paul's clear teaching that homosexual union is 'unnatural' plausibly be regarded as culturally conditioned and thus of very limited (or no) relevance for the modern issue of homosexual relations and the church.

A few additional points about Romans 1 ought to be made in order to avoid misunderstanding Paul. None of what Paul states in this passage offers support of any kind for singling out homosexual intercourse as if this alone constituted a perversion of God's natural order. Nor is Paul's primary intention here to offer Christians instruction on ethical matters (although his teaching has ethical implications). Moreover, Paul's discussion of homosexual intercourse, though poignant and important, plays a fairly modest role as illustrating one of the vices that is both the consequence and evidence of humanity's rebellion against God. In light of Romans 2:1, from which it is clear that all of humankind stands without excuse before God, it would be inappropriately self-righteous for anyone to condemn homosexual relations as if these relations were not evidence of a sinful rebellion in which all persons participate. To miss this would be to miss Paul's point entirely.

1 Corinthians 6:9

In this passage, Paul considers taking another person to court to be appropriate only for 'the unrighteous' (i.e. unbelievers), which the Corinthian Christians once were but no longer are. To highlight the inconsistency of their present behaviour and to remind them that unbelievers have no share in God's kingdom, Paul recalls the unbelieving past of the Corinthians, rooted in the paganism of being, among other things, *malakoi* and *arsenokoitai*.[41] Wrongly translated together in the RSV as 'homosexuals', how should these words be translated? The word *malakos* means literally 'soft', but is used here substantivally in the sense of 'a male performing the female role in homosexual relations'.[42]

There is more confusion concerning the meaning of *arsenokoitēs* than in the case of *malakos*. Scroggs states that the first word-element, *arsēn*, means 'man', and the second, *koitai*, means 'bed', so 'marriage-bed', then sexual intercourse in general.[43] He suggests that the second component probably has a verbal force and that the first is an objective noun.[44] He translates *arsenokoitēs* as 'lying (with) a male', or 'one who lies with a male', translations which Turner similarly advocates.[45] According to Boswell, however, the first word-element is subjective (i.e. 'male' describes the gender of the one engaged in the sexual activity and not the object of it), and the second word-element is a coarse term for 'a person who, by insertion, takes the "active" role in intercourse'.[46] In other words, according to Boswell, in using the term *arsenokoitēs*, Paul is referring not to a 'homosexual' or even to a 'sodomite', but to 'male sexual agents, i.e., active male prostitutes'.[47]

Boswell's view that *arsenokoitēs* refers to a male prostitute has been convincingly refuted by Wright, who demonstrates that the term means 'a man who lies (with a man)'.[48] In fact, according to Wright and others (Turner, for example, and to a certain extent Scroggs as well), the real inspiration for *arsenokoitai* appears to come directly from the LXX version of the laws concerning homosexual expression in Leviticus 18 and 20, in which the words *arsēn* and *koitē* both occur.[49] Turner draws the following conclusions:

> Probably, then, the compound, whether chosen or coined in I Cor., is intended to evoke the Holiness Code with its emphasis on male penetration of the male. Actually as a Biblical Hellenist and Hebraist I should put it more strongly; in the absence of earlier attestation, a deliberate, conscious back-reference by the Apostle is as certain as

philology can make it. (He may or may not have known that he was dropping into 'translationese'.) Fascinatingly, by avoiding the available *paiderastēs*, he [Paul] sees to it that 'loving, consensual, adult relations' are fully covered.[50]

Significantly, then, *arsenokoitai* appears to be a Pauline invention, a direct allusion in the New Testament to the 'all-inclusive' condemnation of homosexual relations found in the laws of Leviticus.

As with the passages concerning homosexual relations in Leviticus, it has been argued that Paul's condemnation of homosexual relations both here and in 1 Timothy 1:10 refers only to pagan ritual practice. In response to this, it must be noted that there is nothing in the context that requires (or even strongly suggests) so specific an application. Certainly the background in the Greek text of Leviticus for *arsenokoitai* offers no support for this. Moreover, based on her judgment that *pornoi* must mean 'at least male prostitutes' in 1 Timothy 1:10 and 1 Corinthians 6:9, Turner states:

> The clinching refutation of the argument that Paul's condemnation of both kinds of male homosexual act[s][51] refers only to heathen ritual practice is that, in both N.T. passages, precisely the 'prostitute-inclusive' word[52] is listed separately, as we have seen. As for the idea that the Fathers condemned only the identical heathen cult-prostitution, as there were no other people who performed such acts, there is no evidence for it. Even if there was evidence, the Greek Fathers would still have called the activity itself sinful.[53]

The broader context of 1 Corinthians 6:9 offers two important additional points of relevance to the issue of homosexual relations. First, through Christ's justification and washing, the lifestyles of unbelief cited earlier in the passage must no longer characterize the Christian (v. 11). Second, Paul goes on to argue that a Christian's body, now part of Christ's own body and a temple of the indwelling Holy Spirit, should not be united with a prostitute, since intercourse involves becoming 'one flesh' with the other person. My point is that there is an operating principle here that is relevant to homosexual relations as well as to inappropriate heterosexual relations: since part of the body of Christ himself is united with another in a Christian's sexual union, that union must be holy, which homosexual intercourse evidently is not.

To summarize the discussion of 1 Corinthians 6:9: *malakos*, 'catamite', refers to the man who plays the passive (female) role in homosexual intercourse, and *arsenokoitēs*, 'sodomite', which invokes the language of the laws against homosexual relations in the LXX of Leviticus, refers to a man who lies with another man. By referring to the passive role as well as to the more general *arsenokoitēs*, by referring earlier to *pornoi* which probably already covered the case of male prostitution, and by not using more confining terms such as the term for pederasty *(paiderastēs)*, Paul seems to be offering a comprehensive (i.e. non-context-specific) condemnation of homosexual inter course. Moreover, there is nothing to suggest that Paul's condemnation of homosexual relations is based on cultic or ritual connections with these relations. The broader context helps to make it clear that relations of this kind are incompatible with membership in the body of Christ.

1 Timothy 1:10

In 1 Timothy 1:10, *arsenokoitēs* appears again, this time in a list that describes the kind of people for whom the law is useful in offering correction. The logic is that the law addresses issues of relevance primarily for the sinner, an example being the murderer who is thus told, 'Thou shalt not commit murder.'

Scroggs suggests that groups of words in this list of vices belong together and that the words *pornos*, *arsenokoitēs* and *andrapodistēs* seem to be a grouping. When seen in relation to each other, the best translation, according to Scroggs, is 'male prostitutes, males who lie [with them], and slave dealers [who procure them]'.[54] On this view, then, we have the same situation here as in 1 Corinthians 6:9 where another word or series of words affects the meaning of the more general term *arsenokoitēs* such that it becomes linked specifically with homosexual *prostitution*.

To evaluate: at least some of the words that describe similar sorts of sins are indeed grouped together in this list, but on what basis? Scroggs argues that the law of verse 8 is possibly civil and that the words in verses 9–10 are grouped together according to the categories of crimes against civil government ('lawless', 'rebellious'); then against religious law ('impious', 'sinner', 'unholy', 'profane'); then against various forms of murder ('patricide', 'matricide', 'murder'), etc. But commentators more often argue that the law in verse 8 is the law of Moses, and that at least the words in the latter part of the list – including those relevant to our discussion – are grouped in relation to the Ten Commandments.[55] On this understanding, the list beginning with 'patricide' and 'matricide' refers to extreme violations against the fifth commandment (to honour one's parents); 'murder' applies to the sixth commandment; 'fornicators'[56] and 'sodomites' refers to the seventh commandment concerning adultery; 'kidnappers' refers to the eighth commandment concerning stealing,[57] and 'liars' and 'perjurers' refers to the ninth commandment concerning bearing false witness.

What are the implications of this for the meaning of *arsenokoitai* in 1 Timothy 1:10? Given the meaning of the word as applicable to homosexual relations in general (and not male prostitution in particular, as argued earlier), its occurrence together with the general term *pornoi* (which quite possibly already covers the case of male prostitution), and its function together with *pornoi* as illustrative of breaches of the seventh commandment, *arsenokoitai* appears again not to be linked in its context to homosexual prostitution or pederasty, but to homosexual relations in general. For these and other reasons,[58] the view of Scroggs that the writer probably refers to something like a group of co-conspirators in a same-sex ring is clearly less likely than the view that the words reflect their more natural meanings of 'fornicators', 'men who lie with men', and 'slave dealers' respectively.

The applicability of the biblical witness

Up to this point, we have been concerned with what the Bible states concerning homosexual relations. It remains to be asked: how does what the Bible says apply in our own day? As noted earlier, the question is particularly important since the Bible nowhere deals directly with the issue of a Christian of homosexual orientation seeking to be united sexually in a covenant relationship with a partner of the same sex.

Evidence adduced in this paper suggests that one must differ with those who argue that there is little or no impediment in the way of condoning covenanted homosexual Christian unions on the ground that the Bible condemns only exploitative or idolatrous forms of homosexual relations such as pederasty or male cultic prostitution. There is no clear evidence for this view. Homosexual intercourse *itself* is condemned in the Old Testament primarily on the basis of the doctrine of creation, and this view is upheld in the New Testament within the theologically substantive discussion of what is 'contrary to nature' in Romans 1. Most likely, 1 Corinthians 6:9 and 1 Timothy 1:10 similarly refer to homosexual relations in general (i.e. they do not allude only to a specific type of homosexual relationship such as homosexual prostitution or pederasty).[59]

How does this apply to the modern situation involving homosexual relations between committed partners? Since the condemnation of homosexual relations in the Bible can nowhere necessarily be identified with or limited to the particularly heinous moral or ritual contexts in which these relations allegedly occurred, the fact that the modern-day context is different (i.e. non-exploitative, non-ritualistic, etc.) is not directly relevant, since the Bible seems to condemn the act of homosexual intercourse *itself as* inherently sinful.

The issue of homosexual relations within the modern church may be addressed further in relation to the church's traditional forms of authority: Scripture, tradition, reason and (according to some) experience.[60] Concerning Scripture, an avenue of recourse yet unexplored in this paper is the invocation of general principles (such as 'all our actions should be guided by love'), or analogy (such as 'just as the early church accepted Gentiles, so we should accept [sexually active] homosexuals').[61] Those who argue along these lines are often at odds with those who invoke specific biblical laws (Lev. 18:22; 20:13) or who appeal to Paul's authoritative and unambiguous depiction of the human condition in Romans 1. In this regard, Hays' response is apt: 'Whatever one may decide about the weight of the appeal to the love-principle ... the fact remains that no biblical text directly contradicts the authority of Paul's teaching on this matter.'[62] It could of course be added that other passages seem in fact to support it, and that providing a sanctioned context in which an inherently sinful act may be given free rein cannot ultimately be considered an act of love.

Concerning tradition, there can be no question that the ethical instruction of the Christian church throughout its history has been consistently opposed to homosexual intercourse.

Concerning reason, as Hays observes, statistical and scientific data describe what is, but cannot alone make moral judgments about what ought to be.[63] Thus, for example, were studies to show that sexual preference is not a matter of choice, as Paul probably thought, but a matter of orientation, Paul could theoretically reply to the effect that this simply supports his understanding that all of humanity is under the 'power of sin'. (To Paul, 'sin' is so fundamental to the human condition that it leads one to involuntary acts of disobedience for which one still remains culpable.[64]) Hays elaborates as follows: 'The gulf is wide between Paul's viewpoint and the modern habit of assigning culpability only for actions assumed to be under free control of the agent ... Scientific investigations cannot provide a *refutation* of Paul's statements; nevertheless it is clear that "reason", in contrast to Scripture and tradition, does provide arguments that may be *counterposed* to the authority of Paul's judgment.'[65]

Finally, concerning experience, certainly this is the most subjective (and debated) category from which to draw authoritative conclusions.[66] Whose experience counts above that of another, and how may this experience be assessed? When individuals claim to be in a supportive homosexual relationship in which the grace of God is experienced, how is this to be measured in the light of Scripture? Was Paul wrong? Has the creator suddenly ordained a new order by which such experiences are now right and valid? Could not the opinion of a person who claims to be in a fulfilling homosexual union simply be a manifestation of humanity's self-deception and confusion as Paul describes it in Romans 1? How could one determine whether or not this is so without reference to a norm such as Scripture? Even if one's 'story' could be assessed in such a way that it functioned authoritatively for the church, would this story stand alongside or eclipse the old scriptural norm? And if Scripture can be eclipsed, on what basis will the church evaluate other people's experiences in the future?[67]

The weight of the fourfold bases for authority in relation to the issue of homosexual relations has been summarized cogently by Hays:

> Arguments in favor of acceptance of homosexual relations find their strongest warrants in empirical investigations and in contemporary experience. Those who defend the morality of homosexual relationships within the church may do so only by conferring upon these warrants an authority greater than the direct authority of Scripture and tradition, at least with respect to this question.[68]

Conclusion

So what might a biblical strategy for ministering to homosexual persons look like? This takes us to yet another question which is worthy of a full discussion on its own. Suffice it to note briefly that a biblically sensitive strategy would clearly take us along the lines of offering love, acceptance, and understanding, and it would include a theology of the shared humanity and fallenness of us all. It would condemn any self-righteous attitude that would suggest that a person should be subject to discrimination or isolation from the church purely on the basis of homosexual orientation. It would include a message in love that, contrary to society's thinking, sexual expression is not essential to human fulfilment, as the example of Jesus Christ and countless faithful single Christians (many of them homosexuals) has shown. It would offer openly and without prejudice or judgment the message of the divine forgiveness of sins for *all*. It would seek to reclaim for the church a more credible, workable and dignified social context for living a meaningful and fulfilling single life. It would call upon sexually involved homosexuals who wish to join the fellowship of the church to join with other Christians in turning away from sin in their pilgrimage in faith. It would seek to hold in balance unprejudiced compassion, on the one hand, with the recognition of the stark reality of sin on the other hand – something our Lord did when he said to the woman caught in adultery, 'Neither do I condemn you, go and sin no more'; John 8:11). The calling for the church is to live up to the high calling of its Lord by holding these two perspectives in balance, for where there is no fallenness, there is no need of compassion, and where there is no compassion there is no escape from fallenness.

Notes

1. P. D. M. Turner, 'Biblical texts relevant to homosexual orientation and practice: Some notes on philology and interpretation', *CSR* 16/4 (Summer 1997), pp. 435–445. An apparent point of intersection between homosexuality as an inclination or condition and a biblical descriptive terminology appears in the word 'homosexual' in the RSV at 1 Corinthians 6:9, but this translation is misleading. (The NRSV is preferable: 'male prostitutes, sodomites'.)

2. As Turner notes (ibid.), only in Rom. 1 does one find a description of a state of mind associated with homosexual practice, but the practice itself is still mentioned along with this state of mind. Moreover, the state of mind is referred to only in general terms and in conjunction with various other 'disordered desires' that lie at the root of outward vices.

   Turner notes two additional reasons for avoiding the terms 'homosexual/homosexuality' in contemporary discussions. First, 'it is unclear whether it connotes (a) the state of mind or emotion, (b) the conduct, whether or not expressing (a), or (c) the condition accompanied by expression'. Turner adds: 'Moreover, the ambiguity now extends to "orientation": is protection being sought for the right to act it out in all situations?' And second, in her opinion, 'in God's providence Scripture reflects a reality of which we are now more aware, namely that the condition [of homosexuality] is not always chosen and that some people have no area of freedom (*except in action*) for which they can be held responsible' (ibid., emphasis mine).

3. Note for example the following excerpt from the Statement by the House of Bishops of the General Synod of the Church of England, December 1991: 'The story of the church's attitude to homosexuals has too often been one of prejudice, ignorance and oppression. All of us need to acknowledge that, and to repent for any part we may have had in it' (*Issues in Human Sexuality: A Statement by the House of Bishops*, London: Church House Publishing, 1991, p. 48). In illustration of the point made in the previous footnote, notice, however, the confusing ambiguity that arises from the use of the term 'homosexual'.

4. This give-away line appears to provide the *raison d'être* for the so-called second creation account.

5. Tom Horner, *Jonathan Loved David: Homosexuality in Bible Times* (Philadelphia: Westminster, 1978).

6. Victor Paul Furnish, *The Moral Teaching of Paul: Selected Issues* (Nashville: Abingdon, 1986), p. 81. Even if there were substance to the claims of Horner, the alleged biblical allusion to homosexual traits and/or same-sex sex would have to be prescribed or set forth in a positive exemplary light for it to be significant for Christian ethical reflection today.

7. Although there is no reference in the Gospels to Jesus having spoken specifically about homosexual relations, Turner ('Biblical texts relevant to homosexual orientation', p. 4) makes an interesting case on the basis of the meaning of *porneia* in the Greek Bible, that homosexual relations would probably have been included in the use of this word by Jesus according to Matt. 5:32 and 19:9. Turner defines biblical *porneia* as coming to mean 'all irregular genital contact except adultery and in some contexts [it] seems to be a portmanteau for adultery too. Matt. v and xix are cases in point.' She adds, 'It is thus not tenable that the Gospel record shows Jesus making no reference to homosexual acts' (ibid.). In any case, the Gospels portray Jesus affirming the traditional view of heterosexual marriage as the divinely ordained order for humanity (see e.g. Matt. 19:4–6; Mark 10:6–9).

8. Even in scholarly literature, one is sometimes led to infer that it would be of no great significance if homosexual behaviour was condoned by the modern church, since homosexual relationships are mentioned relatively infrequently in biblical literature. Although the proponents of this logic would hardly be likely to do so, the same logic could be applied to cases such as bestiality or child sacrifice.

9. D. S. Bailey, *Homosexuality and the Western Christian Tradition* (London: Longmans, Green, 1955). Bailey argues that the men of Sodom were not wanting intercourse with Lot's guests, but

simply credentials by which to judge that the strangers posed no threat to the town.

10. Cf. also Judg. 19:25.
11. The following comment of Turner ('Biblical texts relevant to homosexual orientation', p. 1), made with reference even to those who acknowledge the sexual connotation of the Hebrew word 'know', is poignant: 'Some ... want to make the main moral point the threat of a breach of hospitality. This makes a weak argument. Why should homosexual gang-rape have violated hospitality, unless it were inhospitable?'
12. Gordon Wenham, 'The Old Testament attitude to homosexuality', *ExpT* 102 (1990–91), p. 361. Wenham states, 'It may also be noted that the motive for divine judgment is similar in both cases. The flood was sent because of the great wickedness of man demonstrated by the illicit union of women with supernatural beings, the "sons of God". In the case of Sodom another type of illicit sexual intercourse is *at least contributory* in showing it deserves its destruction' (emphasis mine).
13. The unnatural relations primarily in mind in Jude 7 might possibly be between the men of Sodom and angels (which Lot's visitors were, in addition to being men). It is interesting to note that the implications of this passage from Jude are sometimes downplayed by implying that this epistle is somehow less deserving of a place in the Christian canon than certain other epistles. For obvious reasons, this kind of argument should be allowed to carry very little weight.
14. Wenham, 'Old Testament attitude', p. 362.
15. Ibid.
16. Ibid.
17. Ibid.
18. Ibid.
19. Ibid., p. 363.
20. Works which uphold this view include the following: John J. McNeill, *The Church and the Homosexual* (Kansas City: Sheed Andrews and McMeel, 1976); Bailey, *Homosexuality and the Western Christian Tradition;* and Letha Scanzoni and Virginia Mollenkott, *Is the Homosexual My Neighbor?* (New York: Harper and Row, 1978).
21. See, for example, John Boswell, *Christianity, Social Tolerance, and Homosexuality* (Chicago: University of Chicago Press, 1980), pp. 100–102. It is unfortunate that so highly influential a book as this contains so many misleading lines of evidence. It is no exaggeration to say that many of the arguments rallied in support of Boswell's thesis are based upon misinterpretations of classical and other sources.
22. Even if Israel's negative attitude toward this practice were attributable in part to a xenophobia vis-à-vis the Canaanites, this alone cannot have been determinative, since Israel had no qualms about sharing many practices with the Canaanites, such as many forms of sacrifice (Wenham, 'Old Testament attitude', p. 362). Wenham states: 'Aversion to Canaanite custom no more explains Israel's attitude towards homosexuality than it does its preference for monotheism' (ibid).
23. See e.g. Karel van der Toorn, 'Prostitution (Cultic)', *Anchor Bible Dictionary* 5 (1992), pp. 510–513; Elaine Adler Goodfriend, 'Prostitution (Old Testament)', ibid., pp. 507–509. A possible reference to male cultic prostitution occurs in Deut. 23:17–18. Goodfriend (ibid., p. 508) is nonetheless dubious, while van der Toorn (ibid., p. 512) suggests that the prostitution was possibly cultic only in the sense that the money gained from prostitution was paid to the temple, in payment for a vow.
24. See Richard B. Hays, 'Relations natural and unnatural: A response to John Boswell's exegesis of Romans 1', *JRE* 14 (1986), p. 212 n. 7.
25. Lev. 20:18. The law concerning menstruation is often cited as an example against the applicability of the law concerning homosexual intercourse. Given the fact that many of the principles lying behind Old Testament law concerning sex are expressed in the early chapters in Genesis, it may be that the law about menstruation reflects a more general concern for pollution of the land as the result of the shedding of human blood, a phenomenon which in other contexts usually occurred as a result of violence, as in Gen. 4:10–11. This might help to explain why, as Sperling notes, menstruation is only one of two categories in which blood in itself is a source of contamination, the other category being unjustified homicide (S. David Sperling, 'Blood', *Anchor Bible Dictionary* 1, 1992, p. 762).
26. In illustration of the difficulty with applying this distinction meaningfully, as noted above, Lev. 18:22 and Lev. 20:13 cannot be limited to a law concerning ritual purity alone. For additional problems in so limiting these laws, see the *Statement by the House of Bishops*, p. 15.

27. See the discussion later in this paper of Rom. 1:26–27 and of the Old Testament background to the meaning of *arsenokoitēs* in 1 Cor. 6:9.

28. David F. Wright, 'Homosexuals or prostitutes? The meaning of *arsenokoitai* (1 Cor. 6:9, 1 Tim. 1:10)', *Vigilia Christianae* 38 (1984), pp. 125–153.

29. Idolatry is mentioned in the same context as homosexual relations in Leviticus, but it does not follow from this that the relations condemned involved cultic prostitution in pagan cults. Rather, the Old Testament quite commonly discusses moral-social vices in the same context as religious ones (see for example Ezek. 8 – 9).

30. Robin Scroggs, *The New Testament and Homosexuality* (Philadelphia: Fortress, 1983), p. 110.

31. Ibid.

32. Hays, 'Relations natural and unnatural', pp. 190–191 (emphasis his).

33. p. 190.

34. Hays observes (ibid., p. 211): 'We must forthrightly recognize that in Romans 1 Paul portrays homosexual activity as a vivid and shameful sign of humanity's confusion and rebellion against God; then we must form our moral choices in light of that proposal.'

35. Boswell, *Christianity*, pp. 107–117.

36. As Hays notes ('Relations natural and unnatural', pp. 186–187), Boswell must here assume the phenomenon of sexual 'orientation' which was not recognized until modern times (see further my introductory comments).

37. Cited in Hays, 'Relations natural and unnatural', p. 187.

38. Ibid., p. 194.

39. Furnish, *Moral Teaching of Paul*, pp. 72–77.

40. William Countryman, *Dirt, Greed, and Sex* (Philadelphia: Fortress, 1988); for the works of Scroggs and Furnish, see the references given above.

41. These words occur in a 'stock list' of vices which scholars suggest Paul possibly borrowed from Hellenistic Judaism. See further David Aune, *The New Testament in its Literary Environment* (Philadelphia: Westminster, 1987), for elaboration and other examples of vice (and virtue) lists.

42. Turner, 'Biblical texts relevant to homosexual orientation', p. 4. Turner observes further that 'in such a context straight after the word *moichoi* no-one would have read it differently … "Catamites" is the right rendering.' Compare W. Bauer, W. F. Arndt, F. W. Gingrich and F. W. Danker, *A Greek-English Lexicon of the New Testament and Other Early Christian Literature* (Cambridge University Press, 1952/University of Chicago, 1979), p. 489, s.v. *malakos*: '2. of pers. *soft, effeminate*, esp. of *catamites*, men and boys who allow themselves to be misused homosexually.' Scroggs (*New Testament and Homosexuality*, p. 106) concludes similarly that *malakos* probably refers here to 'the "call-boy", the youth who consciously imitated feminine styles and ways and who walked the thin line between passive homosexual activity for pleasure and that for pay'. Contrast Boswell (*Christianity*, pp. 339–341), who tries to argue that *malakos* 'refers to general moral weakness, with no specific connection to homosexuality' (ibid., p. 341).

43. Scroggs, *New Testament and Homosexuality*, p. 106.

44. Ibid., pp. 106–107.

45. Ibid., p. 107; compare Turner, 'Biblical texts relevant to homosexual orientation', pp. 5–6.

46. Boswell, *Christianity*, p. 342.

47. Ibid., pp. 345, 344.

48. Wright, 'Homosexuals or prostitutes', pp. 125–153.

49. Ibid., pp. 126–146; cf. Turner, 'Biblical texts relevant to homosexual orientation', p. 6.

50. Ibid. Here, as in certain other cases, I transliterate the Greek where the original quotation contains the actual Greek letters.

51. I.e. both the passive and the active role in male homosexual intercourse.

52. I.e. *pornoi*.

53. Turner, 'Biblical texts relevant to homosexual orientation', p. 6 (cf. p. 4).

54. Scroggs, *New Testament and Homosexuality*, p. 120.

55. Note, for example, Gordon Fee (*1 and 2 Timothy, Titus*, Peabody, MA: Hendrickson, 1988), who states, 'Most likely the list is a conscious reflection of the Mosaic Law as law and expresses the kinds of sins the law was given to prohibit.'

56. Or, possibly, 'male prostitute'. In support of this alternative, see Turner, 'Biblical texts relevant to homosexual orientation', p. 4; for references to *pornos* meaning 'male prostitute' outside the New

Testament, see e.g. Bauer, Arndt, Gingrich and Danker, *A Greek-English Lexicon*, p. 700, s.v. *pornos*.

57. Fee (*1 and 2 Timothy*, p. 49) draws attention to the fact that there is a very early rabbinic tradition that links slave dealing to the eighth commandment.

58. For Scroggs's interpretation to be correct, *arsenokoitēs* would have to refer to the passive partner here, whereas he argued that in 1 Cor. 6:9 this same word denotes the active partner (i.e. the homosexual prostitute). In other words, on his understanding, Scroggs has two words for the active homosexual prostitute and none for the passive partner. The apparent incongruity between *arsenokoitai* as active in 1 Cor. and passive in 1 Tim. may be seen in Scroggs's statement that '*Pornos* could effectively function in relation to *arsenokoitēs* in precisely the same way as *malakos* does in 1 Corinthians' (Scroggs, *New Testament and Homosexuality*, p. 120). Later Scroggs seems to allude to the incongruity again in his comment that 'perhaps the effeminate call-boy is also included in the condemnation, but I see no way of making a judgment on the matter' (ibid., p. 121).

59. It is interesting to note that *pornos* and *arsenokoitēs* are the only terms listed in both 1 Cor. 6:9-10 and 1 Tim. 1:9-10.

60. For a discussion of the roles of these various authorities within the context of Anglicanism, and the question whether and to what extent experience is applicable in an Anglican context, see Murray L. Newman and Richard Reid, 'The Bible and sexual ethics', in *A Wholesome Example: Sexual Morality and the Episcopal Church*, ed. Robert W. Prichard (Alexandria, VA: Charter Printing, 1991), p. 1.

61. Some argue similarly for the acceptance of a sexually active homosexual on the analogy that the non-procreative and outcast eunuchs of Matt. 19:12 and Acts 8:26-40 were so accepted, but the analogy labours at the point of the eunuchs being celibate and sexually inactive.

62. Hays, 'Relations natural and unnatural', p. 208.

63. Ibid., p. 209.

64. Ibid., cf. Rom. 7:13-25.

65. Ibid. (emphasis his).

66. Newman and Reid observe that experience, 'if it is to be included', is clearly the 'most elusive and problematic' category ('Bible and sexual ethics', p. 1). They cite Richard Hooker in support of the claim that of the various categories, 'The Bible is first and primary' for Anglicans. This stands in contrast to the growing popularity in some ecclesiastical circles of hearing people's stories and of reflecting upon them as if these stories determine the church's stance – even above Scripture, tradition and reason. This represents a remarkable change from the church's position historically, a change that is perhaps symptomatic of a crisis of authority in society as well as in the church, particularly in relation to a timeless standard such as the Bible.

67. Hays, 'Relations natural and unnatural', p. 211.

68. Ibid.

© J. Glen Taylor 1995

Postscript
Two perspectives on the contemporary scene

The future of evangelical scholarship

A British perspective

Carl R. Trueman

While I am by trade and by training a historian, and thus given only to explicating the past, not to predicting the future, it seems only right that in a volume such as this some time should be spent looking forward to the questions and challenges which are likely to confront the world of evangelical theology in the years to come. Such an undertaking is, of course, highly speculative and fraught with risk. After all, sixty years ago the very possibility of a volume such as this would have been inconceivable – the idea that evangelicals would have been contributing at a high academic level to some of the major scholarly debates surrounding the Bible and theology would have seemed like the pipe dream of only the most hopelessly naïve optimist in the evangelical world.[1] Thus, as I now point towards what I see as the major challenges facing the world of evangelical scholarship, I am acutely aware of giving hostages to fortune and of opening myself up to the risk of appearing as an absurd footnote in any history of evangelicalism which may appear one hundred years from now.

Nevertheless, the risk is, I believe, worth taking, and that for one major reason: the work of evangelical theologians must stand in positive relation to the work of the evangelical church. If it does not, then both sides will ultimately suffer. As a result, my ambitions, concerns and fears for the future of the evangelical church are intimately connected to those that I have for evangelical scholarship; and, as I look forward, the picture is not, even now, without its dangers. Yet not one of these dangers – perhaps 'challenges' is a less loaded word in this context – is insurmountable if it is anticipated and dealt with in a biblical fashion; and if a volume such as this can serve to highlight not only the gains of the recent past but also the issues which loom in the near future, then it may ultimately stand not as a piece of pointless scholarly self-congratulation but as a positive contribution to the future health of the church.

The challenges facing the evangelical church and academy are manifold, but I have chosen to restrict myself to three: fragmentation, accountability, and success. The choice is not entirely arbitrary, representing, as I believe, the three related issues which impinge most directly upon the world of evangelical scholarship, and that at points where its work bears immediately upon the life of the church; yet neither is it in any way intended as an exhaustive account of all the challenges which face evangelical scholarship. Nor indeed is my intention to belittle the gains that have been made in the past or to paint a bleak picture of the future. Martyn Lloyd-Jones, perhaps the most influential preacher of the twentieth century, once declared that it was pointless to spend time worrying about the future of the church: the church's task was to remain faithful to the gospel; God had already promised that he would remain faithful to the church, so why worry? Thus, as I write this I am not overly concerned about the future of the church: God is faithful and will look after his own. My only fear is that the world of evangelical scholarship, which is itself the work of members of the one church of Christ and thus a beneficiary of the same promises, might well exclude itself from that glorious future through seeking the wrong things and labouring for the kind of earthly treasure which will ultimately pass away and mean nothing.

Fragmentation

Anyone involved in scholarship in any major academic discipline will be acutely aware of the fragmentary nature of much contemporary scholarly endeavour, and theology is no exception to this trend. Previous generations often produced scholars who were technically accomplished in a range of sub-disciplines within their wider chosen field. Thus, in the nineteenth century the great Princeton theologian, Charles Hodge, was able to produce major commentaries, a three-volume systematic theology, and a number of pastoral works, all with a high degree of competence.[2] In Scotland, James Denney, an evangelical of a different theological persuasion on a number of points, wrote important books in the areas of theology and biblical commentary, as well as being a noted church leader.[3] These men had their particular areas of interest, but they were able to comment with a high degree of competence in most, if not all, areas of theological endeavour – and in this they were not untypical. Since then, however, the notion of the theological renaissance man or woman has become something of a chimera. Some of the reasons for this are outside the control of the immediate scholarly community: the advent of the technological society and the near-obsession in some quarters with the production and manipulation of masses of information has combined with the (in my view not unreasonable) contractual requirement that all scholars need to publish to retain tenure, to produce a vast amount of literature in all of the theological sub-disciplines. One result of this has been that it has become virtually impossible to keep up to date with even one's own chosen field of narrow specialization, let alone with the broader contours of the theological enterprise as a whole.

In addition, the increasingly generalized nature of undergraduate degrees has been paralleled by the increasingly specialized nature of postgraduate research degrees, particularly in fields such as Old and New Testament. The result of all this, therefore, is a rising generation of scholars who are highly competent within their own chosen field of specialization, but who often lack the background to fit their research work into the wider context of theology as a whole. Gone are the days of Hodge and Denney, where scholars were able to integrate their biblical, systematic, historical and practical works into a coherent whole. Where once we had New Testament specialists who were perfectly capable of competently setting their work within the context of Old Testament studies, systematic theology, and relevant historical trajectories, we now on the whole have specialists on Mark, or Paul, or Romans, or apocalyptic, or the first chapter of Ephesians – many of which scholars are very good at their chosen task but who lack, through no particular fault of their own, the wider understanding necessary for them to contextualize their work, either theologically, historically, or ecclesiastically. Furthermore, lest any should think I have a particular axe to grind with biblical scholars, it has to be said that the same pattern is evident in the other theological sub-disciplines: in systematic theology, for example, it has on the whole been more advantageous in recent years to have an academic background in philosophy rather than in biblical exegesis – a fact that indicates a tragic divorce between two parts of the theological curriculum which would have been unthinkable in the past and which reflects a fundamental change in what precisely systematic theology is understood to be.[4]

This fragmentation has, inevitably, affected the evangelical constituency as it seeks to establish itself within the wider scholarly world and thus has to play the game according to the rules set out by the secular academy. The questions to be faced therefore are: is such fragmentation desirable or even merely acceptable? And, if not, what is to be done about it? The answer to the first question is easier than that to the second. It must be a resounding 'No', and that for the following reasons. First, as will be touched on again below, an increasingly fragmented and specialized scholarship inevitably leads to a situation where guilds of scholars become answerable only to each other, as only those within the guilds have the technical scholarly competence – and the accepted stature – to comment not only upon the work of fellow members but also, and more seriously from an evangelical perspective, upon what the Bible itself says to the church.[5] As the medieval church placed priests between God and the congregation, so modern scholarship is in danger of placing academics in much the same position. Where once Mrs Bun the Baker's Wife could read her Bible every day and understand it in a way that helped her in her Christian life, now the general feeling in some quarters is that she should have at least a postgraduate qualification in first-century Judaism before she can presume to understand anything of what Paul is saying in his letter to the Romans. If, as evangelicals believe, God is a loving God who speaks through his Word in the Bible, then hearing and understanding his voice must be open in some ways to all, whether specialists in New Testament or not. If we find ourselves, either in practice or in theory, denying or even subtly undermining the latter, then it is going to be very difficult to maintain the former in any meaningful and, in the best sense of the word, evangelical way.

Second, if the work of the church is listening to the voice of the living, personal God as he speaks in and through Scripture, and the subsequent communication of his message to the world around, then this activity is simultaneously exegetical, theological, historical, and pastoral at the very least – and all four approaches and perspectives need to be brought to bear in the church's task.[6] To ignore exegesis is to ignore the very act which brings God's word from the Bible to bear on the present church; to ignore theology is to ignore the very content of the Bible; to ignore the historical is to adopt an arrogant attitude to the past which risks all manner of theological catastrophe (there are, after all, few heresies which have not already been confronted at some point in the last 2,000 years); and to ignore the pastoral and practical is really to miss the whole purpose of the church's existence here on earth. If each of these perspectives is pursued in isolation from one or all of the rest, and even in such a way that interaction is actually technically impossible, then the work done by evangelical scholars within their respective fields is ultimately useless to the church – and, one might add, to the world to which the church seeks to witness.

Of course, it might be objected at this point that I am indulging in fantasies regarding a golden age, and that, in practice if not always in theory, the church has always depended upon its intellectual élite – its commentators, theologians, and linguistic experts – to determine much, if not all, of its testimony.

There is some truth in this and, as a historian, I am very much aware of the problem. The Reformation placed the Bible in the hands of the laity, but the Reformers were themselves very cautious about how much leeway was to be given in pratice to the laity when it came to interpreting what the Bible meant. Nevertheless, the open commitment of the Reformers and their successors to the substantial clarity and theological unity of the Bible's message, to an active role in the daily life of the church, to the preaching of the gospel as the ultimate purpose of their theological labours, to educating and catechizing the laity, and to a clear stand on precisely what was and was not consistent with orthodox Christianity, arguably served to reduce the distance between the interests of the élite and those of their congregations, while at the same time giving clear and decisive theological leadership. They also made great efforts to communicate profound theology and scholarship to their congregations without obscuring the message. One has only to read Calvin's sermons to see such an approach in action: when preaching, he adamantly refused to mention Hebrew and Greek on the grounds that such references in a sermon were mere obfuscation, and yet he still dealt with texts with great clarity and precision. Today, when scholars glory in the theological diversity not simply between but even within the Old and New Testaments, when their different disciplines are pursued in isolation from each other and for their own ends, when the daily life of the church and preaching the gospel are not priorities, and when clear doctrinal consensus is at a premium, the gap between intellectual élite and regular church member is greater than it ever has been – and references to the role of the élite in the Reformation, while perhaps relativizing the present difficulties by putting the problem in some kind of historical perspective, cannot disguise the fact that the situation we have is considerably more complicated today than it was then, with scholars in different sub-disciplines now rarely answerable even to each other, let alone to the church at large. In such a situation, recovery of the unity of the discipline, where scholars in one discipline at least become accountable to those in others, while not solving the problem, would at least be a step in the right direction. Evangelicals, with their commitment to the one God who speaks, should be at the forefront of such endeavour.

How, then, is this fragmentation to be overcome? There are, sadly, no quick or simple solutions to this situation, a situation so much easier to analyse than to solve. Nevertheless, some possible ways forward do suggest themselves. First, as mentioned above, scholarly fragmentation is in part due to factors outside the control of the scholarly community, and so it is quite possible that part of the solution will lie with such external factors as well. The intense competition for faculty positions in university departments and seminaries, combined with the financial constraints under which many such organizations work, means that those places which do become available will tend to be given only to those who are able to teach more widely than their postgraduate research competences might imply. One has only to browse the job advertisement section in the higher-education press to see that this is already becoming the norm across many disciplines, including theology. In addition, the pressure on funding and student recruitment means that many theology departments and seminaries are shrinking, and more and more generalized teaching is being demanded of current staff. The result may well be that the increasing pressures on teaching serve to counteract the pressures on research and bring the academic world back to a position where the renaissance man or woman, capable of commenting intelligently beyond his or her immediate sphere of interest, is once again a more common campus phenomenon than at the moment.

Second, the wider community of evangelical scholars can respond by striving to work closer together on theological projects. If the days of Hodge and Denney have gone – and let us pray that they might return! – when an unaided individual could competently relate systematics and biblical studies, perhaps the time is ripe for seeking to acknowledge this situation and to move to a position where evangelical scholars work as teams on particular projects. If no individual can now write a systematic theology, then maybe a team might do so – if they were willing to work together in a spirit of humility, with no one group or guild claiming an automatic privilege for their own approach to the problem. It has to be said that, from a human perspective, the chances of now realizing such a project look slim simply because of the time and organizational effort involved, but we must and should hope that there will be those who can work together to rectify the wider disintegration of evangelical theology into self-contained, self-absorbed, and thus ultimately self-defeating, sub-disciplines.

Third, and perhaps most difficult of all, those of us who aspire to be evangelical scholars must remember that we are to be first and foremost servants of the church. Our task is not ultimately to please our academic masters or to devote all of our energies to answering the questions raised by the secular academic guilds to which we belong – though there is nothing necessarily wrong with either of these tasks in themselves. It is rather to serve the church, to build her up in the faith, and to make sure that we ourselves remember that we too are to be working members of local churches. Evangelical scholars should be as committed to running a young people's Bible study, teaching in Sunday school, or doing any task which their local church requires of them, as they are to writing cutting-edge articles for top scholarly journals. After all, there is ultimately no substitute for humble service in the church when it comes to keeping our theological work in perspective and ensuring that our scholarship is also tailored towards the needs of fellow Christians. If evangelical scholars cultivate within their own professional community such a unified vision of church service, the problems of disciplinary fragmentation may well start to resolve themselves as the different theological subdisciplines are gradually tailored towards the common goal of building up the church. This may also, of course, serve to break down some of the perennial distrust which exists between church and academy over the importance of Christian theological scholarship: if the church, through our actions, can see that our work is relevant, then she is hardly going to waste time asking us to justify our existence.

Accountability

While fragmentation may well be the most pressing academic challenge faced by evangelical scholarship, it points, as has been hinted above, towards another equally serious problem, namely, that of accountability: to whom or to what is evangelical scholarship accountable? Unlike most other scholarly traditions, evangelical scholarship, at least in theory, seeks to place itself at the service of the church. It is concerned with the good news of Jesus Christ; it is therefore involved in the study of the Bible, of theology, and of church history in order to assist the church in articulating the gospel to the present age in a biblically faithful manner. It is thus theoretically accountable in the first instance to the evangelical church on earth and ultimately to God himself in heaven.

Such accountability has proved problematic, however, because much of the evangelical scholarship of the last sixty years has focused less on establishing itself within institutions which are accountable to, and which directly serve, the church and more upon establishing beach-heads in the secular university and the wider academic world (which, I must stress, is in itself a perfectly legitimate and laudable aim). Indeed, much has been made over recent years of the rise in numbers of professing evangelicals holding university – even very senior university – posts in the United Kingdom. A crude headcount does indeed indicate the significant number of individuals associated with evangelical bodies such as the Tyndale Fellowhip who now work within the university system and whose work is taken seriously not just by their immediate evangelical constituency but also by the scholarly world at large. Nevertheless, this apparent success itself brings with it its own peculiar challenges.

When addressing the issue of accountability, it is vital to remember that the secular university is in essence an Enlightenment phenomenon and that its criteria for what is and is not acceptable are not the same as those of the church. This should immediately alert everyone to the fact that an evangelical university scholar is, in some ways, a Harlequin figure, the servant of two masters. While the historical origins of many British and European universities lie in the Middle Ages and thus in a strongly Christian milieu, the immediate roots of their current intellectual culture are of a much more recent vintage. The impact of Enlightenment philosophy upon university curricula and agendas from the early eighteenth century onwards, with its privatizing of religious beliefs and quest for universal categories and criteria of discourse, effectively served to secularize university patterns of learning and notions of knowledge.[7] There was, of course, no absolutely rigid code of what was and was not considered to be *true* – universities continued to be places of heated academic disputes and a variety of scholarly pursuits – but the basic boundaries of what was and was not considered to be *plausible* were set by the secular philosophies of Enlightenment Europe. The result was that the plausibility structures of universities shifted in a way that excluded the supernatural, and along with it the traditional understandings of God, revelation, and salvation, from university discussion. Orthodox, supernatural Christianity became, quite simply, implausible within the scholarly world, given the underlying assumptions of university discourse.[8]

In attempting to penetrate this university environment, evangelicalism has indeed enjoyed some success. It is certainly true, particularly in the field of biblical studies, that evangelicals have made significant contributions to wider scholarly debates and now enjoy considerable credibility within the wider academic world. Evangelical commentaries appear on university reading lists; articles by evangelicals are published in mainstream scholarly journals; and books by evangelicals regularly appear from the major academic presses. The achievements are not entirely unproblematic, however: in order to gain this foothold within institutions whose plausibility structures are basically in- imical to their ideological commitments, evangelical scholars have sometimes had to don the garb of the secular academy in order to be accepted as contributors to the ongoing scholarly debates. This is where the danger lies: it is a fine line between, on the one hand, being all things to everyone in order to win men and women for Christ, and, on the other hand, simply accom- modating to the wider culture in order to be accepted.

In this context, evangelical scholars must strive to be acutely sensitive to the nature of the secular universities' own presuppositions and approved methods. Sometimes it is no doubt possible to demonstrate that evangelical conclusions are, after all, plausible, even within the epistemological frameworks of modern university culture. Nevertheless, sometimes this will not be the case: it is surely no coincidence that one area in which evangelicals have signally failed to make any impact on secular universities has been that of systematic theology, where one's presuppositions are only too evident to all, and where evangelicalism's commitments to an infallible Bible, to supernaturalism, and to Scripture as the epistemological starting-point of theology, would be utterly unacceptable within the current canons of university discourse.[9] Only where it has appeared plausible to claim some kind of common ground, be it in terms of methodology or rationality, between evangelical theological scholarship and the secular academy have evangelicals been able to find a place at the academic debating table. Thus, we have evangelical university teachers in biblical studies, philosophy, church history and historical theology – all areas where some kind of common presuppositional or methodological ground has apparently been found, however illusory such may sometimes be – but very few in systematics;[10] and those evangelical systematicians we do have often work in areas such as linguistic philosophy where positive contributions to university life can be made without touching on central evangelical tenets, or at least in a manner which is separable from such.[11]

It is crucial that we understand that our failure to spend time reflecting on the crucial methodological assumptions of university discourse has led us unwittingly to some unfortunate results. For example, the language and thought forms of our evangelical scholarship have often come to emulate those of our non-evangelical colleagues so that the distinction between the two has become blurred. Thus, references are found in works by evangelical scholars to deutero-Isaiah, to the 'Easter event' rather than to the resurrection, to the author of the Fourth Gospel rather than to John, etc. Now, such terminology does not in itself necessarily imply particular dogmatic commitments – one must avoid adding the 'root fallacy' to the list of crimes of which James Barr has accused evangelical scholarship – but it can lead to confusion. For example, one might choose to refer in a book to deutero-Isaiah even in an argument where text-critical questions are not significant. One might do this simply because such is the accepted terminology when referring to certain parts of the book of Isaiah. Nevertheless, before doing so it might be profitable to reflect for a moment on the origins and purpose of the terminology. The term itself derives from a tradition of scholarship which rejects the original unity of the book, and thus stands against the background of a variety of theological issues concerned with authorship, inspiration, and the nature of predictive prophecy. If an evangelical scholar holds to the multiple authorship of Isaiah and reinforces this with the standard rejection of the early date of certain parts of Isaiah's prophecy, then the use of the term is quite legitimate –

but then that scholar should also make quite clear what the wider theological implications of this view are. If, however, some scholars use this terminology but do not hold to the theory of multiple authorship etc., then we can legitimately ask why they bother to use terminology which has been developed for no other reason than the convenient and precise expression of the view they in fact reject. The reasons could be wholly benign; but if they are using the term simply to appear credible to the wider academic community, then we must ask whether this is necessary or helpful, whether they have unwittingly become sheep dressed up as wolves, unnecessarily frightening to the evangelical community, and scarcely likely to impress any genuine wolf. We must all take care to ensure that the pressure not to appear obscurantist in front of the academic community never proves greater than the desire to present a clearly defined, unequivocal position to the church.

I am aware that some would claim at this point that multiple authorship and pseudepigraphy are conclusions demanded by any fair reading of the evidence. My response would be to argue, first, that notions of what constitutes evidence and how it should be interpreted are critically related to presuppositions. This is not to reduce all knowledge to presuppositions: such a naïve stance is scarcely legitimate, particularly for a historian! Nevertheless, it is to highlight the fact that the relationship between presuppositions, evidence and interpretation is a crucial one which requires careful critical reflection on the part of the practitioner, and that of a kind which seems all too rare in evangelical biblical scholarship. Often, the game seems, at least to an outsider, to be one where evangelical scholars attempt to beat others by operating within a neutral, mutually acceptable framework in order to demonstrate that conservative conclusions are still plausible within the context of modern university discourse. Neutral frameworks are, of course, something akin to the crock of gold at the end of the rainbow. In my own field of history, where Marxists, Skinnerites, deconstructionists and materialists, to name but four, all offer their own readings of the past, I have yet to discover an analytical framework which could be regarded as 'neutral' in any meaningful sense. Thus it would be good – indeed, highly beneficial – to see more evangelical biblical scholars reflecting on the presuppositions and interpretative frameworks they are using, and explaining exactly what they are.

Second, as issues of authorship and so on have dogmatic implications, the implications of asserting, say, the pseudepigraphal nature of a canonical text, need to be carefully delineated. If, for example, it can be demonstrated that letters of the style and genre of 2 Peter were routinely pseudepigraphal in the ancient world, with no deceptive or malicious intent implied, then one might wish to make the argument that the pseudepigraphal nature of Peter would not seem too devastating for the canonical status of the letter. If, however, benign examples of such were rare or even unheard-of phenomena, then significantly more caution needs to be exerted. Even if such examples were not rare, the contemporary documentary evidence we have of life in the first century is scarcely exhaustive and thus not necessarily representative, and therefore it might be useful only as a basis for very tentative judgments. The declaration that 2 Peter is pseudepigraphal would then raise acute questions about its status as a canonical text. Indeed, in this case the existence of one surviving case of malicious pseudepigraphy might be enough to cast doubt upon the safety of denying Peter's authorship. In such contexts, those making a case for pseudepigraphy should feel themselves obliged to address the issues raised by their conclusions regarding authorship for their wider notions of biblical authority, inspiration and canon.

In fact, the ease with which the theologically loaded terminology of the academy, along with much else, has penetrated evangelical discourse is paralleled by the fact that evangelicalism now embraces positions which fifty or a hundred years ago were regarded as typical of traditional liberalism. The virgin birth, the theological unity of the Bible, the historicity of Jonah, the reality of original sin, the existence of hell as a place of eternal punishment, the nature of God's wrath against sin, the illegitimacy of a committed homosexual lifestyle – mutually exclusive positions on all of these can be found emanating from professed evangelical authors, the result of a slow but steady elision of conservative and liberal evangelicalism and the gradual shift in definition of what is and is not evangelical. Indeed, the dramatic evangelical penetration of the academy has been accompanied by the equally dramatic collapse in the theological consensus among evangelical scholars – though not, on the whole, among ordinary church members as yet – as to what precisely an evangelical is. A movement broad enough to embrace writers such as R. C. Sproul on the one side and Clark Pinnock on the other is undergoing a serious identity crisis. This crisis is, in part, the result of a failure by the evangelical scholarly community to clarify in its own mind to whom exactly it is ultimately accountable, and to prioritize and shape its work accordingly. It is also, no doubt, the result of the failure of the evangelical scholarly community to keep its own house in order. Nobody should object to open and honest enquiry, but when that enquiry leads us to break with positions which are definitive of evangelicalism, we should have the honesty and integrity to take the appropriate action in relation to our position in the evangelical camp.

Two questions therefore arise at this point. Does the criticism of James Barr still ring true today, that evangelical scholars are respected by the wider scholarly community only at precisely those points where they are not evangelical in the accepted traditional sense of the word?[12] And does recent evangelical success within the academic world depend to a large extent upon basic changes of definition with regard to what actually constitutes an evangelical position? If the answer to either question is anything less than a decisive 'No', then the grounds for the unadulterated celebration of evangelicalism's academic achievements become somewhat problematic.

In the mid-1980s, in a book intended for a popular, rather than scholarly, audience, Francis Schaeffer pointed to what he regarded as a spirit of accommodation among the evangelical scholars of his day and to the failure of evangelical leaders on the whole to grasp the nettle and do something about it.[13] His indictment still stands, and those of us who claim to be evangelical scholars have still to demonstrate our willingness to give an account of ourselves not simply, or primarily, within the secular academy but within the church as well. If we ever make our academic expertise the basis for exempting our scholarship from the discipline of the church, then one can only assume that we have forfeited the right to be considered evangelical, however orthodox we might otherwise be, because we no longer feel any responsibility towards that which has responsibility for the evangel: the church. Those of us who are evangelical scholars in the academy need to reflect long and hard on the fact that our evangelical integrity, based upon accountability to the Christian community under God, and our academic credibility, based upon acceptance within the plausibility structures of the secular university, may not infrequently prove to be mutually exclusive categories. The only question then is: which is ultimately more important to us? The question of accountability will not go away, and we must ask ourselves if the flimsy consensus that currently holds academic evangelicalism together can be maintained indefinitely if the *evangelical* distinctiveness of *evangelical* scholarship is to be preserved. The rising generation – church leaders and scholars alike – have a duty to create an environment in which the biblical fidelity of evangelical scholarship is strengthened through proper ecclesiastical accountability.[14]

How such accountability would work out in practice is, of course, a very difficult issue, and one which will require the kind of long-term reflection and detailed discussion which is simply not possible within an article of this size. Nevertheless, some basic elements of a solution would appear to be obvious: a theologically literate church leadership; a church that actually cares what its theologians and scholars are doing; and, above all, a clear stand by all concerned on precisely what is and is not evangelical. The last point should be easy: evangelicalism has historically defined itself in part in terms of definite doctrinal commitments which, while allowing for a certain diversity,[15] yet set limits to beliefs. In Britain, the position is summarized neatly in the UCCF

Doctrinal Basis, which was framed against the background of the theological legacy of the Reformation. Today, it is the doctrinal standard of scholarly fellowships linked to UCCF and provides a normative theological stance for those who freely identify with the cause of evangelical scholarship. In terms of the Doctrinal Basis and the issue of accountability, the point is simple: either the DB means something or it does not. The statement on, for example, sin, either means something or it does not; the statement on justification either means something or it does not; the statement on the Scriptures either means something or it does not. Looked at historically – and, one could add, from the point of view of the non-scholarly world of the evangelical church in general – these statements were clearly intended to have a specific meaning and to set boundaries between the evangelical and the non-evangelical; looked at in terms of contemporary practice, they appear to mean very little when the whole evangelical scholarly picture is taken into account.[16] The first move to accountability would seem, therefore, to be the clarification of what exactly such evangelical doctrinal bases mean and how they are meant to function, combined with an acknowledgment that agreement on a form of words, without agreement on what those words represent, is illusory, deceptive and ultimately very unhelpful to all concerned.[17]

Success

The third and final challenge which I wish to look at is, perhaps, potentially the most serious of all: success. Evangelical scholarship has been remarkably successful in the last sixty years, at least within the sphere of academia, where evangelicals have made their mark particularly in the field of biblical studies; but there must be no triumphalism. Many a revival within the church has contained within it the seeds of its own destruction, as a glance at any elementary textbook of church history will confirm, and thus a careful appraisal of evangelical success in the academy is important if the future health of the movement is to be assured.

First, all talk of success must be set within the larger context, not of the academy, but of the church. Here, it must be said, the picture is not so rosy. While we may take heart from observing that the collapse in membership in evangelical churches has been nothing like as dramatic as that in liberal churches, confirming the fact that liberal talk of 'a relevant gospel' has little actual relevance outside of certain scholarly circles, we must face up to the fact that the evangelical renaissance in academia has not been matched by an evangelical renaissance in the churches, where numbers are on the whole in decline (at least in the West) and there seems little appetite for solid theology.[18]

In light of this, there is little basis for complacency in the evangelical scholarly community; there is without any doubt more rejoicing in heaven over one sinner who repents than over ninety-nine evangelical scholars who have their PhDs published by a university press. Further, to draw an analogy with medical research, the success at building up university medical faculties and research institutes ultimately counts for nothing if no more diseases are cured and no more members of the public actually enjoy better health as a result. So it is with theology: if what we do never has any pay-off in the pulpit or pew, then we have little ground for satisfaction.[19] Again, as in earlier sections of this chapter, questions about the priorities of evangelical scholarship, the accountability of evangelical scholars, and the success with which their scholarly pursuits are communicated to the church and integrated into its life become all too obvious at this point. We should not belittle the gains that have been made – but we should not forget the frequent failure of the scholarly community to serve the church which provides the only real reason for its existence.

Second, success has without doubt brought with it respectability – and once a movement becomes respectable, it becomes attractive to those outside. Where once the title 'evangelical' merited scorn and derision, it can now at least command serious attention if not always respect within some academic circles. It also opens up certain publishing presses, journals and conferences to those seeking an audience or who are perhaps disillusioned with the lack of spiritual life found in the more traditional liberal stream of academic life. The result has been that more and more scholars are prepared to identify themselves with the movement, not all of whom, as already noted, hold to what many would regard as classic evangelical positions, yet who are happy to sign up to doctrinal positions which are more and more subject solely to private interpretation. This has added fuel to the process of expanding evangelicalism's meaning to embrace traditionally non-evangelical positions, symbolized by the coining of a new, orthodox-sounding term, 'open evangelical', to replace the older and less slippery category of 'liberal evangelical', as well as by the disturbing tendency in some quarters to go to great lengths to criticize and disparage evangelical theologians of previous generations.[20] Neo-orthodox positions on Scripture,[21] the rejection of penal substitutionary atonement,[22] the abandonment of the Reformation understanding of justification – all are countenanced within the wider movement. To be sure, evangelical scholarship has always defined itself fairly loosely, but it must be said that this looseness becomes more marked as the years go by, something exacerbated by the consistent failure of those of us who are evangelical scholars to define the boundaries of what is and is not acceptable, and at times by the existence of the same academic schizophrenia on our faculties as one finds among students: our uncanny ability to be theologically liberal from Monday to Saturday and theologically conservative on a Sunday. In addition, evangelicalism as a whole (and the scholarly community is no exception to this) has always tended to exalt its great leaders and to place its confidence perhaps a little too readily and too completely in them. Thus, it has been profoundly shaped by the views of significant individuals, which may not in itself always be a bad thing, but it does leave the movement peculiarly vulnerable to change as and when the views of particular leaders shift over the years.

Each of these factors has served to blur the boundaries, to shift the definition of evangelicalism and to make clear and strong leadership in the scholarly world more difficult. Indeed, the cynical observer might well be led to the conclusion that there is now hardly a single doctrine, other than the bare existence of God, upon which the entire evangelical scholarly community, defined in its broadest terms, could agree upon without any hint of equivocation. Such might well be a hyperbole – but not by much. Academic success has brought with it a measure of respectability, but the price may ultimately prove to have been very high indeed. Let us not forget that we strive in the first instance for theological integrity and Christian fidelity, not academic respectability. And, as problems of definition and boundary-marking arise in the future, let us also remember that there is no eleventh commandment which says, 'Thou shalt not under any circumstances rock the boat.'

Conclusion

Perhaps the above seems like a bleak picture. It is certainly not intended as such: my self-imposed brief was to look to potential challenges and dangers of the future, not to the gains and triumphs of the past. Had this been a retrospective, the tone would perhaps have been less that of Jeremiah and more that of Asaph in Psalm 79, for the last decades have surely been a testimony to the goodness of God towards those who have sought, against all the odds, to realize the dream of an evangelical scholarship which can hold its head high in the academic world. Those, such as myself, who are the benficiaries of this legacy, owe a great debt of gratitude to those who, under God, have achieved so much in such a relatively short space of time. Indeed, the essays collected in this volume are intended as representatives of precisely the kind of contributions that evangelical scholarship has made over the last twenty-five years. The careful reader will find that there is much here to rejoice over, plenty of evidence of ground already claimed, and, perhaps on occasion, hints of precisely the kinds of issues I have raised above.

None of the problems posed by the challenges I have mentioned should belittle the very real achievements that have been made, and none is in itself necessarily insurmountable. The important thing is to acknowledge their urgency and to act upon them before it is too late. There is absolutely no reason why the future should not witness the growth of an evangelical scholarship that brings together the fragments of a shattered academic discipline and rebuilds them into a theology which reflects the unity of the God whose revelation made such theology possible; there is no reason why evangelical scholars should not pursue their work in a way which is accountable to the church and which serves the needs of the church; and there is no reason why the success of the movement in academia should not find its counterpart in the growth – both numerically and spiritually – of the churches it serves. What is certain is that such scholarship requires strong leadership – those who are prepared to build on the success of their forebears while at the same time realizing that there is much to be done and that some of it will be difficult, costly and perhaps at times very unpopular, particularly in terms of the maintenance of the difference between what is good and what is bad, what is orthodox and what is heterodox, what is biblical and what is merely designed to soothe itching ears. Let us pray that the Lord will give us just such strong, faithful leadership, and that each of us individually will have the spiritual stamina and discernment to fulfil our particular roles in the drama as it unfolds. We have a great gospel, a great story to tell: may the God of all grace make us humble witnesses to that greatness!

Notes

1. A brief account of postwar evangelicalism in Britain can be found in D. W. Bebbington, *Evangelicalism in Modern Britain: A History from the 1730s to the 1980s* (London: Unwin Hyman, 1989). A popular narrative of various developments, including the growth of evangelical scholarship, is that by O. R. Barclay, *Evangelicalism in Britain 1935–1995: A Personal Sketch* (Leicester: IVP, 1997). A book which has a primarily American focus but which also contains material of relevance for the British situation is Mark A. Noll's *Between Faith and Criticism: Evangelicals, Scholarship, and the Bible in America*, 2nd edn (Grand Rapids: Baker, 1991).
2. E.g. *Systematic Theology*, 3 vols. (Grand Rapids: Eerdmans, 1996); *Commentary on the First Epistle to the Corinthians* (Grand Rapids: Eerdmans, 1980); *The Way of Life* (Philadelphia: American Sunday School Union, 1841). A narrative account of Hodge's life and work can be found in C. A. Salmond, *Princetoniana: Charles and A. A. Hodge with Class and Table Talk of Hodge the Younger* (Edinburgh: Oliphant, Anderson, and Ferrier, 1888); also David B. Calhoun, *Princeton Seminary: Faith and Learning 1812–1868* (Edinburgh: Banner of Truth, 1994).
3. E.g. *Studies in Theology* (London: Hodder and Stoughton, 1895); *The Epistles to the Thessalonians* (London: Hodder and Stoughton, 1892). On Denney, see the relevant chapter in Alan P. F. Sell, *Defending and Declaring the Faith: Some Scottish Examples 1860–1920* (Carlisle: Paternoster, 1987).
4. Howard Marshall has noted the comparative lack of interest in biblical exegesis in the influential approach to systematic theology of Paul Tillich (and, by implication, in those who follow his lead): see his article 'Climbing ropes, ellipses and symphonies: the relation between biblical and

systematic theology', in Philip E. Satterthwaite and David F. Wright (eds.), *A Pathway into the Holy Scripture* (Grand Rapids: Eerdmans, 1994), pp. 199–219; the same topic, the relationship between biblical and systematic theology, is discussed from the systematician's perspective by Kevin J. Vanhoozer in 'From canon to concept: "same" and "other" in the relation between biblical and systematic theology', *SBET* 12 (1994), pp. 96–124. It is worth noting, however, that there is a discernible return to interest in biblical themes and theology in the work of recent systematicians such as Colin Gunton of King's College, London. Whether this represents a long-term trend away from the sterile philosophical approach of Paul Tillich and his epigoni remains to be seen.

5. Ironically, when passing a draft of this paper around for comment, two readers responded by saying that it was unfair of me to criticize the work of biblical scholars because I was not a biblical scholar and thus could not understand the complexity of the issues involved, nor had I faced the kind of critical issues in the academy which such academics face on a daily basis. This is, to an extent, true – but the very fact that such a criticism of my comments was made is itself a dramatic demonstration of precisely the disciplinary fragmentation and lack of sense of accountability to those outside the guild which I was criticizing. My own hope is that the incompetent criticisms of one such as myself might encourage those who are competent in the field to make constructive contributions to solving this problem from a more informed perspective.

6. Cf. the constructive proposals of Richard A. Muller, 'The study of theology', in Moisés Silva (ed.), *Foundations of Contemporary Interpretation* (Grand Rapids: Zondervan, 1996), pp. 533–666. A scholar who had made some provocative arguments for the reunification of the theological discipline is Francis Watson, whose views are neatly summarized in his essay 'The scope of hermeneutics', in Colin E. Gunton (ed.), *The Cambridge Companion to Christian Doctrine* (Cambridge: Cambridge University Press, 1997), pp. 65–80.

7. For a controversial and highly charged discussion of this issue, with particular reference to German universities (though with much wider relevance), see Eta Linnemann, *Historical Criticism of the Bible: Methodology or Ideology? Reflections of a Bultmannian Turned Evangelical*, trans. Robert W. Yarbrough (Grand Rapids: Baker, 1990).

8. For further discussion, see the essay by Paul Helm in this volume.

9. It is worth qualifying this statement by noting that the policy of British evangelical scholarship after the Second World War was to channel its limited resources into biblical studies rather than into the other theological disciplines. Thus, one could argue that systematic theology is actually fifty years behind biblical studies as a result of this particular commitment of resources and will catch up in due course. There may be some truth in this; only time will tell.

10. Some might well argue at this point that, in Donald Bloesch and others, evangelicalism has produced systematicians of note. Two things are worth mentioning in this context. First, it is far from clear that Bloesch's work is taken seriously outside of the seminary context and within the systematic-theology sections of secular universities. Secondly, Bloesch himself represents that peculiarly Anglo-American tradition which reads Barth in as conservative way as possible, and the evangelical tradition in as loose a way as possible, in order to establish an overlap between the two. It is indeed doubtful whether such a reading does either theological stream justice. For some interesting reflections on the reception of Barth in the Anglo-American world see Richard H. Roberts' essay, 'The reception of the theology of Karl Barth in the Anglo-Saxon world: history, typology and prospect', in S. W. Sykes (ed.), *Karl Barth: Centenary Essays* (Cambridge: Cambridge University Press, 1989), pp. 115–171, esp. pp. 146–148.

11. Cf. Kevin J. Vanhoozer, *Is There a Meaning in this Text? The Bible, the Reader and the Morality of Literary Knowledge* (Leicester: Apollos, 1998), where it is arguable that the fundamental defence of 'the author' is separable from Vanhoozer's theological position and agenda, and where it is the former, not the latter, which will gain the book an audience in the secular academy.

12. For a resounding and well-informed critique of Barr's strictures on evangelical scholarship, see the essay by David F. Wright in this volume. A somewhat less tendentious though still hard-hitting and controversial version of Barr's argument can be found in Harriet A. Harris, *Fundamentalism and Evangelicals* (Oxford: Clarendon, 1998). Not all evangelicals thought that Barr was unfair or inaccurate in some of his most controversial criticisms. In an interview in *Christianity Today*, published on 8 February 1980, Martyn Lloyd-Jones commented that 'James Barr's *Fundamentalism* correctly represents some of this country's prominent Evangelicals as having quietly and subtly crossed the line by concessions to higher criticism.' Quoted in Iain H.

Murray, D. *Martyn-Lloyd Jones: The Fight of Faith 1939–1981* (Edinburgh: Banner of Truth, 1990), pp. 719–720.

13. Francis A. Schaeffer, *The Great Evangelical Disaster* (Eastbourne: Kingsway, 1984).

14. While on this issue, of course, it is worth noting that the pressures of the secular world are not confined to scholars working within the context of the university. The massive expansion of higher education in the last fifteen years has witnessed not only a huge growth in the number and diversity of university-based religion courses but also – and perhaps more significantly for the church – a rush for university validation by church-linked and independent theological colleges. This latter development has often in the first instance been driven by basic economic considerations – colleges depend upon fees and it is a basic fact of life these days that a university or university-validated degree is considered better value for money than the non-validated alternatives. In addition, the lucrative overseas market is simply inaccessible to any institution which does not offer its students a recognized university-validated course.

This situation could well prove in the future to be highly ambiguous, particularly for theological colleges. In the past, the immediate point of accountability for such institutions was the church or the churches who supplied their students and whose pulpits their graduates were intended to fill. Such accountability was not in itself sufficient to guarantee the theological integrity of any institution – one has only to look at the history of many church colleges to see that such has never been the case – but it did at least mean that the theoretical chain of command remained within a broadly Christian context. Once university validation has been accepted, however, a new set of criteria apply: no longer is the college solely responsible to the church(es) which it serves; it must also make sure that it conforms with standards applied to it by its validating body – a secular university. The chain of accountability has thus become ambiguous, embodying as it now does both secular and religious elements. What the long-term effects of this will be, it is currently hard, if not impossible, to judge. Indeed, it is unlikely that the results will be uniform – choice of college staff, of validating body, of external examiners, to name but three, are all factors which will have a profound influence on local variations. What is certain, however, is that the increasingly high-profile role of secular bodies such as central government and universities in the life of theological colleges will be one of the major challenges faced by these institutions in the next fifty years, and the response of those involved to this will be decisive for the shape of the theological education and scholarship emerging from this context – and, one might add, for the type of theology and pastoral ministry taken into the churches by graduates.

15. For example, to return to our earlier examples, both Hodge and Denney were evangelical, while yet differing to a certain degree on a number of doctrinal points. Nevertheless, not even looking through the most rose-tinted spectacles would allow any contemporary observer to conclude that the differences between Hodge and Denney are not fairly minor compared to the differences between the different wings of modern evangelicalism.

16. An interesting book in this context is Millard J. Erickson's *The Evangelical Left* (Carlisle: Paternoster, 1998), which is a popular exposition and critique of the work of Bernard Ramm, Clark Pinnock, Stanley Grenz and James McClendon. On the whole, the book is an enlightening, if somewhat brief, analysis of the process of theological revision which has been underway in certain evangelical circles for some time. Two aspects of the book, however, are particularly noteworthy in the light of what has been said above. First, Erickson includes McClendon only because he teaches at Fuller Theological Seminary, an evangelical institution, not because of his theological convictions (p. 40). This represents an interesting shift in evangelicalism's defining character-istics from doctrinal commitments to organizations and institutions. Second, despite Erickson's own commitments to an orthodox evangelical position, and despite his clear realization that, at least in the case of McClendon and Pinnock, fundamental boundaries have been crossed on almost every doctrinal distinctive of historic evangelicalism, he yet refuses to draw the obvious conclusion and still argues that they fall within the evangelical constituency (pp. 139–141). This raises in an acute form basic problems of definition and accountability which Erickson's reference to Zeno's paradox on page 141 does little to resolve.

17. I would stress here that I am not arguing for the end of theological debate, but rather for honesty and integrity in such debate: if, for example, some consider the *broad* tradition of evangelical teaching on sin or justification, epitomized in the UCCF Doctrinal Basis, to be fundamentally wrong, they should feel no shame in declaring that to be the case and in acting in accordance with

their convictions by dissociating themselves from public identification with what they believe to be a theologically incorrect position. What is surely unacceptable is a twisting of meanings or carefree attitude to credal documents which accommodates those who reject clearly stated positions by effectively denying their whole import. My own view is that if the fundamentals of historic evangelicalism are wrong, then we should have the humility to acknowledge this, and, so to speak, pack up our bags, and go on our way; if, however, they are, as I believe, correct, we must stand by them and maintain them with vigour as being of the very essence of the Christian faith.

18. On this issue, see David F. Wells' trilogy: *No Place for Truth* (Leicester: IVP, 1993); *God in the Wasteland* (Leicester: IVP, 1994); and *Losing Our Virtue* (Leicester: IVP, 1998). The argument in Mark A. Noll, *The Scandal of the Evangelical Mind* (Leicester: IVP, 1994), covers similar territory but is vulnerable to criticism on two counts. For a start, Noll tends to view the essential problem with evangelicalism's current academic outsider status as being primarily an intellectual issue. There is some truth in this, but two things need to be borne in mind. First, Christianity, by the very fact that it focuses upon the resurrection from the dead of one who is regarded as the incarnation of the living God, has at its very heart a dogma which is sheer intellectual folly to general scholarly culture – and that is true of postmodernism as well as of modernism. Second, he tends to take secular objections to Christianity as being sincere and having integrity. This is not always the case – the morality of Christian salvation is as morally repugnant to the non-Christian intellectual culture as many of its intellectual commitments, and this, as any evangelical who has ever worked in a secular university department will confirm, provides a strongly irrational and emotional antipathy to evangelicalism among liberal colleagues. In this context, the argument of former *Themelios* editor Stephen Williams, that the Enlightenment represented a moral as much as an intellectual shift, is worth pondering: see his *Revelation and Reconciliation* (Cambridge: Cambridge University Press, 1995). The second point at which Noll's argument is vulnerable, particularly in light of its professed evangelical perspective, is in his failure to define and emphasize what constitutes a biblical outlook. In this context, I find the criticisms of D. A. Carson to be both perceptive and persuasive: see *The Gagging of God* (Leicester: Apollos, 1996), pp. 482–484.

19. I am not, of course, arguing here that all theological research must be directly relevant to the pulpit and the pew: as with medicine, who knows when an apparently useless discovery or piece of research leads to an amazingly useful development (penicillin and the cure for rabies both being, I believe, somewhat 'accidental' in the way in which they were discovered)? What I am arguing for is that evangelical scholars should work with the *ultimate* goal of their work being to bring glory to God through the upbuilding of his church. There can be no place for purely academic or antiquarian motives in the evangelical scholarly world.

20. In this context, the comments of D. A. Carson, on current intellectual tensions within modern evangelical thought deriving from its ambivalent relationship to its past, are both an astute commentary on current trends and a distinct warning of the shape of things to come: 'It [the tension] is reflected in the widely recognized clamor for academic recognition among many of the younger evangelical intellectuals, in their drumming criticism of evangelical "fathers" (like immature adolescents who cannot allow any opinion other than their own to be respected), in their persistent drift from biblical authority, and, increasingly, from other doctrines as well. But most of them still want to call themselves evangelicals: that is their power base, that is their prime readership, and that is the group that funds many of the colleges and seminaries where they teach' (*The Gagging of God*, p. 453).

21. In this context, it is indeed depressing to find in a book published in 1999 the claim that verbal inspiration was not taught by the early Reformers: see Roger E. Olson, *The Story of Christian Theology: Twenty Centuries of Tradition and Reform* (Leicester: Apollos, 1999), p. 566. Whether the doctrine is right or wrong, such a claim is historically fallacious and, in this instance, based upon the long-discredited arguments put forward by Jack B. Rogers and Donald K. McKim, *The Authority and Interpretation of the Bible: An Historical Approach* (San Francisco: Harper and Row, 1979), a book which clearly continues to enjoy influence, if only among those unfamiliar with the primary sources of the sixteenth and seventeenth centuries.

22. Indeed, the fact that atonement now needs two qualifiers within evangelical circles – 'penal' and 'substitutionary' – is itself indicative of how terminology has been forced to change over the years.

© Carl R. Trueman 2000

The past, present and future of American evangelical theological scholarship

Craig L. Blomberg

In 1925, Tennessee public-school teacher John Scopes was found guilty of teaching evolution in his science classroom and fined $100. The token fine reflected the fact that, while Scopes was guilty according to the existing state law, the tide of national public opinion had turned massively in his support as lawyers Clarence Darrow and William Jennings Bryan debated the merits of the case. Bryan's articulation of a special creation of the universe by God and a literal interpretation of Genesis 1 left the conservative Christian worldview looking foolish to a majority of the country. The tensions between traditional Christianity and modernity exacerbated by this 'Monkey Trial,' as it came to be called, account for much of the subsequent history of American evangelical thought.[1]

I have been asked in this brief article to trace some of the past, present and future of evangelical theological scholarship in the US and to respond to Carl Trueman's companion piece in this volume on trends in the UK.[2] By 'theological' I refer to the entire spectrum of disciplines that comprise a typical 'faculty of divinity' or 'department of religious studies'. By training, however, I am a biblical scholar, so most of my examples will come from that arena. I am not the most obvious or most qualified candidate for this assignment, but my work for a number of years on the *Themelios* editorial board and my experiences as a theological student and researcher in both countries perhaps give me some insights worth sharing.[3]

The recent past and the present

The fundamentalist–modernist controversy in the 1920s led to the marginalization of evangelical theological scholarship in the United States until after the Second World War. Carl F. H. Henry's slim volume, *The Uneasy Conscience of Modern Fundamentalism*, is regularly cited as contributing an influence out of all proportion to its size to the re-establishment of conservative scholarship as a cultural force with which to be reckoned.[4] Along with Billy Graham, Henry spearheaded a movement, particularly through his editorship of the magazine *Christianity Today*, that was increasingly ecumenical (in the sense of crossing denominational boundaries *within* conservative expressions of Christianity), that set the stage for the numerous interdenominational parachurch organizations that would spring up and that preferred to call itself evangelical (as opposed to fundamentalist) as it rejected strict, sociologically separatist tendencies.

By 1976, conservative Christians were once again a recognized and respected force within the public arena, so much so that *Time* magazine dubbed that bicentennial year, 'The Year of the Evangelical'. The election of an unabashedly evangelical president, Jimmy Carter, played a large part in this identification as well. During the last quarter of the twentieth century, evangelicals also traded places with mainline Protestants and Roman Catholics in becoming the most affluent wing of the Christian church in America.[5] The formation of the 'Moral Majority' under the Rev. Jerry Falwell reflected a re-entry into the political arena of conservative religion supporting conservative (i.e. Republican) politics. Carter after all had been a Democrat, to the chagrin of many evangelicals. In the summer of 1999 *Christianity Today* assessed the gains and losses of the 'religious right' over the last two decades from a variety of perspectives, but all contributors to the colloquium agreed that it had not nearly accomplished the aims it had set out to, with its agenda of reclaiming a culture for Christ.[6]

Evangelical theological scholarship has grown enormously since 1945, but it too has not had nearly the widespread impact many would have desired. Evangelical churches comprise a disproportionately high percentage of the fastest-growing churches in the country. But Christianity in America has always been more 'populist' than in Europe; most of the power-brokers and trend-setters have not come from the world of academics nor have they necessarily been seminary-trained pastors.[7] Today, with a record number of competing technologies for the dissemination of information, reading 'meaty' theological books does not rank high among the priorities even among academically trained clergy. This is also in keeping with nationwide trends in which all Americans read less and less and watch TV (movies, videos, etc.) more and more. Thus it is arguable that our generation has more helpful resources for the understanding and application of Scripture than any culture in the history of the church, yet has become, even within the circles of the faithful, among the most biblically illiterate in history.[8]

Somewhat unlike our British[9] colleagues, American evangelical theological scholars have not made many inroads into the university scene. Part of this failure is due to the unique restrictions on what can be taught in public education (and how it can be taught) in a country with separation between church and state enshrined in its Constitutional Bill of Rights, although the interpretation of these restrictions has often far surpassed what can be demonstrated to have been the intentions of our country's founding fathers.

Part of this failure is due also to the broader theological spectrum of American scholarship and the large numbers who remain polarized at opposite extremes of that spectrum. Numerous British scholars have remarked that a 'Jesus Seminar' – the group of largely very radical scholars who voted on each segment of the Gospels and colour-coded them according to probability of historicity – could never have formed in the UK as it did in the US. While it is making enormous detrimental inroads into American university departments of religious studies, it is having a comparatively negligible impact in Britain.[10] At the same time, Britain has nothing comparable to the Evangelical Theological Society, founded in 1948, an organization of more than 1,500 scholars with ThMs or PhDs who all annually sign a statement affirming their belief in biblical inerrancy. In fact, it was precisely to create an American equivalent of sorts to the Tyndale Fellowship, with its more broadly formulated understanding of evangelicalism,[11] that the Institute of Biblical Research (limited due to constraints of size to Old and New Testament scholars) was birthed in the 1970s.

Some of this polarization is a factor of size. For example, with more than 15 million Southern Baptists in the US, until recently one could be a scholar at one of their denominational colleges or seminaries and scarcely have to interact with the northern and western evangelical world, which was often suspect if for no other reason than that it was 'Yankee' (i.e., northern)![12] As a mobile population increasingly breaks down this kind of intra-American isolation, we still remain unalterably removed from an entire hemisphere by two oceans. And notwithstanding unprecedented technology for turning the world into a global village, a much higher percentage of 'news' reported in this country, including by Christian news agencies, tends to focus on domestic affairs than is the case in the UK (or for that matter in *any* other part of the world). It is thus more likely for one to be able to receive a PhD in a theological discipline in a North American evangelical context without ever having learned French or German than it is in Britain. We are also less likely to be aware of issues emanating from Two-Thirds World scholarship, especially among inerrantist wings of evangelicalism.[13]

Of fragmentation, accountability and success

In light of these trends that at times set American and British evangelical scholarship apart, I naturally react to Carl Trueman's three main points with varying degrees of enthusiasm. There is no question that our theological scholarship has become fragmented. In non-evangelical circles, one could argue that the situation is even worse than in the UK; witness the enormous diversity of topics and study groups at any annual meeting of the Society of Biblical Literature and American Academy of Religion. Methodologies and presuppositions can be so different that members of various subgroups of the academies can scarcely talk to each other intelligibly. And with universities dominating the scholarly landscape of the UK, the SBL and AAR are perhaps the better American analogies to what Trueman is discussing under the heading of fragmentation than anything distinctively evangelical.

On the other hand, the contexts in which a sizable majority of American evangelical scholars of religion teach – Bible colleges, Christian liberal-arts colleges, and free-standing seminaries – does force most of us to be somewhat more 'integrated'. At the very least we are in regular interaction with colleagues of other theological disciplines than our own specializations; at times we are able to keep abreast of Christian thought in a variety of non-theological disciplines as well. Without the external constraint of having to compete for government grants for their university departments, most American evangelicals feel freer to focus not only on formal academic research, but also on textbook writing, semi-popular and popular-level works that apply to a broader audience the results of their or others' scholarship.[14]

I do think that British evangelicals, however, have better developed mechanisms for formal co-operation and joint scholarly ventures, as illustrated by the various study groups of the Tyndale Fellowship, the special Tyndale House publishing projects[15] and the numerous anthologies that have resulted from conferences in Cambridge of the World Evangelical Fellowship.[16] To date, the Evangelical Theological Society and Institute of Biblical Research have only begun to scratch the surface in organizing parallel activities and publications on this side of the Atlantic. And while American college professors may work right next door to Christian scholars in other disciplines, the teaching load they typically shoulder is greater than that of the average

British university professor, so they may not always have the time to take advantage of their neighbours' expertise.[17]

It is Trueman's section on accountability with which I am least comfortable. Again I know there are American parallels to the phenomenon of British scholars wanting to retain the label 'evangelical' while rejecting doctrines that increasingly impinge on true fundamentals of the faith.[18] But far more often the problem on this side of the Atlantic is that evangelical believers raised in a particular denomination or theological tradition have, through their academic study, come to nuance or define their adherence to a given doctrine in ways that find adequate precedent in other historically evangelical traditions but which are perceived by some to push the boundaries of their own traditions too far. And enormous discomfort can be brought on such professors by a denominational constituency or influential preacher who does not thoroughly understand the issues. For every American evangelical I know who deserved to be fired from his or her teaching post for no longer adhering to an institution's doctrinal statement, I know several who were fired who didn't deserve to be! Had F. F. Bruce taught in an American college or seminary that included 'inerrancy' in its confession of faith, he would have come under fire for (at least) his beliefs in a late date for Daniel and two Isaiahs. Harold Lindsell, who wrote *The Battle for the Bible* in the late 1970s and is probably best remembered for his attempt to harmonize the Gospels' accounts of Peter's behaviour in the high priest's courtyard by postulating *six* denials,[19] published an editorial in the popular Christian press in those years that condemned Bruce on precisely those issues.[20]

That such a narrow, sectarian spirit has not disappeared from the American scene is demonstrated by the 1998 publication of a book entitled *The Jesus Crisis: The Inroads of Historical Criticism into Evangelical Scholarship*. It is edited and partially authored by Robert L. Thomas and F. David Farnell, two professors from the seminary started by megachurch pastor John MacArthur as a fundamentalist protest against the mainstream evangelical, inerrantist perspective of the Talbot School of Theology in greater Los Angeles, from which many of the founding professors came.[21] Thomas in particular argues that virtually all evangelical Gospel scholars have capitulated to liberalism and are, in essence, no different from the Jesus Seminar, because they accept theories of literary dependence among the synoptic Gospels or embrace, even cautiously, various aspects of form, tradition or redaction criticism. Only an additive harmonization that sees all of the sayings of Jesus in the Gospels excerpted from a larger whole that contained massive reduplication of what now appears parcelled out among the four narratives is consistent, in his mind, with inerrancy.[22] I can scarcely imagine such a book ever being published by a major Christian press in the UK, much less its being publicly praised by the *president* of an evangelical academic society, as Norman Geisler did in last year's presidential address to the ETS![23]

Or, at a more grass-roots level, television and radio preachers can through one nationally syndicated programme do more damage to the career of an evangelical academic or institution than years of patient, nuanced scholarship on his or her part do to advance it. The Christian counselling movement in the US is a frequent target for such overstated and devastating attacks. The countercult industry wields similar power; self-appointed, theologically untrained watchdogs can keep books out of Christian bookstores and set constituencies against their scholars through campaigns of misinformation. I experienced how this felt firsthand after I co-authored a book with Brigham Young University New Testament Professor Stephen E. Robinson, entitled *How Wide the Divide? A Mormon and an Evangelical in Conversation*, in which we dared to list everything we agreed on as well as including long lists of disagreements. We also tried to model an uncharacteristically irenic spirit for Mormon–evangelical interchanges.[24] Fellow academics uniformly praised the book; it won an award from *Christianity Today* as one of the top fifteen Christian books of 1997. Several leading countercult ministries, however, severely criticized it, and one of the most influential ones has gone out of its way to condemn it over the airwaves (and in print) on a regular basis.[25] If for no other reason than that national Christian radio and television do not exist in the UK, I again cannot imagine a parallel phenomenon occurring in Britain.

Perhaps it is now clear why I have mixed feelings about Trueman's concern for 'accountability'. In the US we may well have too much of a very wrong kind of accountability. Many of us who were trained at seminaries that were vigorously engaged in labelling (rightly or wrongly) other historically evangelical seminaries as no longer evangelical and who then came to the UK for doctoral study found the breadth of British definitions of evangelicalism and the comparative lack of a polemical environment like a breath of fresh air.

I have the least amount to say in response to Trueman's section on 'success', perhaps because I find myself agreeing with him the most here. Evangelical scholars have had enormous success on many fronts, especially within the church, and that success can make us complacent, too, and less vigilant in defining our boundaries. But, as noted above, we have not made nearly as many inroads into secular academics as in Britain. Large libraries of highly respected American universities often have virtually no holdings reflecting evangelical scholarship, even from those British authors whom Trueman fears are pushing the envelope too far in a liberal direction. Departments of religious studies at times have no Christian professors teaching courses on Bible and theology, although the situation in history and philosophy is sometimes less bleak. And students graduate with degrees in religion unaware of even the most academically responsible of works from evangelical presses, which in all but a handful of cases publish and sell more volumes annually than do their liberal or secular counterparts.[26] So we still have quite a way to go in this country before we can speak of success in the academy.

Church versus academy?

Trueman writes that evangelical scholarship is 'theoretically accountable in the first instance to the evangelical church on earth and ultimately to God himself in heaven'.[27] I would revise this slightly to say that we are *first* of all accountable to God and then to all that God has revealed in his Word we should do. The establishment of his kingdom or reign extends to both the church and the world, and I resist prioritizing the two – as in the endless church squabbles over whether serving the membership or engaging in outreach deserves pride of place. Perhaps differently from in the UK, it is arguable that in the US evangelical scholars have better served the church than they have the secular academy, so that we must continue to work harder on the latter front.[28]

But inasmuch as the church itself is so frequently polarized in the US, fragmenting itself with false dichotomies, our service to the church should often be to help people see the truth in both sides of a theological debate. We do not have to choose between evangelism and social action, between doctrine and ethics, between rigorous scholarship and practical application, between an orthodox view of Scripture and adherence to such politically *and biblically* correct movements as concern for the world's marginalized. We don't have to take 'all-or-nothing' positions with respect to deconstructionism, reader-response criticism, socio-rhetorical criticism, feminist and non-Eurocentric scholarship as so many tend to do.[29] We must be rigorously eclectic in our methods, while recognizing in a postmodern age that it may be left above all to evangelicals to champion the 'old-fashioned' study of history. As Martin Hengel has repeatedly stressed, conservative scholars, who of all people most recognize what is at stake, should strive to master the ancient sources and the ancient languages better than anyone else, so that the next vacuous theory that needs to be refuted can be.[30] Yet in the US at least, the anti-intellectualism that turned the Scopes trial into a débâcle does at times remain rampant, not only as creation 'science' attempts to defend a 10,000 year-old Earth, but as evangelical constituents, administrators and even fellow professors outside the biblical and theological disciplines frequently call for decreased requirements and offerings in the study of ancient civilizations and biblical (and modern) languages.

Conclusion

That six of the ten best-selling Christian books in the United States in January and February of 1999 were about the 'millennium bug' and the devastation it would wreak worldwide, all in fulfilment of some apocalyptic scenario alleged to emerge from Scripture, is yet another vivid illustration of the gap between the academy and the Christian grass roots (and even the larger secular culture) that evangelical scholars in America have yet to bridge often enough. We continue to need men and women called to lives of the most rigorous, even-handed scholarship. We need others who will popularize their findings for a broader audience. Evangelical scholars must be sufficiently involved in the life of the church, locally and globally, as *sympathetic* critics, so that their voices are trusted rather than doubted. Their personal lives must model the integrity that the gospel requires, especially these days in the areas of sexual ethics and financial stewardship. They must bend over backwards to affirm everything possibly true about non-Christian systems of thought, while remaining careful never to compromise the essentials of the gospel (cf. 1 Cor. 9:19–23 with Gal. 2:11–14). Above all they must strive, with the power of the Holy Spirit, to be faithful to their unique callings and giftedness. As we all play our part, we can trust God to work out the results according to his sovereign, good pleasure.

Notes

1. Cf. esp. George M. Marsden, *Fundamentalism and American Culture: The Shaping of Twentieth-Century Evangelicalism: 1870–1925* (New York and Oxford: Oxford University Press, 1980), pp. 184–205.
2. 'The future of evangelical scholarship: a British perspective', pp. 291–310.
3. My undergraduate degree in religion was from a liberal Lutheran liberal-arts college in Illinois (Augustana College); my masters degree in New Testament, from a leading American evangelical seminary (Trinity Evangelical Divinity School); and my doctorate in New Testament from Aberdeen University in Scotland. I have subsequently taught American undergraduates at a Baptist College in Florida (Palm Beach Atlantic College), been a senior research fellow for a year at Tyndale House Cambridge, taught graduate students in Denver Seminary in Colorado for the last thirteen years and returned twice in the 1990s for extended times of research in Tyndale House.
4. (Grand Rapids: Eerdmans, 1948.)
5. Martin Marty, in a public lecture, Denver Seminary, 1988.
6. Paul Weyrich et al., 'Is the religious right finished?' *Christianity Today* 43.9 (1999), pp. 43–59.
7. Outstanding examples include arguably the three most effective evangelists of the second half of the nineteenth century and the two halves of the twentieth century – Dwight L. Moody, Billy Sunday and Billy Graham. In our day, Bill Hybels of Willow Creek Community Church in the Chicago area continues the trend, although he began pursuing a seminary degree after his church

attained megachurch status.

8. Cf. esp. Gary M. Burge, 'The greatest story never read', *Christianity Today* 43.10 (1999), pp. 45–49.

9. I realize that 'British' and 'Britain' by definition do not include Northern Ireland, but it is cumbersome to write 'British and Northern Irish' and it is monotonous to always say 'the UK'. So I ask my readers in Northern Ireland for understanding that I am not trying to exclude them from consideration, or making a political statement of any kind!

10. See esp. N. T. Wright, *Jesus and the Victory of God* (London: SPCK; Minneapolis; Fortress, 1996), pp. 29–35.

11. I.e. biblical inspiration and authority but not necessarily strict inerrancy.

12. Cf. James L. Garrett et al., *Are Southern Baptists Evangelicals?* (Macon: Mercer, 1983), with David S. Dockery (ed.), *Southern Baptists and American Evangelicals: The Conversation Continues* (Nashville: Broadman and Holman, 1993).

13. I made a plea for ETS members to rectify this situation in my plenary address to the society in 1994, subsequently published as 'The globalization of biblical hermeneutics', *JETS* 38 (1995), pp. 581–593; but I have detected no increase in its membership grappling with these issues in the last five years. In February of 2000, Denver Seminary's Institute for Contextualized Biblical Studies will host a conference that will, one hopes, make at least a small contribution to this topic.

14. This point became clear to me in remarks made by Anthony C. Thiselton in a discussion period after my plenary address to the 1994 Tyndale Fellowship joint conference in Swanwick, subsequently published as 'Critical issues in New Testament studies for evangelicals today', in *A Pathway into the Holy Scripture*, ed. Philip E. Satterthwaite and David F. Wright (Grand Rapids: Eerdmans, 1994), pp. 51–79.

15. I think, for example, of the publications of anthologies of select papers from the Tyndale Fellowship's three triennial joint conferences in the 1990s, or the Genesis, Gospels and Acts projects from Tyndale House.

16. Here I am thinking of the series of volumes edited by D. A. Carson on such topics as worship, prayer, the church, and so on, and published by Paternoster and Baker.

17. I realize that this gap has narrowed over the last two decades, as funding has consistently been cut for British universities, but I still seldom hear of academics in the UK having to teach 27–30 semester hours a year (up to five courses in any given term) on top of heavy committee work, as is the norm in many American evangelical undergraduate settings.

18. But it is widely agreed among American evangelical academics that Schaeffer's *The Great Evangelical Disaster* (cited approvingly by Trueman on p. 308 n. 13) was overstated and full of misleading generalizations.

19. (Grand Rapids: Zondervan, 1976.) On Peter's denial, see pp. 174–176. For a more nuanced set of comments with respect to the accounts of Peter's denials, still from the perspective of a strong commitment to biblical inerrancy, see D. A. Carson, 'Matthew', in *The Expositor's Bible Commentary* 8, ed. Frank E. Gaebelein (Grand Rapids: Zondervan, 1984), pp. 557–558.

20. Although I have vivid memories of the contents of Lindsell's remarks, I have been unable to locate the source. But very comparable sentiments appear, with respect to works Bruce edited, in ibid., pp. 156–158.

21. (Grand Rapids: Kregel, 1998.)

22. See esp. Robert L. Thomas, 'Redaction criticism', in ibid., pp. 233–267, which also treats source, form and tradition criticism, even though previous chapters deal at greater length with those topics.

23. Published as Norman L. Geisler, 'Beware of philosophy: a warning to biblical scholars', *JETS* 42 (1999), pp. 3–19; see specifically pp. 13–14. Thomas himself is a past president of the ETS. The overall membership is not nearly as narrow or polemic as these illustrations might suggest, but there has been a fairly consistent tradition in recent years of electing presidents from among the organization's most 'right wing', since nominations are usually proposed by a small committee and seldom opposed from the floor.

24. (Downers Grove: IVP, 1997.)

25. For a detailed survey of reactions to the book, with documentation of all of the above, see 'Sizing up the divide: reviews and replies', *BYU Studies* 38 (1999), pp. 1–27, with analysis by Matthew R. Connelly and the *BYU Studies* staff and responses by Robinson and me.

26. Books that I have published with IVP in the UK are regularly reviewed by a broad cross-section of

British and continental journals of the highest academic level; books that I have published with IVP in the US are barely ever noticed in this country by any but distinctively evangelical journals.

27. Trueman, p. 297.
28. In my particular field, Markus Bockmuehl ('"To be or not to be": the possible futures of New Testament scholarship', *SJT* 51, 1998, pp. 271–306) has pointed some ways forward as well as anyone I know.
29. Again works written in Britain point the way forward better than any purely American counterparts I know. I am thinking here esp. of Anthony C. Thiselton, *New Horizons in Hermeneutics* (Grand Rapids: Zondervan, 1992); and Kevin J. Vanhoozer, *Is There a Meaning in This Text? The Bible, the Reader, and the Morality of Literary Knowledge* (Grand Rapids: Zondervan, 1998).
30. See esp. his presidential address to the Society for New Testament Studies in 1993, published as Martin Hengel, 'Aufgaben der neutestamentlichen Wissenschaften', *NTS* 40 (1994), pp. 321–337.